Darkness before the Dawn

Darkness before the Dawn

Diary of a Changi POW
1941 - 1945

Sgt J N Farrow
(No: 5772439)

5th Royal Norfolks

First published in 2007 by:
Stamford House Publishing

© Copyright 2007
The Estate of J N Farrow

ISBN 978-1-904985-55-6

Printed and bound in Great Britain by:
Stamford House Publishing
Remus House
Coltsfoot Drive
Peterborough
PE2 9JX

CONTENTS

PREFACE

INTRODUCTION

LIST OF ILLUSTRATIONS

. . .

LIST OF ILLUSTRATIONS (contd)

Good Luck.

Darkness before the Dawn.

Adieu.

PREFACE

The campaign which ended in the fall of Singapore in February 1942 has a particular resonance for the people of Norfolk. Thousands of young Norfolk men were captured and many died through ill treatment, disease and starvation. Those who came back from the Far East were both physically and mentally scarred by their experiences. It was very difficult to adjust to family life and the bleak world of post war Britain.

Jack Farrow was one of the Far East Prisoners of War survivors. A Norfolk boy whose father worked as a landscape gardener in Sheringham, Jack joined the Territorial Army and was a sergeant in the 5th Battalion Norfolk Regiment. These Norfolk territorial battalions were locally recruited so Jack found himself serving alongside friends and neighbours from close-knit communities. In 1941 Jack had only been married a few days before his battalion was ordered on active service.

Along with the 4th and 6th Battalions Norfolk Regiment Jack's battalion formed part of the 18th Division, which was sent to the Middle East. Faced with the Japanese attack on Malaya the division was diverted to Singapore where it was deployed piecemeal into a losing battle.

Throughout his wartime experiences Jack Farrow kept a diary. In Changi jail this would have been both difficult and dangerous. We have other accounts of life in Changi jail but Jack Farrow's is quite unique in that he remained in Changi throughout the war. His background as a gardener probably saved his life as he was ordered to supervise the upkeep of the ever-expanding cemetery. Many of his friends were sent up country on work details where the life expectancy was very low.

His diary entries are often laconic and matter of fact, but they document the daily struggle against disease, starvation and the brutality of the Japanese guards. He remembers his wife's birthday and frequently comments on what might be happening at home.

The epilogue by his widow Joan is especially poignant as she describes how Jack had to cope with life at home on his return, and how his experiences as a POW never ever left him. A gem of a diary.

Keith Simpson

MP for Mid Norfolk

INTRODUCTION

In the years leading up to the Second World War the much boasted of 'island fortress' of Singapore was widely regarded as the jewel in the crown of Britain's far eastern empire; an empire upon which the sun would never set. Therefore, its loss in the early months of 1942 to a vastly inferior force of the Imperial Japanese Army came as a devastating shock to an already beleaguered British public. The capitulation and unconditional surrender of the islands defenders, numbering over 80,000 allied troops, despite having been ordered to fight to the last man, was one of the greatest defeats ever suffered by the British Army in recent times. To many ill informed commentators it was seen as shameful, to others simply bewildering.

The British defence of the Malayan peninsula started badly. On the 6th of December 1941 a large convoy of Japanese troop transports, escorted by a number of warships, was reported to be heading towards Malaya. The following morning, in a surprise attack that surely came as no surprise to the British High Command, the Japanese attacked the headquarters of the US Pacific fleet at Pearl Harbour. With Japanese military intentions now clear and expecting an enemy landing in the north of the Malayan peninsula, Naval Force Z, consisting of the battleship *Prince of Wales,* the battle cruiser *Repulse* and four escorting destroyers, left Singapore harbour on December 8th to intercept this potential threat.

In the early hours of that same morning units of the Japanese Imperial Army made the expected landings in the northern area of the Malayan peninsula. The British commanders were slow to react as all but one of the Japanese landings had taken place not in Malaya itself but in neutral Thailand and the British had no wish to violate this neutral territory. This delay was to prove fatal. By the time the scattered British forces had concentrated and prepared to dislodge the invaders the Japanese had firmly established themselves and captured virtually all the airfields in the north of the country. Now without local air support the British troops were at the mercy of the 500+ enemy aircraft that had been assigned to support the land-based operation. The British position was further threatened by their lack of armour. The Japanese campaign, though infantry led, was supported by over 200 light and medium tanks, the British had no tanks anywhere in the peninsula.

The problems facing the British commander on the ground, General Percival, were also compounded by two other factors. Firstly, though his troops looked highly impressive on paper, numbering approximately 88,000 (15,000 Australians, 19,000 British, 37,000 Indians and 17,000 Malayans), they were in reality a highly mixed bunch. Although the majority were fine troops who fought with courage, many of the units were poorly trained, badly led and lacking in even the most basic supplies. Virtually none of them had ever seen a shot fired in anger and the troops they were facing were amongst the elite of the entire Japanese army; an army that had been fighting a war in mainland China for over four years.

General Percival's second problem was one of mobility. The Japanese had made their attack during the monsoon season and all but the major roads had become impassable to large bodies of troops and their associated supplies. However, the Japanese, when faced with British blockades of the main routes, simply took to the surrounding jungle and outflanked their positions. Time after time the British were forced to withdraw after successful Japanese flanking manoeuvres and by December 10th the British withdrawal down the peninsula had become an almost continuous retreat.

That same day a disaster took place that was to prove decisive for the British in Northern Malaya. Naval Force Z was intercepted by the elite 22nd Air Flotilla of the Japanese Naval Air Arm and attacked with a mixture of torpedoes and high level bombing. Despite the *Prince of Wales'* 175 anti-aircraft guns, which could deliver over 60,000 shells a minute, the attack was pressed home with precision. With the northern airfields already in enemy hands and only about 150 outdated allied aircraft to protect the whole peninsula, Naval Force Z had no air support and their fate was sealed. After several hours of sustained attack both the *Repulse* and the *Prince of Wales* suffered fatal damage and sank. Happily, of the 2,800 men who formed both ships companies over 2,000 were rescued by the escorting destroyers.

With the only major British naval force in the area now eliminated, the Japanese were able to re-supply and reinforce their troops at will and without fear of heavy attack. Combined with the vast air superiority that they now enjoyed the Japanese army was able to keep up relentless pressure on the ill supported and ill equipped British forces. Retreat followed retreat and by the 30th of January 1942 the British forces had been forced back into the very tip of the Malayan peninsula. The following day the British rearguards crossed the straits to the fortress island of Singapore and the entire peninsula was now in Japanese hands.

* * *

The conquest of the Malayan peninsula by the Imperial Japanese Army had taken a meagre 54 days to achieve and had been undertaken with minimal losses. The ground forces had lost only an estimated 4,600 men, as opposed to the allied 25,000 (mostly captured), and even the attack upon Naval Force Z, which had cost Britain two of her most prestigious capital ships, resulted in the loss of only three Japanese planes.

However, it would be wrong to look upon the Japanese victory as an easy one - it was far from that. The allied troops put up a massively strong resistance and fought at every opportunity. Unfortunately a mixture of bad weather, lack of supplies, information, air support, armour and experience meant that all such efforts were futile. Inexperienced troops manning road blocks were outflanked, surrounded and captured by Japanese troops travelling through jungle that British Intelligence reports stated was impenetrable. Similarly, infantry based defensive measures such as those taken on the River Slim were of little use when faced by enemy tanks. The tanks burst through the defences, raced to the river, captured the only road bridge intact and effectively cut off 4,000 allied troops who were later forced to surrender. As the troops retreated south towards Singapore they were under constant air attack and supply dumps, stationed strategically along the peninsula to enable rapid re-supply of allied troops, soon became either over-run by the enemy or easy targets for Japanese aircraft.

* * *

As the morning of the 1st February 1942 dawned bright and clear the entire British army of Malaya found itself ensconced upon the much vaunted island fortress of Singapore. Barely a mile away, across the straits that separate the island from the mainland, the crack forward units of the Japanese Imperial Army took up their new positions and awaited their orders to attack across the water. Although the British High Command had managed to withdraw many of its troops to the island their position was not as strong as they would have wished. In particular certain types of ammunition were in short supply and artillery shells became scarcer by the hour as the Japanese bombing took its toll on the supply depots. In addition to this severe shortage it was also realised that the state of the local water supply, barely adequate under normal conditions, was insufficient to cope with the many thousands of extra troops; especially since the enemy bombing had added to its various deficiencies. Food stores were also low and, with many thousands of civilians from the mainland having taken refuge in Singapore City, the situation looked unlikely to improve in the near future. In short, prospects for a long-term siege of the island looked bleak.

The ability of any fortress to withstand a siege relies upon three main factors; factors that have remained almost unchanged since the very earliest development of the fortress itself. The defenders of such a besieged fortress must have an adequate supply of water, they must hold many months worth of food stores in reserve and they must have the manpower and wherewithal to man the defences and withstand repeated assaults. By the beginning of February 1942 Singapore Island could only lay claim to the last of these attributes. Manpower they had, unfortunately, so short was the ammunition supply that it looked increasingly likely that any final defence of the fortress would take place with the bayonet.

On the night of February 8th, barely a week after the final rearguard had withdrawn to the island, the Japanese launched their attack. Under cover of darkness armoured landing craft began the assault across the shallow straits and, attacking on a wide front, the Japanese managed to land over 13,000 elite troops before sunrise. In part this success must be seen as the result of allied failures. The beach defences, which included searchlights and a rapid artillery response, were, for reasons unknown, never brought into use. As it was the landing was opposed by only three battalions of Australian regular troops who were quickly forced back with heavy losses. Crossings continued all day and by sundown on the 8th of February over 20,000 Japanese troops had landed and established themselves in the north west of the island.

Despite this the defenders still considerably outnumbered the attacking forces and looked, at least on paper, to be more than capable of forcing the Japanese back across the straits. However, at this point this was simply not the case. The Singapore garrison had received a not inconsiderable number of fresh reinforcements only a few days (February 5th) before the Japanese launched their final attack across the straits. However, even these fresh troops could do little to help.

The convoy in which they had been travelling had received considerable attention from the Japanese air force en route and had sustained a great deal of damage and suffered heavy casualties. Furthermore, as soon as the convoy entered Singapore harbour it had come under heavy dive-bomber attack resulting in the loss of the *'Empress of Asia'*. This transport, as well as holding several hundred troops, carried the majority of the reinforcements' equipment. The troops, when finally disembarked, discovered that virtually all their weapons and ammunition now lay at the bottom of Singapore docks. The supposed saviours of the Singapore garrison now found themselves having to scrounge, beg and borrow what equipment they could from the already under-supplied Australian troops stationed nearby.

As the enemy artillery and air bombardment grew worse, and the allied ammunition and food stocks dwindled, the situation became desperate. As each stand was made the defenders were shelled, bombed and strafed until, once more they were forced to retire. Finally, by the 10th of February, the allied troops, with little ammunition, less food and the prospect of no water, found themselves retiring to the very outskirts of Singapore City itself.

As the remnants of the army of Malaya took up its final defensive positions around the city they received their orders from General Wavell. They were, he commanded, to fight to the very last man. The officers should lead by example and the Japanese should be pushed back into the sea at the point of the bayonet. However, even as General Wavell's message was being passed amongst the ranks, the truth of the situation was becoming clear. Behind the defenders position great explosions shattered the air as engineers destroyed the docks, harbour artillery and unnecessary oil supplies. The island was lost and the Japanese would find nothing left when, as everyone now believed they would, they finally captured it. The soldiers now knew that the authorities thought they were as good as lost. Their immediate future was simple - they would either die with their backs to the sea or become prisoners.

Later that same day the Japanese commander sent a message to General Percival, the commander of the forces still holding Singapore. The British and their allies had, according to General Yamashita, taken part in many "fierce and gallant fights . . . to the honour of British warriorship". However, the fate of Singapore was already sealed and continued resistance would merely result in further suffering for the enlarged civilian population of the island. For the sake of both his men and the civilians General Percival should surrender his command and end the hostilities forthwith. To continue to defend the island would add "further miseries and horrors of war" and would not "add anything to the honour of your army".

There was to be no vainglorious last stand for the British army of Malaya; no fight to the death at the point of a bayonet. On the 15th of February, at three in the afternoon, General Percival crossed the lines accompanied by two Brigadiers. As set out in the Japanese instructions one of the Brigadiers carried a large Union Jack; the other carried a large white flag. Later that afternoon General Yamashita accepted the unconditional surrender of all British and allied forces then serving in Singapore.

* * *

The fall of Singapore was a defeat on the scale of that received by the British at Dunkirk - but with none of the positive factors. At Dunkirk the majority of the defeated army had, against all odds, been brought home. From Singapore there was no quick way home. It was the fall of an island fortress that could not, would not, be beaten. Some blamed the soldiers, some the lack of air cover, others still blamed the generals and army commanders. Unfortunately, the true reasons for the fall of Singapore can be traced back much further and the blame laid at a much higher level.

For many of those soldiers their fate was sealed the moment that they marched off the boats in Singapore harbour.

The decision to turn the island of Singapore into Britain's far eastern fortress was made in the years immediately following the First World War. It would act as a strong base for the much vaunted British Fleet and add both a great deal of prestige to the empire and act as a major advantage in the game of far eastern politics. However, although the scheme received a great deal of media and public attention, the financial and political realities of the late 1920's and early 1930's meant that actual development of the base proceeded at a snail's pace. Furthermore, an argument quickly developed in the corridors of Whitehall between Trenchard, the Chief of the Air Staff, and Beatty, the First Sea Lord, as to how this new base should be defended.

Trenchard believed that the best way of ensuring the security of the new base was with the provision of a large number of aircraft and their associated airfields. Beatty, on the other hand, saw the base as primarily naval and believed that such a base was at threat only from a major naval force. These could be countered, he strongly argued, by the provision of a large naval flotilla and the installation of several batteries of heavy coastal artillery. Furthermore, Beatty was reluctant to even admit that any large naval vessel could be sunk by aircraft alone. In the end it was Beatty's views that prevailed and the base was provided with massive seaward facing coastal batteries of artillery and few aircraft. Unfortunately, when the attack finally came in late 1941 it was from the mainland not the sea and Beatty's coastal batteries could play no part in the defence of the island.

This threat to Singapore via its 'back door' was not something that simply came out of the blue. Both soldiers and politicians had realised that such a threat was a reality as far back as the mid 1930's but, despite their urgings, very little had been done to rectify the situation. General Percival himself, during his time as Chief General Staff Officer in Malaya (1936-7), had made the same observations and his then commander, General Dobbie, had gone some way to countering the threat by beginning the construction of a defence line across the southern end of the peninsula in 1938. In addition the standing garrison for the island was increased, on the advice of Mr Hore-Belisha, the minister for war, with the deployment of two brigades of Indian regular troops.

At the outbreak of war the defences of Singapore were further strengthened and plans were put in place to rectify the obvious shortfalls associated with the peninsula's air cover. General Bond had stated that the air defence of Malaya would require a minimum of 500 modern aircraft. However, this number was later reduced to 300 and, by the time the attack actually came, the whole Air Force contingent in Malaya could muster only 158 airworthy fighting machines, the majority of which were pre-war machines that were no match for the state of the art Japanese aircraft. This shortage of modern fighter aircraft was to play a massive part in the capture of Singapore and if any blame is to be apportioned anywhere for this shortfall then it must be with the British High Command and, in particular, Winston Churchill.

After the Battle of Britain had reached its dramatic conclusion in the autumn of 1940 aircraft production had been almost wholly aimed at filling the new made gaps in Britain's home defences. However, over the next twelve months there were more than enough new aircraft built to bring the Malaya garrison up to strength. Unfortunately, the political will was just not there and, despite constant urgings from various quarters, the British High Command, and Churchill in particular, kept the new planes back for other operations. The Singapore air defence was constantly shifted down the list of priorities.

The reasons for this are various and still the subject of much debate. However, it is clear that Churchill saw Malaya as relatively safe. Japan had not entered the war and, in the event that Japan did so in the near future, its forces would be tied up fighting the Americans who, Churchill was convinced, would immediately enter the war on the Allied side. In the meantime Churchill was content to strengthen his forces in North Africa, supply Russia with 600 aircraft and build up a bombing campaign against the German homeland. Indeed the coming campaign in North Africa and Egypt weighed heavily upon Churchill's mind. Britain needed a high profile victory and, in the premiers opinion, that victory was most likely to be achieved in Egypt. Years later, writing in his history of the Second World War, Churchill made his position quite clear. "I would not tolerate", he wrote, "abandoning the struggle for Egypt, and was resigned to pay whatever forfeits were exacted in Malaya". Unfortunately, the forfeit that Churchill was to pay resulted in the fall of Singapore, the surrender of an entire army and long years of captivity for those soldiers who, with little support, had done their very best.

* * *

When the guns of the defenders of Singapore finally fell silent there followed several days of uncertainty. Finally, with the arrival on the scene of the Japanese Army, the remnants of the army of Malaya were marched off into captivity. For some, the lucky ones, the captivity would last over three years. The rest, those whose luck had run out, never came back.

Amongst those who were marched off into captivity and an uncertain future was Sgt J.N. Farrow of the 5th Battalion, The Royal Norfolk Regiment. He, along with thousands of his fellows, was destined to spend the next three years confined in the notorious Changi Prison. Sgt Farrow, Jack to his friends, would not have caught anyone's particular attention amongst the many thousands of his comrades. In fact, in many respects, he was probably doing his utmost not to stand out from the crowd. As a sergeant and territorial soldier of some experience Jack knew how to get on in the army - fight hard, always salute an officer and never volunteer for anything. However, there was one thing about Jack Farrow that was, over the next three years, going to set him aside from his fellows; his diary.

Throughout his years in captivity Sgt Farrow managed to keep a diary of his own thoughts and record the events that went on around him. This in itself is remarkable, as all forms or writing material were in extremely short supply, and the practice was brutally discouraged by the Japanese. His diary, made up of a collection of notes written on any scraps of paper that came to hand, grew as the years of captivity passed. Sgt Farrow also managed to preserve many of the other documents that came into his hands, camp orders, newsletters etc, and kept all the material together until his eventual release. Years later, long after Jack himself had come to terms with his captivity, he decided to complete the task he had begun in Changi prison and finish compiling his diary.

Luckily for us Jack Farrow was a lot more than just a diarist - he was a clear and natural storyteller with a keen eye for detail. His account of the battle of Singapore brings the reader to understand, if not what the men went through, then at least the true circumstances under which they operated. Even Jack Farrow's account of three years of captivity, normally thought of as a period when time weighed heavily, has the reader turning the pages to continue the tale. In short Sergeant Jack Farrow's diary is one of the most human and compelling documents to have come out of any far eastern POW camp.

Sadly, Jack Farrow died in 1992. During his lifetime he never gave any thought to having this remarkable document published. It was a personal tribute to those men he left behind in Changi Cemetery; a way of exorcising their ghosts from his memory. However, after his death the document came to the attention of the local museum, who suggested that Jack's wife and family approached a publisher. This book is the result.

Matthew Champion

CHAPTER 1

DESTINATION UNKNOWN

Monday October 27ᵗʰ 1941

A lot of hustle and bustle is taking place here at our station, Marbury Hall, a fine old place in Northwich, Cheshire, it is raining but the atmosphere is one of serious excitement as the battalion under Col. Prattley is preparing to move overseas, destination unknown.

In our kit bags we have full-scale English winter clothing, including balaclavas and also, physical training kit, we have too a complete outfit of tropical kit and what kit! I should think it was left over from 1918, it fits where it touches and some of us must be careful how we bend, whereas, others look like scare-crows in jackets, trousers and topees much too big. We, considering the name of our regiment are disgusted and ashamed, but cannot help joke and laugh at the funny figures we cut.

It is 1.30pm and we are on parade complete for moving. I am Sergeant-in-charge of a reinforcement platoon of B Company. Roll is called and reports given, yet an hour later still no orders to move, it is still raining. The Company Commander, Capt. Self, comes along and the order is to remove equipment and lay it down and cover with ground sheets, then go to huts until called. A stoppage of 2d per man has been made to pay for tea to be obtained at a railway station halfway to the docks.

4.30pm and as the bugle calls us on parade it's still raining. With great coats on, equipment over-top, pack, haversack, entrenching tool, rifle, respirator, gas cape, steel helmet; who said the modern soldier travelled lighter? Look at all the extra gas equipment, a lot of small articles not named, and my kit bag of warm clothes over one shoulder. For the last year we have been training as a mechanical unit, now the war across the seas calls us and all at once we become the P.B.I. with a 3-mile march to Northwich station carrying the above kit.

The 'Norfolk Boys' after the Liverpool Blitz, May 11th 1941
(Sgt. J. Farrow, seated 3rd from the left)

Canadian Pacific Liner 'Duchess of Atholl,' 20,000 tons.
Nicknamed 'The Drunken Duchess'
The ship that took us from the Clyde to Halifax, Nova Scotia, Canada

"COMPA-N-Y! ATTEN---TION!! Company will move to the right in column of Route No 10 platoon B. Company leading etc. etc." We are off and what of our feelings of the past 2 years? Coastal defence, training over the Scottish hills, fire-fighting during the Liverpool blitz, our thoughts of those we are leaving behind. Shall we see them again, or will it be curtains for us? Yes some of us. We badly want to go, we are browned off with training, yet we are sad at heart because of what we leave behind us.

A quiet battalion of men moves across the bleak Northwich flashes silently cursing the weather or a slipping kit-bag. It is dusk as we reach the town, but the townsfolk line the wet streets to wave farewell to a battalion they have grown to love, men from Norfolk. We try to part in high spirits singing "Roll out the Barrel", "We are the Norfolk Boys" and "Farmers Boy" and with shouts of "Cheerio Mother" and "Bye Bye darling, soon be back", handkerchiefs dab the eyes of many girls. The boys made a hit and quite a few weddings took place during our stay here. We arrive at the station but our train is not due till 8.30pm. The platforms are massed with baggage and troops and while we wait rumour runs riot, always the same question, I wonder where we are off to? Middle East? Egypt? What, with all this winter kit? I reckon it'll be Russia. They say our transport has gone to India and conjecture runs, for myself, a little voice keeps saying somewhere around Iraq or the Far East - Singapore? A train runs in and a bugler sounds the "Advance". Everyone stands to and the order is given to entrain, which all goes off methodically as planned. The bugle sounds again and the train pulls out, groaning under its load. Where are we sailing from? Liverpool and Stranraer are the chief guesses.

The night drags on, Newcastle is reached and no tea, perhaps at the next stop. We arrive at Carlisle and still no tea, it is cold and we are tired, a cup of 'char' would do us a lot of good, anyhow we have paid for it! The train has virtually become a racing snoring giant, for most of the men are asleep in huddled positions and the snores are terrific.

Monday October 28ᵗʰ

It is 12 noon, we are arriving in Glasgow station and there is still no tea. It is almost 24 hours since we had anything other than water, only meagre haversack rations on a cold journey. During the morning we passed through Castle Douglas where in early 1941 we were stationed, somehow they had learned that the "5th Norfolks" were passing through the station and many townsfolk lined the platforms, the driver slowing down as we went through.

At 1600hrs., we arrive at Gourock on the Clyde, our port of embarkation. A canteen there manages a half a mug of tea per man, it is thankfully received, over 24hrs has elapsed since the last cup. What happened to that which we had paid for I never knew, someone's organisation was at fault

A tender arrives for us and we embark, for many of us the tender is a big ship and for some the first time on the water. When we push off I am below deck and see little of what's going on. After what seems an age the tender stops and we start filing to the upper deck to find a large liner alongside. She is the *CPS Duchess of Atholl* with already a lot of troops lining her rails. It is 1800hrs and we are going aboard. I am assigned to a port cabin on B deck, with 4 bunks, however, there are five of us, lots are drawn and the unlucky one sleeps on the floor. It is a luxury ship and not yet fitted for troop carrying, a civilian staff still operates. We get hold of a cabin boy and tell him that we will see him alright if he brings us tea at 0700hrs. each morning. Now a parade for blankets, dining cards etc. My card is Berth 5, Dining table 9 and so to bed in sheets and a pillow.

Wednesday October 29ᵗʰ

Aroused by the cabin boy bringing the arranged tea. Washed at the basin in the cabin and then go up on deck and have a look around. To me it is a big ship (22,000 tons) and it seems easy to lose oneself, everywhere is busy as the ship is still taking on stores. We go to breakfast; the Sergeants' mess is 1st shift in the main dining room. Phew! What luxury it must have been in peacetime, this room, its equal I've never seen. The depth of two decks, halfway up one side a bandstand and surrounded at that level by glasswork, partitioning the room off from a companionway or corridor of an upper deck, electro-plate on the tables and a ship's waiter to each three tables (12 NCO's). As I finished with each course he pounced on the empty plate or jumped forward to pour out the tea. I felt too nervous to eat. I was not used to this, being more at home with a tin plate or mess-tin. The changeover from army to luxury hotel was almost too much. We even had a menu and it wasn't just decoration, it worked. Dinner and tea passed us by in likewise manner and I'm getting used to things a bit now. The day has been spent in getting used to the ship and listening to rumour talk.

Thursday October 30th

We pass another day at anchor in the Clyde, several more ships in midstream have been taking on troops. To the starboard lies the aircraft carrier *HMS Eagle*. It is now 1730hrs and the ship's pilot comes aboard. The Commodore has also boarded our ship with British Navy signallers; evidently we are to be the command ship. Lifeboats are being swung into emergency positions over the ships side so it looks as if we are all set to sail, the engines are going and we wait in anticipation but nothing happens, so we turn in to our bunks. At 2330hrs, we are aroused by the ship's siren, we are moving, a rush is made for great coats, we must see the last of the old country. Maybe it will be the last. Well we are off - to somewhere, *HMS Eagle* also slips by, outward bound. The beauty of the Clyde is seen beneath the light of a full Scottish moon. We are quiet, a mixture of feelings surge within us, no one sees us slip away, a few minutes before midnight, maybe to avoid the old superstition of sailing on a Friday.

Friday October 31st

0800hrs and fading in the distance is the North Irish coastline. Well we are on the Atlantic now and our destination has just been revealed - it is Halifax, Canada, so I shall at least see something of a country I've often longed in my youth to live in. The sea has a heavy swell on and some of the men are already sick, I am OK myself (but for how long?). There are nine ships in the convoy, including the *"Stirling"* and I think the *"Dunbar Castle"*, also the Polish ship *"Sobieskie"* is out there rolling very badly. We have a six destroyer escort, doesn't seem much if we run into trouble, but we have great faith in these little ships and their crews. At times they disappear in the troughs of the waves.

It is 1630hrs. - gunfire caused quite a stir throughout the ship before it became generally known that it was a practice. I am feeling all the excitement and romance of a sea voyage as we travel on board this luxury ship which as been nick-named by the crew the "Rolling" or "Drunken Duchess". Apparently she is flat-bottomed to some extent, being built, so rumour says, for the shallow waters of the Bermudas, where she was supposed to have carried rich Americans for week-end bottle parties. These parties starting the moment the ship was outside the three-mile limit. The run was said to have taken 30 hours from New York - snowstorms to tropical sunshine.

Saturday November 1ˢᵗ 1941

The Atlantic is calmer this morning; two bombers are seen flying by in the distance, heading NW. Some small birds are flying close by, I don't think we are very far from the coast of Iceland. Our steward has just informed us that we are now passing over the approximate spot where the *"Empress of Britain"* was sunk and rumour has it that an American destroyer was sunk here only yesterday.

Sunday November 2ⁿᵈ

0730hrs. Troops line the deck rails as fighter aircraft are seen flying towards us and smoke is seen on the horizon. In a few tense moments several questions are asked - are we going to be attacked? Are they Jerries? Through the glasses the American markings are seen and a cheer goes up with the cry "They are Americans". They circle us and drop a message onboard. A half hour has passed since their arrival and the smoke on the horizon now plainly to be seen is causing excitement to run high, through glasses warships can be seen.

0900hrs. They arrive and what an impressive display as the huge American escort of 15 ships take over. They cross and re-cross our bow in a surge of speed and display, they include, I am told, one heavy battle cruiser - *USS Mississippi*, two light cruisers - *USS Mexico City* and *USS* ------ plus the aircraft carrier, *USS Lexicon City*, which is said carries 96 aircraft. The sky is certainly full as the aircraft continually zoom and roll above us, also there are 11 destroyers. This powerful force has taken over and the silent service of Britain has just as silently taken over the huge convoy of merchantmen that the Americans escorted this far and is taking them through the most dangerous of waters to the English ports.

Today we have chicken for lunch, a nice treat. Explosions are taking place and the whole ship shudders, depth charges are being dropped by our new escort, which at present are prone to jokes from us sceptical British. A wit says "Perhaps they've sighted a whale", another says, "A U-boat has just left Germany", or "It's to keep their spirits up" and so forth. We are in mid-Atlantic, following a zigzag course, every few minutes we change direction and the convoy follows, by signal from our ship. The signal, two hoots to port and one for starboard, is given on the ships siren. There is a heavy ground swell on now - many more seasick and feeling a bit heady myself, I go up into the bows, where the wind is gale force and bashes the sea over the sides as the ship dips into it. It freshens me up and I feel better, but on looking back and seeing the stern apparently towering over the top of you makes you gulp and quickly look ahead.

Monday November 3rd

The sea is running very heavy and the "Drunken Duchess" lurches forward with a sideways roll at the same time and the rails are lined with sick men. Feeling sick myself but not enough to miss my breakfast, I find that two of my table companions are missing and many other empty places are seen. Those of us that can stick it come in for extra rations. There is a great display of aircraft from the carrier, they constantly take-off and return, making her resemble a busy bee-hive. It is a wonderfully clear moonlight night which is useful in finding ones way about the ship during a blackout. As we are now considered to be out of danger of an attack by bombers we are allowed to remove our clothes on going to bed, the first time since we left England.

Tuesday November 4th

During the last four days we have put the clocks back 3 hours. I have just found out that in charge of the convoy is Vice Admiral Swabbey, whilst Rear Admiral Hewitt USN is in charge of the American naval escort. Message of the day, which may make history: -

Major General Beckworth-Smith DSO MC to American escort:
British troops proud of honour of your magnificent escort.

Commander American escort (in reply):
The officers and crew of escort appreciate your message and hope to be worthy of your confidence.
Rear Admiral Hewitt USN.

Wednesday November 5th

Guy Fawkes, but luckily no fireworks for us other than depth charges dropped by escort destroyers at mid-day. A quiet day passed playing cards in the bunk.

Thursday November 6th

Our seventh day out from England and I think we must be nearing land as seagulls are floating on the water. It is 0900hrs and eight more naval ships of America join us making our escort total 23 craft. What an escort! The morning has passed quietly with us watching the ships on all sides.

1500hrs and the escort is scurrying about, action stations are being taken up, something has been detected. Escort appears to be searching and moving very efficiently. The ships news say that submarines are working in these (Newfoundland) waters, reports say two transports sunk in this area recently. Everyone is on their toes, keyed up with excitement. The weather is getting much colder.

Friday November 7th

It is foggy and can only see other ships dimly. The convoy slowed right down during the night as one ship had trouble and lost touch in the fog but has since caught up. We are preparing for arrival and it must be considered safe as the lifeboats are being hauled inboard to their normal positions. The night is upon us and the fog persists, which I think is normal in these waters.

Saturday November 8th

Our last lunch on the "Duchess" is once again chicken as we drop anchor off Halifax (Canada). Large American liners are anchored around the docks, which we learn are to be our new homes as troopships from now on. It's a wonderful sunny day for November and the men are full of excitement, although no shore leave is allowed. In the late afternoon we transfer to a nice streamlined looking liner - *USS Mount Vernon*, formally the *"Washington"*, 35,000 tons, speed 30 knots, length 700 feet and at this time America's best liner. Getting back to Halifax, we learned of an interesting but tragic happening to Halifax city in 1921. It was blown up when a ship carrying explosives blew up in the harbour. An American warship there at the time had all her men blown off her decks, also her gun turrets were blasted off and the anchor blown seven miles away, where it is now railed off as

The Liner 'America', later known as the 'West Point', 34,000 tons. One of the ships that took us from Canada to Singapore.

a memorial to the sailors and civilians who lost their lives. As the day wears on the first newspapers for 11 days filter in. These comprised 16 pages so there is no shortage here. It is getting dark now and as blackouts do not exist here it looks like fairyland with all the shore lights and the lights from the liners, looking like giant floating hotels. So uplifting after two years of Britain's blackouts. Water on the ship for some uses is obtained by extracting the salt from seawater, but otherwise a dry ship - a disappointment for the British troops.

The day comes to an end and so to bed, just settling down when a call comes for a volunteer baggage party. I hurriedly dress to be one of them. Our last ship, the *CPS Duchess of Atholl,* has moved to another berth over two miles away and to finish unloading baggage we have to take our trucks through Halifax to reach her. The main street, over a two-mile straight, is ablaze with light. It is midnight and shops of various descriptions are open, it seems cafes keep open all night.

Sunday November 9th

Fights between the American sailors and Canadian soldiers keep the Black Marias busy. By 0430hrs we had finished our task and got in a short sleep before breakfast began at 0630hrs. Dinner comes in at 1030hrs, and tea at 1530hrs, this means a rotation queue the whole day to feed the complete Brigade of 5,000 troops on this ship. We are now paid in American dollars, only to find that we cannot easily use them owing to the shortage of small change in the canteens and no beer!

Monday November 10th

We are suddenly aroused by the shrieking of Klaxon horns, all hatches and doors are closed, we are about to sail. 0800hrs and we are off on our second stage to somewhere. An hour later we pick up an escort of one British destroyer, which later hands us over to six American destroyers and one aircraft carrier. We have a number of black sailors in the American crew, it appears to be the first voyage for most of them and they are a bit nervous. The Yankee cooks certainly serve up some queer mixtures in the food line, including sweet potatoes, baked minced meat, tough pressed meats - one made from goose livers and sausages resembling rubber and raw grated cabbage and pineapple salad.

It is now 1800hrs and we are again in the blackout area, this after so much light from the past few days causes some confusion on the dark decks.

Tuesday November 11th

We find ourselves sailing down the American coastline, the sea is rough but the ship moves smoothly enough. Meals on the ship are a lengthy business, possibly because of the large numbers of troops. Have just been in a queue for a good half hour and then had to stand to eat it. We are still going south towards the West Indies and the weather is getting much warmer. I am casting off my under clothes and physical training has been started on the upper deck as a means to keeping us fit while in a confined space.

Wednesday November 12th

It is very warm and we are now only wearing vest and shorts. On hanging over the ships rails gazing down into the clear blue water you can see lovely green-looking fish swimming by, also the ship is ploughing through masses of seaweed, it seems we could be near the area of the Sargasso sea, that is where the masses of seaweed build up and in the old days wrecked many ships. Night comes in rather quickly and tired out from watching the sea go by we turn to our bunks and hammocks for some sleep.

Friday November 14th

As dawn breaks we are awakened by excited voices shouting "Land ahoy!" Yes, land on both sides or to port and starboard as the sailors say. We are cruising through the West Indies, with porpoises playing and moving in front of the ship, also shoals of white-looking flying fish leaping across the rippling and sparkling sea. We also have for a little while an escort of large Catalina flying boats.

1. **On this day...** November 14, 1941... HMS Ark Royal sank.

Sunday November 16th

More land is seen, the approaches to Port of Spain, Trinidad. These headlands rising high out of the water, reaching skywards with their jungle covered terrain like peaks of a partly submerged mountain range and through the binoculars flashes of colour from flying birds. Around noon we dropped anchor off the port and the task of refuelling and the taking on of supplies began with busy little ships hurrying backwards and forwards between us and the docks.

Tuesday November 18th

The surface of the sea is covered with thousands of oranges, the result of some burst open crates. What a sight! The little ships, the glow of the oranges on the vivid blue-green water with every now and again a glimpse of shoals of electric eels swimming beneath the surface. Another day gone by, night comes fast with all the red, blue, green and yellow shore lights making the coastline look like fairy-land, shimmering with exotic jewels. All the ships in the convoy including escorts are aglow with light, bands playing on some and an open air cinema on ours. What a night to remember outside the blackout zone, a brilliant night, sky complete with tropical moon and the slow slap of water on the ship's side with the light reflections bouncing back, soft music floating over turning ones memories homewards.

Wednesday November 19th

It's now two days gone since we sailed into paradise, we have not been allowed to go ashore and are now moving away along the

Ancient Order of the Deep
- a way of passing time onboard ship

course we cruised in on, an experience long to be remembered. We have been instructed to put our watches forward by one hour.

Saturday November 22nd

We are now three days out from Trinidad and following the South American coastline and back with the blackout at 1830hrs. The sea is aglow with phosphorus, looking like a huge expanse of underwater lighting.

Sunday November 23rd

As dawn comes with a huge red sun rising from a calm silvery sea a large cargo ship passes by our convoy, the only sign of life during the last three days.

It's 0900hrs, we are now crossing the Equator, still going south. The ceremony of crossing the line is now going on throughout the morning and two of my Sergeant friends have been barbered by "King Neptune", each having lost half of their moustaches and many have unusual haircuts. Battles with rival parties with the deck hoses make the ships decks awash. The Brigadier was found, dragged to the throne and painted red with some colorant. Haircuts with a butcher's knife still go on if you are unlucky enough to get caught.

Wednesday November 26th

The days pass with the troops lolling about the decks soaking up the hot sunshine or hanging over the ships side watching the sparkling sea and the long white wake of the ship, or if you are up the bow you can see shoals of flying fish, so much like flocks of white birds leaping away as we plough through the sea. A distant coastline appears and during the day we cruise closer in and drop anchor off Rio de Janeiro, but only to wait for tenders to bring us fresh water. 5,000 men can get through a terrific amount of fresh water in a week. Food is getting a little better, this morning I had grapefruit and two eggs etc. For dinner, roast turkey, cranberry sauce, olives, mashed potato, mincemeat tart, oranges, nuts and tea. At tea, lemon squash, soup, onion and lentil stew, beans and tomato sauce, corned beef, and apples. All very good but then it's not a British Army menu but provided by the American staff.

Saturday November 29th

An American crew member has just been reported drowned, he jumped overboard after learning that he was to face a court martial for deserting his look-out post. Our destroyer escort are dashing around as a report has come in that there is an enemy submarine in the vicinity. Nothing exciting came of it and the only incident other than that was to one of my men who broke a leg while boxing on the deck this afternoon. Some British naval vessels pass by and also our American aircraft carrier is leaving us.

Sunday November 30th

The ships sirens wail out and everybody grabs his needs for abandoning ship, which is his topee, life jacket and water bottle, and then calmly makes for his allotted boat station where the boats hanging in their davits are out over the side of the ship, the position they have been in since we left Trinidad - ready for a quick launch in case of an emergency. The sea is very calm and with the practice over we go our various ways. Today I am Sergeant-in-charge of the Troop deck and have just watched the burial at sea of a Petty Officer from one of the escorting destroyers, also saw a whale blowing, off the starboard side.

Monday December 1st 1941

The sea is flat calm, a brilliant blue sky as I watch Dolphins swim around our ship. A "blowing" whale is seen off the starboard side.
Cpl. Miller lies dangerously ill with sulphur poisoning.

Tuesday December 2nd

It's now a lovely tropical morning and we have just been told that the *HMS Devonshire* has sunk an armed raider in our vicinity. She was believed to be a submarine supply ship. A huge bird has just flown over, we must be a 1,000 miles from land, maybe it's an albatross. The day draws to an end with me hanging over the stern of the ship watching its long wake trailing in the distance. It is strewn with the debris thrown over the side by the crew, which consists of cardboard boxes, orange crates, paper and bottles etc. All of which goes over just as darkness comes down, to put it over before could bring enemy submarines down our way.

Wednesday December 3rd

A destroyer is dashing around laying a smoke screen, but I cannot find out what all the excitement is about. Our time is now back to English time so we must be dropping away from the Equator.

2. **On this day...** Friday December 5, 1941... Britain declares war on Finland, Hungary and Romania.

Saturday December 6th

It has been a bit cooler the last two days and today very much cooler which is surprising as we are supposed to be making for Cape Town. We have been at sea for a long time, 14 days now without seeing land. It's now after tea and all NCO's have been called to the mess decks where we are told by the Regimental Sergeant Major that on getting up in the morning we are to wear all our English winter clothes, also great coats when going on deck. We are instructed to inform our men to do likewise but no reasons are given for the clothing change.

Sunday December 7th

It is very much colder and we feel it, as less than three days ago we were scorching hot. After breakfast we go on deck and watch in some surprise the heavy rolling sea covered in a heavy mist and drizzle of rain. It is so English one would not be surprised if Southampton docks suddenly appeared. It seems that the convoy has been speeding towards the Antarctic in an effort to outwit submarines that were lying in wait for us. It's getting much colder and we are wearing our great coats. We must be hundreds of miles to the south of our normal course as it's now daylight until 2230hrs, while near the Equator darkness comes down like a curtain at 1800hrs. During the day an albatross (the sacred bird of sailors) has followed us. The sea is very rough and the ship is rolling well, also I learn that to date we have cruised in a zigzag fashion across the oceans 12,000 miles. We are on our way back to the Cape and are now being thrown about by heavy seas, being in the area off the Cape where they tell us three tides meet.

3. **On this day...** December 7, 1941... Japan bombs Pearl Harbour, American Pacific fleet suffers heavy losses. Battleships *Arizona, Oklahoma, West Virginia and California* sunk. The battleships *Maryland, Nevada, Pennsylvania* and four smaller vessels also sank. Japan loses 29 planes.

Monday December 8ᵗʰ

There is a lot of excitement among our American crew as they have just learned that their country has declared war on Japan and yet we have been on their ships for a month now.

4. **On this day...** December 8, 1941... Japanese forces land in northern Malaya. Britain declares war on Japan.

Tuesday December 9ᵗʰ

The sea is calming down and the weather becoming much warmer again so gradually we change back to vest and shorts. Land ahead! Up goes the cry and a great rush to the ships rails to have a look, yes there is a coastline with a large flat piece standing above the rest. It is 0600hrs and daylight and as we forge along the coast becomes more visible, it is the Cape of Good Hope.

At 1130hrs, we dropped anchor off Cape Town. It was a wonderful experience for all of us, seeing the lovely coloured houses of the town backed by the high rocky terrain of Table Mountain with the thin mist over the top, known as the table cloth. We've been jamming the rails most of the time watching the shore-line, with little ships coming and going and now with a rumble of anchor chains we are moving again.

Ship docks at 1500hrs. Later we exchange our English money for South African and then are allowed to go ashore by 1900hrs. It's like a new freedom to set foot in a strange land, and what excitement, thousands of people at the docks to greet us and cheering their heads off. Everywhere ablaze with lights of all colours; what a thrilling contrast after seven weeks on a blacked out liner. The buses, cinemas and dances are free to us, free to 5,000 troops! How nice it is to see and mix with civilians again, to see lovely girls walking about and drink an iced beer, to walk like a sailor but to feel terra-firma under your feet. All the ships of our convoy are ablaze with flags as a salute to Cape Town, its first visit by these crews. Many sailors from our own naval vessels are also ashore.

Wednesday December 10ᵗʰ

1030hrs. and a heavenly warm day with slight overhead mist and the troops from all the ships in the convoy, which includes three Battalions of The Royal Norfolk's, form up on the dockside for a march with bands through parts of the town. At once we were greeted with a civic girls' band, 40 strong, bugles and drums from Johannesburg. On return to the ship, something out of the blue for us, iced lemon tea was served.

5. *On this day...* December 10, 1941... *HMS Prince of Wales* and *HMS Repulse* sunk by Japanese aircraft off Malaya. 800 men lost. British forces relieve Tobruk, North Africa.

Thursday December 11ᵗʰ

We were free to go our own way, so a friend and I set off to see some sights of the town. On reaching the dock gates there were hundreds of cars, buses and people waiting to take us on sight-seeing tours, all for nothing. An old gentleman took my friend and me in his car around the Cape suburbs and up a road around Table Mountain. We saw a reservation for wild animals and birds, he also gave us tea at a Dutch farm-like restaurant up the Mountain. Later he left us in the Public Gardens with its wonderful display of colours in its shrubs and flowers. We were picked up again later by a man and his wife and invited to spend the evening with them. We were taken out to "Sea Point" where we spent three hours at the Bay Beach Hotel, with our drink and food at our hosts' expense. Finally arrived back at the ship just after midnight, a little worse for wear after imbibing a little too much Cape brandy, which by the way is only four shillings a bottle.

Friday December 12ᵗʰ

It's Reveille again and the pair of us feel a bit thick headed, but after a cold shower and breakfast we feel more ourselves. We join the thousands of troops on the dockside where we form up for another route march through the town. There are so many of us that we march in double formation, six abreast through the wide streets. After this we spent another enjoyable day in the town. The people here are certainly enjoying having us, their cars and buses are outside the docks in their hundreds waiting to take us off to see the sites. I have never met with such hospitality and am sure never will again. Later that day I was approached by a lady from an organisation that wanted to help. She told me that the mail leaving Cape Town would probably be the last to get to England by ordinary means, so I gave her my home address as she promised to write to my wife. (It was a number of years later that I was to learn that passing through Cape Town was the last my family was going to hear from me for about three years).

6. *On this day...* December 12, 1941... Britain declares war on Bulgaria.

Saturday December 13ᵗʰ

Lucky or unlucky we sail from Cape Town docks and drop anchor in the open sea with all the other ships of the convoy. The weather has turned misty and cool, but no blackout in force here as yet. Our ship puts to sea cruising in a wide circle back to its original position, why? It is said among the troops that the crew told them they were 'boxing' the compass and testing magnetic mine circuit gear.

Finally left at 1630hrs. The cruiser on escort duty is *HMS Dorsetshire*, it is said that she fired the last torpedoes at the German battleship *"Bismarck"*, and recently sank an enemy supply ship. We now have aboard officers and men of the Royal Naval Signals section. Our American naval escort left us and the whole convoy is now in the hands, safe hands no doubt, of the British cruiser. I have just seen my first shark swimming around the ship, hoping no doubt someone would fall overboard, but he was out of luck. We are now entering the Mozambique Channel, between the African coast and the island of Madagascar.

Destination rumours are Egypt, India, Singapore and even Australia. A speech made by the Mayor of Cape Town reads thus:

> *"I will make a great splash in the South African Press about the biggest and best behaved convoy ever to enter Cape Town."*

It seems that previous to us they had some Scottish troops who had to be recalled to their ships and stood out at sea because of the trouble they caused.

Thursday December 18th

Weather is hot as we near the Equator for the second time and it is now rumoured that we may be calling at Mombassa, East Africa. While I write, the 'Ack Ack' guns are barking away on both sides of the ship, we can be thankful that so far we have only heard them in practice.

Saturday December 20th

We have now heard that our destination was formerly Cairo, but orders received in Cape Town have changed it to Bombay, India. We hope to reach India in seven days time as among the men we have assumed the name "The Floating Division". Crossed the Equator again today and have now cruised half-way around the world. During the afternoon a lecture was given by the Brigadier on India. The transport of this water-borne division is supposed to be in a convoy some days behind, although it left ahead of us.

Sunday December 21st

A destroyer appears on the horizon and a ship leaves the convoy to return to Mombassa as it has developed boiler trouble. Our clocks have been put back fifteen minutes instead of the usual forward routine.

Dawn again and in the Indian Ocean, a wonderful day, deep blue sky and sea, enough breeze to temper the heat, a picture as painters and writers would see it. I often wonder if there is a war on, but the fact remains that every day must be bringing us nearer the Eastern conflict, which reminds me of a premonition I had while sitting on the promenade at home one Sunday evening in 1938. I said to my girl-friend (later my wife) that "I would finish up fighting the Japanese in the Far East and finish up as a Prisoner of War".

As I hang over the ships rails watching the sea rolling away from her sides as her bow parts the water, darkness comes down like a blue velvet carpet, later to be pierced by a giant moon that I feel sure can only be seen here at the size it appears to be. In this romantic setting I am dreaming of home and Christmas, which is only two days away. I visualise Mother carving the fowl, perhaps an empty corner with a bottle of beer and not being there to drink it. The pulling of crackers, the laughter and joking, wondering if you are all still at home and if Joan (my wife) is with you. A bit of homesickness perhaps, anyhow it's time to wash the sweat out of my vest and pants then to the bunk for the night.

Monday December 22nd

Awakened by the crew moving around so get up and go along to the galley. You can sometimes be lucky enough to get a jug of the crew's good coffee if there's any left over, otherwise on the mess decks we are served tea made by American cooks - I leave you to think what it can taste like. Usual type of day spent with lecture in the afternoon on use of compass and maps and the evening passed sitting on deck enjoying the present calm of the Indian Ocean.

Tuesday December 23rd

Same old queue for breakfast, the American cookhouse staff has not overcome the problem of 5,000 troops.

It's now 1050hrs and a boat from the escort cruiser is coming over to our ship which has stopped. Full of wonderment, many troops line the rails on one side, so much so that we developed a list. A rope gangway is put out and the party of British signals are taken off and put aboard another ship in the convoy. While we are still talking among ourselves as to what is going on, all sorts of speculations, the convoy of ships and escort cruiser continue their way, leaving us making a sweeping turn and heading back in the direction we came from. The convoy disappears in the distance and we are alone on the ocean and no escort. The ship is now travelling at top speed, vibrating from stem to stern and the order goes out for us to pack our kit. Nobody knows why.

The day passes by with a bit of physical exercise to try and keep us fit, it's a real effort doing it as it is so hot. When you go down for a mid-day meal and sit for awhile with elbows on the table talking away, you find that you leave pools of sweat on the table where it has run down your arms. Your clothing is soaked so you rinse them through in the wash basin, put them on and dry out in the sun. It was during such an occasion that I sat on a bollard and fell asleep, when I awakened later my shoulders, arms and legs resembled a boiled lobster. For several days I was pretty sore.

Wednesday December 24th

It's Xmas Eve and before yesterday's turn about the crew were decorating the dining halls with festive trimmings and Xmas trees, which apparently were taken on board at Cape Town. Ship's doing 23 knots and now the crew tell us that we are heading for Mombassa, East Africa. We have now crossed the Equator three times in the last eight weeks, twice in the last four days. The men are trying to get the Christmas spirit by singing carols on deck, but a dry ship, so it's difficult without a bottle to come to grips with it. We get through the evening in a flat sort of way and finally go off to bed.

Thursday December 25th

Up this morning and as far as I know 5,000 men shake a leg without a hangover - amazing! Well "Merry Xmas" to you all. Just arrived off Mombassa 10.50hrs. It's so hot that 500 turkeys meant for our dinner had somehow become victims of the heat and were thrown overboard, leaving us to pull our imaginary crackers over good old bully beef, potatoes and "Adams Ale". Mombassa looks very picturesque with the various coloured roofs of the houses, the native women tall and colourful in fine silks, soldiers of The East Kenya Rifles in khaki uniform topped by a red fez with gold tassels and police in khaki shorts and blue naval-type jerseys, none wore shoes. I see the ship that left the convoy with boiler trouble is here, also two naval craft, the *"Emerald"* and *"Columbo"*. We are allowed to walk off the ship after tea, but confined to the dock area, where we are eaten alive by mosquitoes. Well here we are just about the end of Xmas day and before I bed down, here's to all your "Good Health" in weak tea.

Friday December 26th

Boxing Day dawns, it seems a funny way to spend this day in equatorial heat, a blazing searing sun and the continuous buzzing of plagues of flies. Some of the lads are taking physical training, phew! Must be mad; for myself I join a bathing party. A four mile ride, the crossing of a wooden span structure known as the "Yahati" bridge brings us to a clearing on the Kenyan coastline, where the native lorries creaking, and some hissing with escaping steam come to a halt The large trees in the area are ringing like circular saws with sounds emitted by insects of the locust family. We emerge from the belt of trees and there in front of us stretches an expanse of glittering silver sand with the gentle waves of the Indian Ocean lapping softly along a coastal fringe dotted with clumps of palm trees, wild orange tangerines, bananas, huge aloes and bamboo giving you a dream beach. Here and there the occasional flight of colourful birds, the exotic scent from the flowers wafting on the still air and looking back, again the coloured roofs of the houses present a quiet picture. Going back to the musical locusts, the natives tell us that they only whistle at Christmas. These natives live in queer hutments with a mud-hole outside the door for washing purposes, however, their women-folk looked clean and very colourful. After taking in our surroundings we finally take to the sea, I cannot swim but a sergeant friend takes me in hand, teaching me to float in what seems like a warm bath. The sea being so full of salt it is very buoyant making floating easy and delightful. After a half an hour splashing around we make for the sand, which is hot to the touch and in the shade of the palms we lie and within five minutes have dried ourselves off. Brushing off the fine sand we make ready to return to the ship and as we leave the beach we are given bowls of nuts, raisins and toffee by soldiers of The East Kenya Rifles camped near the beach. We arrive back and as we board ship we are warned not to touch the metal parts of it. The reason being that lying in dock for two days she has become so hot from the drenching sunshine that it is possible to quickly fry eggs on the metal.

In the evening a friend and I were walking through the area enjoying looking at the sights and ways of the native population when a car pulls up alongside us, its occupant asks us if we would like to go for a drink. Did we hear him right? Those magic words, last heard over eight weeks ago. He opened the car door and we scrambled in before he could change his mind. Introducing ourselves to him we learned that he was an English customs officer working here in Mombassa. On arrival at his club of The Royal Naval Reserve, we are ushered inside to meet his son and Rose-Marie his very beautiful daughter. She could have doubled for my wife, however, I was staggered when told that she was only 11 years old, I would have put her at least 18, must be all this sunshine made her develop so. Further introductions take place to other Petty Officers who treated us very well with Australian beer, which was selling at half-a-crown a bottle, although it did not cost us anything. We had a hectic night out and how we got back to the ship I do not remember much about.

Saturday December 27th

On waking I feel as though I have been hit by an almighty big mallet; if that's the effect of Australian beer they had better keep it down under, but then fair's fair it could be the result of being on a dry ship for so long. Food and fuel are being loaded on the ship this morning therefore we are not disembarking here after all. The native Dockers are whispering Singapore. Besides us, there are also a lot of Swahili soldiers back from the Abyssinian campaign.

After tea John Jacobs and I strolled out to a sort of native market where you could get sundries, fruit and silks at prices as exotic as the perfume of the flowers unless you were prepared to barter hard. I bought a pair of "choppies", native shoes, just a sole and toe strap, could be useful on deck. We also bought one hundred oranges for three shillings. Later we went to a bar for a drink, beer at two shillings a bottle but very potent. The young native barman was proud to inform us he was British and insisted on shaking hands. We finished the night having dinner at the Palace Hotel with a South African soldier also back from Abyssinia. The dinner was ten courses, duck, green peas, roast beef, gorgonzola cheese, coffee, sweet and various trimmings, all for four shillings per head. It has been a riotous night, the potent beer and wine makes us a bit unsteady, well lets admit it - drunk. The Military Police trucks are dashing about picking up such people so we hide behind some palm trees until a taxi comes in sight, which we manage to stop and get it to take us to the docks.

Sunday December 28th

The morning brings a thick and vague memory of where we were the previous night, although, a quick shower followed by a mug of tea sorts out my senses. After breakfast I attend to my regimental duties which, as a Sergeant I do have although in the past I may have overlooked to mention them. This, at the moment onboard ship, is mainly checking any for sick parade, any complaints and general tidiness of quarters. Later I join the beach bathing party for what could be the last time. I have learned to swim during the last few days in this lovely blue water of the Azanian sea, as this coastal strip is known.

In the afternoon I watch railway trucks being shunted alongside, these are full of waste from the galleys of the ships in the harbour. Our kitchen staff is ready to dump our waste into them. The wagon loads of refuse stinks and are a mass of flies, sitting amongst it are native workmen who are picking out pieces of bread, brushing off the tea leaves and then eating it. Empty tin cans are also being licked out, it's utter poverty and to them it seems a Godsend.

Have a walk into town this hot sultry night, where we go to the Marina Hotel and enjoy a supper, getting back to the ship about 2250hrs, to find it all hustle and bustle with the crew preparing to raise the gangways. As we go aboard the dockworkers still whisper "Singapore!" although as yet we have been told nothing. Really it would be a relief to get moving again as the ship is so very hot. It is difficult to get a decent sleep twisting and turning in a pool of sweat on the canvas bottom of my bunk, the cursing and swearing of men in similar conditions. If the ship moves at least we shall be drawing in some cooler night air.

Monday December 29th

It's dawn and the anchor is being raised, ropes tying us to the dockside are being cast off and at 1015hrs to the minute we slowly move away from our hot-house of a home for the last six days. A few cheers from the dockworkers and then we are well away, slowly turning to a due east direction.

Night approaches, sea calm, Very lights fired, no one knows why, what could they be looking for? The cruiser *HMS Emerald* has also left Mombassa and has now joined us as escort. It is now official that our destination is Singapore, if we can get there without the attention of the "Kamikaze" pilots of the Japanese airforce.

Tuesday December 30th

One day out from our last port we are now being joined by a large convoy that has just come into view. Have run into some monsoon-like weather, skies are heavily overcast and there are frequent tropical downpours. The large convoy now closes with us, 19 ships in all and others have moved off in another direction.

Later in the day a further split takes place, leaving us five in number and one naval escort. Last nights Very light signals must have been for the benefit of the convoy. We have also learned that the convoy that we left Scotland with went on to India and with it went our transport. So we are on our way to the war zone, 5,000 men and no transport.

Wednesday December 31st

New Year's Eve and no parties, or drinking and dancing the New Year in, so to bed with memories of the past.

Thursday January 1st 1942

After breakfast we are again told that we are headed for Singapore, only this time it comes straight from the Commodore, he says that we are headed for the Eastern conflict and by all accounts we have some work to do which will be warm in more ways than one. So after 10 weeks at sea the fate of the "Doomed Brigade" is decided (we named ourselves this after being at sea for so long without our knowing our destination). Anyhow let me wish you a telepathic "Happy New Year" and may be with any kind of luck be with you for the next one. Nothing of great importance happening at the moment, but I have just noticed that our naval escort is two ships, the *HMS Dorsetshire* and *HMS Exeter*. The sea is calm and we cruise serenely on our way with hardly a thought among us about the Japanese. The men are lolling around the decks in groups, enjoying the sun and no doubt swapping stories of home, others are playing cards in some shady places whilst on the mess deck there is always a "Housey Housey" game going on. The fellows who run it getting rich on their takings and I wonder when we reach land whether they will be able to enjoy the money that is fleeced from the lads. I was once persuaded to take part in a card game, Pontoon it was called. I made a great start, winning a few hands and quite a bit of money, after awhile however my luck deserted me and I was as they say 'taken to the cleaners' by crafty old soldiers. Too late I realised what had happened, I had no doubt been allowed to win a few games to keep me interested and then like a fly I was swatted. I'm afraid this taught me, a novice, to keep out of card games with soldiers of peacetime battalions. Time passes by and the ships routine goes on, it's a hot afternoon and I am feeling parched so I wander around to a point on the ship where the Americans sell soft drinks. As always on this trip one has to wait a fair time in the queue before getting a drink, two gulps and it's gone only in a few minutes to return through your skin and drip off the end of your nose. All the guns on the ship are now permanently manned by the American crew as we are now within range of the Japanese long-range bombers.

Monday January 5th

Most of us are letter writing as we are going to make a call for water somewhere in the Maldives Island group. There is just a chance that the letters, maybe the last from this convoy, will reach home. You can hear the scratching of so many pencils as we set to work on our writing, at the same time trying to word these letters so not too much will be blotted out by the censors.

1000hrs. Arrive off the Maldives which look to be just flat stretches of sand barely above sea level and covered with coconut palms, to me it looks like the much imagined desert island. Small ships come alongside and our mail is taken aboard and in that bulk of letters are two of mine, homeward bound I hope on an old tanker that is shortly leaving here. The day spent lazily as the ship takes on oil, the tankers supplying it we are told came from Rangoon in Burma. Can see areas of tents among the palm trees, but so distant that we cannot see what's going on there. See two men walking about but even through my binoculars cannot recognise anything about them, guess it must be an army supply dump.

We have finished taking on oil and various goods and we are making ready to sail after standing off the islands two and a half days.

Tuesday January 6th

Flat calm sea and hot sun, for a while my thoughts turn to you at home, perhaps you have snow and with this thought I imagine my younger brothers shouting and laughing as they sledge down Beeston Hill. Two sharp toots from a destroyer bring me back to reality. We are slowly making our way through this tropical air having just recently zigzagged across the Equator for the fourth time.

For the next four days we just cruise majestically on our way to Singapore under bright blue skies and over a calm rippling sea, sparkling like the sunshine on a gigantic mirror. The men are now talking more of the future and what it may hold for them. When we left England war against the Japanese was not dreamt of by the majority of us, well it seems to be our destiny otherwise we should not have been steaming around the oceans since October, this now being January 1942. When I stop to think back it's like a fairy tale. It started with the Irish Sea, the North Atlantic, the Caribbean, the South Atlantic, Antarctic Circle, the Cape and the Indian Ocean and still we plough on. I wonder how we will cope physically when the testing time comes as we must be a flabby lot now with no real training after all these weeks of little activity. As for me I now have a second small boil on my waist at the back

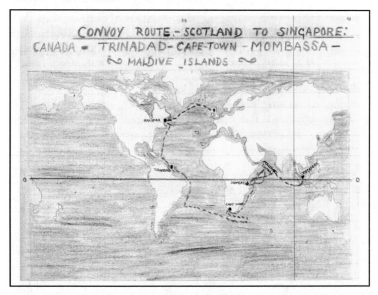

Sketch of convoy route – Scotland to Singapore via Canada, Trinidad, Cape Town, Mombassa, Maldives

and the elastic of my shorts seem to hang on it making it very painful. The first small boil was on the outside of my forearm and it was always catching on doorposts and uprights of the ship until one day it burst.

A large force of the Dutch East Indies navy has come out to escort us also we are once again joined by a convoy of five merchant ships apparently carrying stores although one is reported to have 50 Hurricane planes in packing cases aboard.

Monday January 12th

Another sultry night passes by and the coming morning finds us in the Sunda Straits after passing down the coast of Sumatra. During the day the moist heat has caused so much sweating that I go down to the wash-room to rinse out my vest and shorts and as I stand over a wash basin I let out a howl of anguish as I am grabbed and the small boil on my back nipped out. I turn angrily only to see a grinning medical orderly friend of mine, Well it was ripe for the taking he said, so he thought he would get rid of it before I had to wear my equipment, which wouldn't be long now. As we talk the ships klaxons blare out for lifeboat stations, evidently the last of many on this long voyage. I run quickly to my cabin, put on my "Mae West" (life-jacket) and hurry to my lifeboat station where I check to see that all my men are there and properly dressed for lifeboat drill, or is it a drill? We are passing through the Sunda Straits, a stretch of water between Sumatra and Java, and now for the first time growing fears and the excitement of the whole voyage as the escort destroyer fires at, and explodes, two sea mines. Men are kept below decks owing to close proximity of land and the possibility of machine gun bullets, maybe from fifth column terrorists. As we cruise up the coast of Sumatra, I can see through my binoculars a coastline that appears to be almost level with the water and in places just swamp with trees standing out of it.

CHAPTER 2

BAPTISM OF FIRE.

Tuesday January 13ʰ 1942

Early, we arrive at the naval docks, Singapore. Lucky or unlucky date, what matters is that we have arrived and are all ready to disembark. It is high tide causing the ship to stand high above the dock, this making the gangway very steep. I am coming off the ship onto the gangway, I have on all my webbing equipment, a sea kit bag, also a land kit-bag, a rifle, respirator on my chest, a rolled up gas cape across the nape of my neck, a topee hanging from this, a steel helmet on my head, full pack on my back and side pack etc. Perhaps you are wondering where the kitchen sink was. All morning tropical rain has been falling, this they tell us is to our advantage as enemy aircraft cannot spot us. I start my descent down to the docks, slip on a steel runner, this causes my gas cape to fly up and knock my steel helmet down over my eyes. I was now virtually blind, I had no free hand to push it back but managed to stumble my way to the dockside already wet through but glad to drop, for a bit, some of our gear.

Getting wetter we stand around awaiting further orders, soon we are told to form up in Companies ready to march off. We march for about three miles and with the water running through the seat of our pants and slopping through the lace holes of our boots we finally arrive at an Indian troop camp, close by a large oil dump. We are siphoned off to hutments where we are glad to get out of our soaked clothes. We hang about waiting for the promised tea, but after an hour had passed it still did not appear. We are feeling very fed up after our past hectic and wet two hours, and our grumbling brings the news no one knew of our coming therefore no rations were drawn for us. Our thanks to an Ack-Ack gun detachment in the camp for they provided us with a cup of tea and hard biscuits from their own rations.

Night comes and with it a change of sleeping conditions, complete with my first effort to fix and adjust a mosquito net, which after a while I managed. Next, to get inside and tuck in. I lay for a time listening to the buzzing of the mosquitoes on the outside of the net and to the noise of the various types of repair works going on into the night, eventually almost exhausted I fall asleep.

Wednesday January 14ᵗʰ

Too soon I'm awakened again by noise of movement around, well it's 0600hrs. and time to get about, to find somewhere to get a wash and shave and then hopefully breakfast, which after a long wait does not materialise. It appears we are a square peg in a round hole, no one has drawn provisions for us, a lot of running about by our Officer and Quartermaster Sergeant eventually, through the good grace of the other units in the camp managed a mug of tea, one rasher of bacon and half a round of bread. A starvation breakfast for starving men but we are thankful for it. After our meagre meal I receive orders to get my men on parade bringing with them their greatcoats, topees and other British winter clothing which apparently would have been needed if we had gone to our original destination 'Somewhere in the Middle East'. After 11 weeks as the "Floating Brigade" now they tell us what might have been. Later in the morning we take stock of our remaining kit. Turning out the kit bag we find any leather attachments have already gone green with mould, bits of metal and buckles rusty because of the terrible humidity that prevails here, even my leather wrist-watch strap is green. Grub is at last coming through and we get a decent dinner.

In the afternoon I visit an Anti-aircraft Artillery Battery that is in the camp hoping to hear some news of my next door neighbour, (Jim Tuck) who I have learned, is out here. After extensive inquiries I find that he left during the last few days with part of the Battery for somewhere up Malaya. As the day comes to an end this camp is all work and movement, troops coming and going.

Thursday January 15th

We have just had a raid by Japanese planes on the oil containers, some of which they have managed to set on fire. With the flames, the thick black smoke and the crack of the Ack-Ack guns we have moved nearer the action. All the Sergeants have now been called together. We receive orders to be ready to move tomorrow morning onto the mainland of Malaya.

The camp is as before, a hive of industry, everywhere are sand coloured trucks, evidently worn out transport from the desert. Mechanics are working on the engines and other mechanical parts, other men are busy painting a green camouflage on them for their new venture into the green jungle and rubber plantations of Malaya. What a way to start a campaign, with patched up transport, our own good stuff no doubt still sitting in India.

The day nears its end as darkness comes down as it does like someone drawing a curtain across the sky. Not much we can do with the almost darkness of very strict blackouts except discuss the possibilities of tomorrow and where we are likely to finish up. Not having been told anything about Malaya all our rambling talk does not reveal much to help.

Friday January 16th

Morning has come with the so-called curtain of nature being opened across the sky to reveal it clear blue and a huge rising red sun. Quickly dressed I dash for the wash area to avoid the sleepy-eyed crowd that will soon muster there pushing each other around to get to the taps. Shaved and refreshed I make my way back for breakfast, after which I get my men together in readiness for the move warned of the day before. It does not at this time come off for the men as I am given orders to gather my kit and proceed to the Headquarters Hut where I find I am in the company of some more of my Sergeant comrades. We are told we are going in advance to a place called Jemualang, around two hundred miles up Malaya. We are to take over positions from the Australian 22nd. Brigade.

Off we go in our reconditioned and redecorated transport, a couple of small covered trucks travelling through Singapore, over the causeway and onto the mainland. We make our way unhurriedly through Malaya's rubber plantations flanked on either side of a long narrow tarmac road, which I am told is the only main road there is. Nothing else is going our way but there is a great movement of three-ton Army lorries going past us in the opposite direction, mainly driven by soldiers of the Indian Army. They drive without any due respect for anyone else on the road. A few times they have been so close to us on this narrow road that the flapping canvas covers of their trucks have brushed ours. The further we go into Malaya the more evidence of the mad driving as every mile or so there are lorries overturned by the wayside, upside down over embankments, all this gets us wondering why we are the only ones going north.

We finally arrive at the Australian positions and what a desolate looking place, it's raining cats and dogs, part of the area was I should think an old tin working, great holes filled with water. The village of Jemualang a blackened burnt out mess, enough to put us off before we make the rounds of the defence points with the aid of an "Aussie" Captain. These points are dismal enough, trenches roofed over with branches and palm leaves for camouflage cover. Having completed the rounds I am taken to a native hut to meet the other "Aussie" officers and Sergeants, then tea and cake of all things is given to me. The officer asks me if I have a supply of water purifying tablets or quinine tablets, he was a very surprised officer when I told him that we had had no issue of these things. On his table stood large jars of each, he dug his hand in giving me some of each and then showing me a corner I could sleep in, tossed me a couple of pomelos, large grapefruit-type fruit, but sweet.

I was not asleep for more than an hour when I was awakened by someone shaking me. I was practically exhausted when I got into my blankets so did not come to very quickly, but when I did manage to take in my surroundings I recognised the officer I had last seen, bending over me. He was apologising for waking me so soon but he said that he had just received orders that I was to return to a rendezvous a few miles back and await my Battalion which was not now coming so far up. He did not know why, he gave me a map reference and asked if I could find my way there. What a hope, my first night in jungle country, it's dark except for the occasional glimpse of the moon through the tree tops and no "cats eyes" in the paths unless I run up against a tiger or some such animal. The officer realises my predicament so he gets one of his Sergeants up to take me to the road, our trucks having left earlier. We travel over narrow muddy tracks, through the mud holes of the old tin mine, the night alive with the croaking of countless thousands of frogs, it was almost deafening, slipping and sliding we reached the parting point. He shook hands, wished me luck, pointed down the road and was off on his way back, the journey was not long but like a nightmare to the newcomer that I was. I arrived at the rendezvous at midnight and spent a few hours with the other Sergeants who had arrived and were huddled together in a stinking little hut. Although it was still raining slightly I decide to sleep outside on an Army form standing alongside a table covered with various Army bric-a-brac. We were in a rubber plantation which appears to be the base of the RASC, an Army mechanical repair service.

Saturday January 17*th*

I am aroused at 0300hrs, just as a small monkey decides to steal a small loaf of bread given to me by the Australian officer. I had put it on the table when I put my head down for some sleep. I cursed the little monkey as he scooted up the nearest tree, flinging his supple little body from branch to branch, finally disappearing into the darkness leaving me with hard biscuits for breakfast. Well I had better find out the cause of me being dragged from an uneasy sleep the second time in five hours. It turns out that we may have to rejoin the Battalion who are still eighty miles south of us at a village called Aya Hitam. After an hour goes by nothing seems to happen so I get back on my seat for a bit more sleep, feeling a bit wet and scruffy, I cannot remember having shaved lately. To think that I could lie on a foot wide seat and not roll off proves how tired I am.

Sunday January 18th

Daylight comes with a head that feels like a turnip, also feeling cold and a bit below par so hope I can rustle up a cup of tea somewhere. While I am pondering on this a signal has come through, that after the lost sleep and harassment, the Battalion, that is the 5th Royal Norfolks, are coming up to Jemaulang after all. Why all the indecision? Well perhaps things will get organised now. The other Sergeants and I rejoin our respective companies as the Unit moves through. It's raining hard as we reach the Jemalaung positions, the "Aussies" have left, where to I wonder. Their 22nd Brigade is forward of us at a place called Mersing. It appears that we are a reserve Brigade to the 29th Australian Division.

It's night so with the light of the moon we off-load our trucks and as the fire positions are spread over a large area it's just one hell of a job. As I have already described the place is one of mud-holes and muddy banks fringed with jungle vegetation, the men are swearing and cursing as they slip and slide and many fall into the mud as they carry weapons and heavy boxes of ammunition to the firing points. After plodding around for an hour wet, plastered with mud, scratched faces and hands and a few torn shirts, lookouts are posted. I try to settle down again just where I was two nights ago.

During the night two men are found dead with stab wounds. No one knows what happened; did some Jap creep silently in? No one knows.

Monday January 19th

In the early hours a shot and a scream is heard a little way off near to a flanking Company. It came out in the morning that an officer had moved out at the call of nature and was shot clean through the buttocks. It was thought that the whiteness of his uncovered skin in the moonlight caught the eagle eye of a marksman. Friend or enemy, who knows in this mixed up war?

During the morning we take a look around our immediate area, the place seems to be alive with small swamped back pigs, which must have been left by hurriedly departing natives. This was too good to be true it seemed, we were hungry men, the rations not being too good owing to so much movement. After a lot of chasing around some of my men caught one and amid a lot of squealing a butcher among us soon had him dressed out and hanging from a tree - looks like pork stew for lunch. At the moment we haven't encountered any Japanese, nor does there appear to be any air activity. It's funny, being here, almost in the Front-line, no planes only the odd distant bang of a gun and the occasional rattle of a machine gun a way off.

It's 1800hrs and that heavy mantle of blackness descends on us in a matter of minutes. The mosquitoes are busy taking their daily meal of blood from swearing men who try to swat them in the dark. Some men are busy smearing anti-mosquito jelly on their skin, I don't know whether it's the strong smell or taste that keeps them at bay but at least it is effective.

Tuesday January 20ᵗʰ

The night wears on into the weary early hours, not much sleep for me as I have to make sure that my section on duty do not fall asleep. At 0200hrs in the morning my officer creeps out to find out how things are going "How are you feeling Sergeant". Knowing that he has been swigging whisky, I for once come the old soldier and reply "Rotten Sir, I could do with a strong drink." He took the hint, left me, but soon returned with a stiff whisky in a cup. He says "Don't fall asleep when you have drunk it." "No Sir", I reply, "I am there already but it will help me keep my eyes open". With a quiet chuckle he disappears into the darkness.

A long and weary night passes and with the coming of the dawn, the continuous croak of myriads of frogs gradually dies away as that great ball of fire rises over the jungle. The sky is clear and blue, the rain that has fallen steadily over the last few days has passed. The vegetation steams as the sun rises and the howling calls of monkeys take over from the frogs.

Walking around before breakfast I come upon a small curious shelter built from palm fronds, on taking a closer look inside I find a large half-barrel. It was filled with reasonably clean water, I guess it was the "Aussie" officers' bath-room. I retrace my steps to where my equipment lay, get my towel and hurry back, slipping off my shirt and shorts take a quick dip before anyone else discovers it. A quick rub down and I feel a very much better being, cooling off the 'prickly heat' and ridding ones self of an accumulation of sweat. (I might add that it was soon found by others). Prickly heat is an itchy rash, which Medics tell us we are likely to be bothered with until we are fully acclimatised. The morning passes with general cleaning up, equipment soon dries out in the sun.

Our stay here is short for after a quick handout of mid-day rations we are told to reload the ammunition for a withdrawal 80 miles back. I suppose the powers that be know what they are doing; I don't, having being shuttled backwards and forwards for the last three days. Having hauled the "ammo" boxes once more through the mud and loaded them onto the trucks. We are once again covered in the mud of Jemalaung. We board the lorries and rumble out of the area towards our new destination, where we arrive under the cover of darkness. Camp for the night is made in a rubber plantation alongside a native graveyard. My Corporal complains that he will in all probability get there quick enough without a sight-seeing tour first. Sentries are posted and we settle down to try and get a few hours sleep.

Wednesday January 21ˢᵗ

We find a stream on the other side of the road, where, we are told that, by using extreme caution and quietness we may wash. The weather down here is much dryer, no mud, just rubber trees and odd spots of jungle. Breakfast is dished up and afterwards I check my platoon for rifle cleanliness, for a rifle choked with mud wouldn't be much use if surprised by the enemy. I also check to see that they have their ammunition intact. While this is going on news comes through that the 2nd Cambridgeshires had made contact near the village of Batu Pahat, also the 6th Royal Norfolks somewhere near the village of Yong Ping. Ourselves, the 5th Royal Norfolks, were being held in reserve at Aya Hitam village. The holding of these areas I learned later were the responsibility of the 3rd Indian Corps, under whose control we now are.

Enemy aircraft are very active and we have to keep to cover as one flight has just dropped about eighteen bombs on a nearby road junction trying to blow out an 'Ack Ack' gun position close by. The men are a bit on edge, not knowing what's going on, we are not kept in the picture very well and that's bad for morale.

Around 1800hrs as darkness falls we are ordered to move three miles along a road where we unload our trucks. It's very dark now and movement is difficult, there is only the eerie light from the fire-flies flitting to and fro, which when I first saw them caused me to think that some of my men were moving around smoking against orders. Hardly have we finished off-loading and the instructions to move back one and a half miles are given. We have moved up too far, now you should hear the swearing, what a bloody shambles, does anyone know what's going on, and so on as once again we trail off. Finally positions are taken up, a patrol is sent out and around mid-night firing is heard not too far away and in the early hours the patrol returns carrying two badly wounded men. They had been surprised by the close proximity of the Japanese troops.

Thursday January 22nd

Morning comes, again lifting away once again the almost dark mantle of despair as no one tells us what is happening. After a scrambled breakfast I receive orders to take my platoon forward to a point seven miles on. We were conveyed by small trucks, no enemy were sighted, nor on the return journey, although we travelled slowly through what were mostly rubber trees. As I was searching with the aid of my binoculars for any sign of movement in the interior I noticed that a large part of the rubber estate had recently been worked, small vessels wired to the trees to catch the latex dripping from V-like cuts in the bark were still in position having no doubt been left as the war moved nearer. When I and the patrol arrive back at camp I find it very busy, I make my report to my Company Commander who informs me that the Battalion is to move out again after dark. At the moment we are leading a very harassed life with everyone feeling rather tired and worn.

Away goes the daylight and down comes the tropical darkness and with it the mosquitoes. We are frequently told not to use the anti-mosquito jelly as the very strong smell could now be picked up by the Japanese patrols. Within an hour amid the flitting of the spark-like fire-flies we are again on the move. Slowly in the darkness we push on but after a mile or so are halted. Why, I wonder, have we run into trouble? After a restless wait, no-one speaking above a whisper, we learn that we are to retrace our steps. With grumbles and quiet mutterings we now accept this as our pattern in this fly-by-night life and return to a rubber estate close by a cross roads, where most of us wearily drop to try and grab a little sleep.

Friday January 23ʳᵈ

Morning comes all too soon as weary-eyed, chafed and sore from sleeping in equipment for so many nights we rally ourselves for breakfast and a more than welcome cup of tea. Its just occurred to me that today is the wife's birthday, if it was not for the diary I am trying very hard to keep I would by now have forgotten the date, even the day. (I might add at this late moment that this is not a diary of map references or troop placings, but one of just how I was living day by day.)

It's now 0700hrs, my officer, Capt. Pallister, asks for the platoon to be mustered, this I do and with him inspect the rifles, ammunition and equipment etc., then he says, "Sergeant we are to move off along the Aya Hitam road in advance of the Battalion". We set off calmly, listening to the odd birds and monkeys that were still in the area, unsuspecting that the "Japs" were anywhere

43

close by. As we approach a slight bend in the road with myself at the head discussing the days possibilities with Capt. Pallister, a few spurts of road dust and smoke shot into the air, it did not, being so sudden register. I heard the officer shout that he had been hit, the realisation that we were under fire sank in and yelling to the men to break we dashed, by sections, to either side of the road. Myself and one section fall straight into waist deep water in a ditch, bullets are flying around us, bouncing off the tarmac, the lad next to me slumps forward onto the bank lying motionless. He is dead, with only a small hole where the bullet entered his back, I turn some of the men to watch our rear. We are now in a position to see that a roadblock has been set up around the bend with a few of the enemy running around it. A section of C Company on the right are firing at it. A yellow and black snake swims past, not knowing what he can do we give him pride of place.

Well, I cannot stand in the water for much longer, but must await orders which when they came gave me a bit of a jolt They were to take charge of the platoon and move forward. Capt. Pallister, on the way back had again been hit, in the side of the head. Now in this instance a steel helmet might just have saved him, for on leaving base camp that morning he could not find his. I heard one of the cooks offer to lend him one but he refused to take it. So now I find myself in a strange and dangerous situation, that of being in complete charge of men who like myself are at a complete disadvantage and easy prey to the enemy. We have not been trained in jungle warfare, we wear light khaki dress as against the "Japs" who wear green. They have, also, rubber boots with a separate big toe for easy climbing, which makes for many snipers and with our light colours make us easy targets.

I give the signal to move from the water filled drain to the rubber and scrub. With men well spread out we go hesitantly forward, my teeth are chattering, try as I may I cannot stop them. We carry on, shocked by the sudden onslaught. No doubt most of us are scared, but then we have been told only brave men are scared. As we pick our way through the trees men are falling around me, picked off by an unseen enemy. A young Lance-corporal from a village near my home town jumps onto the roots of a blown over tree shouting, "Where are the little yellow B's?" as I yell to him to get down he topples backwards, his arm shattered by a burst from an automatic. From my right comes a Corporal of C Company, one arm and his side pouring blood, but still carrying a Bren gun. We have gained ground up to the road block, only to find there are more ahead and we are coming up against heavy machine-gun fire. News is filtering through that two officers have been killed from 11 platoon also one from D Company platoon. Three killed (Capt. Boardman being one) in little over an hour and a lot of men. Not being able to move forward without heavy casualties being incurred I send my Company runner back to Headquarters with news of the position, but after an hour, which seemed like a lifetime, he still had not returned. I asked for a volunteer runner and a big lad offered to try and get back.

Around mid-day I came up to a wide and deep monsoon drain running through the plantation, I decided that if I dropped in, the other side being so steep and muddy I wouldn't get out, the only other option being a Chinese bridge. Two stout bamboos laying one foot apart across the gap, which the natives no doubt just ran across with no fear or effort. I felt I would have to chance the odd hidden marksman, so with an off balance act I manage to shuffle across side foot, breathing a sigh of relief as I take to close by cover for a breather before checking with some of the men. With a zigzagging run I return to the area of the bridge, to await hopefully for news from HQ. Enemy fire is still intense, bullets wham into the rubber trees and white latex sap oozes from the holes, others whine by and I wonder just how close they could have been. I spot the returning runner carefully picking his way through the trees, makes his way across the bamboo bridge to my position but before he can utter a word, he falls at my feet shot through the eye, dead. I feel shocked and grieved for the loss of a fine man.

Still not knowing anything of what is going on around us I join a Corporal of my platoon in a hollow behind a tree. In between firing at movement to our front we talk over the events of the morning. He thinks that I should pull the men out, but I don't believe this is right until I get orders from Headquarters as at the moment we seem to be holding the Japs to their area, or they could be waiting for us to show more of ourselves to be picked off like so many sitting ducks. It's now four hectic and tragic hours in what amounts to an ambush. A Company Sergeant Major now puts in an appearance telling me to hold my ground and not to withdraw as another platoon is approaching the enemy from my right flank in an effort to dislodge them; at least some help is at hand. After another hour of this hell the roadblock is overcome but more have been noted so the order is given for me to withdraw my men, who are tired and somewhat shocked at their baptism of fire, but still able to laugh at their plight. We spend the night in the rubber away back, some sleeping, some alert in positions.

Saturday January 24*th*

Morning comes upon us finding a lot of still tired and haggard men, waiting for that cup of tea that seems to work such miracles. It comes eventually, so with breakfast over, we check over kit, restock with ammunition, grenades and such like. There are no aircraft of our own flying around, we have never had any air cover and very little help from artillery either. I wonder what happened to the fifty Hurricane planes we brought with us? It's hot and the sweat constantly runs into your smarting eyes and drips off the end of your nose, but it's not often that you get time to realise it. When I get a moment to relax I feel my shoulders sore where the equipment has rubbed, the webbing dirty and soaked with sweat feels heavy and tight on our tired bodies, still soft after the long sea voyage.

It's afternoon, the order goes out to make an eight mile detour to get to Batu Pakat on the West Coast Road. Some Australians, we are told, are cut off there. This is turning out to be just another day I shall not forget in a hurry. Food is doled out on the trucks as we move. The invidious darkness falls again bringing with it the desire to sleep, some doze but it is difficult as the trucks bounce over broken roads. We soon become involved with a huge convoy of troops and arms, all going towards Singapore while we still move up. This has awakened the men from their dozing and is causing much speculation as to what might be going on.

Sunday January 25th

A little further on we pull off the road, it is around 0400hrs, it is very dark. It's demoralising this hanging about, not knowing what is going on. At 0700hrs we move by truck again to the outskirts of Batu Pakat. By 1200hrs we were told to get off the road for a rest and food.

10 Platoon and I move into what was a racing stable. although the horses are gone, a few Chinese workmen are still there. I am issued on the spot with seven 1lb tins of bully beef to open and share out among the men. The noise of exploding mortar bombs and the chattering of machine guns is going on all around as we question the best way of getting the tins open. Hard biscuits are also doled out, but before we can do much about it the call comes for us to fall in quickly. A very old and wrinkled Chinaman standing close by suddenly finds his arms full of tins of bully beef, and with his grin stretching from ear to ear due to his sudden bonus, we leave. Rushing to our fall in area we see stragglers of 11 Platoon coming in wounded and shocked, having been hit by a third mortar barrage. Now hungry as well as tired and with the temperature in the searing sun around 110°F, I am instructed to take my platoon forward in the direction that No 11 Platoon has just evacuated.

I move along the edge of the road, mortar bombs exploding here and there, machine guns barking to our right, soon I come to a road junction. I lead my men down it and take up positions along a bank still looking forward. Visually we search the rubber trees and scrub in front of us, the heavy machine guns still firing to our right. Men of the Cambridgeshires are withdrawing from that area. They tell us that a lot of their fellows have been shot through the legs by the machine gun fire. It now appears that I have to hold this area until they are out. I see two heads move directly to my front behind an uprooted tree, I open fire but see nothing more. On drawing the attention of the man on my right

(Pte Alexander) to the place, he lifts his head a bit high, suddenly he spins backwards flat onto the road. I jump quickly to his side thinking that he must be dead as I had heard the crack of a rifle, no doubt a sniper in the trees, but I find his steel helmet creased like a Trilby across the top but not penetrated, he was however out cold. Stretcher-bearers picked him up, they say he is concussed then took him off. I am thinking I must have a charmed life, he is the third man to be shot down by my side.

By darkness we move into a native cemetery, this is the second one I have been in, not very reassuring. There is a trench that was hastily dug by the party that recently withdrew so we occupy it. Not a lot can be seen this night except for some blurred grave-stones just out in front, you just keep alert and listen, trying to pick up noises other than the croaking of the multitudes of frogs. We know that the enemy are out to our front but have been told by lecturing officers in Singapore that they do not move much in the dark as the 'Spirit Life' they believe in scares them, also if they have to they will carry lights. He must have thought that we were born yesterday or else since he was fighting the Japs in north Malaya their habits have changed. Down our way it's mostly at night they move in from the coast. As I stand thinking about this a soldier from my left creeps down, "Sergeant, there is a rustling noise out to the front of my position". I go back with him and listen, after a while I hear the noise he described, it stops and a short time passes before we hear it again. It is the only place on our front that we hear anything. With the movement, I can hear what must be laboured breathing, the man next to me wants to shoot, but no it could be a trap to draw our fire. It gets closer and with it a low moan, straining our eyes into the darkness we see a man crawling, almost up to us. I realise that he is wounded in the legs, no doubt from this afternoon's action. I send a runner back onto the road to get a stretcher-bearer, he later returns with them and the poor fellow is taken away.

As the night creeps on I hear more moans and spend a good half hour creeping around in the dark but find no-one. I get back to my trench and standing up to take a breather an amazing thing happens, a tracer bullet enters the wall of the trench just a foot to one side of me. The man in the next position panicked and threw an anti-personnel grenade out to the front, however it hit a gravestone and almost blinded us with the flash, at the same time filling our eyes with stone dust. It was a good job that this type did not have a metal casing otherwise it could have killed or wounded a number of us. The point in mind however, was that the enemy must now know where we are. I was now very alert but nothing happened, there had only been that one shot.

A half hour later, now getting within an hour of dawn, a loud voice comes from away to our front. It said, "We are the 2nd Cambridgeshires and you men out there are to join us". Now I knew that the Cambridgeshires had withdrawn under our covering fire and in any case they wouldn't be using loud speakers, therefore it must be some more Japanese trickery. It is repeated about three times then silence.

Monday January 26th

Daybreak, and with it comes shooting now and again from the snipers. In some of the trees a huge fungus grows where the branches break, forming a huge basin-like structure, just right for a man dressed in green. A number of enemy snipers have been shot in these things once we gained the knowledge of what was happening. Annoyed at being shot at by an invisible foe I took my Tommy-gun and creeping around the thick green screening of the grave-yard I put a burst of fire into all the fungus formations within range, four in all. I cannot say that I scored a hit but we were not sniped at any more. Heavy firing starts up again on my left flank and men are pouring back from that direction, the whole line is in a state of chaos. My men can no longer be held, they break and fall back with the rest, disgusted I grab a Bren gun that has been left behind and stay alone in the trench firing a burst here and there into the undergrowth where some movement occurs. I then decide that as we are now so mixed up I could be shooting at my own men. I am still without an officer and at the same time no information comes as to what's going on. I pick up the Bren gun and run zigzag for the road down which the men have gone. On catching up I am surprised to find hundreds of soldiers gathering, it's a withdrawal to new positions further along the road, in a wooded area.

Just before dark, planes come over, they circle the area and then dive in, strafing the place with bullets. I dive flat behind a tree, as I lay listening to the roar of the planes, the spitting of bullets as they hit the tree trunks, trying to press myself deeper into the ground I wonder if this is my lot. The bullets seemed as if they were coming straight through the middle of my back at any moment. After what seems an age the planes fly off, I slowly get to my feet, feeling dazed I look at the bullet holes in the tree trunk just three feet above the ground and decide what I hate most about war is being strafed from the air, you are so helpless. I also ask myself again, where are our planes, our tanks and big guns, what wonderful company they would make just now. The raid over, darkness encloses on us like devil's fingers clutching for your throat and with that thought in mind we are mass hailed to take up positions again by an abandoned aerodrome at Batu Pakat.

Tuesday January 27th

Morning comes and I take stock of my outlook, an empty 'drome' with oil drums and such like placed around to obstruct possible enemy landings. Leaving are a number of lorries, evidently removing stores, but no planes of ours here.

At 1050hrs on the move again, two miles back on last night's tracks. (If anyone ever reads this I hope that they can take in all our backwards and forwards movements of the last few days.) Hardly sleeping, hungry and dirty we are at a point of exhaustion. Again we halt and are told to take to the jungle and rubber on each side of the road and to keep out of sight of aircraft. Rations of bully beef and biscuits are given out for which we are very thankful, but our drink has to be water. For five hours now we have been hanging around, it is a rest at least for our weary limbs.

CHAPTER 3

FLIGHT, FIGHT AND FALL

Tuesday January 27th 1942

The men wait, some sleeping, others talking both about the events of the last few days and also, occasionally allowing conversation to drift towards home. Finally, the few officers left call us to fall in. They tell us that we are completely cut off and with the troops at hand there is no hope of getting through enemy lines. We also learn that we have been up against soldiers of the Japanese Imperial Guard who outnumber us seven to one, Japan's crack troops, who were fully trained in jungle warfare and guerrilla tactics.

Now the order is given, 'Every man for himself and try to get back to Singapore', which must be sixty miles away as the crow flies. We had now caught up with all our transport, there it stretched, a long line of tankers, guns and all the platoon trucks etc., needed by an army on the march. At a rough count I put the number at 270 types of transport. We couldn't leave all this for the use of the enemy so as we passed some of us damaged it the best way we could. After filling our water bottles we drove pickaxes through the water tankers, cut tyres, smashed lorry engines and setting fire where we could. At the village of Senggarang, some way ahead, was a bridge over a river; we are told that it is to be blown up at 1830hrs. So with the time getting close we have to leave the demolishing of the transport and as we do we pass a fleet of ambulances filled with wounded, others are lying on the ground too bad to walk. They have to be left to the Japs. Hoping that they will be compassionate two men decided to stay behind with them, one a medical officer, the other Padre Ducksworth, once a Cox in the Cambridge boat race crew.

We now have to hurry, for myself and the remnants of my platoon appear to be the only people left on this side of the bridge, with only five minutes to go before it's blown up. We dash across, get about 100 yards clear and with a terrific bang, up it goes, shooting debris high into the air to fall with a splash into the river. With a few mutterings, "Just in time" and "That was close", we now have to think out our next move, and we have to hurry as darkness will soon be upon us. There are about nine of us and four want to go to the coast a short distance away thinking that they will be seen and picked up by a Naval gunboat. I decide to take the long way and face the jungle where I could have some cover, in any case the chances of being picked up on the coast must be very slight with the Japs possibly now in command. We part company with "Good Luck" and "Hope to see you again". Running along the very high riverbank we are greeted with a burst of heavy machine gun fire coming from the other side of the river. As the bullets whine over our heads we quickly jump for safety down the riverbank into mud nearly up to our knees. One fellow jumped too far out and sunk to his waist, it was an effort to get him out. Having coped we carry on down the edge of the river to a point where it made a sharp bend and to get away from the road we would have to cross again. At this point the water did not appear to be so deep. The tallest of us went in first carrying his rifle above his head, halfway across he was little more than waist deep. The others followed, but what about me, being the shortest of them by several inches. Although I can swim a little thanks to my stay in Mombassa, I am in this case carrying equipment. No time to hesitate so I take the plunge, the water is warm and as I get to the middle it's up to my armpits and I have difficulty in keeping my feet on the bottom. A few more yards on and the river bed slopes up towards a very high upright bank, the man in front of me goes up and over with some considerable effort then disappears, not waiting to see if I can get out. He cannot be blamed for this as there are still some bullets flying around. On reaching the bank, because of my stature which no doubt up to now has stood me in good stead, I find the top is beyond my reach and because of the slime I just cannot get out. As I struggle to get to grips, two heads look down from the top and a rifle is lowered butt first. I take a firm grip on it and am pulled to the top gasping for breath. Quickly we run across some open ground to cover where the others are waiting. Only half an hour has passed since we left the bridge but it seems ages.

Darkness is up on us but we have, luckily, the light of the moon. It is good here as the area is treeless being mainly tall "Elephant grass", but it has a searing edge to it and makes exposed parts of the limbs sore. We decide to push on for a bit. Struggling through the vegetation we come to a patch of pineapple, cultivated no doubt by the natives. Pineapple leaves are sword-like with a saw-tooth edge, which badly cut my knees as I crossed the area. The turn down part of my shorts that we usually tuck into the hose tops being badly ripped and still wet affords little protection. On coming out of the patch we hit a narrow track which we decide to follow, but not before cutting small unripe pineapples and trying to eat them. Here we learn something the hard way, not having this fruit fresh in my life before but only from a tin, I peeled it, then ate some of it. It was then that I was spitting blood, I had not removed the skin deep enough and little thorn-like pieces that are seated deep in the fruit badly lacerated my mouth. Throwing the fruit away in disgust and disappointment at not getting something to eat I swilled my mouth with a little water and we carried on down the track. The scrub vegetation is getting thicker with more boggy areas among the trees, at times ankle deep and once with one man up to his waist. It is more difficult to get along among trees, as the moonlight does not penetrate as well.

Wednesday January 28th

After a nightmarish trek, daylight comes upon a handful of deadbeat, mud plastered, mosquito bitten and very hungry soldiers far from home, bacon and eggs and marmalade. Stumbling on we come to a few low growing palms with large green coconuts in the crest of their enormous fronds, which hanging down almost touch the ground. I have learned that this type of palm is known as the "King Nut". We help one of our number up the trunk and with a little effort he is able with his bayonet to knock some down. We pounce eagerly on the fallen nuts, however on cutting one open find no nut only a lot of milky-white mush, evidently a coconut in its early growth. I scoop some out and taste it, find it alright and we all eat some to appease the pangs of hunger. Some nuts have more milk than others so as the green outer husk is soft we find that a V-shaped hole cut by a bayonet enables us to drink easily from them.

Our preoccupation with the main thought of the moment could have endangered our lives although the moments of gun-fire were now distant. I heard a rustle nearby and then a voice, the hair at the back of my neck was standing up when I realised that the voice was English with a Norfolk dialect, "Where the hell have you fell from", it said. Moving towards their cover I saw just a handful of dishevelled men like ourselves, except the voice was that of my own Regimental Sergeant Major, who most of the lads when in England vowed wouldn't live two days once we were in action. He is alive and well and we are only too pleased to see him, furthermore luck is still with us as the officer with him is from the Malay Volunteer Corps, attached to my Brigade as a Liaison Officer. Formerly of the Malay Police Force he is somewhat familiar with this southern part of Malaya. So we happily join forces, which relieves me of a lot of responsibility.

We travel slowly resting now and again under trees out of the hot wearying sun. The occasional aircraft goes over and if out on the track we have to scurry for the cover of the trees, it could be a tragic end for us if spotted. The dark velvety blue of darkness falls, but the large tropical moon as it rises throws a mantle of gentle light over us and just for a few minutes allows us to revel in Nature's romantic settings, then back to reality with a jerk as the mosquitoes begin their dive-bombing of our skin, also a voice saying it's time to move on. Pushing through the tall "Elephant grass" that hangs over the narrow jungle track, probably used by the natives, we stumble on with a short rest every mile or so. Along this tortuous hike we are scratched from head to foot, my shirt now torn half off my back by thorn covered creepers.

Thursday January 29th

In the early hours of the morning word comes down the column, (which has now increased to about eighty through men being picked up as we move along), to halt and stay very quiet. We flatten out in the grass and while laying there I try to remember the last time I slept for more than one or two hours. While pondering over this a message comes for me to go to the head of the column. I am told we have come to a river that is too fast and deep for us to cross at this point. A boathouse is just down the riverbank and the officer of the Malay Volunteers has gone down there to find out if anyone or boats are around. After a quite a time and a few raised voices, he returns with three Malay boatmen at revolver point. Apparently they were too scared of the Japanese to have anything to do with us except at gunpoint. He forced them to take us to their boats, which were two long and one short sampan types. It meant two journeys across the river.

The officer explained to the man in charge of each boatload, that on the other side were rice fields divided by bunds, raised flat-topped banks, on which we could cross to a rubber plantation in which there was a village. He would first check to see to see if it was safe. Each boat on reaching the other side was to leave a man to wait for the next boat and so take the men on over the bund. I was in the last boat but one and climbing up to the path, I could not find anyone waiting to take us on. On looking around I see no sign of him. The last boat lands with my RSM in charge and naturally he wants to know why the hell I haven't moved on, I reply that there is no linkman for us, he must have taken fright and followed his own party. Crossing the bund was easy enough with no fear of falling down the sides as in the moonlight they stand out in relief. It was when we came to the rubber and no linkman there we became a bit concerned as to our whereabouts. The RSM was fuming about the frightened bastard who should have been here. I was wandering around looking for a likely track through these rubber trees when I noticed something white in the moonlight. Getting down to a closer inspection I see that it is latex, the rubber tree sap, oozing from injured surface roots. On looking further to the front I find more oozing, suddenly it becomes obvious that they were damaged by the heavy boots of those in front of us. I report back to the RSM who agrees with me, so feeling like a Red Indian tracker I move on, the remainder following.

After about half a mile we hear voices. The voices are getting louder so must be coming towards us, we move very cautiously and strain our eyes to penetrate the trees ahead. I see that we are now moving along the edge of a deep drain and the voices, now shouting, are coming from the other side. Soon we see many people in white clothing, they beckon us to follow. The advance party must have met up with them, then sent these people, mainly Chinese children to find us. As we move along the bank they keep just ahead, still waving and calling to us. Quite suddenly we find ourselves through the rubber trees and in a clearing, the Chinese cross a bamboo bridge and join us. We are taken to a large hut, the centre of a small village. There is quite a clamour going on and tin baths of water have been provided for us to drink from and on doing so I find it has been laced slightly with whisky.

Our Liaison Officer is speaking to some of the older Chinese, he is the only one who can understand them, to me it seems that they want us to go quickly and in a direction that they are pointing. As we go they hand us cigarettes and our Captain tells us that the villages say the enemy is close behind us. The only thing we can do is move on as in our present condition we would be no match in a skirmish, the majority of us have no ammunition and some no rifles, having lost them in the river and swamps. Not far from the village we run into swamp again and for a mile we struggle knee deep in the mire, sometimes being sucked down waist deep. Two other men are fighting their way through it while dragging a wounded man. Myself and another help where and when we can, but we are in such an exhausted state it is little we can do.

The moonlight is fading so now it is with some difficulty that we move and avoid odd trees. In a mind relaxing moment I find myself wondering if there could be alligators in this slime, just too bad to lose a leg now. To relax was dangerous; a branch from a tree knocks my gun (which I have done my best to keep above water) from my grip. As I grab at it and miss, it sinks into the liquid mud, I flounder and my arms sink to the armpits but make contact and the muddy thing is brought to the surface. Being choked with mud it is unusable, but will clean when time allows as I have always been taught that it is my best friend! The men fall and flail, pulling themselves out, swearing quietly under their breath.

Will the end of this nightmare ever come? Suddenly out of the darkness a voice shouts, "Keep to the right". It was a voice with a foreign accent, but I obey the direction and the next step I am struggling in armpit deep water and mud. "Stop where you are", the voice shouts and at the same time I can just see the faces of two Indian soldiers. They slide their rifle butts towards me, which I grab and am only too grateful to be pulled out of the swamp. Their right to me should have been left! However, I am soon on dry land, in fact a tarmac road. The Indians give me biscuits and water, which I am more than pleased to have. It appears that we have arrived at an Indian Advanced Field Dressing Station. The Major in charge has a number of trucks with which he is now preparing to move his men out. He tells me that during the withdrawal down Malaya he has lost two field stations and most of his men but does not intend to lose this one. According to him the Japanese are about four miles from us.

The Indians are now loading their equipment onto trucks, and the men of my party are resting or sleeping just as they fell on reaching the road, the tarmac holds the day's heat and is warm to the touch. Looking around they resemble a flock of black sheep as they lie dotted about in dark lumps. The lorries move away with a promise from the Indian Major that he will send the trucks back for us if everything goes alright, so we settle down to wait, far too dead beat to move ourselves yet. It is dark but not the blackness of night that one would get at home but a velvety kind that one can see the shapes of the trees lining the road through. I lie with my pack under my head, not sleeping, only a dazed stupor ready to jump if anything happens. I hear the grunts and groans, an occasional shout from those sleeping around me.

Over an hour has passed since the trucks left and as I turn one possibility after another over in my muddled mind the fellow next to me turns towards me saying, "Sarge, think those trucks will come back?" or did I think that we should move on? Didn't want to be caught here like sitting ducks, he says. Giving this some thought I looked for the RSM and on finding him I put my fears to him but he reassures me by saying that they had agreed to wait two hours before moving on. Not long after this conversation I hear the rumble of lorries coming from the direction that we hoped were ours. The transport arrives and begins to turn around which is difficult enough on this narrow road. The men are getting to their feet now and jostling about looking for rifles and such bits of equipment they still have. The order is given to board the three trucks that returned for us. After seeing that no-one was left sleeping by the roadside the RSM and I climbed aboard and we are off on another stage of this nightmare of a journey to Singapore. With the Japanese about two miles or so away it's not too soon.

Friday January 30th

After an uneventful run we reach a transport camp near the village of Skudia at 0400hrs. The place is alive with men ragged and tired but after a drink of tea and rum they soon become themselves. We are directed to a heap of packs and told that if we require any clothing to take what we need. My immediate wants was a shirt and shorts, my own being in ribbons and caked with mud. I dragged out a valise and was staggered by the coincidence that hit me, for a time I didn't move as I looked at the name inside, it was the kit of my officer, Capt Pallister, killed a few days back. When I came to I took a shirt out and put it on, thinking that he would have wished me to wear it. Having cleaned some of the muck off our legs and boots, cleaned the mud from our fire-arms we manage to get down for a couple of hours rest.

Later in the morning we are aroused and told to get ready to move, like all the men I am so hungry that my belly-button feels as if it stuck to my backbone, but no grub is forthcoming here. On the dot of 1100hrs we embus and are transported away once more and in due course cross the causeway linking Malaya with Singapore, and onto a camp at Serangoon Road. We are now shown to long huts constructed or rather covered in by a type of dried palm leaf, inside on either side are double platforms, the top ones reached by short ladders. I staked a claim on one of the top ones, laid out what kit I had then went outside to find out what was happening. There are comings and goings of lorries, bringing in men as they come out of the jungle and rubber plantations. Myself and those with me were three days finding our way out, but then we were very lucky to have had such a good guide, those three days were long enough without proper food or water.

Talking of food, a shout goes up "Come and get it"! Thinking that cry was something from the past peaceful days, I dash into the hut, gather my mess tins and hurriedly join in the rush for the first meal to be served hot in a fortnight. It could not have been better if it had been served in a first class hotel, after washing it down with a good mug of tea, I return to the hut for a towel of sorts. Then to find the water taps and give myself a good wash, after which I feel like a king and a night out for a beer, but no such thing. There are only the hard planks for a bed, or to wander around in the darkness of the oncoming night. Well I have a lot of sleep to catch up on so it's to the hut where I sit with some of my men chatting about the past and trying to sort out the future. After a couple of hours we solve nothing so I climb the ladder and let my weary battered body down on the boards and must have been asleep in minutes for I remember no more until being awakened next morning.

Saturday January 31st

Most of the men were awake stretching, groaning and rubbing stiff joints. Grabbing a mug I make for the cook-house for an early cup of tea, on leaving the hut and its darkness ones eyes are screwed up to slits as they take in the light of the dazzling sunrise. As I pass the taps I have a quick rinse wiping the surplus water off with my hands, leaving the rest to dry in the early morning warmth. On getting my tea I make my way back, sit down to drink and really enjoy it, then wait around for breakfast. This over we parade for inspection, are sorted out and reformed, reverting to 53rd Brigade. On being dismissed we are told we are free to visit Singapore but to be back in camp by 1800hrs.

On one side of the area is the inevitable cemetery, only British this time. At the bottom is the road to town, a few miles away. The other side of the road are a few village shops, one of these is an Indian barber. There are four of us in all with a good growth of beard so we decide to have it off and enter the shop. On setting down on a bench, we are being eyed by a grinning black barber flashing a cut-throat razor as he expertly shaves a client, although he does not appear to be looking at what he is doing but watching us. Perhaps he is pleased at having some extra custom. We watch with some apprehension as his razor flashes to his client's eyebrows, the end of the man's nostrils and then to his ears deftly removing superfluous hairs. My mates argue as to who is to go into "Sweeny Todds" chair first, wondering whether he has any "Jap" tendencies. I take the bull by the horns and get into the chair first, being greeted in English as a brave soldier back from the jungle and in his patter he knows as much about us as we know ourselves, telling us that he has shaved many British soldiers before the war. We were shaved, powdered and pattered and shown the door feeling like new men.

We walk some way along the road, an army lorry pulls up alongside and offers us a lift. The driver is stationed on the island and talks of our doings on the mainland as heroic, telling us that there is a lot of sympathy for us among the troops here. We are dropped off near a huge building known to me as the Cathe. I gather among many things it houses the Radio Station. We roam around the Chinese quarter, tall squalor-like settlements hanging with signs, washing and such like. One of the men with me says that he has read that if all the Chinese population here was on the ground at one time there wouldn't be room for them to stand up. After trailing around in the hot sun for hours we find a little place where we can get some food, mainly eggs. We have a tuck in, later buying a bottle of beer for two shillings, but must not drink it on the premises. When we get outside in the pyjama clad throng of Chinese girls we prise the top off of the bottles, the beer oozes out in a creamy froth, its taste is warm and soapy-like, with only one word for it, horrible! We decide to make our way back to camp, as it is quite a walk. We amble along the embankment of a river that runs through part of Singapore, the water stinks to high heaven and I would imagine that everything possible is dumped into it for as it swirls along it is carrying quantities of floating rubbish.

At last we reach what is home to us, flinging ourselves down on our respective patch of boards we take a rest before tea. I lie looking up into the roof of the palm fronds, dried and brown, wondering what the next move is to be and how soon the little green men (Japanese) will be knocking at our door. How can we possibly hold out in Singapore with no air force or navy to back us, we shall be at the mercy of the enemy in everyway. At this moment the noise of bursting bombs can be heard in the distance, no doubt some bombing of the Naval docks, the largest in the world. As I try to think things out I am disturbed by the shouts that "Tea is up" and that being the most important thing at this time I grab my gear, bound quickly down the ladder and join in the scramble. There is rum in the tea! Only the second time in my two years in the army. Some regiments get regular rum handouts, even in England. It is said, however, that our Commanding Officer is a tea-totaller and this is thought to be the reason for no issue, although there were times in England and Scotland, when half frozen and wet through it would have been a godsend. Tea over and with the usual amble around we get together to talk things over and swap yarns of home. A couple of hours go by and we take to our hard beds which never feel so bad when one is dead tired.

Sunday February 1st 1942

Must have fallen asleep immediately, as I remember no-more until awakened by someone shouting his mouth off about us lazy so-and-so's ought to be awake on this bright and beautiful morning. It's one of the sentries coming in from duty, he is soon told what he can do with himself and his beautiful morning! I lay for another quarter of an hour trying to collect my thoughts, also stretching my stiff limbs, then with great effort of will power I grab my towel, slide down from my perch and make for the nearest wash trough and tap. After a wash and pulling a comb through my tangled hair I take stock of my surroundings, then with the warm sun on my bare back I agree with nature, it is a lovely morning.

Breakfast over I obey orders and inspect my men to see what they need to make soldiers of them again. Many men need webbing equipment and some firearms, having lost or discarded them in the effort to get back to the island. Our needs are in short supply, no Tommy-guns or Bren guns are available and some of the equipment given out included webbing of the 1914-18 war, where did they dig it up! There is little replacement clothing but the best is done and while this is going on, two of my men, amongst others, have just returned from the jungle of the mainland and after five days look more like ghosts than men. Dead on their feet, haggard and with staring eyes they are helped to a hut by a medical party. This over most of us are free to do what we like until curfew.

I look up a Sergeant friend, who when at home only lives a few miles from me. We make for the town and spend time lounging around eyeing the pretty little Chinese girls, also the more beautiful creatures, the Eurasians (offspring of mixed parentage). All of them seemed rather aloof, taking no notice of us, well I suppose we do look a little run down with no Sunday clothes to show off. Perhaps in their minds we are already the beaten Army as there are no Union Jacks flying from the houses as there were when we first arrived, they must, therefore, think that they will soon be hosts to the Japanese soldiers. After looking at a few more of the sights we take a rest outside the "Union Jack" club, which now appears to have had its day. Up to a fortnight ago Singapore was the nearest thing to a film city in this world, where rich, elaborately dressed men and women in expensive cars nightly dined and danced in the clubs and hotels. One more look at the club with its bomb shattered windows and with the thoughts of its past we make our way back to camp.

On arriving back we hear that an officer of my Battalion with 150 men have just returned, having been picked up on the coast by a surviving British gunboat. It is said that they stood waist deep in swamp for a night and a day before being spotted and picked up. Many men arrived in a terrible condition and are placed in the camp hospital.

Tea comes up again followed by the usual discussions. The use of mosquito cream is now allowed again and we need it to keep those dive-bombing little beggars away. No cases of malaria have been reported yet as peace-time operations against the "mozi" were very efficient, but it's my guess that malaria will not be a very long way off now that the precautions have broken down. Talking over, I once again take to the boards, three nights of sleep, it seems too good to go on.

Monday February 2nd

Dawn, and as the huge red sun rises over the camp, its light brings into relief the ant-like movements of men moving to and from the wash troughs. With breakfast over the usual parade and rifle inspection takes place where we are told we are free to go but it could be the last time before the next move. I idle around camp till after dinner then collect my friend and set off for Singapore where we aimlessly wander around until 6 o'clock.

It's now time to return, but feeling rather fed up after three days of relaxation and not knowing what tomorrow might bring, perhaps our lot during the next few days, we try the Continental Hotel which is on our way out. Hoping to get a quick drink we try the front door but it is locked and no-one answers our knocking, so thinking that we've had it we start to leave. At that very moment three figures in firemen's uniform pass us and go round the side of the hotel. "Must be a side door", I say, so we follow them, catching them up as they slide through a side door, which is quickly being shut in our faces. My shoulder gets in first and although a native waiter tries to say no we insist and are let in. Inside the only light is from a few flickering oil lamps because blackouts are now in place and we cannot see the men who came ahead of us. We go to the bar only to find it has Guinness or Johnnie Walker scotch left. We decide on the Guinness and set down for a quiet rest, half-way through the air-raid sirens wail out, the two bar staff panic and try to push us out. We don't want to go so soon but they are near to tearing their hair out and scared stiff, they gabble on so we settle for a bottle of whisky, only four shillings, borrow two glasses and retire to the street veranda to drink it, leaving the waiters to tuck themselves away in their supposedly safe little corner.

We set in the darkness of the night air, calmly drinking and laughing about the antics of the staff and wondering what happened to the firemen. As I watched the flashes from exploding bombs light up the night sky I wondered why we seemed to be the only two beings around. I managed to see that the time was well after 8 o'clock and I really came to with a shock, looked towards my friend, he was asleep, and with the whisky bottle empty nearby I realised I must have slept for an hour as well. Shaking him hard he stirred muttering something about not having been asleep long. I gradually got through to him that we were still in Singapore and shaking and stretching ourselves we set off for camp, but feeling thick-headed and cramped this seemed along way off.

Plodding our way wearily along we were suddenly pulled to our senses by the sharp command of "Halt! Who goes there?", "One come forward and be recognised". On stepping wearily forward I could see first the fixed bayonet pointing at me and then the form of a soldier behind it. Stopping at the point of the bayonet, I was spoken to by the Sergeant-in-charge of the guard post. "Who are you and where do you come from?", "Norfolks are you", "You must be among those just back from up country". I replied that we were, he commented, "You've had a bloody hard time, but you could have been shot here on sight. Don't you know curfew is on?" Heavens, I chilled at his words, we had completely forgotten all about the curfew and had been roaming around for two hours. He directed us off the road, along a track and told us that we would meet up with another guard post. He also gave us a password and said that he would get in touch by field telephone and warn them to look out for us. We later passed through the post after answering questions as to what it was like in Malaya. A little further on and now in higher spirits we had to pass through an abandoned road block and in the light from a sinking moon we could see that it was made up of every type of old furniture and other rubbish that one could lay hands on. From this time on I remember very little.

Tuesday February 3rd

Awakening, I sat up and stared, rubbed my eyes and stared again, for there between us stands a huge Chinese type armchair, looking like a throne. Neither my mate nor I could remember putting it up there, but the other inmates of the hut soon assured us that we did, waking most of them up as we did. They also informed us that we were for the 'high jump' at not being in for evening roll call. We have been here three weeks and so much has happened to us it seems like three months, however, after breakfast we the two miscreants are ticked off for being late in by the Company Officer. As he turns away we hear him say to the Sgt. Major, "Can't wonder at it under the circumstances", so then we didn't feel too bad about it.

Later in the morning new transport is coming into the camp, also some more men are drifting back from Malaya looking in an extremely bad condition. Reinforcements are joining us to make up our losses. I now have after three weeks a new young platoon officer.

At 1600hrs we find ourselves on the move again, this time in defence of the Naval dock, with my B Company occupying the centre position, known as "Beaulieu House area". Just before reaching the positions we leave the transport and march in taking up our positions as we go and are soon joined by the remainder of the Company. We relieve a squad of Indian Punjab troops who before they leave insist on making tea for me and my party. It is very friendly of them and the tea welcome, but so sweet. Later they leave with friendly waves and good luck wishes and I get down to the more immediate things such as appointing sections to take over the slit trenches dug in the lawns of the estate. They overlook the Johore Straits, a neck of sea a few hundred yards across, now dividing us from the enemy. One section was on top of a bank, looking down towards the water, its face covered with tangled vegetation. Having settled the men on duty, I look around for quarters others to rest in. Decide the house seems safe for the moment and its garage could be used as our headquarters.

The night goes on uneventful until around midnight when a few mortar bombs fall short although one manages to set the bank vegetation on fire causing a flanking platoon to pull out of their positions. The area was ablaze but there was no follow up bombardment.

Wednesday February 4th

On looking over the house this morning, I find it had been recently occupied by a Rear Admiral and his family. The breakfast table was laid, a rolled up newspaper by one plate and bacon and eggs still on the plates, just growing a film of green mould, all the signs are that they left in a terrific hurry and early in the morning. On going through the bedrooms I found among other articles of clothing the Admirals dress belt in black leather with brass fittings for sword etc. I decided to keep the belt as it would be something to remember this by if ever I got home again. In another bedroom, possibly his daughter's, hurriedly thrown on the bed were a flimsy pair of silk pyjamas, a pair of white silk briefs and other oddments, amongst which was a tiny Union Jack. For some reason I cut the small flag from its binding and stuffed it into my pocket with the briefs. I then decided while things were quiet I would use the room and have a good nights sleep in that bed.

Some of us taking over other bungalows nearby find lots of silver and silver plate. The plates are taken back to our selected quarters and from then on we feel highly elevated as we eat our meals in this aristocratic atmosphere. The late occupants of this area really must have lived a life of luxury and I feel, just a bit, for the ladies when I wonder where they are now and how they must miss these luxurious houses and grounds. Pushing thoughts to one side I return to my HQ where most of the men are sleeping. There is only one man on duty in the forward section, he acts as a lookout during daylight hours as most of our duties take place at night.

This night in particular I get a visit from my Company Commander who wants to go round the positions. We set off and are walking around the house when he says, "Get off the gravel Sergeant you make too much noise". The fact is, it is he that is on the gravel I am walking on the lawn. He seems a bit on edge so I say nothing as we are both now crossing the lawn towards the first of the positions. As we look across the Straits shrouded in their velvety darkness, he remarks, "Japs could get within twenty yards of you if they are quiet about it". He talks of small beach lights that could be switched on if such a thing happened and also that the water should be wired for a few yards out from the edge. Having satisfied himself he leaves me. I am near a storage area of the Naval docks and discover some boxes of food still there. On getting back I tell some of the men about it and there is no peace until I let three of them go and see what they can get.

Thursday February 5th

The night creeps into the early hours and as it does a lorry comes rumbling in pulling a 75mm artillery gun, the crew jumps off to detach the gun, unload shells and equipment then rumbles back in the direction whence it came. The Sergeant-in-charge wants to dig a position for the gun and decides on doing it in the centre of my area. He tells me that the gun has to be concealed in the daytime and put into position at night. My garage HQ is the easiest point of concealment so I hand it over to him. I look into the darkness across the Straits, all is quiet except for the occasional metallic ring of metal on metal as my men work putting in short pickets and stretching out the barbed wire under the water.

Daylight is coming and with it the men are withdrawn and the lone sentry put on duty. No movement must take place in the daytime; everyone has to be under cover. With this done I wash and shave then go for breakfast which is followed by peaches, apricots etc., brought back during the night and eaten in these unbelievable surroundings. After breakfast the silverware is washed up and set in readiness for the next meal. In the meantime after checking rifles and equipment most of the men sleep and so goes the day.

With the darkness the men take over their positions again while three more go to the docks for more food. They have been gone some time and I am worried for them as the actual dock area is getting some attention, sporadic shelling is taking place from the enemy on the other side of the Straits. A half hour goes by and my worries cease as the men safely return with packs of food, one containing tins of salmon. What a delicacy for the troops! A quick check on positions and back to the house.

My officer thinks I should grab a few hours sleep so I go off to the bedroom and look at the bed I have not yet slept in, with the pyjamas lying invitingly there, I think why not? Once in a while it's reasonably quiet in this area so off came the equipment and clothes, I have lost a lot of weight over the last month, so the pyjamas go on easy and onto those giving springs I stretch more than my tired body. It was not to be my night for I couldn't have been asleep long when I was awakened by the exploding of mortar bombs at the rear of Company HQ. As I lay listening to the whine of them passing overhead there is a crash and explosion not far from the bungalow, at the same moment I am covered with plaster and tile from above. Quickly I roll off and under the bed and when the dust dies down I crawl out, grope around in the darkness for my clothes and equipment, thinking at the same time that sleep does not come easy these days. With a sigh I throw the pyjamas onto the bed then stumbling through the building to the outside I find that my men have come to no harm. They seem to think that a shell clipped the ridge of the house and exploded beyond or else the hole in the roof was caused by a piece of flying metal.

Friday February 6th

A daylight search revealed nothing and later a pair of small searchlights arrived although their erection would have to wait until darkness descends. After sweeping away the plaster dust from our dining table we have dinner supplemented by salmon and tinned fruit from the food dump. Nothing much to do now except get some rest before tea and the forthcoming night work, which comes all to soon.

As soon as daylight fades the gunners get their weapon into position in case of a night attack. As for myself I take two men and set up the beach lights, each close to trees on the bank. The trees afforded some camouflage and one in fact had an adjacent branch slightly pulled down and tied to the light stem.

Saturday February 7th

A quiet night was passed, the new day heralded by the gun being hidden in the garage. With the coming of daylight shells start to explode around our area, two bursting in front of my forward position, throwing up enough mud from the foot of the bank where it met the sea, to unbalance the sentry who had only been on duty for a few minutes. The mud all but covered him at the bottom of the trench and I had to send a man along the communications trench to help him get out. All the time shells were passing overhead, both ways as our own gun, concealed behind us, was answering. A Bofors gun hidden unknown to me quite close by opened up on a low sighting, the whine of its shell close overhead and the wicked crack as it fired, seemed to lift me clear of the ground. The battle of the guns goes on for some time and we certainly get our share, many falling around our positions, the house first being narrowly missed then being hit direct. All the men are in the trenches and luckily this time we have no casualties. We appear to be in a target area so we move Platoon HQ to some concrete air-raid shelters built into sloping ground at the rear.

Undaunted by the day's happening, the men, as darkness comes down, ask that three of them should go for more food from the docks. With a warning to keep a sharp lookout for the duty officer on their way back I agree, though knowing that although the dump is lost to our own people we would still be in hot water if caught. After the days shelling the dump may have been blown up. I decide to take a man and inspect our recent installations, the beach lights. Skirting the trenches but stumbling into the odd shell hole we reach the first of the lights. It is snapped off its stand, we fumble our way to the next one only to find it broken and twisted. What a waste, never to be switched on. The destruction of these lights made me wonder whether the Japanese studied the coastline during the daylight to such detail they could have spotted something that was not there the day before which therefore resulted in the shelling. While out on the bank we could hear the rumble of heavy transport from the enemy side, this we listened to for an hour, must be a big movement up of troops etc., prior to trying a crossing of the Straits.

Sunday February 8th

I reported in to my Platoon Officer just after midnight and am making my rounds of the positions when suddenly all hell is let loose, the night sky is lit up with lurid flashes of red light followed by terrific explosions from the docks. In the flashes the giant cranes and pylons can be seen to be falling, there is the screech of pieces of flying steel as they are blasted overhead. The Naval dock and its installations are being blown up, evidently no effort is going to be made to hold it. Flashes, explosions and screaming steel fill the air for hours. "Jap" artillery has opened up all along the line, all the vegetation is on fire. As I stand for a time shocked by the events, the island vibrates beneath my feet.

Monday February 9th

Later, huddled in trenches, watching the fire-like flashes in the sky we wait for daylight, hardly daring to think what it might bring. If an attack by the enemy across the Straits took place now we wouldn't know about it until they hit our wire because of the noise. As we wait with one hour to go to dawn, the officer comes to me with the news that any time we might get the order to move, but not to say anything to the men yet. Daylight approaches and all the crescendo of the night dies down and we all feel lucky to be still around.

The day passes without event except for our high living as in the past few days. Darkness approaches yet again and the intermittent shelling that's been going on most of the day dies down. A patrol of two officers and three other ranks, which crossed the Straits into Malaya, have returned safely but the result of their 24-hour visit to enemy territory is unknown to me.

It's now 1800hrs and I have just received the order to vacate my positions, this entails clambering around in the dark to move from each position 15,000 rounds of ammunition and cases of hard rations to some distance away and reloading onto platoon trucks. Some light shelling has again started up, probably because of more demolition in the dockyard.

It is now 2000hrs, we are ready to move but nothing is happening. After hanging about for a long time the trucks begin to move out and a bit later we are on our way once again.

Tuesday February 10th

After a four mile hike we come to rest in a mosquito invested swamp. We get into positions as required, then settle down to await the arrival of our platoon trucks, but as time goes on the wait seems in vain. Later I am told that the trucks were hit by mortar bombs and set on fire. That was the end of our little store of extra rations but to me the last straw was the loss of my pack. This containing two years supply of razor blades that I had bought in South Africa, to ensure that I would always have the needs for a shave, plus some small souvenirs I had come by.

Copy of camp orders (1):

February 10th 1942

General Wavell to General Percival

To: General Percival

It is certain that our troops on Singapore Island heavily outnumber any Japanese who have crossed the Straits. We must destroy them.

Our whole fighting reputation is at stake and the honour of the British Empire. The Americans have held out in the Bataan Islands against far heavier odds, and the Russians are turning back the picked strength of the Germans. The Chinese with an almost complete lack of modern equipment have held the greater part of their country against the full strength of the Japanese for four and a half years. It will be disgraceful if we yield our boasted fortress of Singapore to inferior enemy forces.

There must be no thought of sparing the troops or civil population and no mercy must be shown to weakness in any shape or form. Commanders and senior officers must lead their troops and must if necessary die with them. There must be no thought or question of surrender. Every unit must fight it out to the end and in close contact with the enemy.

Please see that the above is brought to the notice of all senior officers and by them to the troops. I look to you and your men to fight to the end and prove that the fighting spirit that won our Empire still exists to enable us to defend it.

Signed A.P. Wavell (General)

Singapore 10-2-42

Copy of camp orders (2):

February 10th 1942

Lt General Tomayuki Yamashito High Command of the Nippon Army February 10th 1942

To: The High Command of the British Army in Malaya

Your Excellency

I the High Command of the Nippon Army, based on the spirit of Japanese chivalry, have the honour of presenting this note to your Excellency, advising you to surrender the whole force in Malaya.

My sincere respects are due to your army, which true to the traditional spirit of Great Britain in bravely defending Singapore which now stands isolated and unaided. Many fierce and gallant fights have been fought by your gallant men and officers, to the honour of British warriorship.

But the development of the general war situation has already sealed the fate of Singapore, and continuation of futile resistance would not only serve to inflict harm and injuries to thousands of non-combatants living in the city, throwing them into further miseries and horrors of war, but also would certainly not add anything to the honour of your army.

I expect that your excellency accepting my advice will give up the meaningless and desperate resistance, and promptly order your entire front to cease hostilities and will dispatch at the same time your Parliamentian, according to the procedure shown at the end of this note. If on the contrary your Excellency should reject my advice and present persistence be continued I shall be obliged, though reluctantly through humanitarian considerations, to order my army to make an annihilating attack on Singapore.

In closing this note of advice I pay again my sincere respects to your Excellency.

Sgnd: Tomavuki Yamashita

1. The Parliamentian should proceed to Bukit Timah road.

2. The Parliamentian should bear a large white flag and a Union Jack.

Wednesday February 11ᵗʰ

Morning, and with it some demoralising thoughts as we do not know what is going on. After a breakfast of sorts we are moving again, whether it be forwards or backwards at this stage I could not tell you. Anyhow our move takes us close by an aerodrome known as Selietui, which as been vacated by our airforce, if there's any left. We dig in when enemy planes permit us to do so, which is not for very long at a time. They appear to have the skies to themselves and every so often we have to rush for cover in the nearby fringe of trees as they swoop to machine gun us, causing casualties to some that tried to hide in bomb craters. This goes on throughout the day until 1600hrs when we are moved again. As we withdraw towards Singapore City, I am thinking that it will not be long before we fall into the sea. We are withdrawing along either side of the main road, which is bounded by a rubber plantations, the sky appears as just a narrow blue strip high above the green of the trees. Looking up at this blue sky I see three aircraft crossing over at a great height but not in view long enough to be recognised.

In a short time we come to a side road running off to the aerodrome from which lorry loads of Indian soldiers are just emerging. At this moment I hear a screaming noise, shells passing overhead? Then flashing through my mind, shells don't scream they whine. "Bombs!", I yell and dash for cover, there's nothing close by, only a grass verge by the roadside about nine inches deep. As I plunge down towards it I catch a quick glimpse of the Indian troops flying into the air as bombs exploded around their trucks. On hitting the ground I collide with someone else but held my ground. More bombs burst down the side road but much nearer us. It must have been the Indian troops leaving the aerodrome that attracted the enemy planes, but being at a road junction we are in line with the sticks of bombs being dropped. Closer they explode, it's all happening in seconds, yet waiting for the one that you think is going to hit you in the middle of your back causes many memories to rush through your mind. A terrific explosion seems to lift me bodily from the ground, I feel a blow on the side of my steel helmet, I am hugging the ground again, then the realisation that the bombing has passed me by and that the explosions are a bit further away. It has gone quiet, the planes drone away in the distance.

New noises reach my ears, cries of wounded men. Severely shaken I haul myself to my feet and the sight that meets my eyes sickens me, at this moment I feel terrible. All around me are dead and wounded men, one decapitated, others just mangled flesh, one man on his feet with flesh hanging from his side. I see my Company Commander sitting on the bank in a state of shock with a damaged shoulder where a flying branch of a tree had struck him. There are men of 'C' Company, who were following us, lying dead and wounded. The man I had bumped on going to ground was my Platoon Officer, like me he was unhurt. Stretcher-bearers and ambulances are among us now, the man whose side is ripped open is wandering away, I run to him, he is so shocked, he does not know what he is doing. I lead him back and am amazed that he is still on his feet.

Our casualties have been severe; I have lost five of my men with two others badly wounded. Still shaken I fall the remainder in as we have to keep going. On moving off, I take stock of myself. One leg of my shorts is wet, my water bottle has a hole in it having been hit by a piece of shrapnel, a bump on the side of my head caused by something that hit my helmet and leaving a large dent in it plus two bleeding fingers that were cut by shrapnel splinters. We had moved about two miles when shells pass overhead, bursting in the soft ground of the plantations. Later we are machine-gunned from some slopes away to our left, but the bullets whine overhead. The enemy must be very close to us yet remain hidden from view although by the sounds of exchange gunfire they are being engaged in some areas. The road is getting more crowded with men and machines all going the same way. After having travelled about twelve miles we halt in the rubber trees, where it is considered safe to stay the night. Heavy shelling continues all through the night but not on our positions.

Thursday February 12th

With the coming of the dawn I find myself holding down an area alongside one of the biggest cemeteries that I have yet seen, it appears to be Chinese and rolls away up and over hills, through valleys until lost to sight. Later in the day we are moving again, this time to a position about a mile away in the cemetery itself. Earlier you will have read how I virtually started in a cemetery and it's beginning to look as though I may finish in this one. Battalions of "The Beds and Herts", "The Sherwood Foresters", "Cambridgeshires" and "6th Norfolks" are also in this area, the last two named still straggling in. Enemy planes are overhead; they are very suspicious and are trying to draw our fire by firing occasional bursts of machine gun fire at us. We are lying in long grass among the gravestones, most of which carry photographs of those interred. On a visual search of a ridge on the skyline I notice some movement, I raise my binoculars to have a look while at the same time a burst of Bren gun fire startles the movement on the ridge into flight, for through the glasses I have seen seven runner ducks! Darkness shuts us in once more and with it comes an order to withdraw back to the shelter of the rubber trees. The talk among the men, rumours no doubt, is that we are drawing back to the docks for evacuation.

Friday February 13th

The night wears on, with the 2nd Cambs. taking over from us, my Company going into reserve for a rest, however, very little sleep is had for in the two hours before dawn all of us are standing to in case of a surprise attack. Red Very lights bursting in the sky gives it a blood-red hue and an intense battle rages all around us, bringing an end to our so called rest. Daylight also brings in the enemy snipers. The 2nd Cambs. withdraw but are ordered back and my platoon takes over new positions.

Saturday February 14th

Talk goes around that Churchill has promised the air will be black with planes tomorrow. Spend the night in line with 'C' Company in defence of Battalion HQ.

Sunday February 15th

Daylight returns and with it the enemy planes, their relentless searching over the area keeps us hidden in the rubber plantation. They come and go at will as our guns are out of ammunition. I remember the talk of the day before, "The sky will be black with planes", but they forgot to say whose. All I can see are those of the "Nips", who all day have strafed the areas about us. A fellow from my home town has just been killed and the Sergeant Major has just brought down a plane with machine-gun fire. All day he has said that he would get one of the "Little Yellow Devils".

Out to our front are two enemy heavy machine-gun posts whose sporadic outbursts of fire remind us to keep our heads down. 'A' and 'C' Companies have endeavoured all day to eliminate these guns. We are told that all types of ammunition had virtually run out and so with bayonets fixed we form a steel ring around Singapore. What a brave quote. We have killed thousands of Japanese during this battle down the mainland of Malaya and on Singapore but we are heavily out-numbered. I and many around me have no bullets for our rifles and now begin to wonder how it's all going to end.

It's now 1600hrs my officer has just come over and instructed us to cease fire, the command has come from the 53rd Brigade Headquarters. It was a complete capitulation of the Island to save suffering and bloodshed to the civilian population, who incidentally had also been without water for two days. We move slowly across areas of rubber trees to another destination. It's a quiet, sad column of men, hungry, exhausted, with clothes filthy, torn and stinking of stale sweat but men still determined that the enemy were not having our guns. Although against orders Bren guns, rifles etc, were thrown into swamps, or given with grenades to native villagers who were only too eager to have them and immediately set about finding a safe place for them. Finally we end our depressing trail and come to rest in a new Battalion HQ, where we have some hard rations. Sentries are posted and instructed that if they hear or see any movement they are just to report it, and with that done the rest of us are told that we can sleep. I can imagine that many pairs of eyes were shut before their bodies hit the ground.

Copy of camp orders (3):

15th February 1942 - General Percival.

Immediate

To. Cmdr 3 Corps (Indian), Comdr. S Area, Cmdr. A.LF, A, "Q" CAAD, BRA, CE, CSO, DDST, DDMS, DDOS, DPM, G1. Staff message control - Chief Cipher Officer.

It has been necessary to give up the struggle but I want the reason explained to all ranks.

The forward troops continue to hold their ground but the essentials of war have run short. In a few days we shall have neither petrol nor food. Many types of ammunition are short and the water supply on which the vast civil population and many of the fighting troops are dependent threatens to fail. The present situation has been brought about partly by being driven off our dumps and partly by hostile air and artillery action. Without these sinews of war we cannot fight on.

I thank all ranks for their efforts throughout the campaign.

(G. Ops)   *Sgnd A E Percival. Lt_General*
15th February 1942   *GOC Commanding Malaya Command.*

Copy of camp orders (4):

15th February 1942 - Beckworth-Smith.

No Commander has led a happier and more loyal team into battle. The Division was sent into a theatre of war for which it was neither trained or equipped, to fight a clever and cunning enemy who was on the crest of the wave. It was sent to fight a battle already lost and had to pass through troops whose morale had been badly shaken. It had to endure long periods of hardship without food or rest, yet it fought with great courage and tenacity, inflicting heavy losses on the enemy. Every man, and I know will, rightly hold his head high, knowing that he has upheld the best traditions of the British Army. During the 18 months I have been privileged to command the Division at home and overseas it has carried out every varied and exacting task it has been called upon to undertake and now I can only dedicate the rest of my life to help in every way the officers, WOs and men of the 18th Division.

God Bless you all and bring you safely home when victory is finally ours, with the knowledge that you have played in its achievement.

15th February 1942   Sgnd Beckworth-Smith
*   GOC 18th Division*

No................................   Army Form B. 104—83
(If replying, please quote above No.)

....Record Office,

....

....19 .

SIR OR MADAM,

    I regret to have to inform you that a report has been received from

the War Office to the effect that (No.)...............(Rank).................

(Name) ....

(Regiment) ....

was posted as " missing " on the...................................

..................at...

    The report that he is missing does not necessarily mean that he has been killed, as he may be a prisoner of war or temporarily separated from his regiment.

    Official reports that men are prisoners of war take some time to reach this country, and if he has been captured by the enemy it is probable that unofficial news will reach you first. In that case I am to ask you to forward any postcard or letter received at once to this Office, and it will be returned to you as soon as possible.

    Should any further official information be received it will be at once communicated to you.

        I am,

        SIR OR MADAM,

        Your obedient Servant,

        Jn Bullock Capt.

        Officer in charge of Records.

IMPORTANT.
    Any change of your address should be immediately notified to this Office.
Wt. 30051/1249 400,000 (16) 9/39 KJL/8812 Gp 698/3 Forms/B.104—83/9

Posted *'missing'* on 15th February 1942

CHAPTER 4

THE GATES OF HELL OPEN

Monday February 16th 1942

We have been here just over a month and I do not remember being static for more than two days and for most of the time having been tired, dirty and hungry. It was like being in a maze, never knowing how to get out, but at this moment we are waiting for our captors to arrive and are not quite sure what their reactions will be when we come face to face. Eventually they arrive, little sturdy, brown, unshaven men in drab green uniform and separate toed canvas and rubber boots (so different from our heavy studded leather ones). Grinning all over their faces they bowed and offered us cigarettes and on learning that we had had no drinking water for three days galvanized baths of the liquid was soon brought and to us it was like wine. They were surprisingly friendly towards us and later through an interpreter they said they were happy to meet such brave men. There did not seem to be many of them around and we spend the day here, with them moving among us with the curiosity of a cat, looking at our wrist-watches, rings and binoculars, however nothing except guns and bayonets are taken from us.

Tuesday February 17th

Next morning after a night of uninterrupted sleep, something unknown during the last thirty days, I form up the remnants of my Company. We join together with others to form a large column of many units, also decreased in number by killed and wounded. The order is given to move to the right and with a quick march we are off on a seventeen mile hike to Changi Barracks at the other end of the Island. These barracks known as the "Hore Belisha" Barracks were built just prior to the war by a Conservative minister of that name who favoured the army. They were said to be the best in the world although at the moment they look a bit worse for wear, mainly I believe damaged by our own troops retreating under pressure. The water and electricity lines had been blown up with other essential things.

Copy of camp orders (5):

Changi, 17th February 1942 - Major General Keith Simmons

After weeks of anxious and steadfast watching you have taken your turn in the fighting on Singapore Island. Some of you had previously done your part most gallantly on the mainland. Throughout the operations on Singapore Island I can only thank you for your efforts to stay the attack. You have had little support from the air: you have been outnumbered and outgunned. Notwithstanding this you have borne yourselves magnificently. Remember this in your hour of trial; you have done your part, your best. You have no need to blame yourselves. Keep your spirits up; good times will come again.

Changi, 17th February 1942   Major General Keith Simmons
GOC 53rd Brigade

(Note - the 53rd Brigade comprised the 5th and 6th Battalions of the Royal Norfolk Regiment and the 2nd Battalion, the Cambridgeshire Regiment. This East Anglian Brigade had fought on the mainland from Mersing down to Singapore Island.)

Wednesday February 18th

After a couple of days spent clearing up the area around the barrack block given over to my depleted Battalion, we are marched down to the sea, which is close by, and allowed to go bathing in a railed off section. This area in Malay is called a "Pagar", and means a space where fish can enter between close-spaced poles. The fish can then be caught by the natives without any fear or danger from the sharks that abound around here. To us it is heaven, just to flounder about in the cooling water and to get rid of the muck and sweat of the last ten days.

The middle finger of my left hand has been stiff and sore for over a week now with a swollen knuckle, which shows a tiny red mark. The little finger is similar but since the bathing this finger seems better and the middle one not so sore, but still swollen. At least we can go to bed feeling refreshed, I say bed but that to us is a three-foot space of concrete floor covered with a ground sheet if you are lucky enough to have one. We have to sleep in our clothes, as we have no blankets. I am on the second floor close to open windows and therefore a night temperature of 80°F down from 110°F in the sun feels somewhat cool to us. It's a long night of twisting and turning in an effort to relieve first one hip and then the other. The hardness of the concrete floor makes it almost impossible to sleep for more than an hour at a time. We now realise that when we were roughing it Mother Earth made a much softer mattress.

Thursday February 19th

Dawn comes suddenly around 0630hrs, just like someone drawing aside the heavy curtains across the window of a darkened room. The sun is rising like a huge fiery cart wheel. No washing or shaving as no water available and with no bed to make we just pile our bits and pieces of kit in a heap at the head of our allotted floor space. We then stand around talking about our enforced situation, hoping at the same time someone will come up with some breakfast.

Around 0800hrs the call "Come and get it" goes out, and with a clatter of mess tins and mugs we rush to the assembly point to partake of an issue of hard biscuits and some tinned meat. This was washed down by a mug of weak tea after which I had to clean my eating utensils with sand owing to the water shortage.

During the morning I take a party and continue to try and tidy up the area, filling up shell holes etc.

In the Barracks area are two churches of different denominations almost completely wrecked by shell fire, the gable ends of both still standing to some extent with battered alters, but with the cross and figure of Christ untouched in both cases, which to many people means a miracle has happened.

After dinner I fall in my party and join the main body for a march to the sea, guarded on both sides by Jap soldiers. This is about all there is now left for us to do for as yet our captors have not decided what to do with us. As darkness is like the dawn in coming suddenly, at 1830hrs there is nothing we can do except sit around and talk until 2230hrs which is bedtime as we have no means of lighting.

Friday February 20th

After another disturbed night we are glad of the dawn if only to get some warmth from the sun, now rising over the greenery of the landscape confronting us. Soon I trudge down for breakfast and on getting my ration, smaller each day, I realise that the food situation must be getting tight. We appear to be living on our own reserves. After breakfast we lounge around in the sun, swatting and swearing at the thousands of flies that seem intent on eating us alive.

Later in the day we go bathing again, the enjoyable part of this is that the water is so warm and that you need no towel to dry yourself, I just lay on the sand and let the sun do the rest. While I am sunbathing I notice something black sticking out of my swollen and stiff finger. I get hold of it and manage painfully to pull out a half inch of shrapnel, about as thick as a darning needle; the seawater has evidently softened things and caused it to work itself out.

Sunday February 22nd

The Nippon General has sent a message to our Commanding Officer saying:

"We fought like warriors and will be treated as such".

He did not say that the odds against were formidable, anyhow it's nice to know what he thinks of us but one wonders what a Nippon warrior is treated like.

Wednesday February 25th

Three more days have passed by with the usual bathing parties and just lying around until nightfall, then the inevitable swapping of stories of our past home life interspersed with the occasional curse and slap as someone smacks at a mosquito. They seemed to have found us and are intent on having their fill of our blood; they whirr around in the darkness just like dive-bombers coming in. There are rumours that our stocks of food are fast running out and that we shall soon be dependent on our "hosts" for supplies.

Friday February 27th

Stiff and now bored we meet the sunrise of another day and await the call for breakfast, which when it comes we find has changed somewhat, just a couple of ladles of watery rice and half a pint of tea. Drink is the one thing we long for as this ration of tea is all we shall get until dinnertime with no water on tap. After a half an hour in the tropical sun you have sweated it out and for the next four hours you are really parched. There is no need to pass water as it comes out through your pores and there drying up to leave a film of salt over your skin.

Dinnertime comes along after what seems a decade as my party and I are very hungry. To our dismay it's a ration of boiled rice and half a herring in tomato sauce for flavouring, plus a mug

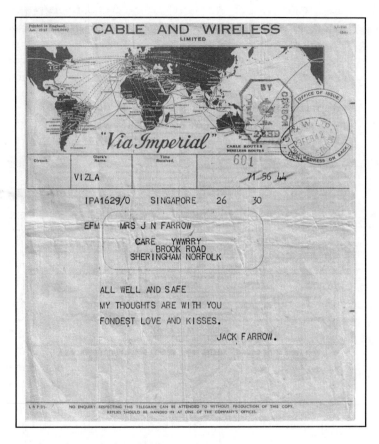

CABLE AND WIRELESS
LIMITED

"Via Imperial"

CABLE ROUTES
WIRELESS ROUTES

601

VI ZLA 71 56 44

IPA1629/0   SINGAPORE   26   30

EFM   MRS J N FARROW

CARE   YWWRRY
BROOK ROAD
SHERINGHAM NORFOLK

ALL WELL AND SAFE
MY THOUGHTS ARE WITH YOU
FONDEST LOVE AND KISSES.

JACK FARROW.

NO ENQUIRY RESPECTING THIS TELEGRAM CAN BE ATTENDED TO WITHOUT PRODUCTION OF THIS COPY.
REPLIES SHOULD BE HANDED IN AT ONE OF THE COMPANY'S OFFICES.

**Copy of Telegram sent from Singapore after the surrender,
February 23rd 1942**

of raw tea, no milk or sugar. Naturally the afternoon bathing party is all discussions about our last two meals and what they consisted of. Today we go to an open beach and have to keep an eye peeled for sharks, although I think the playful yelling of so many men splashing around will scare them off as I am told that they do not like noise. Bathing over we are instructed to find drift-wood or such and take back for the cookhouse fires.

Saturday February 28th

This morning I am ordered to get my platoon remnants together with their bits and pieces of kit and to join the rest of my Company. It seems at last the "Nips" want a work party somewhere, so around 1000hrs we set off marching with all our worldly goods. The march is long and hot with continuous dust raised by passing lorries of the "Nips", each with a little flag, a red blob in the centre of white cloth, nicknamed the "Fried Egg" by the British prisoners. Eventually we arrive at our destination in Singapore. We are leg weary after more than twelve miles marching in the intense heat of the hours around mid-day. On entering the area known as the Passive Defence Club I was somewhat amazed to see my surname on a signpost, "Farrow Park". There is no chance of much rest for us as we are allotted huts which have to be cleaned out. The place stinks and is littered with hundreds of empty food tins, it seems that the last people must have had a party before they left. At last we are called for tea, the cooks have managed to rustle up a meal and some tea. One good thing there is water, however, we are warned against drinking it but extra tea will be available a bit more often.

Sunday March 1st 1942

I see by my diary it is St David's Day. Well as the saying goes, "Better the day better the deed". Anyhow in my opinion that cannot be so, for on this day I with others have just spent nine gruelling hours in the sun putting up barbed wire around Farrow

Park to keep ourselves in. On the opposite side of the surrounding road is a huge hospital. The Queen Alexandra nurses are still hurrying around, Eurasian girls I think. We get a few hurried waves from them when our captors are not too alert. Just before fighting ended here soldier patients were bayoneted as they lay on their beds by the Japs and some nurses also killed.

After heavy overnight thunderstorms the area, in many parts, is flooded and the latrines in some cases are ankle deep with water. I can sit and listen to the calls of bull frogs. These weird sounds like someone in pain takes me back to a night when my platoon were dug-in, in a Tamil Indian cemetery. It was pitch dark and except for the odd rifle shot, when a trigger happy man fired at a sound out front, nothing stirred. I then heard this moaning noise, like someone badly wounded, after putting up with it for a while it got the better of me. Telling my Corporal what I was up to I crawled in the direction of the noise. It was pitch dark so I could only be guided by sound but after a time the groaning ceased and I gave in, that whoever it was had died. At this moment as I sit in this flooded latrine I realise that I had been fooled by a bullfrog, having not heard one before. My search therefore for a wounded man was in vain. Spashingly, I make my way to the cookhouse and partake of vegetable stew and rice, washing it down with the raw tea. Dead beat I lay myself down on a piece of blanket I managed to come by and think of all the comforts of home until I eventually fall asleep.

Monday March 2nd

I am soon aroused, it seems too quickly, by the Sergeant Major shouting "Rise and shine". It's another day, a quick wash and your fingers through your hair for a comb. I have no mirror to see myself in but I must look terrible, a fortnight's growth of beard, a filthy and badly torn shirt and mud covered shorts. Well who's to see me? I gather I look like any other one of us, and what's more to the point my stomach's empty so breakfast is the main priority. With rice and tea inside us, we carry on with the barbed wiring, which is soon finished, then we are set to removing the burnt-out army trucks that litter the compound. They are Indian Ordnance Corps stuff, so it appears it must have been their depot. Natives are also employed removing shells from an old gun position.

At 1500hrs we get an order to cease work and to await a Japanese inspection of our wiring. They find it to their satisfaction and want to be friendly. One asks me in English if I have a wife, I show my wedding snap that I have always managed to keep with me. At the time the photograph was taken I was wearing the red sash of a Duty Sergeant, he was impressed and called some of his comrades to look at it, widely grinning at me and saying top soldier. So far these fighting troops have been keen to show their friendliness. The rest of the day and night pass by with much of the same talk among us, except it is said one of the cooks called a Nippon soldier, "A bloody little yellow monkey", who in turn grinned broadly.

Tuesday March 3rd

Morning comes and with it the noise and bustle of lorries and people on the road adjoining our wired in area. After a wash, and to kill time while waiting for breakfast, some of us walk to the wire perimeter, but are kept far enough away by our guards to prevent us taking to people on the outside. Only yesterday a Chinese girl handed some food to one of our men but was seen and badly beaten up. The men who witnessed this were angry but could do nothing, also the cook who called the "Nip" guard a "Bloody little yellow monkey" has just been beaten up. It appears that he had called the guard this about four times and had had a good laugh, however, on the last occasion another "Nip" soldier understood enough English and that was that. After breakfast of rice and tea we are told much to our surprise to fall in with our equipment as our wiring job is finished and we are off back to Changi Barracks. We have one lorry to carry some of the heavy stuff and on top of the cab is a four gallon petrol tin with a tomato plant, about eighteen inches high, growing in it. It is being held there by one of our men and is the butt of many jokes but perhaps the man hopes to get a tomato meal from it one day. This plant was the most important item being moved, for the square can has a false bottom which contained a radio, which to a few, is a contact with India.

The sun is high and hot as we set off on our march back and soon we are beyond the built up area of Singapore and looking ahead along a road glaring white in the rays of a dazzling sun. Sometimes it runs through rubber plantations and at other times Chinese market gardens or scrub. These market gardens take my mind back to the few days I was in the town itself. There is a place called Lavender Street, once the site of a market garden, and as the Chinese lavatory pans were emptied daily along the rows of vegetables, one can imagine the smell in the hot tropical sun. It no doubt at a later date gave someone an amusing thought to give the area a sweeter smelling name, but it didn't keep so sweet as it became the district's brothel area. Anyhow let's get back to the hot dusty road; having covered about eight miles of the sixteen we have to cover the men are dripping sweat, grumbling, and some dragging their feet. A halt is called for dinner, which consists of four hard biscuits and a small piece of cheese, no tea. We drop by the roadside to eat and rest, only a few have water bottles and these are soon empty. Our equipment is sparse, much having been lost or ruined in the fighting and the remainder handed in at the end.

Soon we are on our feet again, groaning and stretching our stiffened joints and wiping the sweat from our eyes. I finally get my party into threes to join the others and off we go once more. It takes quite a bit of shuffling, swearing and foot dragging before we resemble trained soldiers on the march again. On the way we are passed by a platoon of Nippon soldiers on bicycles and also what appears to be thousands of natives looking very bedraggled on their way back, I expect to homes in the capital that they had left during the bombing. Tired and footsore we arrive at Changi late in the afternoon, get our rice tea, reclaim our bed spaces and get our heads down. Not much noise as I think the majority of the men are feeling just a bit fed up and tired.

Wednesday March 4ᵗʰ

Although we are Prisoners of War our officers manage to keep up formalities. Today I am Battalion Orderly Sergeant and have to accompany the Duty Officer on his rounds of our compound, just to make sure that things are OK and say a word here and there to fellows who are feeling the strain. The officers with us have had their badges of rank removed and just wear a star for some reason, perhaps to bring them all to one level so that they are not picked on by the "Nips" to answer for us in case of troubles with the men, such as stealing the amenities to keep alive if the chances arrive.

Thursday March 5ᵗʰ

We are told that we are going to have a washday. What am I going to wash I don't know. One very torn shirt, which I only wear at night to keep the mosquitoes off, one pair of holy socks and one pair of stained shorts completes the list. Also, of course, there is no soap to wash them with. At the moment we have only the sea to splash our bits and pieces around in, then bash them on a large smooth rock and lay them in the sun to dry, which is very quick. The bashing on the rock idea we learned from the natives whom we had earlier seen washing their clothes in the river and bashing them on specially built slabs of smooth concrete on the river banks. Some of the men are using a camouflage net taken off a gun post to fish with and with great success, they have just counted up their catch - 108 fish. On the menu for tonight we will hope for rice fish cakes.

With bathing and washing over we trudge through the various tropical trees and the dust of the well trodden track to the camp. Perhaps I should mention that the camp consists of three compounds, each separated from the other by barbed wire, Nippon guards and at night searchlights flashing along the wires length making each area completely cut off from the other. The whole camp is occupied by around 20,000 men consisting of those of the Singapore Defence, Forces from Malaya and some from Java. Among us are Dutch, Javanese, Australian and a few American troops plus a few Naval men.

During the darkness of the evening, broken only by the chirping of crickets and the croaking of frogs, the men are discussing a rumour that is going around, this being the possibility of us being sent to the Argentine for the duration of the war. This brings us to bedtime with nothing definite forthcoming except it must have something to do with the Red Cross.

Friday March 6th

With breakfast over a full parade of the area is called for and we are told that we will have to leave the barrack blocks and live in the open. This is the latest order from the Nippon HQ. Later I take a party of men, among many others and from the stores draw some cutting tools from material that has been salvaged over the past few weeks. We march to the area and spend six hours, digging, cutting and pulling at rubber tree saplings, a tangle of creeping undergrowth and thorn covered vines, plus also putting up with the hot pin-like stings of large red ants. At the end of this Herculean effort we drag our weary sunburnt, muck and sweat blackened bodies back to our abode cheerfully enough but with no hope of a wash down.

During the day some men have been square bashing (drilling), this seems hard to believe, but the answer is that it's good for discipline. At times over the past month it has been argued among the men that they have been better treated by the "Nips" than many of our own officers. Rumour is rife again tonight. This time Churchill will release us in 60 days time. We are hearing most days what seems like Naval gunfire, only to be told it's distant storms at sea, which are almost a daily occurrence in these parts.

Saturday March 7th

Next morning arrives and all the expectations to move come to nothing. I wonder why the "Nips" wanted that clearing, not for us that's for sure, but no doubt that was one way to get a good job done. I am now leaving the camp en route for the beach with two of our guards in attendance, on arriving there and to our surprise we are instructed to remove the barbed wire defences erected by our own forces. For two hours we struggle with the untwisting of Apron fence wiring, again in the scorching heat, nothing between the deep blue sky and the dry dusty hot sand except us. Parched, some of the men try sucking small pebbles to keep the mouth moist. We carry on winding up the long wire strands as they are detached from the picket irons, many men have badly scratched hands and are pestered with flies. One of the guards who left us earlier now returns and speaks with gesticulating arms to his comrade, while we wonder what is going on, they shout and point to a spot in front of them and call us to it, saying, "Campo, campo", and so off we go back to camp. For some reason unknown to us the de-wiring has been stopped, not that we are worried, it not being one of the best of jobs even with gloves and cutters.

The time is just 1600hrs and a tropical storm breaks, the rain lashing down like huge whips cracking through the coconut palms. The temperature drops and it feels cool, then someone shouts, "What about a shower". Shortly two fellows are outside dancing completely nude in the rain, within minutes, I with a near hundred more had joined them, laughing, shouting and dancing around like Dervishes on ground that is now mud. This is our first wash for a few days also the first freshwater bath for three weeks. It presents a sight that will never be forgotten, what a pity it couldn't be recorded on camera, anyhow I expect it would have been censored. Feeling somewhat cleaner and happier, when the rain stops as suddenly as it started, we wipe ourselves down with rags, such as we have, old shirts etc.

An enemy bomber flies low overhead and we have just learned that over a thousand anti-personnel land mines have been removed from this area around us. Tea is up, rice as usual, later a sit around in the dark talking about the wire work and having a laugh about bathing in the rain. A bit more refreshed we turn in for the night which makes me wish I had a blanket for the rain has certainly cooled the night air. It has also flushed out the dreaded mosquitoes who buzz around causing me to flail my arms about until I fall asleep and am at their mercy, although malaria, before the war, was stamped out in Singapore.

Sunday March 8th

Morning comes as usual with all its moans and so does breakfast. As soon as it is over I have to go with a party of men to fetch beds from a barrack block taken over by the "Nips". The beds I believe are going to the hospital for our battle casualties and other illness cases.

In the afternoon we are now marching back to the beach to take down a bit more barbed wire. Back in camp and before tea an interesting church service and talk by a Red Cross official. He says it is the first time in the history of the Red Cross that a whole unit of theirs has been taken as Prisoners of war. The Japanese Red Cross, the largest organisation in the world (so they tell us) has just made a request to Australia for $35,000 worth of medical goods (true or false?).

We are back on the beach taking down more wire. Rumour is rife that Italy has capitulated (March 5th, 1942) and Germany is about to give in. Some fellows get excited at this news, the majority take it in their stride but talk goes on about it although only when the Nippon guards are out of ear-shot. Tea today is stew of vegetables and rice which is good by normal standards, we all enjoyed the change. Ten Nippon Naval ships left the docks today and two of our men in a work party were killed. I cannot find out the reason but it's the talking point of the evening as we sit around, some with the odd cigarette that they have managed somehow to scrounge whilst out on a work party.

Monday March 9ᵗʰ

It's sunrise and another night has passed with sleep often interrupted by someone having a nightmare, also terrific snoring by some fellows. Anyhow the early morning is always so nice and fresh and the air a treat to breathe after being huddled together all night with the foul inside air. Breakfast this morning will not get us far, it is some sort of bean juice and tea, one good sweat and it will be gone. Removing barbed wire again today, seventy of us have reeled in 5,000 yards by dinner time. Dinner is just a ladle of plain rice, it is claimed that the officers managed roast meat, rice and sultanas. This has caused the men to take the question of the food up with the Company Commander.

7.   **On this day...** March 9, 1942... Java surrenders to the Japanese.

Wednesday March 11ᵗʰ

Over the last two days much the same has gone on except for awhile we were putting up a heavy screen of wire between us and the block the "Nips" have taken over, evidently they don't intend that we should get up to any funny tricks. Have been promised an extra rice supper tonight. A number of enemy planes flying around during the day. I am told that I can have tomorrow off as I shall be in charge of a night guard on the gate in the wire between us and the "Nips".

Thursday March 12ᵗʰ

My day off goes smoothly lazing out in the shade of the palm trees. Night comes down with its abrupt blackness and with it the start of the all night guard. About 22.00hrs. the night breeze brings a strange smell to our noses and I can hear the voices of men in the distance. This goes on for half an hour as they gradually get nearer to us, also the smells get stronger. At last a large party emerge out of the darkness struggling and cursing as they carry with some difficulty a large gate. They are halted by sentries and on investigation I discover the object on the gate is a dead cow stinking to high heaven. The explanation is that it was knocked down and killed by a Nippon army lorry and was not wanted by the natives, as it is a religious being. We were told we could fetch it after dark, having no wheeled conveyance it had to be carried from the point of the accident to our cookhouse. Holding my nose I told them to carry on saying it seemed too far gone to eat after laying in 90°F of sun heat most of the day. The night wears tediously on and with the nearing of dawn the surrounding area starts to buzz and hum with the various noises of crickets and many other large insects.

Friday March 13th

Daylight blazes out and while walking around close to our guardpost I spot a large crater fourteen feet deep, caused I am told by a delayed action bomb. Night duty over I get my breakfast. This is followed by a clean up of the area and ourselves as best we can, shirts are also to be worn. We are marched to the main road where we are lined each side, later to be reviewed by the Nipponese Divisional General and there we stand, not even allowed to sit, for two hours in the sun awaiting him to make up his mind to come. Suddenly the "Nip" guards get very excited, running around and shouting to us. This is soon followed by the passing of three army staff cars, in the second one, the five-foot high immaculate "Nip" General with his hand at the salute. All is over and we return to camp to collect an hour late dinner of rice and beef stew! Yesterday's dead cow, but for all its stinking carcass it tasted good and was enjoyed by all.

Saturday March 14th

As with the rest of the week the day is given over to taking down the wire from the beaches and I have noticed a number of cargo ships passing on their way to the docks, I hope that one day a Red Cross boat will be among them so that we may have a change of food and perhaps some clothes.

On the way back to the camp I see a monkey clambering over a building with a baby one in its arms, it appears quite tame as it comes close to watch us. Tired and dirty we arrive for our rice tea. Although working on the beach, we are not allowed to bathe in the sea, this is only done on very odd occasions. The next day being Sunday (who said a rest day?) I am told to have my party ready in the morning for the usual wiring work.

Sunday March 15th

Morning comes and after the ritual breakfast we move off to the beach, and as we march rumour is running rife through the ranks. This time it says that Germany has finished fighting, Field Marshal Goering of the German air force is in England and Hitler is in Sweden. True or false it gives us something to talk about.

After tea a church service is being held in an old building, nothing else to do so go along to it. The place is lit by various means, a few candles, and some rope burning in diesel oil and giving off black smoke. The singing of a couple of hymns gives you a bit of a lift even if you can only join in with a couple of lines that you may remember from Sunday School days. The service over, we wander back to our concrete bed spaces and fitfully sleep it out until 0630hrs.

Monday March 16th

Only one month in captivity and it has seemed like a year. At breakfast the powers that be spring a surprise on us. The order for 700 men to get ready to go to Singapore. "Perhaps we are going home", says one, "With what luck?" utters another, and so the small talk goes on until we have collected our bits and pieces and assembled on the gun park. Soon an officer comes up and has a few words with the Sergeant Major, who then turns and bellows, "By the right. Quick march!", and off we go again. I notice a lot of new damage since we marched this way a few weeks ago, caused by salvaged ammunition dumps blowing up, the destruction of almost a mile of built-up area. Accidentally? I wonder. Nearly sixteen sweaty and wearying miles behind us, many very footsore as our boots are no longer in the best of condition. Where is our destination? I can hardly believe my eyes when once again I march through the gates of Farrow Park, the area we so recently worked in. We are to live in tents this time and it has now started raining. It is the season for rain which lasts only a few days, and we are told it will happen again in November, perhaps we shall be home by then. We draw our tea ration and return to the tents to eat it, only to find the canvas already starting to leak. By the time darkness falls the surrounding ground is flooded, much worse than the last time we were here, the men splash in and out of the tent making the night uncomfortable and damp.

Tuesday March 17th

When morning light comes we arise, a cool damp lot of men with little to say except for a few grouses. After the rice issue we are piled into trucks, then driven off to the place of work. The place is a large school and the driveway to it is badly cut up by bomb craters and our job is to level lorry loads of brick rubble to even up the place. Thirty-eight of us have been left on this job and our guards are good to us. They bring us loaves of bread, butter, some two gallons of milk to drink, and later in the day about four gallons of good coffee followed by two more gallons of tea. This is the best day that we have had, the coffee made it a party. Later we get into the trucks and are the first back to camp.

Wednesday March 18th

The next day we are driven back to the same job. We see a lot of the civilian population, but they seem afraid to look us in the eyes. To us they appeared to have the Nippon flags out a bit before the cease fire, but who blames them as they have to live with it. Our job again finished for the day, it's onto the lorries and back to the wetness of the tents for a long uncomfortable night, often being stepped on in the dark by men going out to the latrines.

Thursday March 19th

In a way I'm glad morning light has come so that I can get out in the open air. I do not feel so good as I am suffering from bouts of sickness and diarrhoea. The area around is swamped as it is raining like hell. I don't go for breakfast as I cannot face anything to eat. I get to wondering what has upset me, our guards yesterday gave us bully beef, new bread and sweet coffee because they were pleased with our clean up of the inside of the school building, perhaps it was the tinned meat.

The work party guards arrive and to my relief tell us, "No work today rain too heavy". No one is more thankful than me to hear it as I am now feeling very ill and am glad of the day to recover a bit. I manage to borrow the use of a blanket and get my head down for the day. By tea-time I eat some rice, also down a very welcome cup of tea.

Friday March 20th

I get through the night with only one trip to the latrines in the early hours, stumbling in the dark through inches of water for a hundred yards. As for toilet paper, it is any substitute that comes to hand. By morning I feel much better but a lot of men are still bad. Having eaten my rice I fall in with the work party only to find that I have been given another job of work. Who would believe I am going out as a telephone linesman, not that I know the first thing about it. First we had to clear broken poles and wires, then put up new pole replacements over a length of the roadway that crosses the Straits to Johore in Malaya. This is one of the places where many of the enemy crossed from the mainland to the island. They had to pass through barriers of oil fires set up by the British, the whole area is one of complete destruction.

Saturday March 21st

I carry on through the next day, having been shown how to tighten telephone wires with a hand vice, securing the wires to the cups so that the current can flow through. The "Nip" guards seem pleased and once again bring us coffee, pineapple, jam and bread, also they provided a little sugar for our rice which is welcome. All the time that we are working on this job we are being filmed, for propaganda work no doubt.

Sunday March 22nd

After one more bad night we arise once again hungry and stiff in joints from the climbing of poles and the dampness. The diary reminds me it is "Passion Sunday", what we need is a little compassion for we are about to march the miles back to Changi camp. Many of the men are very sick and weak from the "bug" that has hit us. The road glares white hot in front of us and many men fall from weakness and have to be helped by the stronger men among us. After eight long miles we are halted for a dinner of rice and while we eat this small handout we are again being filmed by the "Nips" from a slowly passing truck. Soon we are on our way again, sweating and footsore we raise a chorus from marching songs to help us to keep going. On the way we pass hundreds of seventy-five-pounder guns that have been salvaged by the enemy, they are twisted and blackened by the efforts of the British gun crews to destroy them at the end. A wired in camp area by the roadside, guarded by Sikh soldiers armed with rifles and bayonets puzzles us, as the Sikhs should be prisoners with us. Further along a queue of natives seem to have been waiting a long time, as the road beside them is stained red where they have spit their saliva dyed by the betel nut that they constantly chew.

All these roadside attractions help us to forget to some extent our own absolute tiredness but we drag wearily along for another mile or so and our hearts are lifted as Changi camp comes into view. Once there and we are dismissed it's off to our bed spaces, and we soon resemble a sleeping flock of sheep. When tea is called it's only the pangs of hunger and thirst that gives us enough energy to make the effort to get up and go for it. We line up sluggishly for our scoop of rice and mug of raw tea; tonight the tea to us thirsty marchers is like a cup of wine. Meals are quickly over as ten minutes will suffice for us to consume our ration. Having done this it's back to bed and the air is soon filled with the heavy breathing and snores of men, broken only by curses as those who, as they hurry to the latrines, fall over others in the darkness. Many are still suffering from bad stomachs.

Monday March 23rd

We arise stiffly in the morning with hangover-type feelings and at breakfast are told it is a day off for those back from Singapore. We take the opportunity to wash our sweat-stinking bits and pieces. We have a few bits of soap among us that we found while cleaning the school building, also a little water is now available from a line salvaged and repaired by our own engineers. The last shave I had was a fortnight ago with a borrowed razor, but during the recent cleaning up operations I was lucky enough to find a folder of razor blades that are marked one for each day, Monday to Sunday. This being Monday I hunt out my razor and start a shaving operation with no mirror, and after a great effort I feel clean and a new man again. I work out that with some care these seven blades could last me seven weeks. I have one pair of underpants that I have somehow managed to keep and I find them useful now whilst my shorts are drying out. The day has almost gone, it's just 1700hrs and we are called to fall in for a 1730hrs practice march past, for a visit from a Nipponese Corps Commander who is coming one day during the week.

CHAPTER 5

BOOT HILL

Tuesday March 24ᵗʰ 1942

This morning there is no work for us, so after the meal I spend a little time writing up my diary and other bits of my war activities. Just before dinner I am lounging around in the sun when my Company Commander comes up to me and asks if I would like a permanent job. I got to my feet and asked him what the work consisted of and what he meant by permanent, he just shrugged his shoulders and said if I was interested I should talk to a Major Bregiel at a certain place in the morning by 1100hrs. As I lay at night I turn the offer of a job over and over in my mind, what could it be?

Wednesday March 25ᵗʰ

I must have fallen asleep with it on my mind as I was awakened later by the fellows arousing themselves for a trek to the cookhouse area for the rice allowance. Later I cleaned myself up, polished up what was left of my boots with the pink blooms gathered from a hibiscus bush. These flowers when squeezed produced a black dye and brought a bit of life back to dusty boots (so much have we learned from men who have done regular service over here). Promptly at the time stated I was at the appointed place for the interview with the Major, who came along at the same time. He was an elderly man with grey hair. Before he spoke however, I realised what I had let myself in for as, just behind us in a cleared patch, I saw two graves and some men were clearing and digging a further grave. The Major then asked me if I would undertake the responsibility of running a cemetery with him. I did not think much to grave digging and burials but thought that it could be better than being pushed around by the "Nips", so I agreed to take on the work. He was pleased at this, having heard he said that I was a landscape gardener and could make the cemetery a nice place.

I therefore start my new job; it will provide me with an interest. I have a pass that gets me and my fifteen allotted men past the guards on the gate. When we arrive the men are set to work, four grave digging, others clearing jungle scrub. I have buried four young soldiers today. They were brought covered by a Union Jack and thousands of flies. Flies must be the world's worst enemy, they are everywhere. If you drop a piece of rice during a meal it is immediately covered with hundreds of them, I am continually waving one hand over my food when eating to keep the flies off. If they happen to get under my guard I throw the piece away rather than run the risk of dysentery, which is now bad among the men. During the day there was a Brigade inspection by our own officers but I did not have to parade. Tomorrow we are told there will be a Nipponese Command inspection.

Thursday March 26th

When the time comes for the inspection, I and my men are exempt, so during the morning we are engaged in moving flowering shrubs from some of the houses in the area to the officers' quarters. This done, we return to the cemetery in the afternoon. The area we have to clear will, when full, hold 1200 bodies and the Royal Engineers hope to build a chapel later on.

Friday March 27th

The weather today is very hot, with heavy storms making it bad for working. In digging a grave the first foot of ground is the easiest, our tools are not the best to dig out what is a red volcanic earth, and which when wet has the consistency of wet clay, and when you throw the soil out from five or six feet down you are inclined to go with the spade as it will not easily part from it.

On arriving back to camp I hear there has been another inspection, but for my part it is nice to miss them as they mean too much standing around. Meals are still very much rice and tea and they are soon over. After an hour or two of discussing what each man's mother makes best in the food line I go to bed, with thoughts of home, and I don't need any rocking these nights.

Saturday March 28th

Remainder of the week spent working on the cemetery. We have 50 new graves, that's just in one week. They are mainly battle casualties, men still dying from wounds, we have very little in the way of drugs and medicines at the hospital. The main road runs alongside us and today I have planted a hedge of Hibiscus cuttings between it and us. Cuttings strike and grow very fast in this hot moist atmosphere.

Sunday March 29th

Sunday comes around again and I get a rest day. Before tea an Indian Army Sergeant friend takes a stroll with me through the camp area, which is full of Flame-of-the-Forest trees, so named because of large racemes of scarlet flowers which form bean-like seed pods. There are also clumps of Allemandes, evergreen shrubs with large yellow bell-like flowers. We arrive back as tea is served up, no tinned fruit or cake for us on Sunday.

After tea we go to church, like a lot of other fellows, to pass the time. The church, once a cold store building was transformed by our Brigade padres, with the help of volunteers, and is now called St Edmonds. After the sermon and a couple of hymns we return to barracks, to a collection of beds made up of beer bottle cases, strung together bamboos and a few Indian charpoys (string beds). Light is also here, a small tin of diesel with a piece of string, giving a little light and plenty of smoke, only previously used in the church. Odd bits of furniture have also been salvaged from some of the bombed houses around.

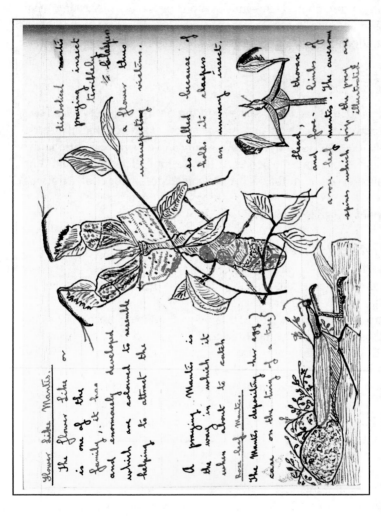

Flower Like Mantis.

The flower like is one of the family, it has enormously developed which are coloured to resemble helping to attract the ...

disturbed mantis praying insect falls ... to flatten a flower thus unsuspecting victims.

... so called because of shape it holds an unsuspecting insect.

A praying Mantis is the way in which it when bent to catch ...

Rose leaf Mantis.

The Mantis depositing her egg case on the twig of a bush.

Head, and fore-legs of mantis. The over... ... which grip the prey ...

Sketches from my diary of some of the local wildlife – Flower-like Mantis and Rose Leaf Mantis

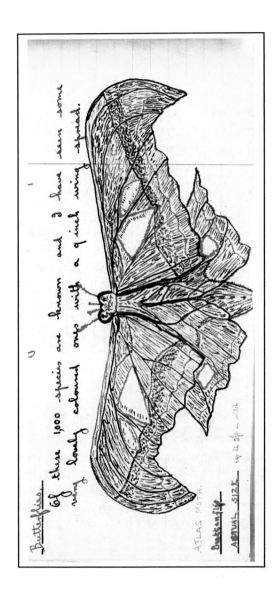

Sketch from diary of an Atlas Moth
One of the largest moths in the world with a wing span of up to 1ft

Monday March 30th

A new week begins and with it new hopes, feeble ones perhaps, but what is life without hope. The ground at the back of the area we are working is somewhat higher because of soil thrown up when a railway cutting was constructed. The line used to take materials and shells up to the huge 18-inch siege guns situated just behind us. The shells were over four feet high and some still lay around the wreckage of the guns blown up by their crews. I don't think that these giant guns ever fired in anger as they were on a 70° traverse which allowed for the cover of Singapore and the Naval dock area therefore not able to be used to fire across the Straits of Johore onto the mainland of Malaya, the backdoor the enemy used to attack through. The firepower of those guns was a tragic loss to us fighting up country. I decide to cut away the soil and form a sloping bank running parallel with the railway line. This is under way and we are now turfing it over. The turf we are allowed to cut from a "Padang", Malay for open space or playing field. This area is across the road from us and then over a narrow bridge crossing a large monsoon drain. The turf is carted on a small truck built onto a pair of Austin Seven car wheels by Royal Engineer friends. No burials today but am told I shall get some tomorrow.

Tuesday March 31st

I have two burials, which means that we have to start digging again. I like to keep four graves in readiness. It is hard work and you can see the sweat bubbling through the lace holes of your boots. The job is now becoming full time and we get a tea ration given so that we can brew up twice a day. This when brewed is little more than coloured hot water, but it means so much to us, who are constantly streaming with sweat. I find it very hard work to keep ahead of things as my squad of fifteen to twenty men are listed as sick and therefore not taken by the "Nips" on work parties. They are not up to my requirements; they are weak, or of "a don't care nature" and it's difficult to get them to work harder. After a few more days I ask to see my Commanding Officer to put my case. I tell him I cannot carry on with the sick men and ask if I can have eleven volunteers from my own Company, with which I could manage. He agrees and gives me the responsibility to pick my men, which I do that same evening. Of the eleven who elected to come with me, one, Pte Alexander, was a cemetery worker in his civilian days at Norwich, another, Bill Bailey, was a burly six foot two timber worker from Wisbech, while the third man for what I had chosen to be the mainstay of the new team was the cemetery Major's batman, a sturdy likable fellow called Ivor Self, a civilian barber from North Walsham.

Wednesday April 1st 1942

Today is the first working with the new team. Everything goes so much better, with much good-humoured banter. The tall fellow, besides being a gravedigger, is allotted the job to draw the daily tea ration and to do the brewing. He is the only one of us who can stand in a six foot hole and still be seen, he doesn't use so much effort in throwing out the earth and as one wag said, " 'Ole Bill could be in a better 'ole". After we have dug our reserve our attention is turned to preparing flower beds and planting shrubs. The grave spacing, up to the present time, has been set out by the Royal Engineers. Have had nine burials this week.

Thursday April 2nd

The Australian Forces have started their own cemetery a bit further along the road and have just buried their first two. They are in a separate compound in the camp and we don't see much of them.

Continue turfing of the bank and around a huge cachou tree that grows from it. This tree is at times useful for its yellow peppery tasting fruit, if you can get them before the red ants.

**Sections of the Australian cemetery,
which was seperate from the British and Dutch areas**

The nuts that grow on the end of the fruit are poisonous if not baked first.

Friday April 3rd

Today is Good Friday and we get a rest day after one burial. Heavy rains have started and I learn that it is the wet season and will rain every day from around 1600 until 1800hrs.

Saturday April 4th

No burials, still raining, a lazy day.

Sunday April 5th

No burials so have another day off. I go to church this morning dressed up in my one shirt, hose tops and gaiters that I have kept. It feels quite good only nowhere to enjoy a pint afterwards.

After dinner a few of us roam around the area, the day is lovely, fresh and clean air after yesterdays rain and a temperature around 80-90°F. After tea church again, twice in one day, is my new job turning me towards religion, or is it something to dress for?

Monday April 6th

It's Easter Monday but work today, we carry on turfing the bank while waiting for two funeral parties.

* * *

A few days pass with much the same work being carried out. Rumour has it that a party of Gurkha soldiers escaped and are loose in Singapore, this could be so as being brown they could mix with the natives. News has been coming in with the work parties that Sikh soldiers who went over to the enemy have been

111

found strangled with their own boot laces and others with their heads cut off and hung in their sentry boxes. This sounds very much like the Gurkhas taking revenge on traitors.

A daft story going around is that Lord Nuffield has bought Singapore and handed it over to Switzerland. Wishful thinking by those already clutching at straws. Also this week, a ration chart has been issued. For three days per man we are to get: 3oz meat, $^1/_6$ oz. salt, 4½ oz. rice flour, ¼ oz. ghee(fat) and 17oz rice. Split the above into nine meals and I will leave you to wonder how we work. The tea is also getting weaker.

Many of the afternoons have been interrupted by torrential downpours but in three days I have done 14 burials and with my men literally soaked to the skin (we wear only shorts and boots, socks have long been worn out).

Saturday April 11th

On the other side of the road are a few coconut palms and we find a nut on the ground so for a few of us our rice tonight will be laced with grated sweet nut for extra flavour. Well we need something to cheer us up as we drag our wet and weary bodies back to camp.

In the morning (Sunday) if no burials I have a day off, but have to attend a medical inspection for tinea, a skin irritation some fellows are now suffering with.

Sunday April 12th

It is being said that the Red Cross in the camp have been allowed to send the names of prisoners to their headquarters in Geneva. This we hope is true and that you at home will soon know who is alive and who is not (that sounds a horrible way to put it) but then we are becoming in most cases a hard-thinking lot. This last piece of news really gets me down to wondering what is exactly going on in the outside world, what do you know of us? I realise that I have been married eight months but what little my wife and I know of it. I have received no letters from her or my mother since I left England and my last to her was from Cape Town. I lay in the shade of the trees thinking around all this and hoping that she does not change in any way during my enforced absence.

My thoughts are suddenly scattered as the sky literally opens up sending me running for cover. It thunders like all the guns in existence going off, the lightning and wind is terrific and a coolness comes over me as the rain drums down. The worst storm I have yet experienced, however it soon passes and I go for my tea. Into the rice I mix my share of the coconut and make it a Sunday tea. Later I go to the church service and listen to the Padre telling us to keep our spirits up and to face the future with the help of God. We shall need someone's backing as our own officers yesterday informed us that we could be here for three years. What a thought, enough to make a man scratch where he don't itch and that spot would now take a bit of finding. Well it's bed time and we go to it with the latest rumour, a 150 mile blockade of Singapore by the allied navies, well time would hang heavy if we didn't have something different to talk about now and then.

Monday April 13th

Morning dawns with the news that I have eight burials to cope with, shall have to get cracking and dig more graves. It's a good job we don't suffer from weekend hangovers. We get to work and the earth and sweat soon start to fly as the holes are dug out. Mid-morning we stop for our cup of hot tea and this always makes ones body become a concourse of little rivulets as the sweat runs down your length to your boots, filling ones eyes and dripping off the end of our noses.

Somehow we cope with the burials and I find I am not completely hardened to this job yet as tears stream down my face as each body comes up for burial, the flag removed, the bearers take over, the Padre chants his piece, "Last Post" and "Reveille" being blown over each one. As they come from all Regiments and

Corps concentrated in the area, each bier is being attended by its own funeral party. The cemetery has claimed over 90 men, in two months. Well thankfully our life goes on, so we fill in and tidy around and plant a few more shrubs before we return to camp.

At tea we each get a small slice of bread, plain rice and a thin green stew. Many are the complaints about the stew but to me all is welcome. After tea as usual we talk. It seems that around 200 men are now being taken daily by trucks to work on the docks where unloading ships is part of the routine, many of these men manage to get some bits and pieces of food, soap etc., hidden on their person and return back to camp with them.

The rumours go on almost daily, the latest being, Japan and Russia at war. Troops leaving for the Russian front. This is supposed to have started on April 6th.

Tuesday April 14th

Our Corps Commander has brought us together and gives an impressive speech, telling us that we were pitch-forked into an already lost war. He also said the "Aussies" were only two days ahead of us in the action. Twenty ships were left at Panang in good enough condition for the enemy to use and that aerodromes up and down the country seemed to be built in the wrong places. If what he says is right no wonder the "Aussies" are not keen on us.

The latest rumour is that the allies have landed twenty-two Divisions of men at Brest. Germany beaten. Oh well, a rumour a day helps to keep the doctor at bay. Anyway I'm tired of all the talk and get to bed knowing that the coming day will bring false hopes and fallen spirits for some.

Wednesday April 15th

Two Captains among the burials today. So far the majority of men have died from gangrene. My Brigade, the 53rd, has now taken over the cemetery from the Royal Engineers, a move that puts me in complete charge of all work.

On the food front, the three day ration included 2½ oz sugar and ¼ oz of wheat grain. The cooks are experimenting with the rice; they are turning out rice pancakes and "efforts" (a variety of things, such as rice pastry with a vegetable insert). The wheat grain goes into the stew.

Thursday April 16th

Today's rumour is that Italy are still in the war and lands six Divisions in Libya, also the Japanese are in India. A work party returns from Singapore and one of them has a note which was concealed in a parcel of bread thrown to them by some Chinese. The note reads:-

"GOOD LUCK. DARKNESS BEFORE THE DAWN. ADIEU".

A cry goes up, "Come and get it", it's tea time, so grabbing mess tin and mug I hurry down the stairs to join the line of jostling humanity. A teaspoonful per man of tinned milk is being issued in your tea or rice as you prefer, I have mine in my rice. It has now got to the point that you eat where you stand so that you are in line for "seconds", if any.

Friday April 17th

Day comes in again with the sad news that Padre Dean of my Battalion, the 5th Royal Norfolks, is dangerously ill with dysentery. We have no burials so we carry on grave digging, clearing scrub and turfing etc., after which we have just enough energy left to make it back to camp. Who said, "Only mad dogs and Englishmen work out in the mid-day sun"? How right he was. On reaching camp we get a nice surprise on seeing that some electric light standards have been erected by the RE's. Perhaps we shall soon "See the light". With the usual routine over it's bed.

115

Saturday April 18th

On arising we learn that our Padre is dead. He will be greatly missed as he was a nice chap. He is to be buried this afternoon. At the moment it is pouring with rain, so heavy that we stay in the barracks. After lunch it is fine and a large parade to follow the Padre's bier is formed up. As I carry the Japanese pass flag I have to march at the head of it, resplendent in my shirt, hose tops and gaiters (full dress). The Padres request is to be buried the opposite way round, why? Some say he has renounced his religion, I wonder if it is to face his flock as in church. We are too busy to think more about it as I see four more flag covered bodies coming in the entrance, so with all hands to the spades we fill in and get the handling ropes ready for the next. I have not mentioned that there are no coffins supplied, but bodies are wrapped in blankets or sheets emphasizing the shapes within. Alexander throws in a handful of soil each time the Padre with the party comes to "Dust to Dust".

Sunday April 19th

Another Sunday comes around and with some hard work as we cope with another five burials, besides digging up some flowering shrubs from a nearby house and replanting them in the cemetery. Later I clean up, wash and shave, then off to church. After the service I stay behind to hear a talk on Confirmation classes. I am thinking that I may be interested.

Monday April 20th

Back to the cemetery, planting hedging, banking up graves and turfing over. I have managed to get a new pair of boots, which are issued only to me and some of my staff because of the grave digging. They are a size nine, I normally wear a seven, but they are better than none at all.

Monday April 27th

Most of the past week has been very much the same routine; burials thankfully have dropped to two a day. The "Nips" now patrol the perimeter wire to stop men buying food from the natives by exchanging watches, rings or anything else of value.

A university course of sixteen weeks is starting and I have just been accepted for it. It covers all stages of agriculture and stockbreeding, also I shall be attending classes to learn something of the Malay language. It all helps to pass away the evenings now that we have some electric light.

The bad news of the day is our rice ration has been cut by half, sugar to 3oz for four days and flour 3½ oz per day. I can already see the flesh dropping off the men; their bones begin to show.

Two men from the compound were caught trying to escape. They were court marshalled by the "Nips" and were flogged. This has caused enforced restriction on the whole camp.

Three of us have had a secret boil up of Tapioca and Sweet Potato tops given to us by an outside worker. This is the first real green food eaten by me in four months. I have also come by a little Red Palm oil and can fry up my dinner rice.

Tuesday April 28th

My Battalion is sent back to Singapore town to work, so I now draw my cemetery party ration for dinner and take it with us to work. Tomorrow is the Emperor of Japan's birthday and we are told to clean up the whole prison camp out of respect for him. I will leave you to guess what a lot of the men said about him.

Rice ration reduced to only 12oz per day, resulting in me feeling weak from hunger.

Wednesday April 29th

The birthday has arrived and with it a few slices of pineapple per man, a gift from the Emperor we are told. A little sugar is also dished out. The rice ration I hear has doubled again, but so far we are not getting it issued, the reason unknown to us. The celebration also gives everyone a day off, but myself and party go to work for the morning and laze around in the afternoon.

In the evening hunger and lack of variety in our food brings the main nightly topic of discussion to, "What mother makes", and you would never believe what mothers do make when you listen to men from practically every county in the UK. Tired and with mouths watering from the things that we imagine, we turn in for the night.

Thursday April 30th

Not long in bed, just after midnight I should say, there is one hell of a commotion. A chap shouting and cursing, a flashing of a torch (something he is lucky to have at this stage). He has awakened the whole floor, the reason being that he was bitten by something. He said it was small and it had an awful smell. We cannot switch on the lights as they are cut off at 2200hrs, so with the help of his torch we search his bedding and to our amazement find some little blood red flat bodies, half the size of a ladybird, hurriedly seeking refuge in dark corners. On being touched they emitted a foul smell, on biting you they sucked your blood, this we are told was the habit of bed bugs - our new acquaintances, the little vampires.

Well after a disturbed night I arise to a great cartwheel of a red sun as it quickly rises above the trees to bring its fresh early morning warmth, and for one hour the joy of living before it starts to burn you up for the rest of the day. Cemetery work is stepping up again as the burials increase, four yesterday and four again today. The officers have started eating snails for vitamin B content, which staves off beriberi, a disease which can make you swell like a balloon until your skin shines as though it has been polished. The snails in this country are huge, comparable in size to the English whelk.

The latest rumour is that the Allied Forces have retaken Java and Sumatra (Islands not far from us) and that the "Nips" are preparing to blow up the causeway again.

Had no rain this week, it's very hot and our newly laid turf is looking very sick. Tidying up after two burials we make for camp, a wash down before tea. Rice and fresh meat stew says the jungle telephone, this was right, but not so fresh meat as I find a couple of blown-up maggots in mine, and the rice, well it's limed rice, i.e. rice dressed for seed, but when cooked tastes like rotten eggs. As hungry as I get that takes some eating.

Sunday May 3rd 1942

It has rained in the night, enough I hope to save the turf we have laid during the last few days. The ground being moist we take the opportunity to plant sprigs of grass a few inches apart on a large open strip. Some of the grass here runs and roots at every joint soon forming a turf. Planted further shrubs and tulip trees.

A convoy of lorries loaded with rice, 125 in all and must be carrying close on 500 tons, maybe the ration will go up.

Had three for burial today and being Sunday I go to church in the evening.

Monday May 4th

The rest of my Brigade, the 53rd, are marching off to Singapore town, my Battalion which is already there is likely to remain. I am told that I must stay to carry on with the cemetery work. I have just completed the fifth burial today. The weather is very hot, in fact it is the hottest day that I have experienced as yet.

We have been getting a small milk ration, but this has ceased, I expect supplies on the island have run out. In the evening feeling a bit fed up I set on my bed space brooding. I wonder if the Red Cross ships will ever come, I'm hungry. In this state of mind I take my thought home to England and realise that it is three years ago today that I first met the girl that I married. I go over those carefree years, wondering if they will ever happen again. I think of home, my father, mother, brothers and sisters, wondering what they are all up to now. I feel rather despondent, perhaps it's because the men that I was close to daily have all left for Singapore; saying my goodnights to what's left of us I go to bed thinking it's the best way out.

Wednesday May 6th

Morning arrives and I face up to things a bit better, get down to work and forget. Numbers of burials on the way up again which doesn't help one's thinking. Commenced lectures on agriculture. First lecture given by Capt Keith who farms extensively at Swanton Morley, near Dereham, Norfolk. At night I attend a lecture on Theology. Well it all broadens the mind and makes time pass more quickly.

* * *

The next few days go along much the same pattern, managed to get some more Sweet Potato tops and have a boil up, very insipid without salt but helps to fill one up. Attended first Confirmation class and it helps to drift my thoughts homeward again to the wife, wondering if she is all right. On getting back to my quarters I learn that 8,000 men are needed to go somewhere overseas, 2,000 from my camp section are warned to stand by. My job again keeps me from being moved, but I feel I would like to go as I now have a roving inclination.

So far this week burials have decreased slightly, only had nine. This has enabled us to clear quite an area of scrub and to set out sections bounded by paths.

I go to another Confirmation class and on returning to my place of abode find myself soon in a great debate on where the men due to move might be going, Formosa or Japan. Not having solved anything I turn in under my half blanket, this mainly to keep the "mozzies" off.

8. ***On this day…*** May 7, 1942… Battle of the Coral Sea begins – 11 Japanese warships sunk by the US off the Solomon Isles.

Sunday May 10ᵗʰ

Not having slept too well I am up a bit before the sun, 0600hrs, get a wash and shave in the half light and now hang around waiting for breakfast. When it comes it brings the news that the 2,000 men from my compound are not now going overseas, but to Singapore to construct a war memorial dedicated to the Nipponese and all other nationalities that fell during the Malay-Singapore campaign. The "Nips" have ordered that the Australians go overseas to Japan, which apparently was the original demand but the "Aussies" kicked against it saying that some of the British should go, however the "Nips" said No.

The weather is very hot with only a rain shower during the last ten days. Tea tonight is a bit better with a Chinese chicken egg (small) and sweet potato to mix with the rice. Later a few of us had a boiling of rice sweepings brought in by members of a work party. Went to church this evening, service taken by Divisional Padre. Men not going to Singapore now, you see how we get mucked around by the "Nips" decisions and indecisions, until you don't know where you stand.

Monday May 11ᵗʰ

A new day brings a burial in from Singapore, one of our men killed when a lorry turned over. The "Nips" brought him back complete with two huge wreaths of orchids hung on standing easels. An officer on the lorry received a broken arm and I was told he had to plead with the "Nips" not to shoot the native driver.

Night comes but with it very little sleep as we are plagued with bed bugs all through it. My mate moves out of the building preferring to try and sleep on an old table. He says he will put up with the mosquitoes in preference to the bugs.

Tuesday May 12th

When daylight comes I find nine large bugs in the folds of my pillow, an old bag filled with grass. On the concrete is a small red patch of my blood, which I have just stamped out of those little red horrors. I believe now the word "bugger" means a soldier who hunts bugs. Other men are now debugging their bits and pieces of bedding with good results. At the moment I am wondering how any of you at home would like my bed partners complete with eggs laid at night. I have to smile at the thought, as I wander down for my rice ration and raw tea.

It's around 0800hrs as we set off for the cemetery and the sweat is already trickling down our bodies, which are now burnt to a dark brown. There are a few among us who still wear shirts because of very fair skin, which if uncovered, get very severe blistering burns. Phew! it seems all set for an extra hot day as I unlock our small tool shed and produce the implements we need for the day's work, very worn spades for digging graves. They will have to get hard at it as there are six coming down for burial today. I have been grave digging all morning, it's so hot in the holes that once again I watch in a dazed sort of way the sweat bubbling through the boot lace holes. The man in charge of our rice ration calls us to come and get it, so with some effort I climb out onto the surface and make for the hut, where we sit around and eat the issue and drink the hot tea. We already feel very tired as we stir ourselves for what's in hand for the afternoon session. The perspiration has already dried to a white salt on our bodies while we have rested in the shade and you can just rub it off. I don't think we get enough salt rations to replace what we sweat out. Leaving off time at last arrives, it's been too hot for digging today and some of us can hardly drag ourselves back to camp, no talk or joking, we are a dead beat bunch who just fall onto our beds and wait for tea.

I learn that disabled men have been on an inspection as there is talk of them getting off the island shortly. There are rumours of good news, but no one knows what. One hundred men leave for Singapore. One of my men has got some green food called "Kang Kong" which we boil up on the QT after dark.

Wednesday May 13th

More classes to attend including one on turkey rearing, but apart from these I use my spare time boiling up "paw paw", a part marrow, part melon-type of fruit which grows on a small palm like tree. I have a bit of ginger root, which also grows around, and I mix this in, in an unsuccessful attempt to make jam. I'm afraid the sugar is lacking, anyhow what I have got will mix with the rice rations.

More men have left camp today for Singapore, it begins to make my area of Changi look a bit thin. The majority left are mostly sick men.

The camp areas, after the heavy rains a few weeks back, have become almost park like with the large spread of green grassland dotted with groups of scarlet flowering trees and the yellow and pink of various shrubs. These are frequented by flocks of birds such as Silverbills, Kingfishers, Mynors, Yellow Weavers and Collared Doves.

Friday May 15th

As I write it is 7am with you at home and I am having my tea, eating with a spoon in one hand and a fly swat in the other, which is constantly waving to keep the swarms of flies from settling on my rice. While I eat I wonder if I shall hear something from you soon. Well I can always go to bed and dream, which I am about to do. Sleeping would be better if we had mosquito nets, they would keep those buzzing night attackers from drawing blood, what with them above and the bugs from beneath, most men have a bloody awful time. Fortunately the bugs don't bite me, what's wrong with my blood! I know they are with me as I can smell them as the roam over me.

Saturday May 16th

Morning comes with its usual freshness, so nice after the problems of the night. I have what is to me a sad burial, Corporal Blunt, a friend of mine has died from blood poisoning after a slight accident in Singapore, his death was so sudden. I made a wreath and on a piece of card I wrote the second verse of "The River", one of the poems in a book that I still have, written by the wife and given to me before I left England.

The River

Onward ever flow
Thou gentle river
For your course I know not whither
On you go hill and valley
Never stops to dilly dally.

So it is in life's sad journey
Never Know what lays before me
Rocky paths, and steep hill climbing
Till at last I hear sweet chiming
Of those Heavenly bells, all pealing
Then shall I from Earth be leaving
All the sorrow, and the pain
Nevermore to see again.

Sunday May 17th

With only about 400 of my Brigade left here now we are feeding from the 6th Norfolk's cookhouse. Food is not too good and as it's Sunday I go to church and with the rest pray for bacon and eggs. It's something we have a laugh about and that helps to keep us going for a bit as back by my bed I find myself thinking of home once again, wondering if you know yet that I am a Prisoner of War, thinking how little I have seen my wife, less than three weeks during our nine months of marriage. "Spela Meloria", its a quotation I have read meaning "I hope for better things to come".

Monday May 18th

A Japanese General has passed through the camp, I hope he caught sight of our ribs sticking through our skin. It's a slightly better diet owing to vegetables now coming in from the garden worked by the sick men. These men do not get a rice ration allowed from the "Nips" as they do not feed the sick, therefore the more sick the less rice we get as it is only humane that we share our rations.

We have been told that the "Nips" require 180 men in a few days to go overseas, as there are only 210 fit men in my section it looks as though I may be leaving the cemetery. With this on my mind and wondering where we might be going, I make tracks for the University hut where I listen to a lecture on Dairy Farming and make notes of it. On walking back to the barrack block I realise it is now May and think how nice it would be to have a rhubarb or gooseberry pie, how one misses these things, we very rarely see any fruit. Within minutes of thinking this one of the men gives me a guava pear, somewhat like a lemon to look at.

Tuesday May 19th

It rained hard today but not on us for it stopped just a half mile away, leaving a straight line across the road between wet and dry. It's three weeks since any fell on the cemetery and the digging is very hard. Burials are between two and four a day now. During the clearing of jungle we have uncovered a large mound about fifteen feet high, which comes right in the way of our cemetery road which we construct as the place expands. What a problem, we shall never move it with the tools that we have, seven small spades and two Malayan hoes (changols). I decide to shape up the foot and go around it, and later if we have time or men to make a feature of it. Have to forget it now as three more arrive for burial, most of the deaths now are from dysentery. Another very hard day in the fierce heat, but maybe we are getting weaker, which would make it seem so. Well it's back to camp and a half hours rest to recover enough strength to have a wash. We are still drawing our rations from the 6th Norfolk's cookhouse, it seems to be less and not so good, so I guess we are sharing with more sick. Well, we are lucky not to be sick, just hungry.

Saturday May 23rd

Three days have gone by and no one for "Boot Hill", so we concentrate on flattening the top of our little hill, moving hundreds of tons of soil over the edge, which I shall later use to form a terrace around the front.

The other day I came across some cucumber seeds, which I planted and in just 48 hours they have germinated, pushing their leaves through the soil. A shower yesterday no doubt done much for them.

News has just come that the shipment of men is off and only twenty needed for Singapore, reprieved again.

Sunday May 24th

On arising this morning I make an entry into the diary noting that it is Whit Sunday. I am remembering a similar Sunday two years ago, I was wiring Weybourne Camp, only two miles from my home. Wish I was there now. At least now we have a bit of music, some Scots are playing "Sing as ye go" on bagpipes in the next compound.

Monday May 25th

Well it's Bank Holiday and what a way to spend it. I am hoping to be home for the wife's 21st birthday next year, I told her I would be, but for once I think my look into the future could be wrong. I seem to be dwelling a lot on home this last week or two, must be the combination of hunger and hard work getting me depressed. We have now been prisoners 100 days and so far I have managed to keep free from tropical ills.

Had one burial today a Gordon Highlander, two men with the pipes preceded it playing "Flowers of the Forest".

Some men foolishly attacked a lorry carrying food and cigarettes destined for the "Nips", they were not from our area but were caught outside their own, I just wouldn't like to be in their shoes. It's been a day of rain and this evening the mosquitoes are a damned nuisance, seem to be coming in clouds.

More men standing by for overseas in a few days and sick men coming in from Singapore.

Earlier today I found another coconut that had fallen from one of the palms close to the cemetery. Not very exciting perhaps but it means a lot to three of us, extra food and flavours the rice, which is not being cooked too well at the moment as it does not swell to the amount it should and soon leaves us hungry.

Saturday May 30th

My Regimental Sergeant Major has gone with replacements to Singapore, he has told me that I can take over his little chalet, so my chum Jack Beales and I move in without delay. It has a fireplace and an oven, what luxury, but then if we only had something to cook. Shall have to move my cucumber plants down to my new abode, they are already in flower. Having fixed up our bits and pieces we look around sizing up our new home. We go up to the main block at night for a natter and after discussing our food likes, no dislikes now as we are ready to eat anything, it's time for bed. Jack and I walk back to our detached home, even doing this is a welcome change. At the moment the death rate has dropped.

Sunday May 31st

No letters from England have reached us as yet, although fourteen months have passed since the capitulation of Singapore, and I don't think there is much hope of the "Nips" letting us write letters. Today I have found a Gardenia bush from which I take some cuttings and a bloom. I always wanted someday to wear a white gardenia so tonight I go to church wafted in the divine scent from my buttonhole. The Padre was so taken with it as it reminded him of his wedding.

Monday June 1st 1942

Today I took him some blooms. We have just survived our most severe storm to date, the rain is so heavy one can only see a few yards ahead, the coconut palms are bent horizontal and anything loose is blown away. When it abates we shall stroll around the camp and look at the damage it has done.

Tuesday June 2nd

The morning dawns quiet after the storm and are told it was a typhoon, which took most things in its path. It seems at the moment with the few drugs at our disposal, brought in by us and used sparingly by the doctors, that dysentery and beri-beri are under control but a new-comer is dengue fever, caused by the bite of another type of mosquito. It's nasty, but only lasts around five days.

After a very hot day working on the cemetery we drag back to camp and on drawing our tea we are informed that the "Nips" have advanced us 80 cents a month, but each man has to sign for it before it can be drawn by our officers. The officer telling us this says that our Command has decided to keep the money and use it at their discretion. He says some will be spent on footballs; this raises a yell from some, "Are you mad? Football in this heat and us starving for food", and so the shouting goes on as he takes his leave, but what he has said is well discussed into the night.

Wednesday June 3rd

At breakfast the night's comments continue to be bantered around, "Any footballs in the rice", asks one. We are called to parade on the gun park and are told that our Command has decided that we are still on active service. It starts with a drill session. Field punishment is being brought back, a structure is to be used as a glasshouse, the irony of it, a jail within a jail. "Have our officers gone mad?" ask the men. Have they? It may be good for discipline but to hungry men it is regarded as an extra torture.

9. **On this day...** June 3, 1942... Battle of Midway, US Naval victory turns the tide of war in the Pacific.

Thursday June 4th

A Sergeants' mess has been sanctioned but we are only twelve in number and very rarely together. My chum Jack is still with me and gets very irritating as during the night he gets out of bed to hunt for something that is disturbing his sleep, finally after much swearing he discovers a large cricket that has somehow got into his mosquito net. To some extent he is lucky to be able to lie and listen to the buzzing of the "mozzies", as for myself I have no net.

Friday June 5th

Today Jack has been informed that he is on the list for up country or overseas and this has not made him any easier to live with. There is a strong rumour that 8,000 men are to leave Changi. I wonder whether I shall be going. Don't know if I want to or not as I have become interested in the cemetery where the gardening side is taking effect. Never thought that I should undertake such a large job as this, it will remain a tribute to my men and myself.

Saturday June 6th

The Sergeants' mess is going well. Cooking for us is done by an ex-London hotel chef, he draws our rations from the stores and the food is a better success due to his ability, pity he has no European food to deal with. Tea was good and as one man said it is something of a novelty to have to pick one's teeth to remove particles of meat. We had one ounce per man. Our morning porridge consists of a mixture of ground rice and pig meal, not much our chef can do with that. There is some concern among the medical staff due to the increase in numbers and size of distended stomachs, "rice-bellies", to us caused by lack of vitamins and too much rice. It is said it will take three months dieting to remove them after the war. A very large number of the men look eight months pregnant.

Sunday June 7th

A French Padre, attached to the British Forces, preached in the church tonight, afraid my mind wandered a bit, thinking of home and that the time is 9.30am with you and 6pm with me. I am getting "down under" and get to thinking that the carrots dad has set will soon be pushing their roots through to me. I come to with a start as the last hymn has begun. I cannot help thinking that my mind is going with such daft thoughts.

Monday June 8th

In the morning I don't feel so good, too much sun I expect, but I managed to struggle through the day with a terrible all-over feeling. I get to bed early only to be called out to parade at 11.30pm for a Nipponese roll call. A man has been seen outside the perimeter wire and they are checking all camps, however, we are complete. I totter back to my bed with a terrible headache, the mother and father of them all, its bursting, my body has all the symptoms of a very bad attack of the flu. I hope I have not got malaria, I cannot sleep, I wish that dawn will soon come.

Tuesday June 9th

When dawn does break I find it very difficult to stand up, no breakfast for me, as hungry as I am, I just cannot face anything other than a cup of tea. I report sick and the Doctor sends me off to hospital with dengue fever, "breakbone fever" the natives call it. A very true description as it feels as if ones bones are being broken in a vice. I really feel damned queer now.

On arriving at the hospital I am put in the only bed available, No 13, I hope it remains my lucky number. This number under prevailing conditions would have scared a lot of people virtually to death, but my birthday is on the thirteenth and I also lived at home in a house of the same number, therefore I have hopes. I am put on a fluid diet consisting of half pint of meat extract followed later by half pint of vegetable stew, a little sweetened tea and a small piece of cheese. This food comes from reserves held by us and go mainly to the hospital to be used for the very sick, however, the special diet only lasted one day for me. I was soon back on rice, par-boiled rice, I hated it, so it was a case of starving. Par-boiled rice is as the name suggests partly cooked then dried by the Tamil Indians that live in this part of the world. The smell from the rice attracts flies by the million and you can observe them following the cookhouse orderlies as they carry the dixies of the stuff to the dishing out tables. Other than the special diet food here is not as good as in our camp. There are more flies here than in our barrack area, they really craze you. The night for me is a terrible one. It seems the longest in my life, daylight seems as it will never come.

Thursday June 11th

When the Malay orderly came to take my temperature at 6am he decided to fetch me some physic, it made me sweat and sleep for a while. The doctor came later to see me, he said I was to go back on the special diet. It's a very wearisome day but I sleep right through the night.

Friday June 12th

On waking up I feel much better. My stomach is dropping out from sheer hunger so I ask to go back on solid food, only to find I cannot face the par-boiled rice yet, so have to starve a bit more.

Saturday June 13th

I shall be glad to get out of hospital now that I feel better. They tell me the "Nips" are going to pay the men 3 dollars a month direct and NCO's $4.50c.

* * *

As the days go by fellow workers from the cemetery visit me, one brings a few spoonfuls of sugar, which is more than welcome, more so because it meant that he deprived himself of it and that is something these days. The Padre and Welfare Officer also came to wish me well. Others that call later tell me that one of my platoon Lance-Corporals died and was buried today.

There are many barrack blocks in this area, they form what is perhaps the largest hospital in the world now, holding about 3,000 patients, each being cared for in the best way possible with hardly any drugs or medicines available. Talk of a large movement of men going up to Burma to help build a railway. Was allowed out this evening to go to a concert in the area, it was put on by some Australians for the patients.

The doctor will not let me out of hospital, as my temperature will not settle down. One man on this fever ward has just been moved to the dysentery section. Poor devil, one doesn't need complications, fighting one disease is enough. The men I have made friends with are mainly Scottish and some of them are being discharged today.

It's very warm, the rain pelts down causing dirty yellow water a foot deep to gush past the steps to this building. What a desolate outlook nothing but water and drooping fronds of coconut palms, but then it changes so quickly to one of bright blue skies and jewelled radiance of dripping water from green refreshed trees. As I watch I think of nature at work with a huge paintbrush. My dreams are interrupted as the ambulance stops at the steps, a stretcher bearing the unconscious body of a young fellow in his early twenties. It is said that he is suffering from some brain trouble, the poor fellow died a short time later without ever recovering consciousness. Another patient has developed diphtheria as a secondary complication and is at this moment being removed to the isolation block, the chances of him surviving are very remote.

With the few dollars now paid to me I make my way to the canteen that has just been set up. I get a pineapple for 10c and two tins of tomato soup for 45c each. These will give the rice a little more flavour for a few days. Wish I could get some more but the quantity and money is limited.

We are very surprised and excited to learn that we are to be allowed to write home, just a small number of words on a card provided by the "Nips". I addressed it to my wife telling her that I was well and cheerful, if that is what one is in hospital. I feel some satisfaction as I hand in my written card and at the same time doubts creeping in, will it ever get home, perhaps one day I shall know.

Sunday June 21*st*

Today I thought I was due to leave the hospital but the doctor says a few more days. It's rather boring also weakening having to stay in bed when you think you are fit enough to leave. Well, I shall have to put up with it, so I lie and dream of Scotland, remembering the winter and early spring when I was up there. I think how nice it would be if we could be back as we had had some good times there. My thoughts are broken as some of the lads call to see me, wondering when I am coming out or waiting to be wheeled onto "Boot Hill". I replied by saying that their spades will be worn out by the time I get there. We are joined by the welfare officer, Major Bregiel, who brings me a new pass, which I shall have to use on resuming work.

Monday June 22*nd*

The morning comes in desolate, teeming with rain, but it will clear in about two hours. The doctor has just made his rounds and tells me I am discharged as from 2.30pm. I have been in this hospital in No 13 bed for thirteen days. After impatiently marching up and down the ward the time of my departure has arrived, a few quick goodbyes and handshakes and I am on my way back to my unit. On arriving I find my friend Jack on his bed resting because of swollen ankles and knees, all tell tale signs of the lack of vitamins. He is hoping that they will be better by Wednesday as he leaves with three other Sergeants and a party of men for some camp in North Malaya or the Burma railway.

Tuesday June 23*rd*

Another rainy morning breaks and after breakfast, having four days excused duties I watch Jack and his new travelling companions out on the veranda grinding rice to flour with two bottles for rolling pins. They have been paid their few dollars before the move so have bought rice from the canteen to supplement travelling rations.

Darkness has once again blanketed out our daily troubles and I take myself off to a concert of classical music. Our entertainments side seems to be finding a few instruments. The music this evening is being played by Dennis East, a professional with a London orchestra. He plays violin and piano and to me he is a genius.

Later, returning to my quarters I find Jack and his three new companions have laid on a farewell supper of bits and pieces, some bought, others scrounged. I am invited to take part in this last supper before they are whisked away into the great unknown. We had just got to the coffee, made from burnt rice, when a lot of shouting informed us that the "Nips" had ordered lights out at 9.30pm and so the meal ends in darkness.

Wednesday June 24th

Morning comes with a touch of sadness for it means the end of a friendship built over the last three years and except for a temporary break during the fighting we have been together all the time. To me this war is like a tragic play, it has now reached its fifth act by my standards. Most of my Battalion have left camp for various destinations, many friends have gone, leaving only a handful of the original unit. Naturally I feel a bit despondent being left behind. Even our cook has been taken with the up-country party, our rations must have gone as well, for today only plain rice has been dished out. This being the first day of the new ration period, usually, extra items are on the menu, anyhow not much appetite at present as the difference between hospital and camp food has upset my stomach. After a stroll around the now much thinned area, stopping for a chat here and there, I return to my quarters, feeling lonely. For awhile I sit and stare at the empty bed of my friend, wondering what can be in store for him and would we ever meet again, with these morbid thoughts I turn in.

Thursday June 25*th*

I awake in the early hours with more stomach pains, these I have to live with until breakfast then I just take the drink of tea which help to ease the gripes.

A little later in the morning I walk down to the cemetery to see how things have gone during my absence. My staff, because of the recent move of men, has been cut from fifteen to seven, but I have been promised parties of "walking sick" to do the clearing of scrub. The grave total has now reached 214 in just four months, other work I find has progressed well. After some light hearted banter from my men I make my way back to camp arriving there tired but feeling the walk had done me good as I had regained something of an appetite.

In the evening I attend my final Communion course and with it over I get back to my bed in the dark as the "Nips" have just imposed an 8.30pm black out, so it's going to be a long night with memories.

Saturday June 27*th*

With the return of daylight and the new hope it always brings, I get through the usual wash and scrape. My few razor blades, even after all the care, such as trying to sharpen them in a "Marmite" jar of water, are now very blunt. After this sore-faced effort and a pan of rice inside me, I make for the cemetery; the walking strengthens my legs which after the dengue fever were jelly bags. The day is lazed away until tea-time, when wonders never cease. I was, as one of the special sick, given a fried egg. No-one seemed to know how they were come by but who cares, it is the first egg since I left Cape Town in December, over six months ago.

The doctor has still not taken me off the sick list so I laze around the cemetery. Today all men except my squad are confined inside the wire perimeter as some high ranking "Nip" officers are passing through the area. Later after the all clear is given I go with an officer to look at some shrubs and plants that I might like to acquire for planting on the cemetery. A Roman Catholic priest says we should be proud of our work. He was very taken with the orderly lay out of the burial mounds and garden effect given to it.

Sunday June 28ᵗʰ

It being Sunday I am on my way to church, the volunteers who have worked on the building have made a fine job of it, the seating and the cross have been salvaged from a bombed church.

Monday June 29ᵗʰ

Monday has started off badly with a tree falling on one of the timber clearing party, fortunately he was not seriously hurt, we also hear that cholera has broken out in Singapore town. All possible precautions being taken here in Changi, as it is the last trouble we need, for it sweeps through taking a dreadful toll. I had to report sick but at last I am taken off the list and can get back to work. The day is marvellous, a bright blue sky, no wind and at the moment not too hot. My first job is the burial of a gunner of the Royal Artillery, killed in a landslide in Singapore.

It's time for a cup of tea and while we drink three large Japanese flying boats pass overhead. They have been around for a few days now. The latest rumour has just come in, it says that beer has gone up by 2d a pint (awful).

A party of "Nips" are coming onto the cemetery; they make their way towards us, where we are tidying up around our newly filled grave. A high-ranking "Nip" officer asks about the grave in English. Two men step forward with a huge wreath of orchids and pink gladioli, they all salute turn about and march off, having paid their respects to the man killed. After all the reports of cruelty coming in from the Malay and Thailand camps we wonder why they bothered but somewhere deep inside there must be some decency.

Wednesday July 1st 1942

The sound of aircraft passing over before dawn gets us talking and later in the day, gunfire, and at dusk planes fly over causing much discussion and a little hope, but this is soon shattered as we are told that it is practice. Perhaps it is, perhaps not, they have to keep us quiet somehow. At least it gives us something to talk about in the cool of darkness, the day has been stinking hot, too much heat for a white man to work around in, more so when he is in a starved condition. A ten-day black out exercise has finished so we can now have a bit more light at night, although my quarters have no power on. My light is still a tin of oil and a smoking string wick, which pours out black smoke and fumes while I write or read but at least it keeps the mosquitoes at bay. As I try and read in this atmosphere I hear the strains of music coming from the men's block. I recognise the tune as a Christmas carol and wonder what is producing a carol in July. I walk over to the building just as another carol is being sung. I find a small gathering huddled around a gramophone. Where did it come from I ask and am told that a work party clearing up in town found it with a few records of Xmas carols in a bombed house and were allowed to keep it. While listening to the tunes I wonder whether we will be free men and home by Christmas, with this in mind and a yawn I realise it is time for bed and so with "While Shepherds Watched" ringing out I take my leave.

Saturday July 4th

The weather is still very dry and I need some rain badly to save the turf recently laid on some graves. We have just been told that we, the 2nd Division, were the British army best when we left England and that Commanders fought over it until it was handed over to Major General Beckworth-Smith. A soldier greatly praised for previous work in France before and during Dunkirk. What a pity such a Division was thrown in at the deep end with no tactical support. Other news is that the Bishop of Singapore is to be allowed to come to Changi for the forthcoming Confirmation ceremony.

Monday July 6th

It's back to work for me as we have a burial of a Gordon Highlander, quite an impressive affair as it approached the cemetery led by a kilted piper and funeral party, to the strains of bagpipe laments. Having completed our mournful task we retire, profusely sweating for a cup of tea. It's so very hot, it is the season of the Southwest monsoons, blowing hot winds known as the Java winds, the natives call them the "Devil winds" because they bring minor fevers and dengue. To date I have buried 217 men.

Wednesday July 8th

Not much of importance today, so a bit about the island of Singapore. Most of its present European quarters in 1905 were sea covered swamp. The engineers pushed seaward and constructed sea walls. Everywhere on the island small and large hills were levelled into the swamps, no machines, they were moved by thousands of Chinese with little baskets working like armies of ants. Now in 1942 people live 14,000 to the acre and it is said that they could not all get onto the streets at one time. It is said that Sir Stamford Raffles founded two zoos, one in Regents Park for animals and the other in Singapore for humanity.

Thursday July 9th

Another hot day starts with the usual rice pap for breakfast, this you drink so the meal is soon over and we are on our way to work. The roar of aircraft attracts my eyes skywards, I count 45 bombers and 13 fighters as they pass overhead, also there is a lot of practice gunfire. The jungle telephone tells us that another 500 men are needed for Formosa or Japan, 40 to come from my unit, including two Sergeants, I shall keep my fingers crossed as there are not many of us left here.

Friday July 10th

Tomorrow is the birthday of our Divisional Commander, Major General Beckworth-Smith. Camp officers are putting on some sort of celebrations and even the "Nips" have sent him whisky and cakes. What a war! Anyhow we must be thankful as yet our captors have been reasonably good to us although we constantly hear of atrocities up country. My day has been spent straightening up the grave crosses, which are made for the cemetery by the Royal Engineers and bear the number and name of the person buried. The trouble is that in this climate the wood soon rots at ground level, or in lots of cases eaten by termites. These creatures abound in the scrub, building very large cones of earth, up to four feet high. They chew the earth, which becomes mixed with the insects' internal juices and then sets very hard. Unfortunately when they are in the way of the cemeteries progress, we have to use a sledgehammer and hard chisel to demolish them. If the termites bit you they left a small painful cut.

Saturday July 11th

This morning I am awakened by the strains of the bagpipes, it turns out to be the Scots in the area come to acknowledge the General's birthday with, "Many Happy Returns to England Sir", and a few reels. A concert was arranged in his favour, he is 56, "Good Luck to him", I think to myself as I turn in for just one more very lonely night.

Copy of camp orders (6):

Major Gen Beckworth-Smith's Birthday message to troops 11/7/42

I have been deeply touched by the many messages and gifts I have received from all ranks and units of the division on this my birthday. From the bottom of my heart I thank you all, not only for these but also the wonderful loyalty and support which you have given me during the two years in which I have had the honour to command the 18th Division. I trust it to be my good fortune to lead you to victory and peace at home before another year is passed.

M. Beckworth-Smith   Major General 18th Division

Sunday July 12th

An hour was taken up this very hot day by a parade and march past as a tribute to the General, who took the salute, I wonder what the "Nips" think, anyhow that is the way of the British, always taking liberties. For much of the rest of the day I have been hunting around the gardens of some deserted houses for shrubs, which, hopefully I can transplant to beautify the cemetery.

Monday July 13th

Phew! We badly need rain if only to keep down the dust and kill some of the glare reflected from roads and buildings by the torrid sun. I never seem to be able to keep my eyelids apart because of it, that I suppose is why the Chinese are called "Chinks". Another impressive funeral by the Gordon Highlanders and a message of thanks from the General for gifts and tributes received by him on his birthday. The message reads that he hoped to lead us to victory and peace before another year is up. We hope so too.

Tuesday July 14th

I have today discovered a fruit known as the durian, it has a very hard skin which protects it when it falls from the great height of the tree. The inside of the fruit has a very horrible smell and tastes

141

like a mixture of strawberries and onions, leaving a garlic-like taste in ones mouth. It is apparently an aphrodisiac which is sought after by animals as well as people, tigers have been known to forage for them. The natives have a saying, "When the durian falls the sarong rises". They also fence around the trees so the fallen fruit are safe from animals.

It is being said that the Bishop of Singapore is coming to the camp tomorrow to officiate at the Confirmation ceremony. There are 180 candidates waiting for the day.

Wednesday July 15th

Today is according to my diary St Swithin's but I don't suppose the legend applies over here. I am one of the very few people to own a diary, it is a tablet type coming from a deserted house, and because of it you can often hear someone shout "What's the day?" or "What's the date Jack?" because it has come to the point when very few people know one day from another.

Thursday July 16th

I am one of the candidates for Confirmation and wait with the others in an old Indian Mosque for the Bishop who after two hours still had not arrived. The "Nips" evidently had decided against him coming. Disappointed. we return to camp, just in time to avoid getting caught in a heavy downpour, the first rain for many days.

After tea I went to a concert at the 18th Div. HQ. It was a play called "Dover Road". I enjoyed it very much, the talent was good and the females (men) were very well dressed with all the bulges in the right places. Halves of coconut shells filled a useful need.

Friday July 17th

I awoke to the usual clatter of a camp coming alive; the morning fresh after yesterday's heavy rain and the sun breaks huge and dazzling over the surrounding trees. At breakfast we learn that all Generals, Brigadiers, Colonels, Divisional and Brigade troops are being shipped to Tokyo. Well even prisoners of war see the world.

Brigadier Duke of the 53rd Brigade visits the cemetery, he tells me that he is very pleased with my work and thinks that it will be the best to be handed over to the War Graves Commission. Our present Padre, Stallard, may have to go to Japan. I shall be sorry to lose him as he is a pleasant chap, takes a great interest and comes along to the cemetery bringing us the latest news and camp chat. He says the Lord Bishop is definitely coming on Monday.

Saturday July 18th

Have had a heavy day with five burials, one was a Chief Petty Officer. Duty Officer Major Bregiel says that the "Nips" are to allow lights around the hospital area. Heavy rain falls again during the night that means that I can start turfing again.

Sunday July 19th

Today the main talk is about the movement of officers and men to Japan on Wednesday. At times I almost wish I were going.

The climate today is very heavy and the effort to speak seems to make me sweat more, especially after the hot cup of raw tea that I have just drunk. My attention is drawn skywards as a formation of five large flying boats thunder overhead.

On arriving back at camp for tea, we are paid $1.10c which doesn't amount to much when it takes $3.00 to buy a coconut.

Tomorrow I have to move some pot plants and shrubs from Brigade HQ to the cemetery; these have been grown by my Brigadier during his time here.

Monday July 20th

This afternoon, dressed in my one shirt, patched and sweat stained shorts I am confirmed among others, some even worse off for clothes. The Bishop of Singapore said that it was an historic occasion for the ceremony to happen inside a prisoner of war camp.

One officer is ordained and I take my first communion. I wonder why I have been moved to take these religious steps. Have I seen the light or is it simply for something to do? Anyhow the day drags to an end with the feeling that something has been accomplished and with that I go to bed ready to wage war once again with the diving and angry buzzing mosquitoes. Thirsting for my blood, they score more hits than the "Nip" dive bombers.

Tuesday July 21st

The new day brings a march to the main road where we line up on either side and await, standing for two hours in the hot dry glare thrown off the road by the mid-morning sun, an inspection by the Nippon General in command of Malaya. At about 12.00pm the "Nip" guards start to get excited, rushing up and down the road, soon a car comes in sight filled with "Nips", behind which comes another in which the "Nip" General stands at the salute as he passes us by, and as the car behind carrying his rearguard passes we are dismissed. Two hours standing for two minutes, that I suppose is the privilege of our captors. Wearily we drag ourselves back to camp and dinner. In the afternoon about 3,000 men are being medically examined for the forthcoming move to Japan. I think I would like to see the home of the "Nips" as I have always imagined it as a land of flowers.

Wednesday July 22nd

The days go by and burials have been low. The cemetery now holds 250, with the deaths now being due to diphtheria, dysentery and a few TB cases. A party of Dutch Naval prisoners have just arrived from Sumatra, only to move on with our party in a few days time. The move has been postponed for a while although reports from dock work parties say that the ships to move the men to Japan are already in port.

I am to move my quarters again tomorrow, but I shall still be alone.

Thursday July 23ʳᵈ

Well the time has come and I have moved my bits and pieces, I also managed to increase my furniture by two pieces, two beer bottle cases make a useable bookcase. I am getting a kick out of this modern furnished room. My bed, left behind by its former occupant, being an old cane bottomed seat and a single cupboard which was once part of a larger unit. While I am arranging my bed-sitter I get to thinking that you all at home must be wondering what's happened to me, six months having now passed.

10. **On this day...** July 23, 1942... Battle of Stalingrad begins

Sunday July 26ᵗʰ

I go to church and communion, after which I take a walk to the cemetery and around gardens in the area. Later I plant some tomato seeds that were given to me. They come from tinned tomatoes and having been processed I wonder if they will grow. Also today I have been paid the princely sum of $1.20c. Later as one of five Sergeants I am on a road picket as Nippon officers, including a General, make an inspection of our camp areas.

Monday July 27th

The previous week ended with thirteen burials, and the overseas party are still with us. Two of us bought from the canteen a tin of herrings in tomato sauce for 62c, these I am pretty certain were once our own army stock. Last week I bought six small eggs, this swallowed up most of my "Nip" monthly allowance, but have to try to keep the body together. Went to bed thinking further of the wife and home, hope she is keeping alright. What a treat it would be to walk indoors for a cup of tea like mother makes. Heavy sighs as I roll over to try for some sleep.

Wednesday July 29th

The morning comes in exceedingly hot and dry which is making our grave digging a very exhausting job. Have just finished a burial and while chatting to one of the fellows with the burial party, I learn he has married a girl from my hometown, from a family I know well. It's a small world but to me and my party as we clear up our tools it seems like the end of one. Sweat and dust-stained and weak from lack of food we trudge back to camp, barely able to move one foot in front of the other. On arriving at the camp, we drop on our beds thinking that we will never find the strength to rise again. A half hour passes by and I manage to struggle to the showers only to find that the water has not been turned on. I get into the line of men waiting and fifteen minutes later the water starts to trickle through, bringing much excited shouting from the men as they dash for the line of eight showers splashing down. The breathtaking cold water on our hot bodies causes us to gulp and flinch as it streams down.

Another weary party has just come in, they have been electric cable laying from Changi jail to our camp, some considerable distance. They are so tired they can barely find the strength to speak. Feeling quite a new man after the bracing shower, I collect my mess tin and stroll off to get my rice and tea ration.

Friday July 31st

The days pass by with my work in landscaping the cemetery getting a lot of praise from the officers, they say that one day the people at home will see it at the cinema.

Tonight I am going to a concert rehearsal by the Suffolk Regiment to commemorate "Minden Day", a battle honour.

Saturday August 1st 1942

Almost six months in captivity and under the primitive conditions that we live in it's a struggle to keep up ones morale, more so as the death rate suddenly shoots up. The total for the week is thirteen and today I have had six burials. They have all died from dysentery. As they are brought into the cemetery the corpses are covered in huge flies, the air is full of them. Padre Stallard tells me that owing to an indefinite postponement of his sailing to Japan he is taking over the church again.

Sunday August 2nd

Sunday comes around again so I put on my shirt and go off to Holy Communion. Went to church again this evening. The Padre stated that the Communion service was so large that in future it would have to be held in two parts.

Tuesday August 4th

Some welcome rain has fallen to lay the dust and freshen up the vegetation, making the atmosphere better for us to work in. A burial I am carrying out at the moment causes me some concern as the corpse bears the name J Tuck, 122 Battery Royal Artillery, his age is 31. I am thinking it could be my next-door neighbour, I know that he was here. I made inquiries about him the second day I was in Singapore only to be told that his unit had left for Malaya the day before. When the interment register was signed I asked

147

the clerk if it was possible to get me the man's home address, he said he could. Later in the day he comes up to me during another burial and hands me a piece of brown paper, bearing the name James Tuck, of "Silvergate", Brook Road, Sheringham. I felt very sad as my worst fears were confirmed, I had this day buried my friend and neighbour, he had died from dysentery.

The grave of my friend and neighbour – Jim Tuck, Royal Artillery, whom I buried on August 4th 1942

Wednesday August 5th

We have had four burials today and I still find it hard to keep back the tears, feeling much sorrow as most of them are only in their twenties.

Tonight to liven myself up a bit I go to the Southern area concert. That is in another section and we have to pass a "Nip" guard to get through the barbed wire. The concert turned out to be very good, it was called "Pins and Needles". Its "women" were so real as to make you blush. "Bobbie" was a perfectly good-looking girl with large impressive eyes, only she was a he. So to bed with the usual fight against the ever-present dive bombing of the mosquitoes.

Saturday August 8th

Morning brings once again a stand by order for the men waiting to go to Japan. A Sergeant working with me has just come to report that he would not be coming to the cemetery as he is going into hospital for an operation on his varicose veins, good luck to him as he has suffered a lot over the past weeks. Had three burials and the work (due no doubt to our weakened condition) is very exhausting, the heat is exceptional and the sweat drips continually from my nose and chin, running into my eyes making them sore. It's time to start our weary trudge back to camp, looking forward to a welcome shower, after which I sit on my bed and dream of home where the harvest is now taking place. How nice it would be to have a picnic in the field, also I wonder if our post-cards have arrived home to you yet.

Sunday August 9th

Sunday comes round once more and I go to Communion, after which I climb to the top of a small hill known to us as rumour hill as it appears all the camp stories begin here. From the top I look towards the Malacca Straits, and also in the direction where I think England might be. Last year at this time I was looking forward to next Sunday, as it was my wedding day, August 17th 1941.

This afternoon I watch what is a camp test cricket match, Barnet, the Australian Test cricketer, captains his side. Result, England 171 for nine declared, Australia 171 for six, light and exhaustion stopped play, Barnet 32 caught out.

Talk has it that liners are in port and that could mean some men will soon be on the move. "Scottie" has shaved off all Bill's hair to stop it falling out and to me that must be a definite remedy.

Tuesday August 11th

During the day a swarm of wild bees swarmed close by and endeavours are made to hive them without success, as for myself I managed to get stung. Other than that things seem fairly peaceful with the "Nips" content for the moment to leave us alone, but time is very monotonous for us.

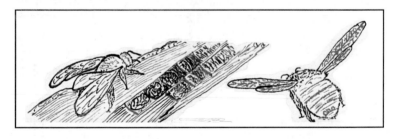

Sketch from my diary of carpenter bees including brood cells

Wednesday August 12th

The morning brings a skin inspection for the 2nd Cambridgeshires with the Divisional General in attendance. Scabies is the suspected trouble. Work-wise I have a gang of men starting to dig out a roadway through the cemetery. Five months ago this cemetery area was a patch of virgin jungle, which is being cleared by the not so sick men, sent down here to me every so often. Sometimes I get a dozen or so, sometimes many more. Tools are often in short supply and I have to work them in short shifts, not being very strong the method suits them. I get all types, some British, Dutch, many Dutch Javanese and occasionally an odd American and as they clear the scrub and vines we are able to dig graves. We have become a British and Dutch cemetery so I am now committed to burials of Dutch soldiers.

Thursday August 13th

Today I have had four quick burials, diphtheria seems to be the main cause of death at the moment, also ulcers. Huge things on the legs of some unfortunate men get infected with the diphtheria germ which becomes very dangerous for the person concerned. While the burials have been taken place it's been raining cats and dogs 200 yards away, never getting any nearer to us and according to my Javanese workers it often happens in these parts. Bill and Puck rig up some bird traps to trap doves or mynah birds to augment our food ration, but no luck yet. Further inspection by the "Nips" of men standing by for Japan.

Sunday August 16th

Have had twelve burials this week, the total now stands at 274, that is the figure for five months, and the way we are existing with little food and no drugs or medicines for the hospital the numbers are going to increase rapidly. With these morbid thoughts passing through my mind I try to switch to thinking of something better. Home and the date, August 16th 1941, come to mind. I have just arrived home on a week's leave, tomorrow is to be my wedding day, the day of days, and here I am a year later burying men dying of hunger and disease. Where will I be in a year's time, who knows? With thoughts of where the wife is and how she is surviving I call it a day and we make it back to camp and a bowl of rice, some chat about various things, the main item being food as usual and then to bed.

Copy of camp orders (7):

16th August 1942 - Beckwith-Smith

Special order of the day by Major General Beckwith-Smith, DSO, MC - Commanding 18th Division.

On my departure for Japan I wish to take what may be my last chance to thank all ranks of the 18th division for their cheerful service and loyal support on many shores and seas during the two years in which I have had the honour to command the Division. I regret that I have been unable to lead you to success in battle to which your cause and sacrifice is entitled, and although I leave you with a heavy heart I carry with me pleasant memories and a real sense of comradeship such as could only have been inspired by the trials and disappointments which we have shared in the last few months.

Difficult days may still be ahead but I hope that the spirit which today animates all ranks of the division will prevail and will form the corner stone on which one day a just and lasting peace will be founded.

God grant that that day may not be long delayed and that we may soon meet again. Meanwhile - GOOD LUCK - HEAD UP - KEEP SMILING.

Sgnd M B Beckworth-Smith
Major General Commanding 18th Division

Monday August 17th

Morning brings before breakfast a visit from Brigadier Duke to say goodbye, for at last the overseas party are to leave. He shakes hands and asks me to make a good job of the cemetery and he turns to go, saying we may meet again in better circumstances. As the party leaves for the dock the rest of us line the road and cheer them on their way. With them gone we return silently to camp wondering who and what's next.

Another sunrise and it's my wedding anniversary, the first, I expect two minds are thinking alike at this moment, wondering when or whether we shall meet again.

I have just heard that a relief ship of some sort has arrived in Singapore docks and naturally a lot of speculation goes on as to the make up of her cargo. Possibly hospital requirements, smokers hope for 2lb tins of tobacco, some jokingly hope for Geisha girls, anyway anyone's guess could be way out. All these thoughts are soon pushed to the backs of our minds as we parade as clean and tidy as we can for a roadside lining to be inspected by a Major General of the Nippon army, now taking over command of the POW camp. After a long wait in the full sun he arrives, and standing in his jeep he drives down the road between long lines of perspiring men who drop to the ground exhausted as he passes from view. Soon we are on our feet again, formed up and marched off to another area to hear a speech from the little General, in which he said in quite good English that he would be a kind and generous General and would treat us as prisoners of war should be treated if we were obedient. It left us wondering what that statement really meant.

Well back to work, we are removing a bunch of coconut palms from the cemetery area as they are in the way of our grave digging, for this, permission had to be obtained from the "Nips" as palms are looked upon as food producers. The central shoot of the palms come in useful for the cooks to put in stews or to be eaten raw, as it is known out here as "millionaires' celery", worth £5 per head.

The afternoon brings heavy rain and we return to our quarters in time to receive a very unexpected issue of food from the ship in dock. I have 1lb 6oz of jam, $^3/_4$lb soup powder, $^1/_4$oz of sweets, containing vitamins A and C, plus some maize flour. These comforts, it is rumoured, were brought here on a ship that carried Japanese diplomats from somewhere in East Africa, anyhow we find them a very welcome addition to our rice. Heavy tropical rain now falling, it makes us feel cold although the temperature is still over 80°F.

11. ***On this day...*** August 19, 1942… Disastrous seaborne raid on Dieppe by Allies.

Saturday August 22ⁿᵈ

I spend some uncomfortable hours just before dawn with the filthy smell of bed bugs and some hot needle-like pricks, so with the coming of daylight I pull my bits and pieces of a bed apart. I find sixteen bugs and a nest of hundreds of tiny red ants complete with a queen and eggs, they must have moved to me during the night.

Day has passed much as usual on the cemetery; we seem to be catching the tail of the NE monsoon as the rain is still heavy. Darkness comes down early because of the grey skies but this evening I shall make my way over to our musical comedy. This turns out to be quite good with the routines backed by a very musical three-piece string band, who made up their own instruments. The good thing is that we enjoyed the show and feel better for it, we talk and joke a bit more than usual as we trudge back through the rain, some saying they could do with a good fish 'n' chip supper, while others tell them to shut up and get to bed. Tomorrow being Sunday they can have an extra hour in bed.

Sunday August 23ʳᵈ

Light breaks with the heavy rain accompanied with storm winds blowing in a whirling manner. I get up early as I am going to Holy Communion, this over I return for a breakfast of raw tea and rice pap. After breakfast I decide to thoroughly pull my old bed of bits of wood etc. apart, as the night again was uncomfortable. I honestly must have found around 500 bugs and eggs. It makes me wonder how much blood has been lost to that red army who in the main now lay splattered on the concrete floor dying it red. I

154

manage to get hold of a quarter pint of diesel oil which I paint over the wood, it helps to keep them off. What a buggy life!

12. ***On this day...*** August 23, 1942... Battle of the Solomon Islands begins.

Monday August 24th

It's work again today, and the rains have given me and my men plenty to get on with, such as turfing the grave mounds and flat areas. Have had four burials, this follows an unusual long period without, although I have noticed deaths seem to follow the rain. After tea once again I climb rumour hill. It is gloriously moonlight only as a tropical night can be, I sit alone with my thoughts, thinking of and gazing in the direction where I think home lies. Nearly ten months since I left and what a lot has happened. How long had I sat there? Hours it seemed in distant thought, the moon is low over the sea as I drag my stiffened body down the slope and to bed.

Tuesday August 25th

Morning brings a change with a bathing parade, these are always welcome for as yet we have no water in this compound except for cooking. As the morning wears on 500 men have returned from Bukit Timah village where the "Nips" have had them build a memorial in memory of the battle and the men who fell there. What curious people they are.

Tea over and it's 8pm; a parade is called which caused quite a stir as it is rather late. It is for a physical check but we are not told why, so it soon sets up a crop of rumours that go buzzing around the compound. So to bed with our thoughts, will it be the Burma railway? Japanese coal mines, or? Well why let it worry me, I tell myself as I try to sleep with a terrific tornado-like wind roaring over and around the buildings. It seems to threaten to tear us all apart.

Wednesday August 26th

Morning finds it all quiet and peaceful except for some disquieting news, 170 cases of diphtheria in the hospital and no serum to treat them with. One of my team, Sgt. Buckley, has had an operation for an abscess on a kidney, but life goes on with always arguments among the men over every topic under the sun.

Thursday August 27th

I seem to have cured my bug problem for the moment as I am sleeping better. In the course of this day I have been fortunate to sample various fruits found growing around, such as the peppery tasting Cachou fruit, a Jack fruit, millionaires' celery and the milk of a green coconut. Surely I must have taken in a few vitamins. Naturally I am vitamin conscious as I hold out hope of getting out of this.

Friday August 28th

Got reprimanded for not saluting an officer, the first time in my army life and it had to happen in a prisoner of war camp. His pip was so dirty I failed to notice it at the 20 yards distance.

Saturday August 29th

I awake this morning realizing that it is my next-door neighbour's birthday, so after breakfast I hunt around the neglected gardens for some flowers and make up a wreath for his grave. His mother would like that if only she knew that he had died, it could be a long time before news reaches her. The rest of the day is spent on grave digging and landscaping.

After tea I visit the Major with whom I work, he is ill but the cause unknown, so he is to visit a hospital specialist.

A warning has also gone out today to all men to safeguard themselves the best way they can against diphtheria, we now have

400 cases this week. What can we do? Only keep utensils clean and flies at bay, which can be a full time job with hands and arms going like windmill sails as they abound here in their millions. Had another de-bugging, but it is better than last week as I have only found one.

Have just heard that a Nippon truck ran over a land mine this morning injuring five of our men on a work party, also two "Nips" injured.

Sunday August 30th

I just lounge around, reading some of the books I salvaged from a bombed out house. Tomorrow we have a rehearsal parade for everyone in the camp as on Tuesday the "Nips" are calling a complete roll call of all ranks. A paper has been sent around to everyone asking them to promise not to attempt to escape from the island of Singapore. In the meantime my Nippon pass flag to the cemetery has gone astray causing a bit of a stir until it was found a few hours later. The weather at the moment is very hot, thankfully burials are down to one a day.

Orders are given to be prepared to move out of the camp. A punishment of some form is possible if we do not sign the non-escape forms. Much argument goes on well into the night, for and against the signing of the forms. Shadowy figures flicker and dance on the walls, thrown by the spluttering of our crude home made oil lamps as we wearily take to our beds. The news tonight has taken the place of our usual discourse of food and what mother makes best.

Monday August 31st

Morning comes all too soon, the dawn with the same swiftness as with the darkness that fell just twelve hours ago. We are called out for roll call to get our feelings on signing the forms. It is soon seen that the majority of the men do not wish to sign them, although escape through 1,000 miles of jungle and many unfriendly natives, or over several thousand miles of sea, if a boat is obtainable, is virtually impossible. The jungle at least would mean starvation and at sea the "Nips" would soon pick up any adventurers. The non-signing of the forms is really a point of honour with most of us coupled with the fact we might lose any entitlements if and when we return home. Later in the day our captors are informed of our decision, by nightfall we get the "Nips" answer, that is we are to stand by in the morning in readiness for a move to another area. We have something to talk about now and discuss among ourselves where we could go, but at night we are no wiser, except filled with wild rumours such as having a rising sun tattooed on our foreheads or being machine-gunned in cold blood. This we sleep on.

Tuesday September 1st 1942

The morning brings the news that the move has been postponed for a few hours. Apparently some discussion is going on at top level, the break gives us a bit more time to air our views on the possible whereabouts of our destination. Knowing our captors and their temperamental attitude towards us, we wander around with a certain amount of despondency undermining our struggling hopes.

Wednesday September 2nd

Mother's birthday. At 2pm it has been decided to move out from the camp and as the move gathers momentum I see that all the walking battle casualties from the hospital are with us. Soon we reach the road from the camp and turn in the direction of Singapore. With as good a show of marching as helping the sick along will allow we set off. There are those among us who have lost arms, legs and sight, and some I passed were being carried on stretchers. Once on the main road what a sight met my eyes! As far as I could see there was an unending column of ghost lorries. I think it looks like a crowd scene from a film in the making, a wagon train without horses, the place of the horses being taken by the straining sweating men and that of the cattle by now the straggling thousands of men. Most of the motor-less lorries carry rice rations, cooking gear and firewood. On some wagons the odd chickens in coops, kept for their eggs, but their owners virtually had to sleep with them or they would soon finish up in somebody's cooking pot. A couple of goats trail behind another truck from which also comes the quack of ducks. The barking of dogs from along the column comes from the dogs that have attached themselves to us. These dogs are truly British in their attitude as they bark and snarl at the "Nips" on roll call. The huge column rolls on its ungainly way up the slope of the road, the sight of it brings good humoured banter and laughter occasionally mixed with some cursing of our captors, as man helps man along.

We seem to have been marching raggedly along for about an hour and now the leaders appear to be turning off to the right and on reaching this point I see a side road that leads to the barrack square and buildings that once held the Gordon Highlanders, which is in an area known as Selerang. I am amused to see standing on the corner a man who judging by the remnants of his clothes is a naval type, holding a large wicker cage, in which is a very colourful parrot swearing as only the Navy can teach him. As we very slowly make our way, due to congestion ahead, through the gates of our new prison camp I see the square surrounded on three sides by seven two-storied blocks. The home in peacetime to less than 1,000 men, soon to be bursting at the seams by around 17,500, almost eighteen times as many and a large number of them sick and weak from hunger and disease. The whole area is encircled by a road.

We finally all get onto the square with hardly any individual space to move in. Two men who move out onto the encircling road and quickly get clubbed back with the rifle butts of a passing Jap patrol, who I note are continually marching around making the road out of bounds to us. While waiting, we are told where to go and I watch the lorries being pulled into position around the square, almost nose to tail. I have just been allotted a space of concrete floor about 18 inches wide on the top floor of one of the buildings in which to lay my bits and pieces plus myself. The sight around me is almost indescribable, tired men stinking of sweat, attacked by thousands of flies, still find the ability to joke and laugh about what is happening to them.

I go down the concrete stairway to the tarmac square and wind my way through the various cook wagons which are already belching wood smoke, turning the whole area into a choking haze. Pushing among the huge jumble of men I manage to get a rough estimate of our new area, which including the ground the barracks are standing on is 150 yds by 200 yds, therefore we could not possibly all be on the square at the same time. My thoughts are broken by the cry, "Tea up". I quickly join the long line of men and collect it, a blob of plain boiled rice and a mug of raw tea. At least I'm glad of a drink. By the time we have eaten darkness overtakes us, and as there is no form of lighting there is nothing for it but to lie down and talk. Sleep is rather a broken affair because of the cramped positions and the hardness of my mattress, a groundsheet on the concrete floor. A lot of noise from outside doesn't help sleep.

Thursday September 3ʳᵈ

I finally nod off, it seems just as dawn breaks, anyhow it is not long before I am awakened by the groans of my stiff and sore comrades. After a lot of stretching and yawning I painfully get to my feet, push my way to the balcony overlooking the square on which a lot of activity is taking place, it also accounts for the noises of the night. It looks as though giant moles have been at work. Trenches have appeared and huge mounds of clay lay on the tarmac. These are latrines, dug across the centre and sides of the parade ground. The various cookhouses are busy with smoky fires heating the rice boilers, only spitting distance from the new latrines. The flies will not have far to hop from one to the other. Going down, with my mess tin in readiness for breakfast, I see on a small plot of grass tucked away in one corner and on it a couple of small marquees with a notice stating "Isolation Area", yet men are sleeping between the guy ropes as there is not enough room in the buildings for all of us.

As the day goes by impromptu shelters are springing up like mushrooms on the flat roofs of the barrack blocks. Bits and pieces of canvas, anything that will give a little shelter from sun and possible rain. All is an effort to get men under cover who had to sleep out last night. The latrine trenches are growing in number, the stench and flies are terrible in the hot sun. The Royal Engineers are busy making latrine covers from doors stripped from the buildings in a desperate effort to keep the flies out and stop a full scale outbreak of dysentery as many men came in with us suffering from this complaint.

On the square it's difficult to get about without pushing and squeezing between men, there's barely a square foot to call your own. There is even a tighter crowd of men at the other end of the ground. I make my way slowly there to find out what's going on. Standing on the surrounding road is a column of lorries manned by the "Nips". They are ration trucks, laden with rice, vegetables and even meat. They it seems will leave the rations if we will sign the non-escape forms, but after some time, with huge grins on their faces, they drive off still fully laden. Tomorrow looks like being a bit thin on food.

Today is also the third anniversary of the outbreak of the war and the feeling among the men is tense. It would not take much to overcome sanity, a spark, I believe, would touch off a mad rush over the road to try and overcome our guards. Mutterings and grumbles everywhere, talk of a case of appendicitis and dysentery, but the "Nips" will not allow them to be removed to hospital. It is rumoured that the appendicitis case has been operated on in the isolation tent. It appears that our captors are being alerted as machine gun posts are now being set up on the four corners of the road surrounding us, a mortar and gun can be seen on a nearby hillside, perhaps they can also feel the intense atmosphere that engulfs the place. Some lorries are standing at the entrance to the area and a lot of gesticulating is going on between a party of "Nips" and some of our officers. The reason for this is soon known to me as I am picked out to take a party and board one of the trucks. What for? Where for? no-one seems to know. Soon we move off followed by the other two lorries also with our men aboard. We soon leave the main road and drive down a rough track through a rubber plantation. The conversation between the men gets a bit wild, such as are we going to be shot so as to induce the others to sign the non-escape forms. Some say lets sign the bloody things and remain alive to fight another day, and so the talk goes on. The truck bumps its way along and we watch the twisting ruts disappear behind us. The drivers are slowing down and finally halt. Our hair stands up on our necks at what we see, cold sweat trickles down our backs as we view the scene, the entrance to a sand-bagged firing range, manned by traitorous Indian troops. A lot of talk goes on between them and the "Nips", meanwhile I'm turning over in my mind all the possible ways of making a fight for my life if the event arose. One of my party breaks down, his nerves under the strain of not knowing what is to happen have cracked, others are strangely silent.

A "Nip" soldier leaves the range and runs down the track towards a house just visible through the trees. By the actions of the "Nips" we think it must be the headquarters of the General commanding the POW camps on the island. A half-hour passes by and the soldier who went to the house is now returning at the double. He reports to the Guard Commander who, in turn, then talks to his men. The guards, with wide grins on their faces, climb back onto the trucks, which are then reversed one by one into the area of the firing range. This fills us with more forebodings as we stop by the sandbagged walls. For a few minutes nothing happens, we are waiting to be told to get down from the lorries when suddenly on a hand signal the trucks move forward out of the gates we had just entered. The "Nips", still grinning from ear to ear, were evidently trying to scare the living daylights out of us and with some success.

With the hair on the back of my neck settling down again, we travel back in the direction from which we had recently come. We are jolted and thrown about as we travel over the rough track but soon reach a main road only to turn away from the parade ground.

At another locality it is evident to us that a firing squad had been doing its deadly work here. Close by in the undergrowth parts of some skeletons were scattered around. We look at our grinning guards with chills running down our spines, they laughed, no doubt at the looks on our faces. Some pointed their rifles at the marked wall; others kicked the bleached bones about and in broken English tell us that they were an Australian and two British soldiers. To my great relief they move us from this area of death and then instruct us to dismantle some barbed wire. With this done the sadistic devils take us back to Selarang barracks, there to tell others of the horrors of the afternoon.

It's tea-time and I am really glad of a drink. Darkness falls over the area, a few flickering lights are seen as men carry on latrine digging. There's nothing to be done other than sit and talk or sleep, packed like sardines in a tin, however before either of these things take place an orderly informs me that I am on a latrine digging party at 2am. Everyone gets a shift during the day or night. These trenches are dug to a depth of sixteen feet in an attempt to keep out the flies.

Friday September 4ᵗʰ

I join my party still stretching and rubbing my sore hips to get some circulation into them. The trench I am sent to is already deep and I have to descend by ladder to its floor which is lit by a hurricane lamp swinging on a rope from the top. We shovel the sticky latorite clay into buckets which are hauled to the top by ropes, emptied, and then dropped back to us and so it goes on. Two hours have passed and my shift ends, I make for the ladder only too pleased to get out of the stifling heat at this depth. The amount of earth piling up on the square is enormous and is quickly cutting down our walking space.

I make my way back to my quarters, the place is in complete darkness and I have to navigate the stairway, which is full of sleeping men. Amid grunts and curses I climb over them to reach the top floor, my boots hanging around my neck to avoid hurting anyone. I finally reach my allotted bed space and soon fall asleep from exhaustion.

Reveille sounds all too soon and with the others I go down for my breakfast of rice and tea. The cooks have kept their fires going by cutting down all the small trees that were growing between the blocks and are also using any wood, which is left in the buildings, such as door frames which are stripped completely from their fixings.

Copy of camp orders (8):

Changi 4th September 1942

Special Order No 3. Dated 4 September 1942

1. On 30th August 1942 I, together with my Area Commanders was summoned to the conference house, Changi Gaol, where I was informed by the representative of Major General Shimpei Fukuye, GOC Prisoner of War camps Malaya, that all prisoners of war in Changi Camp were to be given forms of promise not to escape, and that all were to be given the opportunity to sign this form

2. By the laws and usages of war, prisoners of war cannot be required by the power holding him to give his parole, and in our army, those who have become prisoners of war are not permitted to give their parole. I pointed out this position to the Japanese authorities.

3. I informed the representative of Major General Shimpei Fukuye that I was not prepared to sign the form, and that 1 did not consider that any officers or men in the Changi Camp would be prepared to sign the form. In accordance with the orders of the Japanese Authorities, all prisoners of war were given the opportunity to sign. The result of that opportunity is well known.

4. On the 31st August I was informed by the Japanese Authorities that those personnel who refused to sign the certificates would be subjected to 'measures of severity', and that refusal to sign would be regarded as a direct refusal to obey a regulation which the Imperial Japanese Army considered it necessary to enforce.

5. Later, on the night of the 31st August / 1st September, I was warned that on 1st September all prisoners of war persisting in refusal to sign were to move by 1800 hours to Selerang Barrack square. I confirmed, both on my own behalf and in the name of the prisoners of war, our refusal to sign.

6. The move to Selerang Barrack Square was successfully accomplished on the same afternoon
.

7. I and the area commanders have been in constant conference with the Imperial Japanese Army and have endeavored by negotiation to have the form either abolished or at least modified. All that I have been able to obtain is that which was originally made and, accompanied by threats of 'measures of severity', has now been issued as an official order of the Imperial Japanese Government.

8. During the period of the occupation of the Sererang Barrack Square the conditions in which we have been placed have been under my constant consideration. These may be briefly described as such an existence herein will result in a very few days in the outbreak of epidemic and the most serious consequences to those under my command and inevitable death to many. Taking into account the low state of health in which many of us now are, and the need to preserve our forces intact as long as possible, and in full conviction that my action, were the circumstances in which we are now living known to them, would meet with the approval of His Majesties Government, I have felt it my duty to order all personnel to sign the certificate under the duress imposed by the Imperial Japanese Army.

9. I am fully convinced that His Majesty's Government only expects prisoners of war not to give their parole when such parole is to be given voluntarily. This factor can in no circumstance be regarded as applicable to our present condition. The responsibility for this decision rests with me alone, and I fully accept it in ordering you to sign.

10. I wish to record in this order my deep appreciation of the excellent spirit and good discipline which all ranks have shown during this trying period.

I look forward to all ranks to continue in good heart, discipline and morale. Thank you all for your loyalty and co-operation.

Signed T.B. Holmes
Colonel, Commanding British and Australian troops, Changi.

Saturday September 5th

I am awakened at dawn by men falling over me as they move from their cramped positions to get down for some fresh air. Up here it stinks of sweat from unwashed bodies as the only water we have is for cooking.

It's our fourth day jammed together here and dysentery and diphtheria takes a hold among us. The doctors fear an epidemic and in the circumstances an effort is to be made to obtain a letter from the Nippon authorities to the effect that if we sign the non-escape forms it will be under duress. In the meantime news has come in that the "Nips" intend to send prisoners from other camps in Singapore to join us and later all the hospital patients. One can easily guess the ultimate result of such an inhuman move. I have visions of the dead and dying in their hundreds or a mass breakout, resulting in a quick death for many of us.

So the day wears on with rations of rice short and only of the worst quality. I feel dirty and angry as I make for my bed space, only to be called out for another bash at latrine digging. A church service is being held among the huge dumps of earth. Before I finish my digging I hear that the order has gone out for us to sign the forms, the letter asked for by our Commanding Officer has been promised. I creep back to my spot just as a thunderstorm breaks, with all the rain that only a tropical storm can bring.

Sunday September 6th

The morning comes in fine but what a terrible sight meets my eyes as I look out over the barrack square, the parts that are not latrine trenches are inches deep in water, held by the gigantic heaps of muddy clay. Articles of kit lay around in the water, left by men soaked while they slept out in the open. The day is spent by the roof top dwellers and those outside in drying off their bits and pieces, also the signing of the forms, which say:

"I solemnly promise not to try and escape".

Within the hour we are ready to move away from the filth back to the comparative comfort of "Changi" camp. The unwieldy convoy of ghost lorries and thin, half naked, dirty, but once again somewhat cheerful men in long columns amble away from the mud and stench and shattered barracks which have been our prison for the last five days.

13. **On this day...** September 6, 1942... German advance into Russia halted at Stalingrad.

Monday September 7th

Sleeping last night was heaven after the cramped conditions of the previous few nights. The day seems extra bright and the trees and bushes greener as we walk unjostled, enjoying freedom from tortured thoughts. I have just been told that four men were buried in the hospital grounds, as we were not allowed to work on the cemetery. Tomorrow I have three burials to take care of.

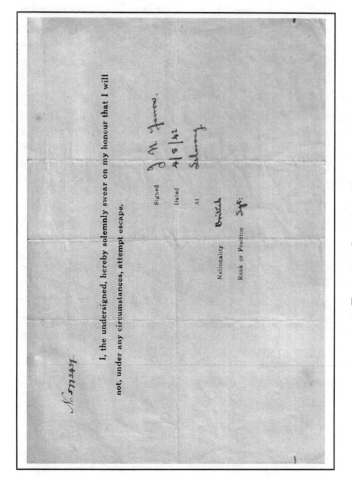

No. 577244.

I, the undersigned, hereby solemnly swear on my honour that I will not, under any circumstances, attempt escape.

Signed   J. M. Jarrow.
Dated   4/8/42
At   Salonaz

Nationality   British
Rank or Position   Sgt.

Escape document

Tuesday September 8th

The day arrives very hot and the bodies as they come along the cemetery drive are followed by a great stream of flies, although it's heart breaking work, it is a pleasure to be back as the results, in a morbid way, are rewarding. Only hours after arriving back from the prison barracks of Selarang I learn that all the men from the southern area of our camp are to return there but under normal conditions, the reason being that a Japanese force of 1,000 men are taking over the southern camp.

Some "Nip" planes are zooming overhead engaged in practice fights. Reports coming in say that all inside area barbed wire is to come down, this will bring the hospital area, the gardens and cemetery into bounds and permit flags will no longer be required to allow movement into these areas.

Wednesday September 9th

Morning comes and men are detailed to start taking down the barbed wire but the "Nips" have decided that after all, the cemetery is to remain outside the free area, so I shall have to continue carry my permit flag, bearing its message in Japanese. The officer who has worked with me is in hospital so I have been given complete charge of the cemetery.

It is said that a shortage of food on the island could cause a cut in our rations, this would prove disastrous, also rumour has it that we are to be sent to Lorenco Marques, in Portuguese East Africa, a neutral country. Our Padre however, doesn't think so as he has approached the "Nips" about Xmas to see if they can muster a few extras in the way of food. They tell him there could be plenty of pork, also two bottles of beer for each man, but if we get drunk and disorderly only one bottle will be given next year, this sounds to me like a sadistic joke.

An armed force of Japanese troops have just passed on their way to the southern camp area watched by my cemetery workers, the comments of some are unprintable. After this the talk turns to the latest rumours, such as things are bad in England, the coast is being evacuated, an invasion of Scotland by the Germans, who it is said are marching through Glasgow. Not knowing how true any of this is you can imagine our thoughts.

Well it's bed time and I crawl onto my bug ridden boards, twisting and turning trying to find the best position for my hip bones. I think about the day's events and rumours, my drowsiness broken by the monotonous "Klonk Klonk" of the knocking of the ice bird, whose neck one would eagerly ring if you could get to him.

Sunday September 13th

I awake and a huge red ball of a sun is rising in the sky. It's my 30th Birthday, I wish myself "Many Happy Returns", thinking that if I am lucky I might get some "leggie" rice (a second helping). I expect all at home are thinking of me today and my thoughts are with my wife and mother, as I go for my half pint of liquid rice and raw tea. After breakfast I now make my way to the church and Holy Communion. This ritual out of the way I decide to go to the hospital to see Sergeant Buckley, so as it's Sunday I put on my only shirt and a pair of hose tops (footless stockings). On the way I see Japanese troops training. The day passes wearily away with nothing to toast my new year of life with, and only to wonder if I shall make it to my 31st.

Monday September 14th

Morning greets me all too soon, as its back to the back-breaking job of grave digging and earth levelling after the scrub has been cleared. Talk among the men says repatriation of the wounded and limbless men, also that the Germans are now in Carlisle. At this moment I am suddenly in the flight path of a swarm of Peningats (Wild Bees) and I have to make a hasty retreat to an open grave until they have passed by.

170

Tuesday September 15th

The night passed with the first real rain for a long time coming our way and it keeps us from working this morning. The afternoon brings us one burial, the total is now 300 buried here. As we march back to camp it feels cool after the dampness of the day and with the temperature around 83°F I shall be glad to put on my shirt.

Wednesday September 16th

Heavy rain is still with us this morning, but we have to work. It is ideal for cutting and laying turf on the completed part of the cemetery.

The night brings the dress rehearsal of the first entertainment that my group have been allowed to put on, "I killed the Count". It was very good, excellent parts played by all. Lt Mackwood playing the part of Rene Lovaine represented the almost perfect woman.

A rifle shot is heard on the precincts of the boundary wire and it makes me wonder if someone strayed from camp. Later in bed I am thinking of home again and trying hard to remember the sound of my wife's voice and I have to concentrate very hard to get a picture of her in my confused state of mind.

Thursday September 17th

Another day has passed and the night sees me in a sorry plight. I have contracted sickness and diarrhoea and spent the whole night with such convulsions of the stomach that I thought I was suffering from acute appendicitis.

Friday September 18th

Morning arrives but have had no sleep and am excused work.

Saturday September 19th

Today sees an influx of POW's that were captured in Java and Sumatra or, taken there by the "Nips". They are using our camp as a transit base as they are en route for Japan to work in the mines and docks.

I am feeling better but crave for the impossible, a bottle of beer, as I feel so dehydrated, but shall have to close my eyes and use my imagination to the fullest extent. Have just been told that the "Nips" want our height, chest measurements and weight. Why? Perhaps at last they are going to supply coffins, quipped one happy soul. It's near teatime so I go off to fetch my mess tin and mug and to myself I say, "My God, how I hate rice".

Sunday September 20th

Morning comes with a roll call followed by a weighing and I turn the scales at 138lbs with boots on. Many pounds of this is rice blubber, my height remains the same - growth is stunted. Spend the rest of the day, it being Sunday, resting, something I can do with, as our meagre ration does not induce much energy.

Monday September 21st

Monday is here all too soon, so it is back to grave digging and clearing. Came across a huge spider that actually attacked one of my men, jumping at him and on him. As I work I think of my imprisoned existence of which I am desperately tired. The climate is nice but to have to work through the mid-day sun is killing and makes me long for the changing seasons of England.

A new line of work comes along to make life a bit more macabre. We have now exhumed four bodies of men shot trying to escape and buried by the "Nips" outside the area. For this permission had to be obtained. Two we buried in our cemetery at Changi, the other two being Australians were taken to their own cemetery. I will not enlarge on the gruesome details of digging up those that have been buried for some time.

On the way back to camp the jungle grapevine tells us that a Red Cross ship has docked and has mail on board. It would be a great lift, after a year, to receive some news of home, for at the moment morale is rather low, there being a big increase in the sickness here this week. It seems that the lack of vital vitamins is causing the body to succumb to new troubles such as scrotal and skin diphtheria, ulcers, beriberi and also some blindness that could become permanent. We are fighting a second war against disease and still with no weapons; no medicines or ointments.

Thursday September 24th

Work goes on as usual today I buried a marine, probably from the *"Prince of Wales"* sunk off here a year ago. Rumour says another Red Cross ship is in and so the rumours go on, more often building up to nothing. Have just seen a party of Thailand troops, wonder what the "Nips" have them here for? More POW's from Java arrive late tonight. It's rice for tea again, for a time we did get the odd egg but they seem to have finished.

Saturday September 26th

This past week has brought thirteen burials. The days go by now with only the daily routine of prison life and as I write I think again how I wish we were at peace and at home with the changing seasons instead of just one long hot summer.

Sunday September 27th

It is Harvest Festival time at our church and it is decorated with such fruit and vegetables as can be found here. Canna lilies, Frangipani, Flame of the Forest etc., Sweet potatoes, tapioca, yams and such from our gardens. Quite a lot of fellows have turned up for the occasion, not so much religion I think, but it's something to do to break the monotony.

Monday September 28*th*

The weather is hot and dry, the rainy period has not yet arrived. Work goes on much the same from day to day although at the moment the main clearing party is working on "Controversy Hill", so called because on clearing scrub it came to light and being right in the way of our road through the cemetery called for a lot of discussion. What to do about it, should we level it? It would take us weeks with worn down spades and one small two-wheel handcart. After a day thinking about our little hill I decided if left I could make a feature of it, so I set to work with about 30 sick men to remove the top and level it, then to cut two four foot wide terraces on its face and shape off the banks in preparation for turfing. No-one but us could realise the difficult and arduous work for men with more guts than strength, the relentless sun beating down during the midday hours, the sweat running down into our eyes, dripping off our nose and chin, and down arms and legs, later drying off to salt which could be rubbed from our bodies. Tired we wearily marched back to camp each day, just ready for tea and bed. This hard slog went on for a week, at the end of which, the hill is ready for turfing but will have to wait for some rain.

Another small job has come my way, I have been asked to mark out garden plots on an area of land in readiness for the walking sick to work. By growing vegetables they supplement our diet, as the rations for the sick are split from ours, the "Nips" do not supply food for the sick.

Tuesday September 29*th*

Buried today the first Javanese soldier from the many with us. The "Nips" want a kit inspection, it's a real laugh, 1 shirt, 1 pair patched shorts (being worn), one pair hose tops, no socks, one pair of worn out boots, a razor but no blades and one comb, what a lay-out! Perhaps when the "Nips" look at it, it may open their little hearts and we might get some new boots. I get back from the cemetery in time for the inspection and on the door of the chalet, where, at the moment, I live alone as many men have been removed to Singapore for work, is this chalked message:

Ghouls unlimited, Prop. Sgt. FARROW.
Graves to measure,
Bring your own Shroud,
Family Ghosts Supplied at reduced rates,
Die now and save cash,
Address: Boot Hill, Changi.

Very funny, but no time to wash it off as the "Nip" officers are only a few doors away. On reaching my door an officer asks through an interpreter what it says and the rather embarrassed man reads it to them, at this they are very amused. One "Nip" officer was very interested in my wedding photo and I thought for a moment he was going to keep it. They leave me for next door where they have another laugh as a Sergeant there has his bits of kit marked up as for a bargain sale.

Wednesday September 30th

Red Cross supplies are arriving at a camp depot, although only the hospital has received anything as yet. This, the "Nips" tell us, is due to Japanese kindness in allowing the ship to come into port. We are still hoping that it has some mail on board. Our hosts have now come up with index cards and require full name and address at birth, wife and parents names in full, when and where taken or capitulated as a prisoner, plus ones occupation. Having given the required information I return to the cemetery to see to burials of three men exhumed by us from areas outside the camp. The remains were in sacks. This is followed by two other burials so we have to set to and dig more graves as we like to keep three ahead. The main clearing party is digging out soil and levelling for the road to bend around the foot of "Controversy Hill".

A medical examination has been carried out on men from Java whose move away from Singapore is imminent.

Thursday October 1ˢᵗ 1942

I have been promised a mosquito net by a friend working on the other side of the barbed wire surrounds, apparently he has somehow managed to get hold of a few. How? Well it does not do to ask questions. It is arranged for me to be at a certain place at the wire, now for those who do not know about barbed wire fencing it consists of two coils running alongside each other and a third on top making it about six feet high and wide and to crawl through it with clothes or equipment on is impossible. I arrived at the point as arranged, absolutely dark except for the light of the stars. The man had just arrived on the other side with the net, he rolled it into a ball and threw it but a bit came unrolled and caught on the top wire. I had most of it but to pull it would have torn it badly. My friend ran off into the darkness leaving me in a dilemma as about every twenty minutes the "Nips" played a searchlight down the wire. I was left with about ten minutes to retrieve the hooked net before it was seen in all its whiteness in the beam of the light, quickly I stripped off my shirt and shorts, got down on my knees and crawled through the spaces in the wire to its centre where I managed to reach up and unhook the caught net and work it clear. I turned in the tunnel of wire and got out only to have to fall quickly to the ground to cover the tell-tale whiteness of the net as the beam of the searchlight played along the wire. I dress and make my way back to my billet thinking of the sleep I shall have instead of swiping at mosquitoes half the night, although will have to wash a few scratches first.

Sunday October 4*th*

Rations appear to have decreased somewhat over the last few days and we are hoping that the Red Cross ship will supply a little change of diet, although it is a very long while reaching us.

A burial this afternoon and it was another from my Company. The hospital has been put out of bounds owing to an outbreak of diphtheria.

The reasons for the cut in our rations has just found its way over the jungle telephone. Apparently the "Nips" have just discovered a reserve stock of tinned food brought in by us at the capitulation. It was being held for hospital emergencies by the Service Corps. They say it has to be used up.

Monday October 5*th*

A sudden storm has blown up, terrific in its intensity, bending the palm trees almost to the ground and ripping away wooden roofs and everything loosely fixed. The rain and wind go on into the night, it is the worst storm so far experienced.

Tuesday October 6*th*

The morning comes and with it a sparkle everywhere as the sun glints on the moisture laden trees and vegetation. I am happy to have had the rain as I can now get on with turfing "Controversy Hill". This means cutting the turf from a Padang (Playing Field) with spades and transporting it on our two-wheeled handcart from across the road, a distance of 600 to 800 yards, an energetic job of work for those in the best of health. The majority of us have the cemetery at heart so we do it with a will. On arriving at the guard hut on our way to work I am given a new and larger pass flag. Red Cross relief still arriving at the hospital but nothing for us yet.

Wednesday October 7ᵗʰ

The early hours bring more heavy rains, this is good for my turf. Burials are increasing mainly from diphtheria, skin and nasal forms. A report says troops working in the Singapore area are now receiving Red Cross goods.

* * *

The daily work goes on, weary and hungry, only the interest in what we are doing keeps us in hope of early release, although we have been warned by our Colonel that it could be three years. We have not done a year yet so we feel a bit down in the dumps at his comments.

Red Cross relief lorries still going to camp. Get my $1.50c amenity pay so I go to the canteen and by a pint of soya bean sauce, 1lb of peanuts and get no change. The goods that I have obtained I am led to believe contain certain vitamins that my body needs to prevent it breaking down.

Another Dutchman died soon after arrival from Java so it is decided on request to keep to one section of the cemetery for Dutch and Javanese men. A rumour is going around that the ship *"Lisbon Maru"* carrying British POW's to Japan has been sunk in a battle at sea and only 200 from 1,800 have been saved. More men from Java leaving us for Japan, they are mainly from the RAF. I had four burials this afternoon, deaths mainly from dysentery. Red Cross supplies in the news again, it is said that sixty cigarettes a man are to be issued, however in the meantime an issue of the food has been made to the cookhouse comprising 3½ tins bully beef, 1 tin milk, flour, fat, ¾lb of sweet biscuits, ¼ lb cocoa, 1¾lbs sugar, tins of meat and vegetables. As this is per man it will make a good change and supplement the rice for a while. Some cigarettes have been issued and with thousands of men suddenly smoking again, the night air is thick with smoke. I have not yet received any but I have made up my mind not to smoke again.

Sunday October 11th

This morning the air is very hot and on waking the sweat is already trickling down my body, perhaps all the thousands of cigarettes smoked last night has heated up the atmosphere. The day moves towards night and everyone has been lying around, heat stricken by what is reported to be the highest temperatures since we landed on the island, it's well over 100°F in the shade. Glad I'm not digging graves today. A mug of cocoa with a biscuit was issued, and yes, with milk and sugar, reminds one briefly of supper at home.

One of our men was killed and another injured when a truck overturned on Changi road. A report says that the sick and wounded men taken to Kuala Lumpur, Malaya, after we left Serangoon are to be brought back to Changi.

Monday October 12th

The day is another very hot one and as I dig, not for the first time, sweat is bubbling through the lace holes of my boots. The Major who works with me has left hospital after a few weeks illness with an issue of vitamin sweets which taste of cod-liver oil extract. Red Cross goods are still coming in and these should at least stem deaths from vitamin deficiencies and give us all a little more energy.

Tuesday October 13th

A report that wounded men are to be repatriated is very strong. I don't know how these rumours start but none have come true as yet. Another man was killed today when the steering gear of a "ghost" lorry broke down.

Wednesday October 14th

Had five burials today, the death rate due to more men arriving from Java. They are in transit to Japan, here one day gone the next. I shall have to put more men on grave digging. The main cause of death is still dysentery.

Sold my issue of cigarettes for enough to buy half pint of real palm oil, which I can use for a few fry ups of green leaves or mix with my rice.

Thursday October 15th

Four more burials and sick men are returning to Changi from Singapore, and 30 men from our camp are immediately sent back in exchange, including my big six foot two chief gravedigger, Bill Bailey. He will be greatly missed as grave digger and tea boy.

Friday October 16th

A party for "Nip" work up country Malaya, standing by. Heavy rain has been falling all morning and this red volcanic earth soon turns to a sticky mud. It's just a year since I returned from embarkation leave and in all that time never a letter from home. It is said that the officers are to receive more pay, which is to be deducted from home accounts later. A few American prisoners have been brought here. Burials are up the highest yet for one week, 21 deaths.

The "Nips" have allocated land near Changi jail for extra garden, the more vegetables we can grow the better. A few months ago some of the rations brought in by us were issued and amongst them were some tinned tomatoes from which I saved some seeds and hoping to grow some plants from them, but at the same time not really thinking that I could do this from processed fruit. You can imagine my pleasant surprise at the sight of seedlings pushing their way through the soil after only a few days. These were religiously seen after and they have grown showing many trusses of green fruit, some just showing signs of turning colour. As far as we know they are the only large plants in Changi.

Saturday October 17th

A Japanese staff officer visited the cemetery today and took a number of photographs of it. Have just buried the first from the RAF. As we finish filling in our attention is drawn to the road where a column of men are straggling along, a dishevelled mixture of RAF, Australians, Americans, Javanese and Dutchmen, where to and what for nobody knows or much cares.

Sunday October 18th

As it is raining heavily we are forced to stay in. I spend some of the time turning over my few photo's which have somehow managed to keep although somewhat stained with sweat. They are of my wife, my wedding and my family, but they only make me feel low and homesick, also done some writing and brought my diary up to date. With tea over I try to smarten myself and go off to church where the address is given by Padre Duckworth, a small but forceful fellow and one whose brave activities we have heard much about.

Monday October 19th

More sick men come back from Singapore and more of the fit leave our camp as their replacements. The burial rate has been lower this week, which is a relief.

Tuesday October 20th

Today brings a wonderful surprise, the "Nips" are allowing parties of us to go to the beach. It is simply marvellous to get into the water, as yet we have little means for washing ourselves except when it rains. We run from the sea and sprawl on the soft sand to dry in the sun; it makes you think you could live here in peacetime. Can see quite a lot of small islands way out. Back in the camp area hundreds more POW's are coming in, some are said to be Canadians. The Red Cross ship is unloading boots, they are badly needed.

* * *

Burial of one of my Battalion, a soldier with thirteen years service and his life ended by dysentery. I made a cross of flowers and made up a card with the simple words "Soldier Rest".

Late in the night another draft of men arrive from Java, our share to feed is 100 men and five officers. They are staying long enough to receive warm clothing before they travel to a land of frost and snow, I think it must be the northern island of Japan. Tomorrow all the 11th Division are having a medical inspection prior to going off to Japan. Many of my own Division, the 18th, are going up country to work on the Burma railway.

14. On this day... October 23, 1942... Battle of El Alamain begins allied offensive in North Africa.

Saturday October 24th

I have had five burials today with much ceremony, they were from the Royal Army Medical Corp, Royal Engineers, Light Ack-Ack, a Dutchman and a Gordon Highlander preceded all the way from the hospital by two men of his Battalion playing the bagpipes. Fifty-two men told to stand by to join the up country party, because of the job I'm doing I still remain exempt.

Sunday October 25th

The day is another wet one. There's not much to do except listen to the men telling stories about their home life and the main topic is what food they ate. I am thinking that a year ago today was my last Sunday in England and wondering when my next one will be.

Monday October 26th

Men from all camp areas moving away all day. Others being medically examined. Three of my cemetery gardeners and three grave diggers are taken to join the up country party. It makes me a bit short-handed, still with so many leaving there should not be so many to bury. In our hospital there are 1500 chronic sick and 2,000 with minor sickness, the chances of many are small while we have little or nothing to treat them with.

The Royal Engineers who run the cemetery office are off up country today. More Java men move out to Japan, we are thinning out a bit.

Tuesday October 27th

It's the rainy period now and we are getting tons of rain, not very nice moving about, as the slight drop in temperature makes us feel cool. Many more wet and dishevelled Dutch arrive from Java, at the moment it is a ceaseless shunting around of men. Buried a Dutch Major this afternoon and a Dutch Padre officiated. It is the third Dutchman I have buried now.

Wednesday October 28th

My men left with a large company of others. They went off singing, waving and cheering, God knows what for as they are weak and hungry and knowing that the immediate future holds nothing good for them. As for myself I feel a bit dejected and lonely after it all quietened down, seven of the men working with me on the cemetery have gone, they had been with me eight months and it is quite a wrench to lose them.

Thursday October 29th

The weather at the moment is cloudy and after the heavy rains everywhere steams and I am completely bathed in perspiration. This all helps to make me rather depressed and homesick. The "Stagamine" (footballer mosquito), black and white stripes, are having a heyday in this humidity. If one is unlucky it could mean dengue fever from their bites.

Friday October 30th

The week has gone by with only nine burials. I have just been told that I must not cut any more turf from the playing field. These are orders from the "Nip" Command. This is rather disappointing for we only need about 150 turves to complete a section. We talk this over and my men want to take a chance tomorrow to cut what we need.

Saturday October 31st

The day and time for action is with us so we cross the road, cut and transport a load to the cemetery, on our way back with a second one we hear shouting and looking to where it was coming from we see a man emerging from a wooded area, he was shouting and waving his arms. We were just about to cross a bridge over a monsoon drain when he reached us, he was it seemed very angry, first pointing to our load of turf and then at us. He was a "Nip" Sergeant Major, this we knew as he trailed a sword at his side much too big for him. He jumped and shouted, we stood still not understanding a word, then he drew his sword swinging it around his head. We stood rooted to the spot, for one moment I wish I was not wearing a Sergeant's stripe. I had heard of "Lollie Lopping" and thought this was it, down came the sword right through, not my neck but the tyre and tube of our handcart wheel. While we gazed in stunned silence he sheathed his sword, grunted and strode off. The men, four of them returned to life, but feeling a bit weak at the knees at the passing of the horrific two minutes. We managed to get the turf to the cemetery and finish the job, still wondering if the risk we had taken was worth it, we thought so, and returned to camp satisfied at our days work but minus a handcart for a time.

Sunday November 1st 1942

Units of men still leaving for up country tours, in most cases mystery ones with no return. I am busy collecting some flowers and greenery to make a wreath for my Company, for tomorrows Remembrance Service, for all those who have died in this campaign and in the POW camp since its end.

Monday November 2nd

The wreath is finished and placed in the church. I attended the service. An officer has been sent to carry the pass flag. He speaks like a "Yank" looks and walks like a farmer and is very noisy. What is left of the 1st and 2nd Cambridgeshires moved away today.

Three more burials, two of these are more tragic than usual; one was a suicide, the other a father, whose son was at his funeral. The third is a Lt Colonel from the Dutch, the first officer to be buried in the Dutch section now in use.

Tuesday November 3rd

A day or two passes by just mainly clearing ground and turfing over and around graves, however, it is not long before something different comes along. My men have just dug up a member of the Royal Engineers who died on the march in. According to his chums he drank too much whisky and died of heart failure. He was a big fellow and they had slid a six by two foot sheet of tin under him, then lifted him with his boots still on, onto the handcart and brought him to the cemetery, where I had a grave enlarged to take the body and the sheet of tin he was on. We had a difficult job to get him off the cart, with ropes under each end we manage to get the corpse over the grave and started to lower it down when a rope broke. One end dropped suddenly and one boot went up into the air and fell back into the grave, we all felt rather upset over this but soon regained our composure as we filled in the grave.

Wednesday November 4th

At breakfast today 2ozs of rice polishings are issued per man. This is the skin off the rice which in the box looks like a heaving mass of bran because it is riddled with weevil maggots. We are told to put the polishings in a mug with a little water and drink it down. A lot of men cannot face the little maggots so I get three rations of this so-called source of vitamin B and feel like a little pig wallowing in a trough. My stomach is strong and I mean to do my utmost to keep alive.

Tonight is an enforced blackout, no lights at all are to be allowed but we are treated to searchlight display by the "Nips". Many more Dutch and American POW's arrived earlier.

15. On this day... November 4, 1942... Rommel's army in North Africa in full retreat.

Thursday November 5th

I now have only one regular cemetery gardener left and two gravediggers so I am back digging and helping with the burials. It's pouring with rain and I have a Dutch burial and the Padre borrows my hat to keep the rain off his Bible. The blackout has continued for a second night and it is still very wet, November being our wet season.

Friday November 6th

It's breakfast with rice pap again. Quite a bit of talking and activity as 400 Royal Army Medical Corps men and 20 doctors are about to leave for up country duties. We can ill afford to lose these men with such a large hospital of sick and disabled.

Breakfast over we line up for a hat and boot inspection, prior to drawing Red Cross items. Hats are really khaki trilbies. We have had no more issues of food or cigarettes since the ship arrived some weeks ago.

Saturday November 7th

Have had four burials today, mainly Dutch. I have been promised a work party from the Dutch for Monday. At the moment I am kept busy filling in and shaping the mounds. I have, also today, turfed over my next door neighbour's grave. Another day is completed as we march back to camp, we always march as it gives us some self respect, especially if we pass any "Nips".

Tea over we sit and talk for a few hours and then to bed free from mosquitoes now, thanks to the net. Bed bugs for some unknown reason don't bite me anymore but if I disturb them when I move they give off a horrible smell. I have a cushion I use for a pillow and I never fail to find young and old bugs in all four corners most mornings.

Monday November 9th

The day brings an order to move to another part of the camp area. We are sorry to leave our present quarters, after six months have got used to them having made them as comfortable as we possibly could with salvaged bits and pieces.

Four burials today, nine for the week bringing in total in this British and Dutch cemetery to 400. I am sorting out the Dutch work party, only five have turned up as others objected to working on such a morbid place. Only two have boots, the others in their bare feet. They have no discipline and in the main only a year's service with the forces, two of them are black boys. Rumours of another 6,000 needed for the trip to Japan. A party of Royal Engineers have arrived, they are to construct a lych gate at the entrance.

Wednesday November 11ᵗʰ

It is Armistice Day and we held a two minute silence before we started work. Eleven Dutchmen turned up today so the others must have told them it was not so bad working here.

I am spending tonight in new quarters, they are lousy with bugs and the men are really at it hunting them out. Some of us search around to find water for a wash, it is very scarce here. How glad I will be when the lads that are fighting this war get to us. At the moment I am more fed up than I have ever been. Maybe it because so many men that I knew have moved on, working in the mid-day heat doesn't help. The scorching heat absolutely saps you, the natives not under "Nip" rule squat under the trees. Our theatre into which the artistes have put so much work is being taken over by the Command Officers. The top floor is to be used as an officers' dysentery wing. Our church also is now in the Command area.

Friday November 13ᵗʰ

Burials have been heavy this week, so far they number 17. One was Stoker Vann from the ill-fated *HMS Prince of Wales*, sunk by the "Nips" just before I arrived in Singapore.

Saturday November 14ᵗʰ

Owing to shortage of staff and an interfering officer we have no open graves in hand and with so many men dying the few of us have to work hard digging down six feet. The clay-type soil refusing at times to leave the spade when thrown up, it's at times like this that the equatorial sun really knocks you out. Twenty-two British and Dutch buried this week.

We now have to parade for roll call, morning and evening fully dressed. This means wearing one's only shirt.

Sunday November 15th

Someone appears to have gone mad around here as physical training has been ordered before breakfast and drill once a week. Most of us already work from 10 until 5 o' clock, on two handfuls of rice. Apart from the rumours we know nothing of what's going on in other parts of the world and what is the truth about Russia, Libya and the Far East.

Monday November 16th

Heavy rain showers and I have had four Dutch burials this afternoon. The high death rate now causes me some concern as we only manage to keep graves just ahead of them. On the way back to camp I was almost run down by a car driven by a grinning "Nip" officer. I called him some harsh things, but under my breath.

Talking with the men at night it seems that the majority of us now dream nightly and mainly about home and family, these dreams to us are as a mirage to a thirsty man in the desert.

* * *

Five more Dutch burials, three of them with one service, which is just as well because of the smell and hundreds of flies. No more Dutch graves left open, the men will have to graft to keep up. There is no more labour to be had for the cemetery although they can manage to find 60 men to move fittings from the old concert hall.

One of my Sergeants and staff were caught and charged because they were after mangoes, the trees now being in the area taken over by our Command Officers.

Friday November 20th

Our recent move to other quarters seems a bad one, it appears to be a vast breeding place for the dysentery carrying fly.

No burials, a clear day for once gives us a chance to get ahead, especially as they have now let me have four more men. As they come from the Northumberland Fusiliers it is hard to understand their accent at times. My only socks are now showing signs of wear so I try to work without them but had skinned toes inside of fifteen minutes and that finished me grave digging for the day, having to find a lighter job.

It has been announced that Major General Beckworth Smith has died on his way to Formosa from heart failure brought on by diphtheria. His death occurred on November 11th 1942, just nine days ago. I feel sad about it as with the cemetery we had something in common. The new men, the Fusiliers, tell me that like myself they were Territorials, also they were at Dunkirk and now, very unlucky to get caught up here. Cemetery again photographed by a "Nip" officer. I was well within shot, it would be nice to have a photo, but no such luck. First section is now completed, each grave carrying a cross bearing name and Regiment. These have been made by the Royal Engineers and all the section has been turfed over by us. Sixteen buried this week but deaths lower the last few days.

Sunday November 22nd

Today we entertained some American soldiers to dinner. Our band, "The Nitwits", performed, they included Geraldo's first cornet and Dennis East, first violinist to the London Philharmonic Orchestra. He, also, before the war broadcast with his own

**The Changi lych-gate at the entrance to the cemetery,
Built by members of the Royal Engineers (18th Division)**

quartet. Later I attended a memorial service to the late Major General Beckworth Smith.

Monday November 23ʳᵈ

Today, I remember is my eldest sister's birthday, "Many Happy Returns" to her.

I have been sent a lot of half-caste Dutch to work on clearing land for the cemetery. They don't appear to get on too well with their white brothers, who admit that the others have had a better education and were allowed to go to school till the age of 21 years, they certainly speak very good English.

A wag has just come in saying that aircraft are only allowed to fly over England four days a week so as to give some time for the sun to shine on the crops.

Wednesday November 25ᵗʰ

Dutch technicians standing by for move to Japan, they have just had a medical inspection, some more of our men may be going with them. Rumour has it that mail and Red Cross parcels may be coming to us, but its all been heard before.

A fight broke out between my Javanese Dutch today. Quite lively for a time but soon settled. We are turfing as heavy rain prevails.

Thursday November 26ᵗʰ

A full account of the burial of Maj Gen Beckworth-Smith in *"Syonian Times"*, cremated, four senior ranks as pall bearers, mention of Brigadier Backhouse, General Wainwright (USA), also 100 Nipponese attended and laid a wreath, buried in Formosa.

Friday November 27th

Petty things happen in this camp such as some men of the Royal Northumberland Fusiliers fined from 10 to 20 cents for being late on dinner parade, this fine has to come from their very small amenity grant. Rumour is rife that another Red Cross ship in dock, but I can only hope it's true as the food is getting bad and scarce. Only six buried this week.

Saturday November 28th

Some 1,000 of the Java men left today for Japan. Another "Nip" roll call. Later I was told by an officer that the cemetery was the most unique among war cemeteries, so unconventional is its layout. Concert parties are gaining ground, each area of men putting on their own shows and invitations are sent out so we can watch them. The hospital area has a good hall going, it is called the "Changi Palladium".

Sunday November 29th

A Red Cross ship and three repatriation boats have arrived, what wishful thinking. Another "Nip" roll call, also managed to buy 1lb of peanuts and 1lb oranges with my amenity grant, something to flavour the rice with for a few nights. In the tea queue heard that 50 Cambridgeshires working in Bangkok during an air attack by allied planes were bombed. Still strong reports of more Red Cross parcels and that the "Nips" have signed the Hague convention, for what I wonder.

Monday November 30th

I am as full of pimples as I was at the age of 18, although I am in fairly good health, working hard and doing a worthwhile job, even if it is so terribly hot, it seems to make life more interesting and does not give me time to worry. With the help of my staff I erected a tent from palm fronds to give us a bit of shade from the sun while eating our midday rice. The lads call it "Bertram Mills Freak Show of Humanity". Well I suppose we do look a bit freakish with elbow and knee joints trying to get through the skin, coupled with rice bellies.

Tuesday December 1st 1942

Going to work today I feel very weak, with my leg muscles giving way through lack of vitamins. Buried a Dutchman who fell from a trailer and was killed. The weather is exceedingly hot and I am completely bathed in sweat. Nine senior British Officers have to go to Changi jail to congratulate Lieutenant General Fukuye on his promotion and Lt General Heath left with a Dutch party for Japan.

Saturday December 5th

The rumour about the Red Cross ship on Monday appears to be false. As yet nothing has come our way although we still keep hoping. All the earlier stores are just about used up. The officers attending yesterdays' Japanese Commanders celebrations were congratulated on their part in running the camps, he told them that he would soon be leaving and another coming to replace him. He did not think we would be prisoners much longer. Why? Are they winning the war or will they kill us all?

Sunday December 6th

It's St Nicholas Day and the Dutch appear to be celebrating Xmas. They have arranged sports but unfortunately it is teeming with rain, as it has been during the past two days. The wet November produced 14 inches of rain.

Monday December 7th

Another day comes in with rain still pouring down, the huge monsoon drains are flooded and if I was in England with rain like this I should feel I was about to drown. The "Nips" call for a roll call and when we get to the area they did not want us. I think the little brown devils delighted in getting us wet, later they routed us out of church and we finished up with a complete blackout. Still tons of rain falling and we feel cooler at night.

Tuesday December 8th

It's the 8th anniversary of the "Greater East Asia War" and the "Nips" have a roll call to let us know. There is to be a count up tomorrow of all Dutch in the camp so we have to take over all the work duties. Still no sign of a Red Cross ship so it looks like a rice and rice Christmas. I have forgotten the day of the week and on enquiring I find that I have got two days behind, at the moment the days are so much alike with the rain just pouring down night and day. Only turned out for burials, a good job that we have graves in hand again. My boots are saturated, I take them off and pour out the water. Turn into bed early as we are fed up with sitting around.

Thursday December 10th

Morning brings the same incessant rain, all through the day it falls in sheets, I have never seen such rain, everywhere is flooded and streams rush down the slopes ending in miniature waterfalls. It is said that such continuous rains have never been experienced in Singapore.

Friday December 11th

At last a day dawns with a sunrise and as the hours went by everywhere steamed, the humidity is terrible. Our open graves are full of water and a burial is due so we start to bail out. We could not get lower than two feet as water rushed in from the sides. Bailing continued until it was time to lower the corpse, it floated and was soon at the top, it was wrapped in a white sheet and almost sitting up. The officer in charge of the escort party had gone to the hut to sign the register and rather than have the poor fellows watch us trying to cope I turned them about. We have to hold the body down with a pole while we fill in.

Saturday December 12th

I learn a bit more Malay and a few words of Dutch. A Nipponese lady journalist called at the officers' mess and asked for "Charlie", this seemed to cause a bit of embarrassment but we never found out what it was about. It is very strongly rumoured that mail has arrived also this ghostly ship in again, I wonder which of the two is true, maybe we shall have fowl for Christmas. Over the last three nights I have passed my time away by going on lectures on music and politics.

Sunday December 13th

At last it's happened, some letters have arrived but are said to be a year old. It is just a year since we left Cape Town, so we must have missed these letters. As it is Sunday I go to the Free Church where I heard a very good and wise service delivered by the Rev. Foster-Hauge.

Monday December 14th

Back to work and still bailing water from the graves. A Gordon Highlander buried during a heavy rainstorm and because of water a similar burial to the last.

Attended a lecture this evening on the welfare of mothers and children. Learned of a husband's duty to a pregnant wife, her troubles and pains at birth, spoiling of a child and other things appertaining to life. We should be quite knowledgeable chaps if we survive.

Tuesday December 15th

Another day of rain and no work done on the cemetery, the men spend their time debugging beds. Have just heard that we have a new Nippon Commander who called for a parade of all men, and then just as quickly cancelled it. Went to a music lecture given by Signaller Renison of Wigmore and Albert Hall fame, he is a great pianist.

Wednesday December 16th

As I pass out of the camp to work this morning a party of Royal Engineers are erecting a big archway of coco-nut palms over the entrance as the "Nips" want it to look nice. I was invited by the Sergeant-in-charge to look over the Australian cemetery, only 78 graves but then their force is not as large as ours. The Sergeant tells me he is a Londoner, fought in France in the First World War, later emigrated and now with the Australian forces and caught up with us in Singapore. Our total burials have reached the figure of 437. Another lecture, well it's somewhere to go, it is on "The Progress of War" and Hitler's part in it 1941-42.

Thursday December 17th

Morning brings an order to turn out for parade and to look our best. We have to line the road for a drive past of the new "Nip" Commandant. For once it's a fine morning and what a relief for he kept us waiting, standing most of the time for the three and a half hours. Some of the men were so weak that they kept falling down, they were suffering from severe 'flu-type colds and now I've managed to get one even though I've tried my hardest to keep clear, but to no avail.

Friday December 18th

Burial of Argyle and Southerland Highlander preceded by wail of the bagpipes. I feel very ill and after filling in of the grave is completed I make for camp and bed after pressing a medical orderly for help, he got me two aspirins also two quinine tablets. I think dengue fever has struck me down again.

Saturday December 19th

This morning comes and I do not feel as bad as I expected to, although pretty low, I manage to get to the cemetery. We have completed the turfing of banks left by the levelling of the slope and planted a terrace on "Controversy Hill" with shrubs salvaged from the gardens of bombed houses.

A Sergeant in the Dutch clearing party invited me to supper the other day, he had caught and killed a dog. I declined the invitation, I would have to be very hungry, in fact getting no rice at all, before I could stoop so low as to eat a friend. The next day the Sergeant did not turn up for work, and on enquiring as to his whereabouts his friends tell me that their officers have put him in prison for eating the dog.

Sunday December 20th

Sparrows have been flying in and out of my bunk house, they must be hunting for bugs, there's nothing else. They seem to be with us from the time we left home, like us they can live anywhere. Our band of odd instruments are striving to install some Christmas spirit by playing carols around the area. I lay back closing my eyes and listening, soon my imagination builds up a picture of England in snow and cold wind frosts instead of a constant tropical sun beating down. Tomorrow I move house again, getting like musical chairs.

Monday December 21st

The new quarters are our officers' old ones, they have electric light. This is really a miracle to us after burning a length of string in diesel oil and smoking ourselves like kippers. Our one day a week meat issue is to finish so it will be all rice and a few greens now. Went to have a look at our old church which our Command took over, they have constructed a beautiful high altar. I had a talk with Padre Sandy who was a Methodist missionary. Have heard that my Battalion is coming back from work duties in Singapore on Sunday.

Thursday December 24th

It's Christmas Eve and the boys are singing carols as they did a year ago on the ship heading for Mombassa. This is our second festive season abroad and the strongest drink is milkless cocoa. Divisional HQ has come up with two Victory V cigarettes for each man, which is certainly a great surprise, although when I think of our good times at home I feel very homesick.

Friday December 25th

Christmas Day is with us and we hold a service on the cemetery where 37 wreaths were made and laid by the area Signal Corp. "A Happy Xmas" to you all at home. I have made a large cross of orange and yellow flowers and placed on my next door neighbour's grave. The rest of the day is spent making our own fun, NCO's fetched the men's rice from the cookhouse on a handcart with our band leading. Later went to an open-air concert followed by community singing.

Saturday December 26th

Boxing Day and work. About 700 men visited the cemetery yesterday and around 100 wreaths had been made by the men.

Two funerals with large followings from the RASC and RAMC.

I have not yet said what my Christmas dinner consisted of, well it was a rice pastry pie containing bully beef, a vegetable pie and a maize flour sweet. Not at all bad.

Sunday December 27th

The Battalion as I stated earlier have now arrived back, eight months away have changed the men's looks, haggard and thin and because of their arrival I have to move once again to another room. Am I browned off, four moves in seven days. Water situation is still very bad here and we have to rely on a rain to get a good bath - the ritual dance of the nudes!

Monday December 28th

Six hundred Dutch have moved out today and a lone British soldier was seen coming into camp with a "Nip" guard carrying some of his kit, a little good in some of them it appears. A "Nip" patrol did not like us cutting turf so far away from the cemetery permit flag and made us return to it. We lay off the turf for the day hoping to return tomorrow when things quieten down.

* * *

Camp Commandant calls for roll calls on the gun park from now on and we have to march twice the distance to it because the officers of the Royal Army Medical Corps object to us going past their mess. The men just back from Singapore seemed to have had a good time food-wise. The CO told them that he did not mind them pinching stuff but he did not want it to appear that they were about to stock up a store. Some flour and currants brought back by one of the men was mixed in cakes and cooked on an outside fire but they set like concrete as the flour turned out to be plaster of paris, luckily there were no broken teeth!

Thursday December 31st

The "Nips" have been kind as they have given us a New Year's present of two tins of pineapple between seven and one bottle of brandy between ten of us. As it is New Year's Eve the Scots near by are making merry with song but nothing to quench a thirst. I feel restless as I send a thought transmission across the world to my wife and family wishing them a "Happy New Year", and may it be a happy one for all of us here.

CHAPTER 6

A LETTER FROM HOME

Friday January 1ˢᵗ 1943

It's the beginning of the New Year and with it a lecture from our CO, in which he told us we had better pray for a Red Cross food ship as things were getting bad. He said that lice had now got with us and that they were carriers of typhoid fever, what a horrible thought. More men have arrived, perhaps from Java as the Dutch Army Commander is among them, also one of our men who was with a party that tried to escape, and it is said that he is the only one left alive.

Monday January 4ᵗʰ

Went to "Ko-Ko Nut Grove" concert last night, quite a good show. "Slogger" Haines, a big fellow with a huge leopard tattooed on his stomach (now a rice belly) brought the leopard alive as it wobbled up and down with his movements.

This morning I find myself on a Nippon medical inspection, they are looking for diphtheria germ carriers, but after a long wait we are dismissed as the doctor failed to turn up. The Governor of Java and the Dutch Army Command visited the cemetery.

Tuesday January 5ᵗʰ

Before I left for work this morning I had to join in a PT parade, our officers are still full of red tape, my rice pap breakfast will not stand up to that and work. Visited 40 graves found in an overgrown scrub area among which is a Nurse Sugden, killed in an air raid, we would like to bring her body into the cemetery, also the others in due course but owing to the heavy rains the area is a bit water-logged so will have to leave it for now. Had another visit from the Governor of Java, who is very taken by the Dutch Section.

This evening I go to a concert in our own hall known as the "Changi Palladium". The bill was topped with Courtinnies Magical Eye, he is a top class illusionist. It is very surprising the extent of talent in our midst.

Thursday January 7ᵗʰ

This morning we followed a Javanese party on medical inspection to have our delayed throat diphtheria check. Had a visit to the cemetery of four Dutch Major Generals, who all shook hands with me and added their thanks. One said he had an English name, Maj. Gen. Cox. They thought they would like a plaque put down sometime, but would think it over.

Friday January 8ᵗʰ

Receiving another visit from the higher realms, this time from Air Vice Marshal Maltby. He tells me that he lost his son in the battle of Singapore and asked us to keep a lookout for his grave if we do any work that way.

The Dutch lads with me have told us that they are leaving on Sunday. I am sorry to lose them, for as we got used to each other we got along well. I have received congratulations from many more departing officers today and they hope I will stay with the cemetery.

Sunday January 10ᵗʰ

A new party of workers for clearing ahead of us started this morning and a goodbye visit from those leaving. An officer, Lt Adams, Royal Indian Army Corp, was re-interred today, more to follow. For tea I had a surprise, it was a shark steak, never thought I would be eating this. I wondered how many humans it might have eaten, anyhow I would not mind if it came up more often. Church tonight for some reason was over-crowded, perhaps thanksgiving for the shark tea.

Monday January 11th

Weather has turned very hot and dry which has put a stop to the turfing of graves. We started to exhume another body but came to water and had to give up.

Later I went to a concert party by the 18th Division men, their band "The Nitwits" was quite good. In bed tonight I wonder what is going on in the outside world, rumours are all we hear. I wonder if they know of the squalor we live in, the long lines of men looking haggard and thin, like poles with clothes on, many with not much life left in them.

Tuesday January 12th

Physical training again this morning but no vitamin foods to replace lost energies. Rice is about all we get now so we are still praying for that food ship to arrive.

Wednesday January 13th

Anniversary of my landing in Singapore, perhaps hopefully by the next one we will be free. I think however, that those of us lucky enough to survive will look some awful wretches, come what will we must carry on, so today I have been laying paving stones on the floor of the lych-gate. This gate is a large four post teak shelter, with teak tiles, it has two bench seats inside and just under the roof on all sides are quotations from the bible including the emblems of each country of the UK, all done by a wood carver. All the construction was done by the Royal Engineers and it is a very professional job. These same people are going to supply me with road gutters so I can lay drains on either side of the cemetery main drive.

Tonight I saw my own Battalions concert party, "Jack and the Beanstalk", which was with an up to date script and very good.

Thursday January 14th

Letters are at last coming in but not for me as yet. I don't know which I want most letters or a food ship, one will boost my morale and the other will comfort my stomach as we get very hungry, anyway a letter from my dear wife would raise me above despair. A Sergeant Major received a letter stating in a roundabout way that Norwich had been heavily bombed, which made me wonder if one of my sisters was still working up there. A few more letters filter in some with bad news, deaths at home, some wives in trouble and so on.

Friday January 15th

Re-interred a soldier from an Ack-Ack battery. Weather is still very dry and for my turfing work I need a rain. Passed the evening at a "Brains Trust" meeting.

Sunday January 17th

This morning I went to Holy Communion at our church, St Edmunds, many in attendance. I was also at the evening service, which had a queue resembling one at the second house of the London Empire, they actually pushed to get in. I wonder when on their knees in prayer what are they asking for, there are so many needs, the main of course is food, the right sort could answer all our prayers.

Monday January 18th

Letters still slowly filtering through, I have hopes that one has been posted in Sheringham, my home town. One man has received four and hands some round for us to read.

Played in a darts match on a board made up in the "Nip" workshop by a chum of mine, he also made the darts and our team won four to two.

Tuesday January 19th

On the cemetery I am supervising the construction of a monsoon drain along the front, these are at least three feet deep with sloping sides, large paving slabs are used for this work.

I am still taking the issue of rice polishings, closing up my eyes and drinking down its lively little maggots, well they say it's a source of vitamin B and also for A. I manage a drop of red palm oil occasionally; they must help to keep the skin on my bones. Played darts again and won, then I go off to a lecture on "How to keep alive", given by our medical officer. Two ounces of "kicking" rice polishings a day seemed to have been his main point. Read another letter received by one of my roommates and it is evident that up to June 27th 1942 his wife had heard nothing of him.

* * *

Party of Australians leave for up country. It is said that a railway is being constructed in Burma, and apparently that is where men in the past have been sent and are still going. Two burials this week, one a Dutch suicide. Have had a new handcart body fitted to our Austin Seven wheels and with the inscription, *"British Military Cemetery - Changi"*. More Dutch have left the camp.

Saturday January 23rd

My wife's 21st birthday. What a time to celebrate it, all the thousands of miles of conflict between us both. It is also a year to the day of my baptism of fire, so this date gives me plenty to ponder on, which is just as well as we have been kept inside our own buildings the whole day, we are not allowed to look upon a Japanese Royal personage who is touring the area.

16. **On this day...** January 23, 1943... Tripoli occupied by the 8th Army.

Sunday January 24th

This morning attended Communion, later watched an Australian side beat an English team at cricket by 27 runs. Barnet, an "Aussie" test team player captained their side and J Edrich of England for us, he made the highest score of 47 runs. Church again in the evening, congregation larger than ever, not an inch of room, this must be a clergyman's dream.

Monday January 25th

Slight rain has fallen, I am still laying drains on the cemetery, there is a lull in burials. Went to a dental inspection by our own Dental Officer who is still with us. Three burials and a re-interment of a Royal Artillery man brought in from a scrub area outside the camp. TAB inoculations started. Went to a lecture on "The progress of work in Singapore 1930-41". Another Dutch party in and some move out.

* * *

The weather is very hot and dry the longest drought since I have been here, making grave digging very hard work and a serious lack of water for personal use.

Saturday January 30th

Out of curiosity I went to the so-called "Changi Races", it turned out to be a bit of fun, the lads had made large cut outs of horses which they sitting astride raced. They had a totaliser so I bet a few cents but was unlucky.

Yesterday I had my TAB jab and I am just feeling the effects, a rotten headache, painful arm and tiredness so I am relieved to get to bed and sleep it off.

*17. **On this day…** January 31, 1943… Battle for Stalingrad over.*

Monday February 1st 1943

Morning brings very heavy rain, breaking the drought and giving us the chance to do a nudity dance in it, at least we feel clean and very refreshed. It's still raining heavily so roll call has been cancelled, we set around before bed and talk of rumours, home and the usual food.

Tuesday February 2nd

Extra sick men are being sent to work on the gardens which can only do good by producing a bit extra in the way of vegetables. The "Controversy Hill" section on the cemetery is now completed, one terrace a grass walk, the other planted with shrubs and the top is a grass flat.

Received notice of "Nip" medical inspection, dysentery tests and second TAB inoculation, what prospects!

* * *

Weather is hot and dry again but still no roll call. After breakfast of watery rice I parade for medical inspection. On reaching a table, at which a "Nip" doctor and two orderlies are in attendance, I am told to drop my shorts and bend down, then a short glass rod is jabbed up my behind causing me to take a step forward, much to the amusement of the boys watching. Later I also saw the funny side and we quickly called the inspection "The Order of the Glass Rod". Following this I got my TAB injection painfully in the muscle, this over off to work in the cemetery. It's been a very low week for deaths, have had only one burial, it's really good news.

More Dutchmen moving out, but with so many constantly coming over from Sumatra and Java our numbers don't thin very much.

Tonight I feel more depressed with my rice and vegetable tea than usual, roll on the end of the war and lets have some bully beef and biscuits.

An internal Command order that men of the 18th Division are to stop using St Edmunds church, this has caused a lot of bitter argument as we made the church what it is. A battle royal later ensued between our officers and those of Command still with us; the outcome finally leaves us in occupation.

Shaving has now become a problem, going back to the days I spent in Cape Town I guarded against this possibility by buying 200 razor blades only later to see my pack containing them blown up as mentioned earlier, during an air raid. With the help of an old stone type "Marmite" jar used as a sharpener I still use the seven blades found earlier. I religiously used these blades for a year ending in tearing scrapes and sore skin, in the end I had to throw them away. Now I try out a table knife which well sharpened does a fair job.

Thirty men have been chosen and taken off to Singapore to take part in a Nipponese film. Rain has come again and as usual we are glad of it. The new drains I have put in on the cemetery work well but not much else going on here at the moment because of the wet weather. I have been asked to give a talk on how to construct a small garden, felt rather nervous when I got on the stage, but need not have been as it went off well enough. I was asked to give another talk at a later date on flowers, colour and schemes for bedding work.

Wednesday February 10th

I awoke this morning to the sound of a bugle at 6.30am, so unusual was the sound after so many months I thought I must be dreaming, but as I gathered my thoughts I realised the bugler was sounding "Reveille". Why? I ask myself and a half an hour earlier than we normally arise. Word goes around that breakfast is ready and as we collect it we are told that everyone in the camp areas have to parade at 8am, that means around 15,000 of us. It's raining cats and dogs, but amid a bit of excitement and the wildest of rumours we make for the parade ground, a motley looking lot already half soaked, the few lucky enough to own capes are enjoying the comfort of them. After waiting half an hour the parade is postponed with no reason given, more bedraggled than ever we trudge back to our quarters, get off the wet clothes and get on the beds and under such bits and pieces of covering as we have. Feeling a bit chilled and depressed no one is saying much so the place takes on the look of a large mortuary, all we know is that we have to stand by, only in our present positions it's a lay by. The day passes with the rain never letting up and no parade being called, someone must have enjoyed watching us get soaked. After tea and having roughly dried out, a few of us make for the "Ko-Ko Nut Grove" concert hut where five (male) girls put on a great dancing show which puts us in a better frame of mind, we laugh and joke about the nice "girls" as we make for home and bed.

Thursday February 11th

The morning comes with sheets of rain falling and still no parade, most of the men are still on their beds, so we have become known as the union of spine bashers. In my room I call them the silent six, among which there's "Horizontal George", "Unconscious Charlie", "Somnolent Sutton" and "Tired Mitch". Saw another play called "Journeys End" it was very good, we certainly have some good actors among us.

* * *

It has rained all night, but now it's left off in time for the parade called for by the Japanese Command. We make our way to the padang (sports field) and eventually 15,000 of us are lined up, all ready for the 9.30am review only to told half an hour later it is called off once again, but we are to stand by, the weather is hot and steamy so we just sit around waiting, discussing mainly as to what this long awaited parade could be about. I'll not write down the ideas that were put around, as they were so many and fanciful. It's 11.30 and we are told that the gathering of the clans is now definitely at 12.15, and we are to be there dressed in our best bits and pieces. A Nipponese film crew arrived, they take photographs and movie films, it must be for some propaganda film that they are doing. During the day more Dutch arrive from Java, also some British RAF and RA men.

Sunday February 14th

I went to early service and then spent the rest of the day lazing around and walking through the Flame of the Forest trees that were formerly planted over a large area of the camp, their long racemes of flowers hanging down below the fern-like leaves gives out a feeling of relaxation.

Monday February 15th

It's the first anniversary of the capitulation. How many more months or years I ask myself, many men failed to make the first year and in our present state of health who knows how many more will die. Saw the first woman for eleven months, goggle-eyed we stood and looked as she, a rather pretty Japanese, actually waved to us as she passed by with a party of "Nips". She became the sole topic of conversation for the next hour.

* * *

The Australians held a memorial service in their cemetery today and our lads wonder why our officers had not done so. Later we are all inoculated against dysentery, it is said that the "Nips" are worried about it possibly spreading to them. I have just been told that one of the recent RAF. arrivals is a close neighbour of mine at home, I am hoping to meet him. Have buried two Dutch today.

Our food is getting bad and I am absolutely fed up with the constant plain rice three times a day, when will they send us another Red Cross ship? It is six months since the one and only came in.

Saw a play this evening "Badgers Green" excellently produced, it was enjoyed by all. When a crowd gets together one hears so many rumours, some of which gives us hope and others make you think that we are going to waste away here for a further three years. I have seen my RAF neighbour, a Flight Sergeant Roydon Duffield, now nick-named "Bessie" because he played very well the part of a woman in a camp play in Java.

* * *

At the request of the Dutch Command I have constructed a suitable base and laid a memorial tablet inscribed by them, it was cut from a marble top of a wash basin stand and the letters cut by a stone mason among them. This they will unveil on the coming Sunday. Have just heard of another lad living only a stone's throw from me at home, has always been in this camp, he is Willie Fields and with the Royal Army Medical Corp, but as yet we have not met.

Saturday February 20th

The week goes by and I get the men to smarten up the area around the Dutch burial section as well as we can in readiness for the unveiling. Before tea I went to the "Changi Races", lost 50 cents but it was a bit of fun. Some wit was there dressed up and calling himself the "Mayor of Changi".

Memorial Plaque set up for the Dutch dead in Changi cemetary,
which I unveiled in the presence of three Dutch Brigadiers.
The plaque was made from a marble washstand top with the words engraved

Sunday February 21st

I am invited to attend the unveiling which is watched by 700 Dutch who have paraded for this moment, also British and Australian Command Officers and a few Americans. A Dutch Naval Officer made the speech in which I was thanked for my work and great help in preparing for this day, I certainly felt more than gratified.

The "Nips" have allowed us another card to send home, just 29 words, we do not know if our first cards have been received yet. It's quite a job for us to form a text to tell as much as we can, we have to be careful because of the censors, among the usual endearments I manage to say that I am okay, not wounded and waiting to receive letters.

My darts team, *"The Gravediggers"*, emblem crossed spades, played and won, we stand high in the camp league however our newly formed bridge team lost its game.

Wednesday February 24th

I awake this morning with my crutch itching and sore, it's tinea so I have to double my intake of rice polishings for its vitamin B. Get my second dysentery inoculation, which has made me rather dopey. At work my staff has been gradually increasing over the last few weeks, six more this morning bringing the total of diggers and scrub clearers to 45. Played darts again this evening and again won easily.

Thursday February 25th

Morning again finds me in a drugged state but my men are to start digging to exhume eight bodies buried in one grave so it's no rest for me. At one end of the cemetery the "Royal Engineers" have started to construct a small platform for the cremation of bodies

214

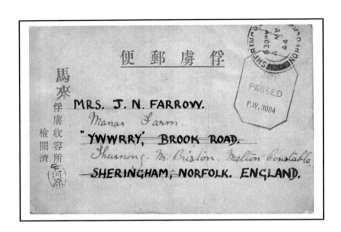

便 郵 虜 俘

馬來 俘虜收容所 檢閲濟

MRS. J. N. FARROW.
Manor Farm.
"YWWRRY", BROOK ROAD.
Sherning. Nr. Briston. Melton Constable
SHERINGHAM, NORFOLK. ENGLAND.

PASSED
P.W. 3084

5772439. SERGEANT. FARROW. J.N.   24/FEBRUARY/1943

DEAREST JOAN.

AM CHEERFUL, UNWOUNDED, ALWAYS THINKING

OF YOU.   NO LETTERS; HOPE YOU ALRIGHT.

LOVE MUM; DAD; ALL AT HOME. DONT WORRY.

LOVE Jack.

Postcard sent from Changi 24th February 1943

Copy of the Changi darts league 1943-44

as the "Nips" have ordered that all who die from dysentery must be cremated, also typhoid and some other victims. Have re-interred two bodies, more to follow tomorrow. Only one death this week, a Dutchman.

Our CO. spoke to the men tonight praising us for our state of fitness which he thinks we should strive to maintain for another year, also he stressed that all men should eat their rice polishings and any peanuts they can get.

Friday February 26th

A pair of shorts that I handed in for patching were returned today and a number of patches were put on but not sewn as we have no cotton, they were canvas bits from an old tent and stuck on with latex from the rubber trees. I look as though I have been badly punctured.

We have heard that the ATS are manning Britain's Ack-Ack guns, it makes me wonder what the wife and my sisters could be up to.

Saturday February 27th

This morning I awake knowing that I have quite a job on hand, the re-interment of ten bodies. The moment arrives with four Padres of different denominations officiating, a Gordon Highlander piped the "Flowers of the Forest" and the last post was sounded by a Corporal on a silver bugle. The bodies even after a year of being buried are in good condition. Nurse Sugden was also re-buried, a white cross is put on her grave.

Sunday February 28th

This morning I attend Holy Communion, the last time was some weeks ago. Spend part of the day repairing the cemetery hand cart and later go to evening service, twice in one day, I must be feeling low.

The grave of nurse Sugden (marked with a white cross) - the only woman to be buried in Changi cemetery

Monday March 1st 1943

Today's meals were as follows:

Breakfast - Rice pap and polishings (for who can stomach them). Half pint raw tea.

Dinner   - Plain rice, a chunk of rice with greens baked in it. Raw tea.

Tea-time - Rice, half mug thin green stew. Raw tea.

Wonder what they would think of the menu in the Ritz.

Tuesday March 2nd

The day starts again with rain, during the morning I saw a large liner enter the Straits, but I don't hold out any hope that it may be carrying cargo for us. The rain has given us the chance to start cutting turf from the Padang and convey it to the cemetery for covering up more of this red clay area.

Wednesday March 3rd

The crematorium is finished, it is not what I expected, just an iron gate fixed to four steel corner posts about three feet high, the body will be placed on the top and fired by wood underneath. It reminds me of mother grilling a fresh herring. Our observations and thoughts would appear callous to you at home but I'm afraid we grow harder as time goes by.

Plenty of plays and concerts now as each unit competes against the other. Saw a play this evening in which all the cast were high ranking.

Thursday March 4th

Cremation of the first body today. The wood for burning is in place, it is from green rubber trees and only so much is allowed with a little oil by the "Nips". Two and a half hours has been allowed for the cremation which began at 2 o'clock, but when we left for camp at 4.30 there was a strong smell of burning pork and it seems that the job had hardly started.

Friday March 5th

This morning I learn that more wood had to be begged from the "Nips" and that the burning took the best part of six hours. Must have been horrible for the lads concerned.

During the day I discover that I have two small patches of ringworm on my waistline, many of the men have huge patches of it.

Have had three burials this week but have not yet received the ashes from the cremation. After tea I borrow a cut throat razor from a friend and start on my first attempt to shave with one. By the time I had finished I had a few cuts and blood was running freely.

Sunday March 7th

By morning I had dreamed that I was on the beach at home shaving the wife with the same razor. Dreams of home are frequent and in many ways funny. Amazing news has just come in that 41 bags of mail have arrived at Changi jail. Will I get a letter this time? Other news not so good as 5,000 men stand by to move up country, 1400 from my Division, the 18th. They are due to move on Monday week, at the moment I am exempt from moving because of my work here, but appears that my men are to go. As I leave church this evening I hear that a further 1100 men are to join the move.

* * *

This morning brought with it 70 men for my use on the cemetery to get as much clearing and maintenance done before they leave, this goes on the next day when the number is increased to 80 but one must remember a lot of these men are sick and weak and it makes for a low turn over of work. The weather is thundery with storms, which often sound like distant battles at sea and always get us straining our ears and hoping but nothing ever comes of it.

The mail is still being sorted and I am still full of hope, also hope for some better food as I am developing spots all over with some ringworm and tinea. What a mess to be in, it's so demoralising. More letters have just arrived for my unit. A friend of mine from my hometown has just received one. Tonight I go to a concert put on as a farewell to the men leaving, also these men have just been inoculated against cholera.

Sunday March 14th

It's Sunday and I am resting, trying not to sweat, hoping it will help my skin complaints which persist in spreading, now to my face, forehead and legs. More mail arrives, one man gets five letters in three days, still none for me. Church this evening is overcrowded and the Padre ask men for addresses so that he can send souvenirs after this war is over.

Monday March 15th

Another inoculation and the "Order of the Glass Rod" (dysentery check) for men standing by for the move. I managed to get a consultation with the medical officer about my skin problems. I get two pints red palm oil from the canteen, this I am pleased about as I am told it's full of vitamin A, which is good for skin and eyes.

Much mail still coming in but I am still unlucky, one fellow from home learns that he has become a father. Lots of letters are bringing surprise news of births. One Australian has learned that his father has married the girl he left behind, another Sergeant receives a photo of his girlfriend and shows it to a Sergeant friend who recognised it as his wife and a sharp fight ensued. A close friend of mine gets four letters which I am privileged to read, the same friend has dreamed that I have also a baby born to me, which I know is impossible although a letter to a fellow living nearby at home contains the information that I am an uncle to a baby girl, so the dream was slightly true.

Over three weeks now the mail has been coming in but still nothing to give me that lift in life that I feel I now need.

The men are off up country today, Burma I expect. All my friends and all but two of my gravediggers are going. This does not help to cheer me up, also all my Territorial comrades are included in this big move, I have become a Changi pensioner. Tonight I am so browned off I could weep. In my state of mind my thoughts turn to home, to my family and my wife who I spent so many happy times with, it all seems so long ago, the days are so monotonous, the nights so long, the food is tiresome, when will it all end. The only good thing about the week is that there have been no burials. The weather has turned very hot, soaked with sweat down to my toes and the fellow I shared a razor with is gone so I am back to a sharpened table knife, to grow a beard would I think in this climate be horrible. One of the men has done a nice sketch of my neighbour's grave, which will be nice for his family if I can manage to get it home. Those that are left here find that they have to evacuate the buildings at night and sleep on the flat roofs or the ground as the place suddenly abounds with bugs, they no doubt miss the men they had been feeding on.

222

* * *

The officer responsible for overseeing the cemetery wants me to move to quarters nearer the place of work. I refused, but he insisted that I should go; I said that I would quit the job if he was so adamant as I was quite happy where I was with the two others of us that are left. Our present conditions are cleaner and healthier and the move would take us to a low swampy area and I said our health comes first. This little incident gets me an interview with my Colonel, he tells me that the Major says I am using the cemetery as a pistol to his head, but I am allowed to remain in my present quarters.

With all the shortage of food we still have "Tiger" the mess cat around, he annoys some of the men because his yowl resembles a baby's cry.

I am still without mail although letters still come in. I am trying a bit of sunbathing in the nude hoping it will help dry up my tinea, which is spreading over all of my un-sunburned body. The itch with this tinea is terrible, with all the will power in the world you cannot avoid scratching, in fact some men sleep with socks on their hands so they do not do themselves damage while they sleep. The men are sleeping out still as the bugs are well in procession, but a concerted drive is being made to kill some of them off today.

The weeks' end brings a sudden rise in deaths, five burials for me, two of which arrive in a terrific storm, the graves are full of water and my two men and I are also streaming with water and feeling cold while the Padre does his service.

Friday March 26ᵗʰ

Another day dawns with two more burials and one cremation.

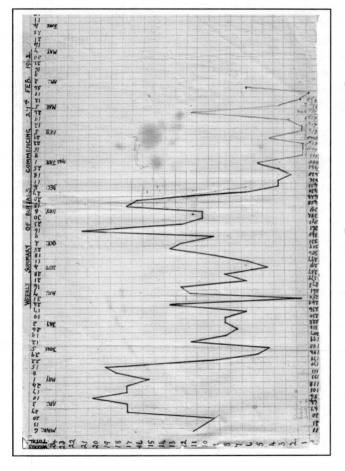

Weekly summary of burials 27th Feb 1942 to March 26th 1943

Saturday March 27th

I am getting a lot of tinea on my face also my legs or "Changi Crutch" as it is commonly known here, it is now in a discharging state.

Sunday March 28th

It is Sunday and I am spending my time trying to make myself a pair of shorts from an old khaki twill slop, they come out alright and the boys call them 'Cutie Pants', they really are cute.

Dawn comes quickly with a huge red sun, the first two hours of the mornings are really lovely, but on this one I feel rather miserable as my tinea is worse and I am reporting sick. After my half pint of rice pap for breakfast I go to the sick room where after an inspection by the medical officer I get a sharp ticking off for not going before. I have 30 ringworm spots and some nice "Changi balls", I have persisted in taking my rice polishings and 4 ozs of red palm oil daily for the past month for their vitamin value, so it does not look as though it works. I am medically C1 and that means I have to spend most of my time on my bed, which I have done for the last four days and for which I get no measly few cents of pay. Tinea around my backside and private parts still discharging so badly I have to wear a piece of towel instead of shorts to ease the chafing. I have another khaki slop which I salvaged some months ago. I think they were Naval gear, anyhow I have made it into a skirt. Now I look like an ATS girl walking around, a friend of mine is likewise attired and we are already known as the "Changi Highlanders".

Thursday April 1st 1943

Reported sick again this morning and get another three days C1 (bed). I am still in a nasty mess with all my underparts well coated in calamine which I have to keep intact on my skin for days on end causing more itching which I must not scratch, it is really maddening. Well here I am in a skirt and the wife no doubt wearing the trousers.

Friday April 2nd

The cemetery officer came to see me last night, he told me that my few men were managing very well. Have increased the mucky rice polishings to eight tablespoons a day, will do anything to get rid of these demoralising skin troubles.

Saturday April 3rd

It's a very wet day, have read through most of it, apart from my daily hobble for treatment.

Sunday April 4th

The last two days have passed slowly and all I can report is that I am bloody browned off.

Monday April 5th

Report sick again, get another three days spine bashing. Am restless all night so I get up at 4 o'clock and mooch around, the desire to scratch almost driving me to distraction.

Tuesday April 6th

Another early morning and the same feeling that I want to scratch myself to pieces and as I shuffle around in the dark, I ask myself where is it all going to end? Not even a letter comes my way to lift my moral. My meagre breakfast over I go for treatment, my face is dabbed with a solution of formalin which gives me a half hour of torture as it burns very much. Improvement in oneself is very slow, the food does not help as it's so plain and monotonous. Am seriously thinking of collecting snails as a meat diet.

Thursday April 8th

Another sick parade and a further four days C1. When I walk past the long lines of men waiting to use the latrines, I then realise that I am much better off than these dysentery sufferers as there appears to be very little hope for a lot of them, they move always followed by streams of flies. As I slowly make my way back to my bed space I am told 7,000 British and Dutch men are to stand by for a move. At this time I hope I am not picked to go, in any case it will not leave so many in this camp. Laying around and thinking about all kinds of things, amongst them is the possibility that if red palm oil is so good to eat, what could it do on the outside. I set to and wipe some over my legs and parts, it cannot do any harm I hope.

Friday April 9th

Tomorrow all of us have to parade for a malaria and dysentery test, those okay will no doubt make up the up country party.

Saturday April 10th

The time arrives for the medical tests, which I attend in my skirt and not looking too ladylike, as my beard is very rough looking, my face being no better. I am not classed as fit enough to move and get a further three days C1.

Helping to pass the time away I make a cross for Captain Campbell-Ord who is re-interred today, I remember seeing his wedding photographs in the local paper during the early days of the war. I believe he married a local girl.

Twenty more bags of mail arrive, will I be lucky? I feel I just have to get one to survive.

Thursday April 15th

Sick again this morning and still C1. I was given a solution of Permanganate of Potash to wash away the casing of calamine from my under parts. As I was making my way back, my face showing the agony I was in, I met my Captain Quartermaster who stopped me and asked what was wrong. I told him what had happened and he then asked me to go back to the doctors with him where he explained what I had said. The doctor looked at the seat of the trouble, called the orderlies concerned and really tore into them, the preparation they had given me was neat, they should have diluted it. This set my recovery back some weeks as all the good was undone.

Friday April 16th

It's raining heavily just now and everywhere is very wet, the place is coming alive with mosquitoes which no doubt will increase malaria. This has not caused us too much trouble to date as the island was almost free of it in peace time, but with men all moving about from one country to another it looks as though it could soon become a major problem.

Saturday April 17th

One of the men engaged in sorting mail has told a friend of mine that he has seen a letter addressed to me but I am not raising my hopes too high.

Sunday April 18th

A memorial service was held this morning for our late Padre Dean. I made up a wreath and cross to be laid on his grave from the 5th/6th Norfolks. It is also Palm Sunday and small crosses of palm were handed out.

Monday April 19th

I begin another week on sick parade and get my category raised to B1, excused roll call and can walk about a bit more still wearing my skirt. Mail is still coming in but not for me yet so I will have to just hope. Hope is not a very big word but it means so much, without it I think you could say one is near the end.

A few men are still being sent up-country, but my small party is still intact in fact they have exhumed five bodies from outside the camp and re-buried them within the cemetery.

The electricity has broken down so tonight we are in darkness, huddled together in groups, talking as usual about mum's bacon and eggs and other mouth watering things that each of us remember. It's time for bed and with jokes and curses we fumble in near pitch darkness for our sleeping places and sleep which is often broken by cries and yells from restless and dreaming men.

Wednesday April 21st

The day begins with the usual trek for breakfast but this time with a mail issue and an almost heart stopping moment as my name is called, my blood runs hot and cold as I move forward to receive it wondering who it is from, wife or mother or perhaps some one else. With some excitement I tear open the envelope and find it is from you Mother dear. I am sad to read that you have not heard from me or anything about us, but that you believe me to be alive and kicking somewhere. If only I could put your minds at rest, my poor dear wife what must she be thinking. I hope she can lose herself in her work and not dwell on me too much. But for me news is good, as another letter I am told has been seen for me, perhaps this time it is the one I am hoping for. My Mother's letter I have already read six times today. We still have no light so I cannot read it tonight. It has greatly cheered me up, but at the same time I feel a bit down to realise that none of you know about me, but I trust God will fulfil your hopes very soon.

229

Saturday April 24th

Perhaps I should mention that this is the first letter from home since I left eighteen months ago and I have not learned so much from it except that the dog has had puppies, but the morning finds me reading it again, to me it is a ray of sunshine, so different to the scorching rays here. It brings back memories of home, although I now find it hard to capture in my mind pictures of you all. Tomorrow is Easter Sunday and I have been making wreaths for a cemetery service.

More men are going away on Monday, which will include fifty of my Battalion, some of them leave throughout the night in parties of 1,500, bound they think for Japan, all movement is in the dark as it is now the fourth long and dreary night without light.

Sunday April 25th

Attended Easter Communion, although I sometimes wonder why I bother.

Monday April 26th

Morning brings another letter from mother, which I am only too pleased to receive although disappointed that it is not from the wife. The letter is short, I would have liked to have heard about Joan and my brothers and sisters, but I suppose censorship keeps the letters to the point.

We are moving again to the garden and wooded area by Changi jail, which is to be our camp area. Padre Duckworth leaves us for the up-country journey. The camp is somewhat sad and quiet as trailers are hauled by gangs of men, who have already sweated away their breakfast rice. They are almost too weak to raise a laugh about the oddly assorted camp equipment that they have loaded.

We have a few banana plants that we have tended, they have some small green fruit which I cut off. At least we can fry them, the officer taking over the area was not very pleased about it, but then we grew them and it is food. I am excused walking so travel on a trailer and assist how I can. The new camp is filthy, the huts stink, our chicken sheds at home are hotels in comparison. The move is completed in two days, myself riding backwards and forwards as the move goes on. The men are little better than slaves, similar to the Israelites, way back in history. The huts are hot and stuffy situated in a rubber plantation, rubber trees are all one can see for miles, no colourful flame trees here. The place is infested with centipedes, three or four inches long, scorpions, bugs and rats.

Friday April 30ᵗʰ

The sun comes up this morning on a bedraggled looking company of men, who set to and clean up the filth left by the late residents. The mosquitoes at night are a plague, if you have no net.

Saturday May 1ˢᵗ 1943

Not much time has elapsed since we took over our new quarters but already it looks as if our numbers will be severely cut as the "Nips" now require a further 3,000 men for another up country party. I attend a special sick parade, but the medical officer will not allow me to go in case there is too much marching.

Roll call is on again for a check by the "Nips", but two nights have passed by and so far they have not appeared.

Some of us are invited to an Australian concert, "In the nude for love", I leave you to guess what it was like, anyway we had a good laugh and that is as good as a tonic.

Monday May 3rd

My cemetery party which I had got back to eight men looks like being depleted again as only two are left off the up country list. They have managed to get the mess cat over here, like us it is its third move, everything is very upside down. More men are needed for work than there are fit, we have to police the camp gates and battle casualties have been pressed into service for the job.

Tuesday May 4th

The men that are leaving have received the "Order of the Glass Rod" (dysentery check). I take over the duties of the Military Police Officer so as to relieve him for inoculations, never know what you are going to be asked to do next. A long-standing territorial friend of mine, Sgt. Ted Mallet, has been to hospital, like me he is bad with tinea and ringworm.

Wednesday May 5th

On sick parade this morning and the doctor gave me a further seven days, no work and I have now been wearing a skirt for five weeks. More men being inoculated. We are still very unsettled in this camp, it is in a hollow and very hot as we have started the dry season. The men due to move have destroyed their old beds to get rid of the bugs and now the move has been postponed for 24 hours and they have to sleep on the floor.

Thursday May 6th

It's six o'clock and the whole area basks in a subdued golden light, It looks like a vividly painted picture somewhere in the south seas, the naked-to-the-waist men glow like Red Indians as they sit around, with the trees looking a deeper green under a deep blue sky flecked with little white clouds. The news that the waiting men are to move early tomorrow, Sunday, brings me out of my poetic dreamland. I am only losing acquaintances this time as all my friends left with the last party.

Friday May 7th

It's two o'clock in the early hours and the camp is alive as the men move off, to where and to what no-one really knows.

18. On this day... May 7, 1943... Tunis captured by the Allies in North Africa.

Saturday May 8th

The food at this time is as follows:

Breakfast	watery rice, a little flour roll and raw tea.
Dinner -	two dixies of rice for 115 men.
Tea -	same amount of rice, some green, third of a mug of almost meatless stew, one spoonful of wheat (as fed to chickens), one teaspoon sugar and a half pint tea.

Where else could one get such a diet!

Sunday May 9th

Camp very quiet, weather hot and sticky. No church services started here as yet and we still have no electric light. My tinea has a new name, scrotal dermatitis, what the difference is I don't know and couldn't care less, all I wish is that it will soon clear up. I am so bored lying around, so against doctor's orders I go to the cemetery, walking around and seeing what's been done, does me a power of good and finally I waddle back to camp feeling a bit more at peace with myself.

* * *

The "Nips" want another 3,000 men and unless more arrive from Java we shall really be thin on the ground. I am not included on the list. A complaint from the "Nips" that the cemetery is becoming too public, they do not like too many men roaming around it, well there will be less as a lot of sick men are on the party to move soon. It's raining very hard and we are thankful for the cooler conditions. The rain causes the cancellation of a roll call, which is followed by the order that the "Nips" do not wish for roll calls until further notice, which brings some relief.

Friday May 14th

The first anniversary of Jim Tuck's death (my next door neighbour) so I make and place a wreath on his grave. While on the cemetery I manage a little light work which is lifting my morale. On arriving back to camp for tea I find the men waiting to move, very busy getting together the bits and pieces that they can carry. They are off any minute, the grape-vine says, moving by ship to a colder climate. Our officers are continuing roll calls, why? Do they think we might break camp or try to escape, which is not likely.

Saturday May 15th

Off to work this morning, with news that we are moving camp once again.

Its been a dull day in more ways than one as the camp is very quiet. We are few in number now, eight of us occupy a sixty foot long hut and just as darkness falls we are joined by two more bodies who evidently require company, a large black and white dog, and a tortoiseshell cat expecting kittens or suffering like us, from a rice belly. I expect they were left by the men who recently moved on, who among them spared enough from their scant rations to feed them and no doubt we shall do the same. Like us the dogs here hate the "Nips" barking and growling whenever they are near.

Thursday May 20th

Reported sick this morning and was officially given light duties. A letter received by one of the men says a medal has been struck for the Singapore campaign, this causes a bit of a laugh, we wonder what it will be awarded for, perhaps for existing for so long on rice. The weather is very humid causing me to sweat a great deal and this does not help my skin problems.

Friday May 21st

The "Nips" have ordered us to march to Selerang barracks together with all other areas for a mass roll call, all walking wounded to go as well. The old place of imprisonment was familiar. On the roll call we were informed that the barracks would be our new home, it means a bit of a crush as it will be 500 to 600 men in each building.

Saturday May 22nd

It is a very wet day, also a very busy one for us preparing for tomorrow's move.

Sunday May 23rd

No rest day this Sunday as we load the engineless trucks and prepare to do the job of old cart horses. The one I am harnessed to was once an Army workshop so it is a rather hefty chassis and three times today I have helped pull it the few miles to Selerang barracks. At the end of it we were absolutely all in, the pulling team included nine Sergeants, seven of whom are battle casualties and myself still on the sick list, like slaves we are glad to sink to the ground for a rest. We managed to bring the two cats, one still looking as if kittens are imminent. With tea over we take to our beds and we don't need rocking

Monday May 24ᵗʰ

Morning comes all too soon and we are still moving, later I get my permanent bed space, at the top of a three story block, which means climbing 52 stone stairs. From this position we have a good view of Changi jail, although a jail it really is a good sight with the lights from many cells shining out coupled with the greeny glow from its flood lights. I am one of a few who can read the time on its clock which because of the distance is proof of still excellent eye sight.

Tuesday May 25ᵗʰ

The cemetery is lacking workers so letters have been sent to the various areas asking for officer volunteers to do maintenance work. The letter states that the British and Dutch cemeteries are at a very high standard and it is wished to keep them that way.

Wednesday May 26ᵗʰ

This day I have climbed the steps to my bed space 18 times, a total of 936 steps, and my poor knees are letting me know it. Tonight I go to an Australian concert which gives me some relaxation, although the concert theme was built around a morgue and was called "Bible Class", a bit sinister. Funerals have been low which is a good thing so we have been able to get on with clearing work.

Thursday May 27ᵗʰ

Have been saving my few weekly cents and today was able to buy a pineapple, two bananas and some goola malacca (unprocessed brown sugar). Purchases are not everyday happenings, just a rarity.

I worked a whole day on the cemetery, the first for a long time, had two burials. To keep busy without too much exertion I sharpen up the reap hooks and shears.

Spent evening at Australian band concert, very good show, marvellous how they came by the instruments

* * *

Reported sick this morning, something gone wrong with the old rectum. After a doctor's inspection I am still on light duties, he did not say what was wrong but I have to visit the skin clinic.

There has been a trailer accident in which five of the pulling team have been injured and taken to hospital. Six new prisoners dressed in battle dress have been driven through the camp and it has caused some discussion as to where they have come from.

Monday June 1st 1943

I have got hold of a piece of tent canvas from which I am trying to make two pairs of shorts, whether I shall wear them remains to be seen, as they may be too stiff for my skin condition, which reminds me that it's time to visit the Australian doctor for an inspection. After looking me over he seems rather concerned with the scrotal dermatitis and tells me to report to him again tomorrow. Many men have this complaint in some form and in various places.

* * *

The whole camp area is being cleaned up, the parade ground is almost back to normal as all the latrines that we dug across it during our enforced stay here have been filled in. The grapevine tells us that a Red Cross official is being allowed to visit us.

Have seen the Australian skin doctor for the third time this week and have to report in three days time. In the meantime, I with all other Sergeants have to move to the centre floor. We shall lose the view of the sea and encounter more mosquitoes, but I shall not have to climb so many stairs.

Friday June 4th

We have a visit from a Nippon General and a Red Cross official, don't know if he is European or not and knowing our captors he could be bogus. He was told we wanted repatriation of battle casualties, correspondence with home and a food ship. It is said we may get the last two requests.

Saturday June 5th

I report sick yet again to my own doctor and ask if I can get back to work, he says it's not advisable for a few more days. All the time I have been off work my right-hand man, Alexander (who lives in Norwich), sees me every night and reports on the work done and burials carried out.

Sunday June 6th

Getting quite good at tailoring, today I have altered a pair of long khaki trousers which were to big in the seat. Later I see the "Aussie" doctor who is very pleased with my progress. This evening I went to church, the only light being a hurricane lamp standing on the pulpit.

Monday June 7th

The morning brings the surprise of children shouting and laughing close by, on investigating I find a school for Chinese and Malay has been opened up almost on the camp boundary. The noise of the children takes my thoughts back home and to you all wondering how you are all getting along. The Colonel spoke to us last night, told us a bit of news that had come over a secret wireless three weeks ago. No doubt he was trying to cheer up a lot of very low and tired men.

I have just had a short sharp attack of lumbago, also my backside is very painful, I seem to be going to pieces, although in myself I feel fit. Made four wreaths for friends of RSM Everret who died a few days after being admitted to hospital. Saw the Australian doctor again, he tells me that I shall have to see a surgeon for an inspection, as he himself cannot see what is wrong with my behind. I had been thinking that the trouble was piles, but he says no.

Thursday June 10ᵗʰ

I have spent a painful night, fed up in general I go for my breakfast of watery rice and weak raw tea. After which I go to my own doctor for a routine check after which he also tells me I will have to see a surgeon as it could be a fissure (a split inside the anus).

Nothing much else going on today so I get thinking about you all at home, especially the wife as I have received no news or letter from her as yet.

Sunday June 13ᵗʰ

As I arise this morning, it is, I am told Whit Sunday, so much different from my past memories of it. The men are saying they hope the war will be over before it comes around again. I remember one such Sunday three years ago, I was, with others erecting barbed wire along the coast at Weybourne in Norfolk. Saw the skin doctor again and thank God he doesn't think a surgeon will now be necessary. It is with a lighter heart that I return to my quarters. It's three months since I have done any serious work.

Since the electric lighting was put back on its power has been very low, and this has curtailed our amusements, concerts and other forms of relaxation. Our Command have now issued an order that our heaving boxes of rice polishings will now be taken under supervision as so many men are missing them. Tonight we invited some "Aussie" friends over for a game of cards, it was very entertaining. A Regimental Sergeant Major went from

England to Australia in 1921 and now owns 25,000 acres of sheep farm, three other men went out also in the late 1920's. Well it's time for bed and after tucking in my "mozi" net I don't remember much more.

Thursday June 17th

Next morning it's the usual noise of fed up men getting out from various types of beds, grunting, groaning and with some swearing they put on their rags they call clothes. After breakfast I report to the sick room, during the morning I saw two doctors, mine passed me fit for work but not the "Aussie", so I'm between the devil and the deep blue sea.

Later I went to an exhibition of war pictures by the official Australian War artist, who like us was caught up here. His sketches are very good, they include many of our camp life. Spent some time with Australian friends this evening, they are getting me Australian minded.

Friday June 18th

At last I get back to a full days work, the first full day for three months. Nineteen officers have volunteered to help on the cemetery on a part time basis, this is a great help in keeping the graves tidy. Glad to get into bed after my day out.

Saturday June 19th

On arising I feel rather stiff and sore from sunburn. I am badly burnt in places as it was my longest exposure to the sun for a long time.

Saw cabaret at "Smoky Joe's Canteen", staring "Judy Garland", she was very good but then our "girls" are very pretty and well dressed in our shows.

Monday June 21ˢᵗ

Mid-summer's day at home, it's almost permanent summer here and can get monotonous. Further visit to the "Aussie" doctor who says a further three days treatment. While there I heard that the "Nips" had just got around to censoring our cards that we wrote in February and they are awaiting orders from Tokyo to send them off.

I attended a talk on Australia. I arranged it with RSM Williams from that country to tell us of the possibilities for returned soldiers and a very interesting lecture took place.

Thursday June 24ᵗʰ

Today the Changi Road is being wired in and put out of bounds to us, as the cemetery is on the Changi end we are wondering if we are to be allowed out. The "Nips" have made what seems to us an incredible demand, they want us to supply men to instruct them in the use of Bren and Tommy-guns. A party of medical men have left for areas up-country where malaria is rife.

Friday June 25ᵗʰ

I was awakened in the night by the meows of a cat, which by the weight was sitting on me, but I could not move a muscle, I was paralysed. Suddenly its cries ceased and I was able to move but no cat and there could not have been as my mosquito net was tucked in all around. My mind went back 16 years when the same thing happened at home, only in that case I saw the ghost of a cat walk through mid air.

Saturday June 26ᵗʰ

I am now free of doctors having been struck off the "Aussie's" sick list. What a relief, three morale-sapping months have at last come to an end. During the evening listened to a gramophone recital.

Cemetery once again outside the camp area so we have to resort to another pass flag.

Sunday June 27th

We awake to a wet Sunday, anyway it's a rest day so we do not worry too much, but a surprise awaits us at breakfast, a small egg is issued to each one of us. A flock of chickens have been built up, although chickens are small in Singapore we are supposed to be getting an egg a week if no one knocks them off for a stew.

Monday June 28th

The start of another week and with it comes inoculations for TAB and dysentery. Later we move out with our pass flag to proceed to the cemetery and a passing "Nip" lorry stopped and gave us a lift. For this we were thankful as the march to the cemetery is two and a half miles. This means a round trip of ten miles as we have to come home for dinner and then back in the afternoon, all this on our pittance of rice and greens plus we also dig graves and do other physical work.

Thursday July 1st 1943

After a delirious night I have had a bad day, the symptoms due to the dysentery jab and now after a day of marching and work I am dead beat and it is an effort to go for my tea. Tea over I fall into bed unwashed as I cannot bother to find water.

Friday July 2nd

This morning I feel much better and get myself washed before going off on the trek to the cemetery. On the way I saw a Hooded

Cobra slide into a brick heap. They say it is the only snake that directly attacks man.

Saturday July 3rd

Saw Australian concert for second time, it is the last show and it ended in a crazy game. Bits and pieces of news seep through from the men who have hidden radios and it appears to be good.

Sunday July 4th

American Independence Day and the "Yanks" here are doing their best to celebrate it. A British band known as "Jack Greenwoods" is doing its best to help. As for me, a bit of soap a few inches square has been issued so I think I will wash my shirt and shorts, it will be nice to get the sweat out of them. I try bashing them but not too hard, as what I have, just might fall to pieces.

Monday July 5th

Today the meals are:

Breakfast -   two ladles of watery rice, half pint of raw tea.

Dinner   -   a ladle of plain rice and one of towgay beans, tea.

At night -   Towgay and green stew, plain rice rissole, boiled rice duff.

At least our cooks do try to change the rice into a variety of shapes.
Had a second TAB injection and the result was another very bad night, hardly any sleep, some men were screaming, others moaning, talking and even singing in their delirium. The place stinks as the bugs move around and get disturbed.

Tuesday July 6th

I make a trip with the handcart and two men into Southern Area to dig out some drain inverts from a broken-up roadway. It was very hard and heavy work for us, but we needed them for our road running through the cemetery. As the days pass we retrieve quite a lot of drain inverts, but it's hell in this heat and with lost sleep over the past few nights, we tend to stagger around under the weight of them.

Before tea I debugged my bits and pieces I use for a bed, I cleared out quite a few of the little red devils and brushed a light film of diesel oil over the wood joints to kill the eggs. Should sleep a bit better without their company.

Wednesday July 7th

Morning comes and with it my fourth and last dysentery inoculation for this period.

While recovering drain materials I heard a crashing of something coming through a piece of jungle covered land. For a minute our blood froze, what could it be? A tiger, but then we had been told that the last of these had been killed long before the war. We listened to the crashing and suddenly four large Gibbon monkeys bounded out, crossed the road just in front of us and passed into the trees on the other side. We breathed again and joked about our scare.

Sitting around at night talking of home as usual, we realise it is July, high summer and wonder how the crops and weather are in Norfolk.

Tomorrow we are to dig up three bodies buried in the Selerang area during our earlier enforced stay here.

Thursday July 8th

Well the bodies were found, taken to the cemetery and buried there. In the area that I exist in there are around 1,000 men and 800 of them are unfit to work.

Friday July 9th

An Australian lad has died in Outram Road jail, Singapore, whilst serving a ten year sentence for trying to escape. This jail has a terrible record for cruel punishment and if anyone is released from it and sent back to the camp hospital he is probably blind and there's little hope of him surviving.

Saturday July 10th

A Dutch Captain working with me has been caught up in an incident with a "Nip" soldier and gets his face slapped.

For security reasons news is not referred to as such, we call it "Griff" and what we hear are encouraging items, even if they are rather old.

19. **On this day...** July 10, 1943... Invasion of Italy by Allies begins at Sicily.

* * *

Went again to Southern Area for pipes, took a lorry trailer and eight men. After loading it we had to lever it up a hill with iron bars to get it out. I bet no Britisher has worked as hard as us just above the Equator for the sheer interest in creating something.

Seem to be a lot of Nippon soldiers around, just sight-seeing as they are new troops. A warning has been issued against getting messages out of the camp. If anyone is caught the "Nips" will take reprisals. Another party of troops pass by, they are very young but cheerful and friendly towards us.

One of our recently formed bands has lost a very good base player, he has been taken to Singapore to play in a Eurasian band, he is an American.

The Dutch have made up a "Heath Robinson" type juice extractor, they throw in lalang grass and various types of leaves and it produces a dark and vivid green juice which is given to sick men as a form of medicine and by all accounts tastes just as horrible as it looks. The Dutch are good at compounding medicines and ointments from the plants growing around and are a great help because of the almost non-existence of the real stuff.

Saturday July 17th

Another day of near exhaustion as we gather more drains and pipes for our cemetery road, which now begins to look like a professional job. A rest day tomorrow is looked forward to as it is Sunday.

Sunday July 18th

On arising I manage a tough shave with my table knife, smarten myself up as best I can and attend Holy Communion for the first time since we left Changi several weeks ago. I attend later, a talk on "After the war and the possibilities", also classes were started to teach men clerical work, afraid it does not interest me. A cricket match is also taking place between the crippled men, a case of mind over matter.

Monday July 19th

The rest day over it is back to work in the gruelling heat. Many men are now without boots and they are coping with slats of wood with a canvas toe piece, a form of Chinese "choppies". Socks are a thing of the past. It is said that some men are returning to us.

Tuesday July 20th

Had to report sick again as the pain in my behind gets unbearable. The doctor gives me a note to see a surgical specialist at the hospital.

Wednesday July 21st

This morning instead of work I go to see the specialist but am unlucky as he is operating, so I am given an appointment for 2.30pm tomorrow. I see that the natives are taking over one of our old camp areas.

Thursday July 22nd

Well I have seen the surgeon and don't I know it, I had to strip and crouch on a bench while an orderly held an unprotected electric light bulb on an extended flex within inches of me. The specialist pushed something up my rectum that felt like a six inch shell, at the same time the orderly touched my behind with the hot light bulb, only my head hitting a wall in front of the bed stopped me from taking off. The memories of this torture will for ever remain, but there is more to come as he informs me that I am suffering from bleeding internal haemorrhoids and proceeds to inject them. Having finished he pulls out his instrument and to me it seems my innards are following. He tells me to report again in a week's time for a further injection, five of these and he says he can cure me. I cannot say that I am looking forward to this breech loading form of treatment.

The natives in camp close by us are being subjected to the glass rod treatment for dysentery, both men and woman are in the queue.

*　*　*

247

The word is going around that we are to move again; in the meantime, we are all confined to barracks as a Japanese General is coming to make an inspection. When he comes, later in the day, he only looks over one room.

Tuesday July 27th

It's four days since the near-by natives had their tests and inoculations and now they are leaving, so it looks as they are travelling up-country, may be to the Burma railway area. Our talked-of move has now been postponed.

Wednesday July 28th

Rumours are still going around about the possible exchange of civilian internees and more Red Cross supplies for us, this could be wishful thinking.

Thursday July 29th

Attended hospital this afternoon for another injection, but it was not so painful this time. I also get a day excused duties.

Friday July 30th

I awake this morning to find that I can hardly hear anything, is it anything to do with yesterday's injection I ask myself? I just don't seem as though I can break out of the wood of ills, I have to see the doctor again. After looking in my ears he tells an orderly to syringe them. This is done and on walking out into the open I am amazed at what I can hear, small sounds that have not registered for months. This certainly lifts my sinking morale.

Saturday July 31st

The "Nips" have large working parties clearing ground of scrub and palm trees on one side of the cemetery and some of our men are allowed to gather a few coconuts from the uprooted palms, it seems that they are starting the construction of an aerodrome here at Changi.

Sunday August 1st 1943

As the days go by we manage to gather a few more coconuts, which are a very welcome addition to our meals as the food is bad just now.

Monday August 2nd

A surprise visit by "Nip" soldiers, they are searching all camp areas, apparently they are looking for cameras and any form of arms. All the men are searched and our bedding scattered around.

Tuesday August 3rd

The mail sorters say that 22 more bags of letters have arrived, dated June to October 1942. Will I get one from the wife this time?

Wednesday August 4th

A notice has been put up stating that a move is talked about and it may involve the hospital from Changi, and the remainder of the men still based there.

Thursday August 5th

I attended the hospital for another injection for haemorrhoids, am getting used to it now. I have been given a tin of 150 vitamin C tablets as its owner could not stomach them, they certainly screw ones mouth up, as for me I'll try anything if it's going to help me keep alive for the day of victory which I know will eventually come.

Friday August 6th

I could not but notice on roll call how our clothing has changed. It is a parade of colours. Many shades of khaki shirts and shorts, shades of blue, green and camouflage colours in clothing made from tent canvas, patches are visible on almost everyone. The night wears on to 10.30 and many are in bed when we are noisily disturbed by "Nips" rushing in and searching us again, it is said they are looking for cut-throat type razors.

Saturday August 7th

This morning started with the burial of Col. Morris, Royal Corps of Signals. In peace time it appears that he was general manager of Telephone and Cables in Singapore and Malaya. Well over 100 officers were at the funeral. The day passes the same as many others recently, marching the two miles back for dinner along a sun bleached road that dazzles the eyes. The sweat dripping off our chins and leaving a salt deposit as it dries on our bodies. We march back in the afternoon, do a bit more work and then trudge wearily back to camp for tea, at this time of day we are at the point of exhaustion and we fall on our beds to recover enough strength to go and collect tea. For once it comes as a pleasant surprise, it was meat and vegetable (tinned food) and marmalade tart. This was the first meat for ten months. You may wonder how we come by this food, no not from the "Nips" but from a reserve stock held by Divisional Headquarters and now must be used up, but to us it was a godsend.

A mail sorter tells me that he has seen four letters addressed to me, I asked him if the writing sloped backwards, he said it does, so it seems as they could be from the wife. Could it be at last, after two years of hoping and longing of news of her? I just cannot wait to get those letters in my hands. After my good news comes the bad, that dreaded terror of the East is flaunting its filthy wings over Singapore, it is cholera. All possible precautions are being taken to keep it from our camp areas, as I think it would polish us all off in no time at all with our resistance being so low.

Chinese female coolies are seen passing to and fro outside the boundary fence, they are dressed in black and wear very wide brimmed hats.

Wednesday August 11th

I was awakened in the early hours by a distant threshing in the trees, I listened to it for twenty minutes, then it seemed to change direction and came towards our area, very soon we were engulfed in the heaviest torrential rain that I have experienced here as yet.

Thursday August 12th

The "Nips" are complaining that our manners are getting bad and that too many fit men are walking about the camp, I forget what a fit man looks like. A fellow gets 28 days in the kennels (barbed wire cage) for passing "Marmite" destined for the hospital and the newspaper, "Syonian Sinbun", states that after the war is over all prisoners will be sent to Germany to remodel and build up the bombed cities.

Friday August 13th 1943

A day with a bad date, but it has passed uneventfully and I am still waiting for those letters. The "Nips" have stopped the volunteer officers from using the hospital road to the cemetery, apparently it is their only exit, so I have to do without their services.

Saturday August 14th

Debugged my bed this morning and got rid of a crowd of the little red devils. It looks as though we may have to move back to an old camp area as we are told the hospital will have to move to Selerang barracks.

Sunday August 15th

Today deserves a special mention as it is two years since I was married so it brings emotional thoughts and a telepathic message to my wife to keep smiling as it cannot be too long before we meet again. Word is going around that we are moving tomorrow.

Monday August 16th

After breakfast the place becomes a hive of activity as we gather together our bits and pieces once again. Soon we are on our way and looking like so many Irish tinkers we make for old married quarters in this Selerang barrack area which are to be our home. As we do this the hospital people are already taking over. We take the day to settle in and after all the ups and downs I am only too glad to turn in.

Tuesday August 17th

A new day starts and with it a present from the "Nips", a tin of pineapple between four of us and a bottle of some kind of cognac between eight. It is so that we can join in their celebrations 18 months after the fall of Singapore, it's what you call rubbing it in. Well food is food no matters how it comes, but with the brandy we drank toasts to all of you at home. Still no letter from my wife but another from my mother has turned up. She informs me that two of my sisters have babies, this makes me an uncle twice over. This news hardly makes me jump over the moon as I am disappointed not having got one from the wife as she must have written many letters, at the same time she may even be feeling as I do, not having heard from me. Moving house is still going on, trailers loaded with the incredible junk that we call furniture and utensils.

Last night I went to a show at the Hospital "Palladium" where I saw a show called the "Little Admiral". It was very good, complete with waterfall, fountains, rain and excellent lighting effects, scenery and nice dresses. The boys that played the female parts were, to us, very attractive. It really is very surprising the acting and the many effects that the Prisoners of War can put over with odds and ends collected from around the area. Six Nippon officers were at this show and appeared to enjoy it. I have also, during the past week, twice seen the Australian show "Everybody's Swinging It", a superb entertainment.

I am at last settled in my new quarters, just two of us on a small veranda. We seem to have the biggest poultry farm in the world as so many ducks and chickens are kept. The early morning noise of these birds is terrible, how they manage to survive is a mystery.

Message just in says everyone for cholera inoculation tomorrow, rumour says it has broken out a quarter of a mile from us and the "Nips" are worried about their own troops, hence the precautions.

Wednesday August 18th

This morning I received a letter from my mother, who believes that I am alive and kicking somewhere. After two days of moving have now resumed work on the cemetery and while doing so I am thinking about the news from my mother regarding being an uncle. I get to wondering if I shall get out of here before someone makes me a granddad. It's amazing what things go through a fellow's mind when looking into an unknown future.

Thursday August 19ᵗʰ

Another day comes and with it the inoculation for cholera, if they were giving away free passages home there could not have been a bigger stampede to get done. Being such a dreaded disease no one was going to miss out. The hospital move is in full swing, men straining on ropes, panting and sweating pints as they haul the loaded trailers to the new quarters.

As a lorry load of Chinese women goes by, we watch with staring eyes as it's a sight we don't see for months on end, and to us starved of female company they really looked good. Someone shouts tea up and that brings us quickly back into the world of rice and raw tea.

It's a nice fresh night after showers so we sit in our usual groups again discussing food, and I think what wonderful mothers we left behind as they make so many nice things to eat. You will notice it is mothers not wives, evidently she is the first and last in many men's lives.

Friday August 20ᵗʰ

The strength of my cemetery workers has now got to 20 which enables upkeep and extensions to go ahead, the place is now looking very neat with the grass cut and graves trimmed (we have a few old grass mowers that are kept in trim by a Royal Engineer). The extra help gives me the chance to start the digging of another monsoon drain down one side of the cemetery.

Saturday August 21ˢᵗ

There are some Chinese women under guard working near by, some of the men say the "Nips" are bringing them close just to annoy the fellows. I see two of the older women climb a tree to gather fruit from it.

Sunday August 22nd

Nippon troops are moving into our vacated Changi camp. This brings the war closer and we wonder why countries want war, will it ever end? We are now at the state that any boots left are now being repaired with wooden soles and being unyielding we walk like Lancashire cloggers. I expect at home things must be getting a bit hard for you, but I don't suppose your food looks like the rubbish that we eat, it would more than likely make you sick.

Monday August 23rd

Commotion at midnight when we catch a rat running among the beds and I don't seem to have been asleep long before shouts awaken me, it was 3am and excitement was running high when another rat was caught but got away again, so back to bed to make the best of a bad night.

Grass and leaves are being collected in greater quantities for use as vitamin extracts and medicines, the Heath Robinson masher constructed from sheets of corrugated iron creates an awful din as it is manually worked. When I was a youngster anything green, I was told was poison, it's a good thing that I have overcome that belief, else I would never touch the produce that comes from the masher. We have a brush factory that is turning out marvellous brushes from jungle materials such as bamboo and other growths. If you are fortunate in having an old toothbrush they do a very good reconditioning job. The rubber factory now makes rubber sandals and repairs spectacles. We also have men making artificial limbs and sewing needles. Ointments are made from natural sources; all these things are proof of the great resourcefulness and ingenuity of the men here. The engineers have repaired the bombed sewers and water mains so that the Selerang area now has plenty of showers for our use. This is a godsend after a days sweating to stand under one, if only to be momentarily shocked, as the water feels ice-cold after the heat of the day. We are getting more and more self-supporting.

Tuesday August 24th

Over the past few days tents are springing up on all the vacant ground as more and more men are sent to the area. One hundred medical men are leaving us today and with the party goes Surgeon Major McDell. This means that I do not get my fifth and final injection for haemorrhoids, which he told me would make a complete cure. Well I shall just have to hope that the four will cure me, anyhow these men will be greatly missed by us.

I had a de-bugging hour to start the day and killed off a large number of the little red devils. Tonight I attended a talk given by an American airman who was shot down on March 31st 1943. Before turning in for the night I sew another patch onto my patchwork shorts.

Wednesday August 25th

Headquarters have presented 35 chickens to us, from those that they have reared. Tonight's tea was good, "HQ chicken" stew, and how lovely it tasted, I seemed to have got most of the skin, but it went down well.

Thursday August 26th

Another morning dawns wet and three of us try our hand at roasting snails. First we boil the snails in a can of seawater (brought back by one of the men on salt production) which produces a thick green slime, this is poured off, then we heat them up again producing more of the slimy mucus. Next they are washed, cut into pieces and fried in a drop of red palm oil, after which we are ready for eats, only to find that they are so very tough and more suitably could be used as leather.

The "Nips" have been good today as we have been told they issued the hospital with some milk.

Friday August 27th

Well, it is another day of rain but during it I spend a lot of time reading my fifth letter from mother, it proves to be more interesting than the others as she tells me something of my brothers and sisters, which is news that I have been waiting for. Quite a lot appears to have happened to them. Fancy Arthur in the Home Guard, he was still at school when I left the country. How are they off for beer, pretty rough being on half a pint, is it a day or for a week? I still have not heard from my "own" yet, I expect she has eloped with a "Yank", or should I have said took the chance to run away from me.

Saturday August 28th

Today brings another 200,000 letters, to me it's like getting the pools up to get a letter, anyhow I can always turn to the ones from mother for a re-read. She tells me that the wife has gone to work in a shop in a village I know, she could learn of my previous flirtations in that area!

Sunday August 29th

Today is my neighbour's (Jim Tuck) birthday so I have made a wreath and placed it on his grave with a card bearing the following words:
"A Mothers thoughts are of him this day as he rests in some corner of a foreign field which is forever England".
Our boots are falling to pieces as no more suitable material is available for repairs, this is bad news for those of us that dig graves as it is tough going in this volcanic earth.
This evening I listened to the "Aussie" band play extracts from "Rose Marie".

Monday August 30th

Burial today for Captain Harrison RA, for some reason the "Nips" supplied an escort, turned themselves towards the east and presented arms. This is the first time such a thing has happened.

Tuesday August 31st

Nippon roll calls are restarted; parades have now to be sorted into units of ten, it's easier for them to count.

Heard talk on Japan, given by a Padre who spent 30 years out there.

Wednesday September 1st 1943

I've had a day off so I put my mosquito net through boiling water to kill off the bugs and their eggs. I received a pair of white wool socks and underpants, it seems that some things are still coming through from our one and only Red Cross ship of 1942. Well, the things are more than welcome as it's a long time since I have had either items.

Thursday September 2nd

This day finds my thoughts with my mother whose birthday it is, hope she can make something of it. Maybe I will be with you next year. A year has gone since we came to Selerang, but the year has passed quickly, working on the cemetery keeps us busy and keeps boredom at bay. Went to see a friend last night, George Batey by name, he fused his area's lighting in trying to make a cup of tea in an old electric kettle. This evening I went to an Australian concert called "Girls", a smashing success. A John Wood plays a marvellous actress and Tommy Cottrill, with English and Russian background I am told does a wonderful acrobatic dance, also juggling. It is said that he has appeared in Hotel cabarets from Africa to Australia, incredibly he is at this moment working for me on the cemetery. One scene in the show was complete with "Ladies" wearing bustles and pushing penny-farthing bicycles.

Friday September 3rd

The fourth anniversary of the war, lets hope that we shall be home by the fifth one. An old *"Nippon Times"* dated April 21st 1943 has been seen by one of the men, it states he says, that Norwich and Yarmouth have been bombed.

Here we are Prisoners of War, yet this day I have watched a march past of Australians to commemorate the fourth anniversary of the war. This you would have to see to believe, with this spirit who can lose?

* * *

There has been another bad trailer accident, Australian wood cutters, 12 are injured, three of them seriously. One Australian had his face slapped for not saluting a "Nip" patrol.

We are to get an issue of 1oz. marmite, but on collecting, it had dropped to ½ oz. as the remainder is being kept for the sick.

Tuesday September 7th

Heavy rain has fallen over the last two days making work a bit uncomfortable, we had to cremate an RAF lad. The Major gave me an egg, I also had one for breakfast from the unit fowls, two in two days, shall have to go easy or I shall be sick.

Wednesday September 8th

The rain has passed leaving it very hot and steamy and all day I have just streamed with sweat. My boots, now wearing very thin, are soaked.

Thursday September 9th

Letter sorting started again, well Joan my dear, will I be lucky this time? It's nearly two years, perhaps it's the same for you at your end.

Friday September 10th

Military band just formed played on the hospital square tonight, listening to it was quite a change. Chickens in the stew again for us 5th Norfolks, it was very rich and I am suffering for it, my poor stomach cannot stand it.

Saturday September 11th

It's very hot and early this morning a "Sumatra" blew (a local storm) with all the intensity of a tornado, shifting everything loose and a lot that was not, the coconut palms were bent in a bow before the terrific wind.

Sunday September 12th

Still no letter from the last batch. No news is good news the saying goes but I don't think it applies under war conditions.

Monday September 13th

My birthday. Ye gods I seem to have grown old at 32, which means four years in uniform for me. I also have a heavy cold, and a temperature of 102°F and sun heat of 120°F at midday leaves me flat out and lifeless. Who said "Many Happy Returns", well I've not got enough strength to throw anything at him. I feel next door to death as the news comes in that the "Nips" are going to supply coffins, at the moment we are using tent canvas to wrap the corpses in.

Tuesday September 14th

After a restless night I greet another day just alive and as it approaches midday the same terrific heat is still with us, but I think I will come through as I am feeling a bit better and am able to face a bowl of rice.

The odd papers that got into camp, *"The Syonian Sinbuss"*, is to be stopped by the "Nips". A contingent of prisoners from somewhere outside the island is expected to arrive at our camp today.

Have just received a sixth letter from my mother who does not know much about me or my whereabouts. Well Ma, I'm in Singapore and the food is rice, which we have learnt to use in a variety of ways, but then I don't suppose this thought could possibly reach you.

Wednesday September 15th

Today with my small amenity grant I have bought a couple of bananas and some towgay beans. Glad to get news of Joan in your letter mother and am sad to think she has heard nothing of me. Poor kid, expects she worries. My cold has left me and I'm in fine spirits, working hard landscaping the cemetery, which gives me little time to worry in, although I am looking forward to the day we are all re-united.

I have just learned that the barman from my local "The Robin Hood" is in hospital and have arranged to visit him on Sunday. Other prisoners are now arriving from Batavia, a mixture of British, American and Dutch. There may be a reason for them being brought here as it is said that the "Nips" are to construct an aerodrome close by the cemetery.

Thursday September 16th

The morning brings definite news of this as we are told that 1,500 men are required to work on the 'drome. Fire restrictions to be enforced, no smoking allowed anywhere except on the open verandas of the barrack blocks and then tins of water have to be left handy.

Friday September 17ᵗʰ

With 900 men off to work on the aerodrome, this leaves me with three of my 22 cemetery workers.

A letter sorter tells me that he has seen another letter for me, will it be the one that I patiently wait for. A "Nip" patrol watches us very closely as a lorry load of Chinese girls go by, as usual it was overloaded, some riding on the running boards and even one astride the radiator which must have been warm for her bottom. Perhaps the patrol thought we would down tools and make chase.

Saturday September 18ᵗʰ

When I get back to camp for tea I am given another letter from my mother which I am grateful to receive if only for the news it brings of you Joan dear, without this I could but think that you have given me up for someone else or for dead. Well mother it's your letters and your news of the wife that gives me heart to keep going. Ours is a small world, no outside, the same faces day after day and worse still the same old food, basically "rice". Tonight as I listen to the band, one song, "A Teddy Bears Picnic", revives memories of you dear.

Sunday September 19ᵗʰ

The men who came from Batavia recently have left us for Japan taking with them a Capt. James, interpreter and liaison officer. Our Commanding Officer has requested that the Japanese broadcast to the British Isles the fact that letters are now getting through to us. No letters from the wife, I wonder if her letters are being returned to her for some reason. Well I must try to retain the memory of her although it's now got to the stage that one can no longer visualise either voice or looks.

The time of roll call is to be changed to 7.30pm so as to give aerodrome workers more time for tea. Went to an Australian concert this evening it portrayed a Prisoner of War who arrived home and had turned slightly mad due to his enforced stay in the tropics. How well this could apply to most of us if we are caged up here much longer.

Tuesday September 21st

When the recent party left for Japan, eight officers were left behind as room on the ship had to be found for a pregnant Korean and some Nippon women. The officers were no doubt pleased that the "Nips" population is increasing. The air raid sirens have been going most of the day, so it seems that we might soon become involved more actively in the war.

A song written and composed in the camp, "I am happy because I have a memory of you", is being whistled and hummed among the men, I should think it keeps their thoughts at home.

Wednesday September 22nd

A very heavy storm hit us in the night bringing down a number of coconut palms so a few extra nuts for us. Had a burial this afternoon and it rained cats and dogs, at least as soon as we had filled in we were able to get out of it, not so the poor bloody 'drome workers. They looked the picture of utter despair when they came in, water running off their sun-burned bodies and tattered bits of clothing sticking to them, it makes me thankful for the job I'm doing.

The eighth letter from mother has just arrived. I sit down to read it before I go to tea. She writes of my brothers and sisters who are lucky to be getting enough to eat, also leave from the forces. Her letter also brings welcome news of Joan, this alone puts a spring in my step as I go to collect my tea, followed by a couple of hours comparing extracts from our letters before turning in for the night.

Thursday September 23ʳᵈ

Morning comes around and as I arise, pick up my boots, which I now realise can be worn no more, as yesterdays rain has just pulled them apart. I have a nice brown pair that I bought from a fellow at the time of the Capitulation, but only wore them a couple of times as they were too tight, I get them out to try on, inside them, tucked away is a pair of white cotton socks which I pull on followed by the boots which to my pleasant surprise are quite comfortable. The reason being that my feet after two years of sweating are much smaller. As I walk to work I am envied by all and sundry, the white socks sticking out from the tops of the shining boots make me feel like a giant, but at the end of the day they will be clogged with volcanic clay.

Friday September 24ᵗʰ

An exciting moment this morning as a bus pulled up outside the cemetery and many Japanese girls alighted, they looked lovely to us dressed as they were in short white dresses and hair in waves falling around their shoulders. They brought flooding back all the memories of home and as my thoughts wander across the oceans I am brought back to time by the passing of lorry loads of Chinese coolie women. Haven't seen so many females in years, it makes us think of the outside world as we laugh and joke about the mornings events.

A tractor is causing some comments after its native driver tries to extract it from some army barbed wire along the roadside, so it has been quite a day with the brown-black and all clear alerts taking place.

Saturday September 25th

I have just finished the laying of 200 feet of water pipe on the cemetery, hoping to get fixed up for water. The camp has just been told that it will take part in three nights of black out practice with the following restrictions, no moving about the area, no smoking, no singing and no unnecessary noise, so the best we can do is sleep them out.

Monday September 27th

Morning again and back to the sweating toil of grave digging and levelling of the area ahead. We are still a small squad with much to do, so when the air raid sirens suddenly rattle off like the drumming of a threshing machine we take a rest under some trees. It doesn't last long before the all clear and we are back to work, only to repeat the exercise as it goes off again within the hour, all this gives us renewed hope as any time now we expect to see our own aircraft overhead.

Tuesday September 28th

A large liner was seen leaving the island this morning, perhaps she has bought more mail or with luck Red Cross parcels.

After tea I was looking at my few tattered photos, your face Joan dear looked a bit mud stained. I gave it a wash, you look much better now, I wonder if you have changed much. I don't feel like bed as I am hot and itching from prickly heat all over my body, it's depressing and uncomfortable.

The aerodrome workers caught a snake, a python, nearly 10 feet long so at least they have some meat for their stew, they say it tastes like bacon. I'm getting very tired of vegetable stew and rice, give me home and a nice salmon salad. As I think despondently of these almost forgotten foods I must have fallen asleep.

Wednesday September 29th

I'm awakened all too soon by noises of men stirring, it is morning again with rice pap breakfast followed by the usual march of two miles to work through the gruelling heat. Later back to camp along a road blazing white in the midday heat, half pint of rice and raw tea and back we go again to the cemetery sweating profusely as the tea tries to escape through our ever-open pores. Working as well as our general weakness will allow for a further two and a half hours and then back to camp, too tired to bother to go straight to the showers, we lay for a while in our grime and stinking sweat. Everyday is a repetition, except that some days we are much more tired than others, but then we are a lot better off than the poor devils we are burying.

Tonight I am reading a war book, Cambridgeshires 1914-18. As a matter of interest it states that the 62nd Home Defence Battalion was stationed in my hometown during that war, as some of that regiment has been this time.

Thursday September 30th

As another day dawns and we set off on our usual route march to work during which we are stopped by some "Nip" soldiers who accused our officer of saluting Indian soldiers driving "Nip" lorries. They shouted and jumped around waving their arms to demonstrate no saluting, the Major just stood stupefied until the "Nips" thinking they had made their point marched off. The lorries driven by the Indian troops were bringing in men, 2500 of them coming from Java, also we hear that there are 200 Italian prisoners in Singapore. A convoy of tractors passing by, all stop because the native drivers spot a mango tree full of ripe fruit. They leap from their machines and rush to gather what they can, at the same time their head man gesticulates with his arms for them to come back. They do not return until they have had their fill, then with mango pulp and large grins on their faces they start up the tractors and with a wave to us move on their way.

Friday October 1st 1943

Another month comes in, hot and dry and I think you would laugh if you saw me now. I am working in the cemetery, dressed only in my underpants, a hat and boots out of which protrude my toes, anyhow, I think I am in the eye of the Chinese girls that pass by with their "Nip" escorts, already two of them became too attentive only to get their faces smacked by the guards. I'm as brown as a native so perhaps I was worth the punishment.

Arriving back at camp at the end of the day I was given a letter, it being the ninth from my mother and just 17 months old. I am looking for a much later letter, for more up to date news, also for the first one from my wife.

After tea I had a chat with a fellow from New Zealand, he was with an airforce unit, he was wounded and got left behind when they moved out. The time has moved on quickly to 9.30pm, talking to someone different for a change helps. I have a bit of lumbago so I turn in for the night and lay listening to the buzzing of the mosquitoes and calls of a night bird, not much noise from the human side except some snores and occasional shouts from restless bodies.

Sunday October 3rd

Day dawns yet again, followed by the usual routine but I do manage to get to a camp concert and hear an Australians new song, that he says one day he will get broadcast. It goes something like this:

"We are waiting for something to happen,
For someone to take us away,
For we can't go on a tram,
It may be an American,
Or it may be Chinaman,
Or the "Nips" may tell us to scram.

We've had malaria, we've had beriberi

267

And now we have a nasty rash that makes it hard to walk,
So we are waiting for something to happen,
But maybe we will wait for years."

Monday October 4ᵗʰ

A Red Cross grant said to have been paid to the Japanese for our benefit has been cancelled and what monies still available will be pooled and paid out as follows:

> Officers $12 a month
> WO's 25c a day
> NCO's 15c and privates 10c per day

with 21c to be paid into the camp mess fund for buying bits and pieces to supplement rations when possible.

Tuesday October 5ᵗʰ

Today the cemetery is visited by high ranking officers of the Dutch army and navy who congratulate me on its layout and upkeep. This at least gives my men and me an uplift as we stand in line streaming with sweat to hear their comments. This over it is back to digging a few more graves, we rarely go a day without one or more burials.

Tonight I'm going to see a new show the "Aussies" are putting on. The concert was very good, it brought many sighs and good-humoured banter from the audience, especially when six smartly dressed "He-females" appeared on stage, they looked ravishing. It puzzled me as to how the producers came by the clothing and other props. Like all good things it ends all too soon, we stroll back to our quarters still talking about the "He-females", no doubt they will be in some of our dreams during the night.

Wednesday October 6ᵗʰ

The night seems to go very quickly as I once again awake to the usual noise of men banging their bits and pieces to get rid of the

268

blood-sucking bugs. The rest of the day passes quietly and after a shower to rid us of the grime, it's tea time, and as in hundreds of times in the past, it's raw tea, plain rice and an "effort" - something made mainly from rice, anyhow we are glad of it. After the feast I attend a darts conference to form an area league and part of the outcome sees me as captain of the cemetery team. Well it gives us something to talk about. The time is around 11.30pm and a sudden commotion arouses us from the fitful slumbers, the noise appears to come from a small room occupied by some RSM's. A man rushes from the room, shouting and swearing, charges down the stairs and into the night, he seems deranged, he is eventually caught some distance away in Command area. A hunt is still on for one who broke out of the mental ward earlier in the day, we also have one who is quiet, he just stands by the side of the road waving his hand and chanting, "Holt bus", poor fellow. I think that maybe we are all slowly going the same way.

Thursday October 7th

Another uneventful day slides away and I attend tonight a preview of a play for which I was given an invitation. It is called "Outward Bound" and was produced by a one-legged officer, Major Osmond Dalby of the Royal Artillery. It was funny, it typified a ship loaded with dead souls on their way to the next world. Major Bregiel plays a half-wit ships steward, who has done the trip 5,000 times, but is not accepted at the gates of heaven because he is a suicide. It records the reactions of the travellers when they find out that they are dead, well it was a good laugh and I retire to bed in a more light-hearted mood.

Friday October 8th

The day comes bright and very hot, sweat streaming down my body as with two of my men I prepare a grave in the Dutch sector for a burial, it makes 525 that I have now buried. What a surprise the body is actually in a coffin, a bulky rectangle of a box, the first allowed by the "Nips". After the burial I pause to reflect on the number buried, what a waste of young men's lives, just dead from disease because of the lack of food and drugs, which could have saved many. It's one thing to die in battle but inhuman to allow men to slowly rot away. The day over we march back to camp, always very quiet at this time of day, exhausted, sweat drying to salt on our bodies, our thoughts perhaps on a cleansing shower or wondering why we are going through this hell. Well we are soon under the showers, after which we again feel fine.

The very occasional sugar ration takes place today, it amounts to a teaspoonful per man. It has ranged from white to almost black and now it's brown, anyhow it's enough to sweeten two rice rations which makes a change.

Saturday October 9th

Another bag of mail has turned up so I keep my fingers crossed, maybe one from the wife. The area sounds very musical tonight as four small orchestras are either practising or playing at concerts, it's amazing how these instruments have come to hand, even a solo trumpeter can be heard in the distance. The music helps to relieve one's depression. The dart league kicks off with a narrow win for my team, this again breaks the monotonous long nights of darkness.

Sunday October 10th

Another day has started and with it a terribly browned-off feeling, we are getting very low in spirit just waiting and waiting for something to happen. It doesn't help when you pass queues of men lying around the latrines, because they have dysentery and cannot move from them. They are wasting slowly away, being pestered all the time with hordes of big flies. Hardly a man walking around without an unblemished body, many are afflicted by skin disease. The hospital is full, around 2,000 patients suffering from beriberi, malaria and pellagra. The last named means the body is going rotten, it smells and a mosquito net has to be used to protect the patient from the flies which are always with us. To cheer myself up I go to an "Aussie" concert party for the second time, at least it gives me a good laugh and I feel better for it, and so to bed with bugs as companions.

Tuesday October 12th

Passed close to the aerodrome that the "Nips" are constructing at Changi, using our men as labour. I noticed that two light railways were operating, moving soil. It's hard work for the men loading the trucks on meagre rations. Trailer loads of bombs pass on their way in the direction of Singapore.

Wednesday October 13th

Some details received regarding the 20,000 men that have gone up country. It is said that seven officers and 200 men died (cause not known) during the period July- August.

Friday October 15th

Saw a mango tree with fruit so we spent half an hour trying to knock some off. I managed to get five rather bruised fruit, these will mix well with the dinner rice.

Sitting around in the evening, talk is about the civilian internees in Changi jail. We have heard so many rumours about their possible moves, that they have become a mystery to us, some say repatriation is on, time will tell.

Monday October 18th

Some 1,300 men in transit from Java to Japan left us today. Strong rumour has it that Red Cross ships are coming into port, maybe we shall have bully for Xmas. Anyhow, "Red Cross ships are coming" crops up so many times but they never arrive so I think they are like mirages in the desert to some men.

Tuesday October 19th

A lorry drove over a mine on the 'drome and three of our men were slightly injured, the "Nip" driver is not expected to live. One of our dock working parties have seen two aircraft carriers loaded with planes.

Wednesday October 20th

Still plenty of talk regarding the Red Cross ships, but work party says they have seen nothing, but report that the aircraft carriers have left port.

Thursday October 21st

One runway being constructed on the 'drome leaves my cemetery practically in the centre angle of two runways, it has been said because of superstition the "Nips" actually planned to leave us where we are. Two Red Cross buses went by on their way to the aerodrome, I expect it was some form of exercise with the "Nip" troops there. The work party safely uncover another mine. Tonight I took my dart team to the show I recently saw, "Outward Bound", it was greatly enjoyed.

Friday October 22nd

Morning again and a roll call, to tell us that air raid precaution exercises will be carried out during the next seven days which will bring black-outs, after this Island exercises will begin, this I expect means "Nip" army manoeuvres. During the day I saw bulldozers pushing over huge trees like so many matchsticks, our lads are there cutting and clearing them, huge earth graders soon move in and level off the ground. A lot of air activity today.

Sunday October 24th

A day of air activity. Saw a mock battle taking place over the Naval dock area. Our peaceful days seem to be shattered by the roar of planes the whole day long, it's so noticeable after 18 months without any, but it must be sign that something is moving in our direction.

Monday October 25th

Food is not very plentiful but we are getting a little fresh fish. Five ducks kept by some officers for their eggs have been stolen. They were later traced, having been taken by an Australian and sold to one of his officers, outcome not known.

Tuesday October 26th

Terribly browned off, so went to "Aussie" concert for second time and had a good laugh and felt better.

Wednesday October 27th

It's just two years since I left Marbury Hall in Cheshire, lets hope that we have done two thirds of our time as prisoners. I doubt whether we can last much longer as illness from starvation will kill us all off. Well a little relief comes tonight with my darts team beating the Officers' Mess staff.

Thursday October 28th

Our work on the cemetery is very hard at this time as we are running out levels involving the moving of a four foot depth of soil, it's hard clay. I could just carry on over the undulating run of the ground, only my need for perfection will not allow it, so we sweat and toil on with plenty of ribbing and swearing about my methods. The night was interrupted with a black out, breakdown or "Nip" exercise, we never knew. It gave the rats a chance to scurry about among us and most of us have been awake anyway long before dawn.

Friday October 29th

The Japanese Imperial Army have issued an order asking us to look for places suitable for digging slit trenches in case of air-raids. This news gives us a definite lift as it seems that long range allied bombers must be getting within range of Singapore.

Saturday October 30th

We are to lose another 100 men and one officer, Lt Munnings of the Suffolk Regiment. The men include fifty "Aussies"; they are going to Blackang Mati Island. Rumour has it that 7,000 men have arrived back in Singapore from other work areas.

Sunday October 31st

No work, no recreation, it sends you rather crazy. I have spent the afternoon drawing cows in various attitudes on a wall beside my bed. On looking at these specimens later, I concluded that I must be going into my second childhood.

Monday November 1st 1943

The "Nips" inform us that they will tell us when to dig slit trenches. Are these hopeful signs? Anyhow it gives us something to talk about. We play darts tonight and beat a Malayan command team.

Wednesday November 3rd

A couple of days pass by with nothing of importance to note except that life gets more boring daily, at work I can get involved, it's the time in between when we all seem to be waiting for something to happen.

Thursday November 4th

The weather has become very heavy and depressing and I have headaches every day, it does not help that I have a Dutch cremation on. It's break time for dinner, a small amount of plain rice and a cup of hot weak raw tea, which on drinking just does its best to flow out of every pore. Work over and it's the drag back to camp.

We are now getting the tail end of the monsoon, so we are getting rather a lot of rain, it makes it bad for the aerodrome workers, some 600 from my area, who after a day out in it return home wet and miserable. The few degrees drop in temperature leaves them feeling cool.

Friday November 5th

Had to go to work today as had some burials on hand. After these had been attended to and two more graves dug we return to camp wet and mud covered. The showers strike a bit cool, it would not be so bad if we had something more than rags to rub down with. Anyhow it is tea time, the cup of hot tea warms me up, the rest of the meal is quickly swallowed. This over I collect my dart team and off we go to play the Company B team, winning after a hard game.

Saturday November 6th

A week has gone by with nothing of importance happening except the daily effort to keep going. The grind has just been relieved by a visit to another "Aussie" concert. It's rather moving, one act depicted a bride in floral setting, she was deep in thought and on either side of her a trumpeter played, "Sweetheart", a romantic melody during which "she" danced a rhythmic movement, after which "she" resumed her seat in an attitude of prayer. The audience was captivated, I feel that it turned their thoughts homeward to their dear ones. The overture certainly took me back to my courting days, it was "Who's taking you home tonight".

Still strong rumours of possible return of 10,000 men from Burma.

Sunday November 7th

Saw another "Aussie" show depicting a Sheik and his harem, very good. I think the "Aussie" lads love dressing up as "Sheilas", but our own B Group has the best female impersonator as yet, "she's" Kay Bell of the RAF. Our concerts are coming over many nights a week now and parties of men are invited to the various compounds to see the shows of each group. Competition is keen and everyone gets better, they keep us from sitting around at night and brooding.

Monday November 8th

A show I have just seen was the funniest thing for years, it depicted a man playing a twelve month old baby, a good laugh, even the "Nip" guards enjoyed it.

Tuesday November 9th

At a lecture I attended, the Medical Director tells us that owing to our enforced living we all have new stomachs (I think empty ones) helped by the lack of alcohol. He says this will, if not ruined by us later, add ten years to our lives. Comments from the men include, "Whose he kidding, we're half dead now".

Wednesday November 10th

We try to run things so that my permanent staff get a half day off, today it is mine but a body for cremation is suddenly brought along and gets me rushing around somewhat, so it is goodbye to a rest. After a fairly long stoppage the "Nips" tell me that I can resume cutting turf for the cemetery, a nice gesture on their part.

Thursday November 11th

We were so busy cutting this turf that we fail to notice that the workers on the fighter runway had stopped work, as it was November 11th they were holding a two minutes silence, the "Nip" soldiers respected this silence.

20. **On this day...** November 12, 1943... German battleship *Tirpitz* sunk off Tromsø, Norway.

Saturday November 13th

At last our piggeries are producing, for we each had about 5ozs of pork with our rice for tea, well, miracles do happen. The pigs have been kept on what waste there is from the cookhouse and garden rubbish. During the last two days my four main staff have cut and hauled 2,000 sq ft of turf to the cemetery. This is hard work on a near empty stomach.

Sunday November 14th

A day off, a time to wash the sweat and stink out of my few bits and pieces of clothing, also my two ragged bits of blankets. It comes to mind that it is someone's birthday in the family, afraid I can't remember who's any more than I can barely muster up pictures in my mind of what you all look like, must be the diet causing one's brain to blot out. Over two years now and not a letter from the wife, she must have given me up for lost. Letters have stopped coming in for the past few months.

Tonight I went to an armistice parade, First World War.

Monday November 15th

There are eight special prisoners in a hut in the garden compound, no one is allowed within a 100 yards of the hut, also a week ago two men were successful in making an escape from the camp. This has resulted in ten former prisoners being taken back to the Singapore Outram Road jail to complete their punishment and that jail is really terrible. These men were formerly sent to us in a horrible state having suffered starvation and beatings. They were hospital cases, nearer dead than alive but the medics restored them to a reasonable state of health only to see them taken back and endure more punishment. When they decide to send people back from Outram Road they are as good as dead, not many survive.

The Changi Road is being closed for an hour later this afternoon, so have to quickly finish off some burials so we can get back to camp for tea. Maybe the "Nips" are moving something to the 'drome. Some of the men have an exchange of words with my Dutch scrub clearing party, apparently their opinion of British girls is that they are gold-diggers and good-timers. Perhaps they would have changed their minds if they had seen the girls on Ack! Ack! guns and driving open trucks in really freezing weather.

Tuesday November 16th

I am still allowed to cut turf for the cemetery so work in covering the ground and graves is moving along fast.

A man returned from the notorious Outram jail has died.

Wednesday November 17th

More huts are being erected in close vicinity to us, rumours says they are for the long expected men from up country.

Another good laugh from an "Aussie" show, a "girl" sings, "Tease You", at the same time uses a reflecting mirror on the audience whilst displaying a daring leg.

Friday November 19th

Two humdrum days pass by, the only highlights, my team beat the dart league leaders, all good for morale. Later saw a show at our own "Little Theatre", called swing time. J J Porter's band including Jack Payne's drummer, Jack Greenwood first trumpeter with Geraldo and others well known in the dance band days. It's surprising the talent in the bag out here.

Saturday November 20th

Talk among the men today is that we must be going a bit funny, we call it being a "bit tropical", some fellows are already advanced.

Sunday November 21st

Rest and wash day, but the more we wash the less we have, also the tiny soap ration has to be carefully used. It is not a "Nip" issue, it's another of the many things made by fellows in the camp. I am not very happy today as I have a re-occurrence of internal piles and they are very lowering.

Tuesday November 23rd

Saw Australian concert party, heard songs from Judy Garland sung by "Ginger and Slim", our drag artistes - who are very good.

Wednesday November 24th

Two days have passed and I am feeling better so spend the afternoon in the wood yard helping to saw a disc from a rubber tree to make up as a dart board, a friend will supply the wires made up by him as he works in a "Nip" workshop.

Thursday November 25th

We beat my friend's Royal Army Ordnance Corps team last night, but we still got our wires. Passed the "Nip" sentry at the gate this morning, he stopped us, shouting and gesticulating. We wait rather apprehensively wondering what's wrong. In his Pidgin English he says, "You no salute proper", and is not satisfied until we have marched and saluted three times. Dimmed lights tonight, it's a "Brown-out".

Saturday November 27th

Tea tonight, a small pork ration instead of the recent fish. Col. Holmes, Commander of British POW's here has been punished by the "Nips" for complaining about prison treatment in Singapore. He has to do 14 days ground levelling on the aerodrome. The day has been wet but we have worked through it, finishing turfing over of the 528 British and Dutch graves. A football match has been arranged between England and Scotland on Sunday.

Sunday November 28th

I go to watch the game and see England win 3 - 1. Some good amateur and professional players represented. A Scot's piper and a drummer turned out to give it added interest. These sports annoy the "Nips", they think we are getting too much food and really mean to cut our rations if we don't stop playing games.

21. *On this day...* November 28, 1943... Churchill, Stalin and Roosevelt meet at the Tehran conference.

Monday November 29th

It's been a week of black-out tests, they make my thoughts return to all of you at home and wonder if you are still getting as many. I think perhaps the wife has given up hope of seeing me anymore, just at the moment I am optimistic enough to think that I will turn up sometime in the future, like a bad penny. Maybe I shall be toothless, with a long beard and around fifty years of age, my God what a thought!

Tuesday November 30th

The morning feels cool as it is pouring with rain, so no work until it breaks. I have just heard that the order has been given to get on digging air-raid trenches, so the war against the "Nips" must be coming nearer.

Wednesday December 1st 1943

Well its got to December again, lets hope the next one will see us home for Xmas. It's still raining heavily and as we do not come under the same code of strictness as other work parties we can spend a few hours spine bashing, providing there are no burials to take care of.

Some men have come back from up-country camps. It seems that cholera broke out in one area and 280 died, those that have arrived are haggard, dirty and weak.

Our rice ration has been cut but supplemented with soya beans. These are better for us, but you have to chew every one otherwise they don't digest.

What few dogs we have left here, the "Nips" say have to be registered, but for some reason "Andy", the group pet was overlooked so the "Nips" says he will have to die. Feelings

281

among the men ran high, in the end a petition was raised and sent in to the Japanese, we have since been told a reprieve has been granted.

Saw Command show tonight, "A murder has been arranged", quite hair-raising.

Saturday December 4th

I heard this morning that six officers had been poisoned after eating lima beans, they had not been cooked correctly. They had temperatures of 104°F but have since been told that they are out of danger.

Sunday December 5th

Four officers have arrived back from Malaya, I heard that they told grim stories about conditions and treatment of men, also back from Blackang Mati (an offshore island) are some men who were recently sent there, they are very sick and they have to be replaced with fit men immediately. Have to parade tomorrow for a throat swab as diphtheria is on the increase once more. The "Nips" want more men for aerodrome work. Almost all men of any use are now out of camp daily.

Tuesday December 7th

So much for our soya bean ration, it's a wonder they didn't cause trouble at the latrines, in a couple of days everybody was on the run as though they had been dosed with Epsom salts.

Tonight as I write notes in my diary all lights go out, on enquiry, I am told it's a real air-raid warning. This news sets the men talking, weighing up what might be happening and where, in a few hours there are enough conjectures to fill a book.

Wednesday December 8ᵗʰ

It's the second anniversary of the East Asia war, again I ask myself, how many more years? A shout brings me to my senses, it's my friend from the "Nip" workshops, he brings me a set of metal darts that he has made for me and they are really good, with the help of him and his pals we have finished the second dart board, the first one has been painted and looks as though we have just bought it from a shop. We are allowed to write another postcard home, 24 words. You cannot say what you wish except that you are alright and good wishes to one's wife and relatives.

Thursday December 9ᵗʰ

An order has just come in from the Japanese Imperial Army asking us to take down and destroy all pictures of the Royal Family and allied leaders.

Friday December 10ᵗʰ

Had a good win over the medical men in the darts, we are high in the league table.

Saturday December 11ᵗʰ

Our group has raised a good number of chickens for egg production, but chickens over here are rather small therefore the eggs are tiny although useful in the cookhouse. It is being said their numbers may have to cut owing to the difficulty in finding suitable food for them.

One of my friends has proved to be a diphtheria carrier, I'm lucky not to have caught it. Fourteen of the first 100 men who had swabs taken are said to be carriers and have gone into isolation for a period. Feeding like cattle now on beans and bean flour mixed with the breakfast rice, at least it has a smell like Quaker oats that is if I haven't forgotten the smell.

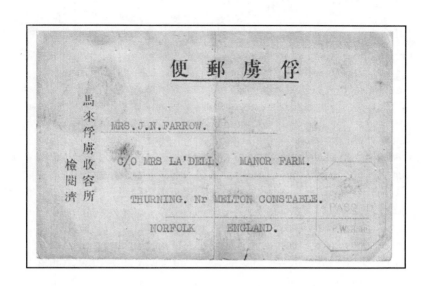

便 郵 虜 俘

馬
來
俘
虜
收
容
所

檢
閱
濟

MRS. J.N. FARROW.

C/O MRS LA'DELL. MANOR FARM.

THURNING. Nr MELTON CONSTABLE.

NORFOLK   ENGLAND.

PASSED

P.W.

5772489 SERGT J. FARROW. 5/R/NORFOLK.R.10/12/43

DEAREST JOAN.
            AM WELL, CHEERFUL. MY LOVE TO MY
MOTHER AND FAMILY, ALSO NEICES. ALWAYS THINKING
OF YOU. KEEP SMILING.

                LOVING YOU ALWAYS

                    Jack

Postcard sent from Changi 10th December 1943

Monday December 13th

This morning I hear that the group has lost four men to hospital with diphtheria, hope it does not get out of hand.

Tuesday December 14th

One of my officers, Major Bregiel, has got rheumatics and may have to have his tonsils and teeth out.

A number of "Aussies" arrived from up country looking all in and filthy, the poor devils will delight in a shower. They have worked on the Burma railway.

Wednesday December 15th

One of the returned Australians, an officer, died and was buried today.

Friday December 17th

A hundred men were allowed by the "Nips" to visit the cemetery for a service. Colonel Holmes the camp commandant praised the work of myself and my men on what we had done on burials and lay out of the cemetery. He said it was greatly appreciated by all the officers.

Recordings were also made today in some parts of the camp for broadcasts to England and Australia. Sounds very nice but knowing the "Nips" they may never be transmitted.

Saturday December 18th

It is getting near Christmas and I have just seen a display of toys made in the camp for internee children in Changi jail. They are beautifully made, and painted from bits and pieces of material that could be pinched, found and scrounged. There were dolls, pedal cars, mechanical toys, ships, railway trains, dolls houses and even dresses, prettily done for the little girls there. The British toys really excelled and I never cease to be amazed at the talent in our ranks.

Tuesday December 21st

Men still coming back from Burma and Malaya, many are very ill and even dying. They are stretching our hospital staff to the limit.

Friday December 24th

I have had four burials to cope with over the last two days and another today, this means that we have to dig five graves to keep ahead, what a sorrowful job on Xmas Eve, our second as prisoners. With the conditions enforced upon us the men have, it seems, lifted their spirits a bit for Xmas. The "Nips" have helped this by a gift of twenty cigarettes per man, also three "Woodbines" each from our own Command reserves. Lights have been allowed for churches until 12.30am.

Saturday December 25th

Another Xmas day is with us, it's gloomy no matter how you try to brighten things up, the food is reasonable, as the cookhouse has endeavoured to save a bit from the rations to make a few extra rice, bean and vegetable pasties, the well-known "efforts". The "Nips" gave us a small pork ration so the food brought about a few smiles. Saw a comic football match this afternoon in which the "Aladdin" pantomime party took part, it also provided four dogs much amusement. A band was also playing which helped to enliven the watchers. Well in my thoughts I send Christmas Greetings to my wife, Joan and my mother, hoping the next one will be their happiest ever.

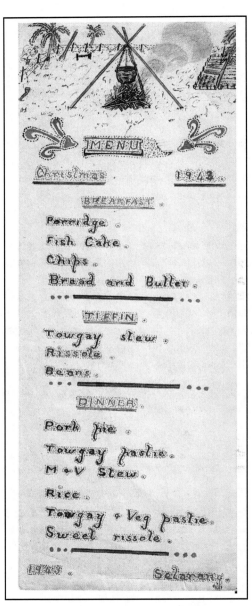

Menu for Christmas 1943

Sunday December 26th

I had some camp made "hooch" last night, enough to give me that million dollar feeling, first alcoholic drink for two years and didn't I feel merry. I feel a bit muzzy in the head this morning. I forgot to mention that yesterday I had to turn out for a cremation, duty calls even on Xmas day. Also to top the day the electricity supply broke down, this affected the water and barely a trickle comes from our only two taps. My men and myself had a good Boxing Day breakfast, mainly through our own efforts through saving a little from our weekly cash allowance, which with the terribly inflated prices in the canteen do not allow for much. We managed to save enough between five of us to buy a tin of fish, $2.85, some sweet potatoes made into chips, fried bread, made from a mixture of sago, maize and rice flour and two eggs. It made a smashing meal for us that was fried up over a fire of sticks outside. We feel good, but this is soon tempered when I am notified of another burial. I expected a coffin but not so, just wrapped in canvas. Rest of my day spent in constructing and preparing beds for flowers in the grass of the centre section of the cemetery. This work engrosses me and I can forget all around me.

22. On this day... December 26, 1943... *'Scharnhorst'* disabled by *HMS Norfolk* and then sunk by *Duke of York.* 11 other Allied warships involved.

Tuesday December 28th

Another morning comes in wet and with bad news that 83 men of the 5th Royal Norfolks, my Regiment, have died of cholera etc, somewhere north of Malaya, including my old friend Jack Beales of Territorial days, also some of my platoon. Rumour again says that a Red Cross ship has arrived, if it has we do not seem to get the contents.

Wednesday December 29th

There are some smallpox patients in the hospital, they have come down from Malaya. Vaccinations for everyone tonight. Extra men to work on the 'drome, I may have to go. This is done so that we may have a day off to celebrate the New Year.

CHAPTER 7

ROTTEN NIGHTS AND BAD DAYS

Saturday January 1st 1944

This eventually came in with plenty of music, lights were allowed until 1am. The old year faded to the strains of "Old Lang Syne" and the new one was hailed with ringing cheers, no doubt all were hoping that the next would see them home. Once again my thoughts are with you all at home, we long for home so much, I expect this is because of the degrading conditions that we live with.

As it is the first day of the year 1944 I clean up my corner of the abode. I debug my bed, bits and pieces and wash my mosquito net. It's a wonderful day with bright hot sunshine, maybe it feels better because today is taking another step forward, perhaps for the better, well I can only hope.

A smallpox suspect has been found in the hospital eye ward, isolating it for the next six weeks. I visited the hospital to see a fellow who used to work as a barman in my home town. He has a bad spinal problem and lies on a bed specially made for him by the Royal Engineers group. He has laid flat on it for seven months, they let him get up for a short time at Xmas.

Sunday January 2nd

No burials so I get a rest day and phew! It is so much hotter up in the 100°F area. I met Mr Legget, a Malay States volunteer who tells me that he was a rubber planter before hostilities broke out, also that he comes from Edgefield, a village quite near my home. He also tells me of another planter that came from my home town, a Mr Aldis of St Peter's Road.

We still receive our amenity grant of 15 cents a day, this allows one to buy the equivalent of a coconut a week.

Some of the bank notes issued by the Japanese

Tuesday January 4ᵗʰ

Weather has changed to heavy rain and after seeing to one burial we pass the time dart playing. Later I go for a voluntary vaccination as the first one did not take then I went to the canteen and spent a fortnight's savings on 1 lb of coarse brown sugar and a few unsavoury looking biscuits.

Wednesday January 5ᵗʰ

The very wet period continues, the tail end of the monsoons it brings just a very small drop in temperature but we feel rather cold or should I say cool. We throw what bits of clothing we have across our shoulders seeking a bit of comfort to our skinny bodies.

Thursday January 6ᵗʰ

The days pass with just routine work; a few more burials as some recently returned men are not making it.

Monday January 10ᵗʰ

I have been soaked twice today trying to keep ahead with open graves, the trouble is finding dry clothing. I do have a pair of trousers I'm keeping to wear on the hoped for day of our release, but I think I may be forced to cut the legs off if things get much worse.

Wednesday January 12ᵗʰ

Tonight I went to the "Aladdin" panto' for the third time to try and keep my spirits up.

Thursday January 13th

Today is my second year round after landing here.

Friday January 14th

One of my men, "Titch" Tunmore, from the 4th Suffolk Regiment died at the table, choking on some soya beans. He slid under the table and by the time we got him out he was dead, it was a great shock to us.

"Nippon" officers inspected the area today, hope they find everything to their liking. Another burial making 11 this week, that brings my total to 540.

Saturday January 15th

Went to another show tonight called "Roman Rackets", a skit on Cleopatra. It is good to see even make-believe girls.

Tuesday January 18th

Toilet paper issue is half a sheet of newspaper per week and sometimes an issue is not made. It does not last some men long as it is used mainly to roll dried leaves in for smokes. So what happens at the latrines? Well animals don't have toilet paper do they, also dry soft grass, water etc., come into use. The lines of dysentery cases grow daily, making the latrines as busy as Piccadilly Circus, without the noise of car engines but with the buzzing of millions of large flies who could easily be the death of you if you lacked cleanliness.

Wednesday January 19th

Today the cemetery was invaded by two-hundred "Nip" naval men, a few showed interest but they were really passing through to view the large naval guns at the back of us. After looking at our ragged selves, their white tropical uniforms are dazzling. A black cobra, over five feet long, is caught just outside our boundary. It is the second in two days, the catchers and their friends will enjoy fried or stewed snake.

Thursday January 20th

As the day draws to its close the sunset is rather unusual instead of large orange ball, a small golden one set amidst thin cloud, giving off a queer golden glow that covered the landscape in its eeriness. After tea there's nothing much to do so we sit around outside in the starlight talking on the same old topic, food and mother's cooking. We no longer discuss to any length the ending of the war, we have accepted the fact we could be here for another year or two. A fellow from our group office drops down beside us imparting the news that six of my group have been admitted to hospital with malaria. This has lately been on the increase and we think the reason is that our largely immune mosquitoes are biting the men that have come back to the camp from Burma and Malaya with the complaint and therefore spreading it among us, this is not a happy thought. An air raid exercise sends us all running to our slit trenches.

Saturday January 22nd

Another day and with it the news that I have two burials on hand, and having dealt with them we carry on digging more graves and clearing ground ahead for more. A sad outlook that gets one wondering who's next. The work day comes to an end and once again we trudge wearily home, mucky and streaming as always with sweat. We cannot wait to get to the showers and when the cooling water falls on our bodies the yells and dancing of the men are like Red Indians on the war-path.

After tea I went to a gramophone recital, seems a rather tame sort of thing, but it turned out to be entertaining. The area is surrounded with tall pink-flowered trees called Casserina, I think it would make a nice name for a house some future day.

*23. **On this day**... January 22, 1944... Allied landings take place at Anzio.*

Sunday January 23rd

As the day dawns my thoughts turn homeward to my wife Joan, it's her birthday and the third that I have been away on the day. Well if my thoughts can be transmitted they are on the way bearing good wishes.

Monday January 24th

The day is spent levelling off another section of ground for Dutch burials. In the filled section we have buried six of their officers.

Wednesday January 26th

It seems that supplies must be scarce as the "Nip" General Arimuty has ordered that sufficient men be withdrawn from the aerodrome workers to maintain the garden supplies.

Had another TAB jab this morning and this afternoon was spent fighting a bush fire on the uncleared part of the cemetery ground. Phew, it was bloody hot, after we had dealt with it we dragged ourselves back to camp, with ash sticking to the sweat of our dead beat bodies. After tea and a couple of hours rest I felt more my self.

Thursday January 27th

Eggs are sought after by the hospital authorities at the rate of 1,000 a week. They will pay 20c each for hens and 25c for ducks, in the past many eggs were donated free by the officers and men who are still able to keep chickens and ducks. Another jab for dysentery only a day after the TAB jab.

Friday January 28th

I feel rather ill on arising from bed this morning, no doubt a reaction from the jabs. Weather terribly hot, even the wind sears you. It's now 17 days without rain and without it the heat is just getting unbearable. I expect being January, at home you are shivering with cold.

Tonight I am putting a patch in my towel, from an old piece of material that I picked up. Everything I've got is patched now, socks, shorts and my bits of blanket.

We had a 3oz meat ration and rumour has it that it was yak.

Saturday January 29th

It is still dry with the hot wind, but it helps in one way that it dries up any pools of water and that stops the egg laying mosquitoes, thereby slowing up the malaria. The cooks now make a substance called "Tempo", they say it's prepared from half rotten Soya beans. Marvellous how we survive on the rubbish we eat. A mess meeting is called as men are dissatisfied with the food rations. The accusations are that three mess cats are eating a percentage of our rations and that some men's chickens and ducks are getting more than swill. Small talk also has it that a racket is going on between the cooks and the keepers of fowls. I think some of the accusations are made from a jealousy point of view.

Sunday January 30th

Today the meal was made up of four types of beans, soya, dizzu and two others unknown to me, anyhow it made a nice change.

News has just reached me that two of my past cemetery workers have died up in Burma. Picked up a six-month-old newspaper, *"Nippon Times"* and saw in it a small piece referring to the cemetery. This keeps us busy with almost daily burials, maintenance and landscaping. It is still very much hotter than usual, every movement makes me drip sweat, it runs into your eyes, off the end of your nose, in fact it runs off everywhere.

Monday January 31ˢᵗ

It's now 20 days of drought, usually a storm hits somewhere locally every few days, until the rain does come, however, we will have to put up with this incredible heat. It is making everyone irritable and weak. Anyhow another small addition to the dinner rice cheered us up, it was a ration of pickled whitebait (tiny fish). The food has certainly improved since the complaints.

Tuesday February 1ˢᵗ 1944

Have just been told that 27 bags of mail have arrived and that five of them are for the British Forces. Once again my hopes are high and that there will be just one for me, from the wife.

Just five minutes rain has broken the drought. This evening I had my second TAB inoculation and then off to an "Aussie" concert depicting a western story and Apache dance starring our excellent version of Judy Garland.

24. On this day... February 1, 1944... American forces land on the Marshall Islands.

Wednesday February 2ⁿᵈ

I do not feel very well this morning, again no doubt due to the recent injection, but I still have to go for a second dysentery one later today. The "Nips" are more free now with the vaccine issue, it's believed that they are worried about possible contact with their own troops.

Thursday February 3rd

Food gets a few more interesting variations as the cooks use their initiative to disguise the rice into "efforts".

Friday February 4th

It's still very hot and dry but I cool off with a shower which was only a trickle as somewhere, something has gone wrong with the water supply. At least I feel clean and fresh as I set out for yet another show at our own Little Theatre, it was very entertaining, "Hay Fever", story by Noel Coward and produced for us by Oswald Dalby, an officer with one leg and one eye. The show featured John Woods, the celebrated "Aussie" "female" actor, who played the leading lady, Major Bradshaw said to be a stage and screen actor, Private Rye a professional actor who played a difficult part of a tom-boy girl, and Oliver Thomas of old Etonian amateur theatricals played the Bohemian lass known as "Moonlight Maggie". He has his hair to almost shoulder length for the flapper part, in which he excels. The hair is a mass of dark golden ringlets. As I write up my diary the lights fade almost out, it is a brown-out so it's an air raid alert and now the best place is on the bed with my thoughts until I drift off to sleep.

Sunday February 6th

One hundred men are to be allowed to write a message for broadcasting to their homeland. Lots are drawn for the privilege, my name does not come out of the hat, not that it bothers me for I do not think for one minute that the "Nips" ever put them on the air.

Monday February 7th

Working close by us on the aerodrome is a light railway. The men are shovelling sand into its trucks for removal to another area. It brings a little light relief to us as it puffs and grunts along with its load, it's around three years since we saw a train.

Tuesday February 8th

The month-long drought has at last broken and tonight it's a real tropical down-pour.

As the barrack blocks have no windows, only large apertures to allow for circulation of air, there is no way that they can be covered, this means we have to shade our lights, which rather darkens things down. All doors and door frames and anything else wood have long disappeared to keep the cookhouse fires going.

Wednesday February 9th

At last the long awaited mail is sorted and letters are handed out. I receive one and with a shaking hand I carefully tear it open to find it is from my mother, whom I'm always glad to hear from. There is no mention of my wife or my father but it is a relief to hear that the rest of the family are alright. But what is happening to Joan's letters as I know that she must be writing often? I feel very depressed at not hearing anything about her, it is over two years now, to me two very long ones, at the same time I wonder if she has had any news of me, why can't these swaggering pig headed little "Nips" let letters move freely, I suppose in their eyes it helps to break morale, that could be so but not for long as we are capable of overcoming these things. I forgot to say that this last letter is over a year old and I must go waiting for the one I want.

All of us have to write an essay of 150 words on an episode during the Malayan campaign for the Japanese. Why, remains a mystery to us.

Thursday February 10th

We have had a daily 2oz meat ration for the past week and even on that small amount you can feel the difference in yourself. Yesterday it was pork from our own piggeries but none on the menus today, let's hope it has not come to an end. The rain is still with us and when it is not too heavy we plod on with the cemetery work, a half an hour of sun and you are dried out.

Friday February 11th

My right hand man, Pte Alexander, has gone down with malaria and is in hospital. He comes from Norwich and is a cemetery worker in civvy street. When I think of him on parade one morning in England, the thought brings a smile. The officer doing early morning inspection asked him, "Have you shaved this morning?" "No Sir, I don't shave yet," Alec replied. "Well start now, before parade tomorrow. You look like a bloody nanny goat!" Poor Alec, the sun shining down the ranks brought to light two or three blond hairs that he had never bothered to cut.

Saturday February 12th

Two years ago today since my platoon was hit by aerial bombs, I pause for a while to reflect on that tragic moment, something one will not easily forget, the loss of men that one has known for a number of years. Asked the medical orderly about Alec, I was told he is rather bad.

I have managed during my time here to gather together some books, some salvaged from bombed areas, some given. At night I read when the light allows, what a mixture I have got through, I turn nothing down. There are as far as I know no Bibles among the men as the thin paper they are printed on was ideal for rolling tobacco.

Monday February 14th

Went to a lecture after tea, given by Staff Sergeant Goodlife, late of Daniels Nurseries, Norwich, he talked on methods of fruit farming. I have already attended lectures on a large number of subjects, including Welsh hill sheep farming, at least it keeps the intellect alive.

Camp life goes on in its humdrum way, with the canteen prices becoming exorbitant. With the little money we are paid it's almost beyond us to buy so food tends to deteriorate.

Tuesday February 22nd

The Japanese Imperial Army staff has warned the Camp Commander to buy up black beans because of a food shortage. It is said that $35,000 worth were immediately acquired. To pay for them an advance of the IJA controlled officers' bank balance was necessary.

Wednesday February 23rd

A Dutch burial this morning and how it rained, once again I had to hold a giant umbrella over the black-bearded Dutch padre to keep his huge Bible dry. Not so many men in our camp now, so the deaths have levelled out to around 10 a week, the total amount now buried in this cemetery is approaching 600, the peak was around October 1942 due to battle casualties still dying, I was burying around 20-odd a week for a time.

Thursday February 24th

The heavy monsoon rain continues, everything is wet or reeking with the damp, even the bits and pieces one sleeps in. Tobacco rarely comes to the canteens, but this is one of the moments and the queues are over 100 yards long. With so much pushing and squabbling it has been decided to issue it to the heads of individual groups to hand out. It's rumoured that a part cargo of Red Cross goods have arrived in port. A court martial is being held by our officers on a fellow caught who contrived to rob the cookhouse of rice in the early hours. A Federal Malay States Volunteer was caught selling hospital drugs over the camp wire, another court martial pending. He deserves severe punishment as these drugs are in very short supply.

Tuesday February 29th

It has just been announced that there are some Red Cross parcels, 1300 in all for American prisoners, but it has been decided to pool the contents, although rumour has it that there is some discontent among a few "Yanks". We have already received 28 cigarettes, brands such as "Chesterfield" and "Camel", also in the issue package is a half cubic inch of chocolate and one cubic inch of soap. I took the small piece from the package, it was white, I presumed that it was white chocolate, but as soon as I began to chew it I realised that I was eating soap. You can imagine my surprise, I spent the next few minutes spitting and cleaning the stuff from my teeth. I fished out the tiny bit of chocolate, just enough to get rid of the soap taste, there is not much of that left either after I had partially chewed it.

I have not smoked for three years, but under the circumstances it seemed the time to start again although I have received offers to exchange them. This I may do as food means more to me.

Wednesday March 1st 1944

The remainder of the cargo has been issued out to the various groups, among the food are large quantities of $3\frac{1}{2}$oz tins. These were tinned especially as a ration for American service men and ranged from salmon, cocoa, coffee, pink (something) pate, small trays of sugar lumps, dried prunes, bully beef, meat, tiny tins of jam - grape and damson, Kraft cheese, ham and egg, biscuits and orange juice. Milk and vitamin tablets have gone to the hospital. The whole works out at 1lb per man throughout the camp of 8400 men. Anyone who reads this at the some future time may wonder why I mention all the foods, well to talk of all these things, to us is like a taste of civilisation. It also gives us a bit of an urge to struggle on towards the day when these foods once again become a daily reality.

Thursday March 2ⁿᵈ

Morning brings news that the hospital A mess have had all their Red Cross goods stolen overnight, how mean can some people get, stealing from sick men?

Monday March 6ᵗʰ

The "Nips" are at their propaganda stunts again, they are going to photograph us at play and work. I have been asked to make a wreath so that they can take pictures of five men laying it on a grave. It's a very bright moonlight night so I walk around the area to find what flowers I can.

Tuesday March 7ᵗʰ

With two of my men I was up before reveille to make this large wreath, which was later laid by five strangers. It was rather a disappointment to us as we were permanent cemetery workers; naturally we wondered why we were overlooked. Through the day the photographers continue to cover all that is going on.

Friday March 10ᵗʰ

I find myself confined to bed today with dengue fever, I feel terrible, aching bones and the king of all headaches. I spend a hot, half delirious day and a similar night.

Saturday March 11ᵗʰ

Another hot stifling night, but a bit better when daylight comes. After breakfast I make it to the cemetery, thankfully on my feet. By midday I'm just all in, the sun has taken its toll, so slowly I drag myself back to camp and drop covered with sweat onto my bed. One of my men fetched my tea for me when he came in.

Tuesday March 14ᵗʰ

There is no water or light as the transformer has broken down, it's now two days without the comforts they bring. The dizzu bean ration is off and maize is on issue, the nourishment value of this food is not up to the beans, in fact the men think it causes some of our skin diseases, anyhow that's breakfast over.

Wednesday March 15ᵗʰ

No cemetery work this morning as we have to parade for an inspection by the new Japanese General, Shito. Somewhere along the line something must have gone wrong for after one hour he had not put in an appearance, after one more hour, nothing except the sun growing hotter. The guards would not let us sit down, they were jumpy and on edge. Three hours go by we are sweat soaked, irritable and strained, the hordes of flies are worrying us to a frazzle. The fourth hour has just gone and the weaker ones among us are now falling to the ground overcome by heat and fatigue, but the "Nip" guards are now running about and shouting at the officers in an excited manner. We are called to attention and our lines straightened, after some minutes several army cars swung onto the square filled with red taped "Nip" officers. The General took up position and made a speech in English about not changing the principals of the camp. He then carried out an inspection of two companies, this is something that no former Camp Commandants had done. As he passed me I noticed that he was still proud to wear the ribbons of the General Service and Victory medals of World War 1.

With the parade over we get a late dinner and then it's work for me and my men as we have to deal with two burials and dig two more graves, we eventually get through an uncomfortable day. During tea we learn that there is to be an inspection of all officers in the morning by a representative from Tokyo and the men are to have a day off.

Friday March 17th

The day dawns and we spend it lazing around, as dinner approaches we learn the parade has been cancelled and I have to see to another burial. Spent an hour this evening listening to CPO Evans, he talked of life on the *HMS Prince of Wales* and the sinking of her, the brave fellows who went down still firing their guns, an unlucky ship.

Sunday March 19th

The chickens in our area have got fowl cholera, those bad are dead within 48 hours, this will mean a serious decrease in eggs. Our rations are now boosted with the issue of whole maize. We get it mixed in the rice, in stews and as a porridge, hope they don't expect us to lay eggs. Beans have gone off the ration and banana skins have found their way into the stews, they can also be made into jam if you have the sugar.

Tuesday March 21st

Today is to you at home, the first of spring, perhaps the sun is shining or may be it is snowing. To us here it is a marvellous morning, a huge red sun is rising above the trees, the sky is deep blue, the greenness of the surrounds, the regality of the coconut palms, their fronds glistening in the sun and not a breath of wind to stir them, or the sparkling waters of the distant sea. The early day temperature is a comfortable 80°F in the shade. At least I can still enjoy nature and make things a bit more pleasant.

Thursday March 23rd

News has just come in that the new Camp Commandant is to provide us with bedding, shirts, shorts, underwear, boots and shoes also hats, overalls, towels, toothbrushes, paste soap, toilet paper and increase the rations. A few mosquito nets have been issued, I wonder if this is pie in the sky, well time will tell. I have slight tinea in my crutch again, I do hope it will not be as bad as last time.

Saturday March 25th

There has been a shortage of palm oil for frying, but today 8lbs have been acquired it will not go far but at least one meal will be worth eating.

Sunday March 26th

The two day black out has ended and we have light again, what a comfort it is.

Today I and 20 men had to move from our quarters, which are to be taken over by eight officers. They arrive with seven trailer loads of furniture, then they tell us there isn't enough room in the camp for the men.

Thursday March 30th

A "Nip" government official is to look over the camp area today, I hope he finds that there is a lot he can do for us, also the "Nip" Commandant and his guard have moved in with us.

Friday March 31st

The guards have taken over gate duties from us and this has brought a change as we now have to give orders in Japanese when saluting them, so tonight we had quite a laugh doing some practice before turning in.

Saturday April 1st 1944

All camp notice boards have to come down and all our living compartments are to be clean and tidy. Some 2,700 men are to be accommodated elsewhere as houses by a camp road, which is due to carry main road traffic, are to be evacuated. The cemetery has been closed for the day and also tomorrow, so I spend my time sawing up timber for the cookhouse fires. Moving around has created some chaos in the camp and the "Aussie" concert is cancelled owing to sickness.

Tuesday April 4th

I have now been allowed to return to the cemetery and had to catch up on a few burials, a bit smelly and followed by myriads of flies.

Friday April 7th

Some moving still goes on in the camp and it's Good Friday and the "Nip" General has given us an Easter Egg of $7,000. It's a move in the right direction but will not go far among us, because of the high inflation.

Sunday April 9th

It's Easter Sunday so I think perhaps a visit to the church for Holy Communion is in order. It will be the first for eight months so at

7.30am I set off for that mouthful of wine, that is if I can hang onto the cup long enough to get it.

Monday April 10th

A new order has been issued restricting us to working only three mornings a week on the cemetery in future and we are to have a "Nip" guard, no reason given. To cope with the work I have been allowed 15 extra men (officers) but I was soon to see that the majority of these did not want to work. My time away from the cemetery is taken up at first laying some acquired paving in front of the Officers' Mess and later helping out on the unit gardens.

Tuesday April 18th

Today is the second anniversary of my Padres death (Padre Dean), I gathered some flowers and made a wreath for his grave.

Wednesday April 19th

Saw a show tonight, "On the Spot", a good gangster show. Afterwards on walking back to my quarters I felt rather weak. Food has been on the light side for the past week so I gather that I am hungry. Beriberi is on the up-grade.

Saturday April 20th

As we are a work camp we have just received 700 fit men from Sime Road camp, Singapore and 700 of our unfit have left to take their place. The camp has now gone back to its earlier formations of 18th Division, "Aussie", Dutch and Southern Area Commands.

Monday April 24th

Today I get a change of work being attached to the aerodrome work party. I spend my time shovelling earth onto railway bogey trucks. Not a bad day but tired out. The food on the 'drome was better than in camp.

Tuesday April 25th

Working shifts are to be changed, three seven hour shifts, I am on a 7am shift today. The weather is very hot and on this job with no shade. I get back to camp about 3 o'clock with just enough strength to stand up and listen to the latest news, which is that we are to move to Changi jail by May 10th. Exempt are hospital serious cases and the limbless.

Wednesday April 26th

To top yesterday's move order, the greatest news that has excited the men is the fact that 50,000 British letters have arrived, but I fear most of them will be for men departed from this camp. At least we will get some, and maybe at last I will get one from my wife, Joan.

Thursday April 27th

There has been a lot of "Nip" air activity over the island today, we discuss it while sitting around at night and come to the conclusion that the war is getting close to us. Another frustrating day of loading earth on the 'drome for me tomorrow.

Friday April 28th

The day passes with the incessant shouts of the "Nip" guards and my sweaty body covered in a fine silt, making me very eager to get under the showers, this done I feel myself once more and join the queue for the proverbial rice and raw tea. It is here that I learn of the unexpected return of 300 men from Thailand, with them is the well known Padre Duckworth, said to be suffering from cardiac beriberi. It does not appear that any of my battalion is among them. The return of these men in a sorry state gives us more thought for speculation.

Saturday April 29th

A new day takes me to the gardens which is much better for my peace of mind, news here is that another 100 men have come back from up-country and this time they include three of my unit, two of whom were believed dead. Other talk is that the move to the jail is put off until May 30th.

Sunday April 30th

The week passes by mainly in an uneventful way, except that today trailer hauling parties have began to lug bits and pieces of past-salvaged furniture and anything that is movable as some of the houses we have been living in are to be blown up to make room for aerodrome establishment. Tonight for tea, chicken stew, some of the unfortunates are not going to the jail with us.

Tuesday May 2nd 1944

I am back on the cemetery today, a lot of maintenance to be done, more graves to be dug and some bodies for burial. A hard day over and back to camp to hear some good news from the letter sorters, they have four for me. I am keeping my fingers crossed. Saw a show this evening called "I'll take you", a good tale of changed identities.

Wednesday May 3ʳᵈ

The morning brings another work pattern, wood sawing and fetching unit rations from headquarters stores. It was rice, dried fish and coconut oil. While I was there a load of mud fish came in, this has earned the name of "Modern Girl" from the men. Tea brings another ration of chicken stew, which leaves us with only three hens and one was very obliging for it laid an egg on my bits and pieces of blankets that were laying out to air.

The letters are being handed out and I have received three from my mother and one from my wife Joan. I hurry back with my tea to my quarter's eager to read the letters, one especially as it's the first for two and a half years from you Joan dear, the first during my captivity. I turn the letter over and over looking at the many various stampings etc. on the envelope, it seems as though it had had a very hard time finding me. Then with eager and trembling fingers I carefully opened the one thing that I had waited so long for. I pull out the letter and as I read that all is well with you, that you think of me as much as ever, in the stillness of the night to me it seems that we are so close not 11,000 miles away. Tonight I shall go to bed with happy thoughts of soon being with you again and seeing your smiling face. One of the letters from mother tells of news reaching her so I expect that you are both joyful to know that I am still kicking around. Well it is true that I am around although rather thin, tired and weary but still hanging onto the lifeline of hope and what a word that is. Without it many have passed on, but this night because of your letter dear my hope has soared, it makes life worth fighting for. I read your letter yet again as I get to bed and sleep with it under my grass filled bag of a pillow.

Thursday May 4ᵗʰ

The men are moving with groaning and cursing as they stretch their underfed bodies and the noise of some bug killing heralds another day. I search for my cherished letter, read it again and feel I'm lucky to be alive.

Friday May 5th

The hot weary grind of grave digging seemed to pass much quicker today and while we were working at this, my men decided that the few chickens that we had left would have to go as we could no longer find feed for them so on arriving back in camp it was left to me to kill the six poor thin creatures. The chickens out here are very little bigger than bantams and the skin very soft. During the killing I manage somehow to pull the head off one, it flutters from my hands, runs around headless, flies up, hits a man on the back spurting blood over him and then falls to the ground. Later I cooked him and all agreed they were a tasty meal. During the week we had eaten our source of eggs, although they had made our food less boring we no longer had the producers of what to us were golden eggs.

Saturday May 6th

Day dawns yet again and with it two more burials and to make matters uncomfortable for me I have internal piles. We have got down to one open grave so we must dig out three more, as I like to keep four in readiness. Now as there are only three of us I give a hand at digging in this hard volcanic earth. At the end of the day I am sick with pain from the piles within so I decide sick parade for me in the morning.

Sunday May 7th

Sick parade only gets me some physic and return to work doing lighter jobs.

Monday May 8th

Today we decided to collect material to make a green stew, one of my men, Alec, put on some climbing irons and clad only in a pair of underpants climbed a coconut palm to cut out its growing point. This is like a giant head of celery, up to four feet high (millionaire's celery) we would have been in very hot water had we been caught by the "Nips" or even our own officers. Anyhow all goes well, the "celery" is on the ground and the man who cut it out is yelling his head off and descending as fast as his iron-clad feet will allow, on reaching the ground he falls down and starts to roll over and over. We who are watching his antics suddenly realise he is covered with large brown ants, hurriedly we run to him and start brushing these stinging creatures from him, his face and ears, his body, we had to remove his underpants to get the ants from the cheeks of his behind and other unmentionable parts. While up the palm tree he had disturbed an ants nest and could have been in serious trouble if we had not been with him, anyhow after the stinging effect wore off he enjoyed the stew with us. Others had picked the tips from a creeping passiflora plant, making a good stew with the nutty flavour of the "celery" and a bitter taste from the green tips, but can you imagine it without salt, still, it's all good when you are really hungry.

I am in charge of British and Dutch workers here as both officers (Major Bregiel and Capt. Jonchere) are sick, but as for me and my troubles I am expected to carry on, "Good old Norfolk Breed", we can stick it. My right-hand man, Alec, is not very happy having received a letter telling him that his wife has a baby and it is three years since he left home, he has not enough fingers to count off the months. Major General Siato (Nippon) sends a letter to congratulate us on the laying out of a new camp site and the way it was carried out, lets hope that he backs it up with a ration increase, which I doubt. The latest news is that we are to move to Changi jail, in fact most of my group leaves tomorrow, but myself and cemetery workers are to remain until it is decided to move the hospital. It also brings me extra work, as I have to take over the cleaning of area drains in off time from the cemetery.

Friday May 12th

Three days have gone by and men from the various areas are still moving to the jail. Tonight the lights failed causing chaos in some places owing to the move still going on.

Saturday May 13th

This morning the hospital urgently required 18 beds, a search was made and they were found and taken whilst their owners were away working on the "Nip" aerodrome, they were replaced with various bits and pieces.

Our work on the cemetery this last week has been cut just to burials but as the move to Changi jail is now well under way we have now been allowed back to work full time, that means a backlog of further digging and maintenance can now be got on with.

Sunday May 14th

Tonight the lighting system breaks down again and apart from a few flickering bits of string in oil it's a very long night of darkness.

Tuesday May 16th

Rumour has it that 7,000 men are returning from Burma and Malaya. I spoke with some men from the jail, they were not very happy with prison life. At the moment they are spending the time erecting huts in the immediate area of the jail for the officers and some overflow.

Changi jail

Thursday May 18th

Watched a "Nip" trying to fix a water point, it was quite funny with him stripped to the waist and water pouring over him and his two helpers, couldn't help thinking that the skin protected by their clothes was as white as ours.

The Dutch officer working with me managed to obtain a pass so that he could (being a Botanist) search for a wild coffee flower. Being interested myself he took me along, however, his passion made him plough through thickets of thorns. He eventually found one flower and finished his search, although having been scratched, torn and stung by ants I wished that I had stayed at work.

I am instructed to report to our Control HQ to fetch a plaque made in the camp to the memory of Major General Beckworth-Smith DSO, MC, our late 18th Divisional Commander. The officers there treated me like a long lost brother, maybe it's because I was carrying on the work that the General himself had asked me to do on the morning that the "Nips" took him away.

Memorial Plaque set up in Changi cemetery in memory of Major General Beckworth-Smith (18th Division). The plaque was made from local hardwood

Friday May 19th

Later this afternoon I was to help sort mail that had just arrived in the camp, didn't find any for myself but there were 13 for Alec, my right-hand cemetery worker. After his recent news of wife trouble it really seemed an unlucky number to get.

Saturday May 20th

This morning I take the plaque to the cemetery and place it in position in readiness for tomorrow's ceremony, then I am off looking for flowers to make a memorial wreath. After tea of rice and green stew I spend the evening making up the wreath, which turns out to be quite a large one. Tired but satisfied I turn in and think of those at home and wondering how long now before we meet again. It is very difficult now to bring pictures to ones mind of those you left behind nearly four years ago, maybe the memory has been dulled by the hard and hungry life we live.

Sunday May 21st

It is daylight before I know it, around 6.30am, time I was moving as I have a busy morning, being invited to the ceremony. First I wash and shave rather laboriously with my sharpened half table knife and very little lather from the camp made soap. So re-faced I collect my mess tin and mug and set off to collect my meagre ration of pappy rice and raw tea. This over I dress in my decent shorts and shirt that I keep stowed away for the great day of freedom.

8.30am I collect my men and set off for the cemetery showing my pass to the "Nip" guard post. They have a laugh amongst themselves pointing at me as I move away resplendent in my hose tops and clean clothes, but no boots only camp made rubber slip-ons. I keep away from any dirty work, and around mid-morning a small squad of men led by several high ranking officers arrived and halted in front of the plaque, these I joined carrying with me the wreath I had made. A short service of dedication then took place by the attending Padre, and at the precise moment I stepped forward handing the wreath to Colonel Hutchinson who laid it at the foot of the plaque. A few moments of silence then I was thanked for what I had done. The party then moved away. For a few moments I felt elated at taking an important part in all this but then depressed to think that it had to happen, but I don't get much time to dwell on thoughts, the morning has gone quickly and the men want to get back to camp for midday rice.

After lunch I change back to just my ragged shorts, the rest of my body burned brown by the fierce sun. I return to the cemetery for the burial of Lt White who was one of our best female impersonators, one part he was very good at was the Princess in "Aladdin". He died of pellagra due to the lack of vitamins. I never know who I may have to bury next, hardly a day goes by without one or two burials but it is a lot better than the days of five or more.

The Royal Engineers have now built us a brick crematorium, a small rectangle building with a grid iron shelf. Now with a small amount of wood and oil we can cremate a body in 2½ hours. It is quick and not horrific like the outside one. It is used for dysentery deaths. The few of us who are left to do this work have become hardened to it so much that we can joke about it such as one man standing with one foot in a freshly started grave saying, "I've got one foot in my grave", or "Which one of us are you digging that one for Bill?". One of the men used to lie in an open grave for a rest at break time. It was crude humour but such things keep you going. It's now time to finish for the day, we clear up our worn out tools. Kipling's "IF" was typed out by an officer and posted on the camp notice board in the early days of our captivity and I made up my mind after making a copy of it to try and live up to its standards. We make our way tired and sweating back to camp, the showers seem short of water as only a trickle is coming through, but we manage to get the grime off.

After tea I learn an order has been given to strip the gardens as we shall be constructing new ones nearer the jail.

Thursday May 25th

Another batch of letters have arrived, better luck for me this time as I get nine, five from my mother and four from the wife, this pleases me but I wonder what has happened to the many scores of letters that I know she must have written.

Monday May 29th

We are out all day and have been issued with our ration of dried rice and a dixie to cook it in. During the morning I search round for some edible weeds that the man doing the cooking can boil up as a bit extra for us. The camp cook-house is turning out some unusual stews, pineapple curry tastes quite good. Naji Goring is tasty; a curry mixed with garlic and onions and fried in a milk substance is a nice addition to the rice.

It is said that the hospital patients move in a week's time, on Sunday to Changi camp. Minor cases will stay for a time at the old Selerang barracks in the area. We, that is myself and team, should move to the jail tomorrow, Tuesday.

Tuesday May 30th

The day has arrived and with our bits and pieces we set off, looking back with feelings of regret at leaving the area of Changi Barracks, which has been our home for most of two and a half years. It's around two and a half miles to Changi jail and on reaching there we are assigned to a terrible looking tent erected on an exercise square within the high walls which are surmounted by machine gun posts and searchlights in turrets manned by "Nip" soldiers, they are situated on all four corners of the outside wall. There are far too many men within the jail for any chance of comfort. I now look upon grey concrete instead of green trees. Meals at the moment are just rice, later I went as escort on a ration trailer to the patients left at Selerang.

Thursday June 1st 1944

Well life goes on every day the same, mainly large parties of men to work on the Changi aerodrome construction. This is back breaking labour, shifting railway wagons filled with sand, many men working waist deep in sea water building up rock walls to contain an infill of earth. Other parties are transported by the "Nips" to the docks to unload cargo ships, some of these men risk grave punishment when they get a chance to steal drugs etc. for the hospital, or small quantities of food for themselves. Going back to the aerodrome, the first four "Nip" warplanes have managed to make a landing mainly on hardened volcanic earth.

Friday June 2nd

Today our first visit to the cemetery from the jail, we have haversack rations, one pint per man of rice and fish hash. It's a forty minute march to get there, that's our breakfast of rice pap sweated out before we start grave digging and maintenance. As the morning goes and it's rice time, we set around laughing at the experience of a picnic like meal, but not looking forward to the march back.

At 3.30pm we set off on the return journey, by halfway there are mutterings and dragging feet, not much guts left in us now, our pint of rice has long since gushed from our pores and ran off the ends of our noses and in constant streams down our brown and grimy bodies, our shorts are wringing wet with sweat. In the distance we can now see the jail and I wonder how long we shall be able to stick this routine, it's more will power than food that keeps us going. At last we arrive at the gates, dead beat, with just enough strength left to reach our tent where we fall exhausted, laying for some time to recover and then to the showers. Feeling refreshed I lay on my bed for half an hour while waiting for tea call. My thoughts are about a village we now pass through on our new route. It's about a Chinese family living close to the road, they have a family of tiny children, seven I counted, but what amazed me was that they looked like dolls running around, they reminded me of my mother's dolly pegs with black tops.

26. ***On this day…*** June 4, 1944… Allies enter Rome.

Monday June 5ᵗʰ

It is morning again and I am away on my trek to the cemetery, we have British and Dutch burials today, also the Australians have some, it's the first from the new hospital area and the Dutch are from a party returned a few days ago from Thailand. Any returned parties are always in bad shape and normally would be hospital cases.

Arrived back in camp during a tropical downpour and the occupants of some tents were washed out. When the rain ceased they moved to what drier areas there were, laying out rain sodden effects to dry in the sun. The day passes much like the rest since we moved here, things have not settled down so as yet we have no entertainment in the evenings, we just set and talk about what our mother used to cook for us, hardly ever does one raise the subject of when are we going to get out of here.

27. ***On this day…*** June 6, 1944… D-day, over 4,000 ships begin landing thousands of Allied troops on the coast of Normandy.

Wednesday June 7ᵗʰ

One more day on the cemetery, am getting accustomed to the daily march now. The days are much the same, grave digging, burials, mounding and turfing graves, creating flower beds and paths, turfing remainder of area and general maintenance. For help to do this I get many not too sick men daily, but they cannot do much as the march almost exhausts them.

On returning to camp this day I am told to move the two gravediggers and myself into jailhouse quarters. I finally finish up in a cell situated on the top (3rd floor) in the last cell along the parade path. These cells were meant to house one native prisoner. I will try to describe it to you. It was about nine feet by six feet, in the centre is a raised concrete bed with curved concrete neck rest, this bed is about three feet wide by six feet long and eighteen inches high which leaves a hollow eighteen inches wide on each side. One of these is my bed space which will leave me hardly room to turn over, a little way from my feet is the doorway, by this, in what area there is left is a floor level urinal. There are in this cell four of us, one man on the concrete bed, one each side of him on the floor and the fourth across the urinal which puts that out of use. In case of accidents I did warn him not to sleep with his mouth open, also the door had to be closed at night as it was in the way. We agree to take it in turn to sleep on the raised bed one week in four. What a first night the moans and the groans throughout the night as we try to ease our bodies about in an effort to get some comfort, with only a groundsheet between us and stone.

Thursday June 8th

Morning finds us very stiff and sore and not very happy. With breakfast over we get on our way to work, at least outside the jail we are among the green trees and this alone helps to raise our sagging hopes. As I march along I think of England, its June and it must be about Derby day and I think "Prisoner's Hope" would be a good name for a horse. Ruefully I think it would be a rank outsider. Putting this thought from my mind I come back to the realities of the moment, we are coming up to what is left of the old gardens. I decide to send two men to scrounge what might be left in the way of vegetables; they come back with enough to provide us with a good stew to help out with the dinner rice. After eating we work on feeling more satisfied with a belly full of cooked greens and are more contented on the march back to the jail.

We spend the evening in the same nightly discourse of what mother makes better than someone else's. Food, if you cannot have it to eat it seems to help talking about what one used to like best at home. We miss the shows that some of the men used to put on in our old camp, so far nothing has got going in this confined space and it's getting more so as men are still being squeezed in. I have heard that 5,000 men are now in the jail, it normally held 500 in peace time.

Sunday June 11th

I no longer go to Communion having just about lost all my faith in religion so I wash my sweaty shorts, the remains of my towel and a tattered piece of blanket, lay them out to dry but not letting them out of my sight for even these rags would disappear. The "Nips" have given the aerodrome workers a Sunday off but our own Command has taken a lot of them to wire in an area. The men used for this are kicking against it, I cannot say that I agree with it either as they need a rest from the hard work that they do.

Monday June 12th

We don't know much about the Monday morning feeling as we march out of the jail gate. We get another chance to search the old gardens and find enough for another stew up, lucky for us they lay on our route and nobody has stopped us from getting what we can.

The day passes and I am back in camp, I have a bad head and am glad to get my cup of raw tea, this I drink and not feeling like eating rice I get another mug of tea from a sympathetic member from the cookhouse, this I take back with me, dragging myself up the 70 iron steps of the prison stairway to D4, my floor. I reach my cell and after drinking my "leggee" tea I take to my confined bed space but do not sleep well.

28. *On this day*... June 12, 1944... First V1 rocket (Doodlebug) lands on British mainland.

Tuesday June 13th

Morning comes and I feel very feverish, I think an attack of dengue fever is coming on. Looking at my diary I see that it is exactly two years ago to the day that I was transported home from the cemetery to hospital with a bad attack of this fever. I join the sick parade and am told to go to bed until it wears off.

Wednesday June 14th

I spend a horrible night sweating with the fever, am delirious at times according to my cell mates. I know that I had a dream that my wife was stroking my brow, what a dream, anyhow it had its results as this morning I have recovered from the horrible stress on my bones, my head is also a lot better but I don't feel like food, just the drink of tea. I lay on my bed most of the day, it's hard although I have managed to scrounge a couple of "Biscuits" (small square mattresses) which help relieve my shoulders and hips, my pillow is my valise which contains bits and pieces.

Thursday June 15th

Have a bit better night and it is now the third day, try to eat a little as I am rather weak and tottery. Am told that dysentery is very bad in the area owing to thousands of flies breeding around the boreholes (latrines). These are bored into the ground manually to a depth of 18 feet. This is supposed to be a safe depth to prevent flies breeding, they are covered by wooden traps constructed from doors taken off the cells. When you go to make use of one you are confronted with the white behinds of men squatting over these fly ridden holes. When you lift the trap you are met by a gush of hot air and flies, what a state we are in. How much longer is this damned war going on? Time drags. I suppose I am suffering from a bit of depression due to the fever. I think I will try to get to the cemetery tomorrow, just to get clear of these concrete walls.

Saturday June 17th

Morning comes, I am ready but still a bit weak. I join the lads and march off. I've nothing left in me for work so I just sit around until it's time to return. I make it with an effort and drop on my bed exhausted but my mind at peace at having been out among the trees again. Having rested I have a shower, survey my bones which I seem to have more of than flesh, I certainly have lost a few valuable pounds over the fever period.

A notice has been posted with the words:

"Picking over swill at the incinerator for edible pieces will cease forthwith".

Sunday June 18th

The hospital patients left at Selerang have now been established here, in huts in the outside area.

Many of the days are routine except that burials have stepped up a bit, may be due to so much moving about. We have a small market for snails, the officers pay 1 cent each, as they require them for their ducks. After a rain we can usually collect plenty.

Sunday June 19th

Talk of another move, but I hope not, I have been in the jail a month and moved four times to get where I am. More huts going up outside and there is a reshuffle going on, trying to get regiments together but as my end of the floor is already mainly 5th Norfolks I do not get moved. Meals are now to be taken in the exercise yard, it started with breakfast rather early this morning, before daylight.

Wednesday June 28ᵗʰ

The day brings 60 survivors from a torpedoed ship, but cannot find anything about them as there is no contact. No work today as all flags (passes) have been taken in by the "Nips", but I am called to take a burial party out with a "Nip" escort to bury one of the ships survivors who died soon after arrival here.

Tuesday July 4ᵗʰ 1944

After a few days off main cemetery work we have now made a fresh start, we are to go out with the aerodrome spread over party, which means I have to be up by 6.00am, when it's still dark. We march off at 6.30am as it is just getting light, and on our way we see the sun rising like a giant red wheel, it rises very quickly and soon beads of sweat trickle down my forehead. As the party reaches the cemetery we break off from the rear, watching them going on with long trails of smoke coming from tins of smouldering coconut fibre that they take to light the fires for rice cooking, we are just one stage from rubbing two sticks together as no matches are available to us.

We work a long morning catching up on grave digging, as with the stop and go method adopted by the "Nips" I am worried that I could be caught with no graves open. At 2pm the 'drome early shift comes by on its way home, we form on the rear and march in with them. I feel rather weary and fed up, this method makes a nine hour day for us by the time we arrive back in camp.

Friday July 7ᵗʰ

This has gone on for four days and now the "Nips" say that we are not to go out as we are still without a pass. Later I have to go with an escort as I have a burial.

Saturday July 8th

This I have to do again today, for a Dutch burial.

Sunday July 9th

No rest for me and my burial party as another Dutchman has died and has to be buried. Both these men were from the torpedoed ship's survivors, one an officer the other the ship's surgeon.

After tea there is a welcome change, an Australian road show has arrived to entertain us, which relieves the monotony of things for an hour.

29. On this day... July 9, 1944... Caen captured by the Allies.

Wednesday July 12th

Tomorrow I have to parade for a check up by a medical officer to find out my physical state:

GRADE 1. Can march 15-20 miles.
GRADE 2. Fit to guard lines of communication.
GRADE 3. Barrack room duties etc.

Our command must think that something may happen in the near future but all I can think is they must be better fed than us if they think that they can remake a force out of the skin and bones left around here. Most are living on hope and will power, without these half would already be dead. One of the morale builders, letters, have seemed to stop coming in.

A dock work party tells of a ship in Singapore, just arrived from North Malaya, it carries 750 men, 60 of them from my own Regiment and a close local friend of mine has been seen. These men rumour has it are on their way to Japan.

Thursday July 13th

I reported sick this morning with what I thought was heart trouble as I have been having a lot of pain at nights when breathing. The medical officer told me to run about 50 yards then he put the stethoscope on me, after a few seconds proclaimed me as having the strongest heart in Changi, then giving me a chit for some indigestion mixture and at the same time re-grading me from A1 to A3. My complete recovery from dengue fever has been slow.

After tea the air raid sirens blare out and at the same time all lights go out. After a half an hour they are switched on, we are told it's a full-scale practice.

Saturday July 15th

This morning the "Nip" guard would not allow my party through the gate, so no work for us. When word was got to the "Nip" Commandant, Takahachi, he laughed and said the rest would do us good. Around 1,000 men are still working shifts on Changi 'drome.

Tonight to pass away the time I went to a Communist lecture entitled, "What about the workers", this seemed rather unusual to me in an army camp but the reception he got made me think Roberts (Barracks) appear definitely red.

Monday July 17th

The new "Nip" Commander (Takahachi) appears to have a softer outlook as when I took a corpse for burial through the gates the guard turned out and saluted. Later we were joined on the cemetery by a Nippon officer and escort who presented arms at the graveside. It's nice to see some respect shown. The night goes by much as usual.

Tuesday July 18th

The morning brings another surprise, a day's holiday for us and the 'drome workers, no reason given why. The day brings heavy rain for the first time in 25 days, it is badly needed. Some more letters in, I am pleased to receive four more from my mother and two from the wife.

30. On this day... July 20, 1944... Bomb plot on Hitler's life – failed.

Saturday July 22nd

One of our officers escapes from Changi and is caught in Singapore by the civilian police, apparently he left a Chinese wife there, the camp authorities did not report him missing and they came in for reprisals from the "Nips". They were dropped from their positions and replaced by another Colonel and new staff, even some of the men think this could be better for us.

Sunday July 23rd

I have been practising on the office typewriter, managed to type out a few bits and pieces. Tonight I went to a lecture on Churchill by a Major.

Monday July 24th

We are off to work but have to join the rear of the aerodrome party. We are marching along a lane-like path, suddenly we are attacked by hornets, evidently disturbed by the smoke from the 'drome men's fire-lighting cans. The hornets left the nest and flew amongst the 600 marching men stinging a number of them. It was suddenly a stampede as we took off for a hundred yards or so like a herd of buffalo, three men had to be taken back to the camp hospital. I myself was stung on the back of the neck, which

Roberts Barracks Changi

stiffened up my shoulders for most of the day and gave me a bad head so I was glad when the day came to an end and I could relax on my bed. Two more letters from home helped.

Wednesday July 26th

Have spent my day constructing a flight of steps and some retaining walls in the cemetery. On arriving back at the jail I learn that 200 men are to go to Singapore which gets me wondering how many I shall lose from my clearing party, these are sick men, working so that the rations can be kept up to strength as the "Nips" do-not allow any for non-workers.

A visit to the boreholes (latrines) phew! What a pong, they now stink to high heaven and the lines for hanging out bits and pieces are so thick with flies that they look like ropes.

At tea we are paid nine dollars, but to give an idea of its value it will buy little more than a coconut.

Saturday July 29th

The Australians today buried their Camp Commandant, the "Nip" Commander attended. A new road from the jail to the aerodrome is being constructed, in its line of route is a small hill but the road is not going over it or around. It is being levelled by hundreds of old Chinese women dressed in their uniform like black trouser suits, their heads covered with huge coolie type straw hats. They use small baskets holding about two shovels of soil which they convey to other areas, all by hand. To us it is like watching ants on an ant-hill.

Our recently new camp officer, Col. Newy, in charge has changed most of the officer administration; this has caused some bitterness between his following and the old.

331

Tuesday August 1st 1944

The cemetery grows in size and my work party are now busy extending the road that runs through its centre. We have a source of rubble and roadside drain gullies from a broken up road in the area but it is arduous work carting it with our equipment and poor physical condition, but our bit of willpower and the interest of some makes the cemetery worthwhile. To one side of us the area of the aerodrome is now a vast place.

Dreamt of home last night and that the wife could not cook rissoles, why rissoles, perhaps it comes from getting rice ones here when we get a bit of grease to use, they call it "ghee", the men say it's what they put in the train axle boxes, anyhow it goes down.

Wednesday August 2nd

The remnants of the Suffolk Regiment keep up their spirits by a celebration of "Minden Day", one of their battle honours. I make them a wreath in their Regimental Colours.

Sunday August 6th

The days drag slowly by and I am feeling very browned off and fed up with everything, no news coming through from the outside and all we seem to talk about is the food we used to eat at home. I have just grated a coconut to help out my rice for a couple of meals, just to change its taste a bit is worth something.

Monday August 7th

Another public holiday comes round but not for us, we are hard at it, streaming with sweat we arrive back at camp only to find no showers as the water supply has been cut off, a notice says no washing until further notice.

Two days pass us by and still no water, we are now at the stage we were in at the start of our prison life, waiting for a thunder storm so that we can run out to bathe in its refreshing water. Three days sweat, we must stink, it's a good job we all smell alike, it's not so noticeable.

Tuesday August 8th

Today we made some tea on the cemetery and brought back to camp as the ration here is cut, it kept fairly hot in the rice dixie. We are allowed our fourth letter card, in the few words I am allowed to write I send love to you Joan and mother and I hope that you can puzzle out my veiled message to let you know that my next door neighbour has died here, that is if the card ever reaches you.

Thursday August 10th

Received two or more letters from my mother and one from my wife. My mother states that my wife has been ill, but doesn't say much about what was wrong. I go to bed thinking about it.

Copy of camp orders (9):

Bulletin No 3 issued by camp office 10th August 44

Conversation between Camp Comdt and the Rep Officer.

1 RED CROSS SUPPLIES: Lt Takahashi said that he desired to dispel from the minds of the POWs that the Japanese Government was preventing Red Cross supplies from reaching them. He added that it was up to our countries to send the goods. The Camp Comdt. said that we were permitted to receive Red Cross funds, but in our case it was stopped as we were being paid by the ITA. As regards the civilian internees, it was understood that they were still in receipt of Red Cross funds.

Lt Takahashi said that "exchange ships" were the only available means for carrying the Red Cross supplies. In this connection he pointed out that as 7 L.I.A. Red Cross ships had been sunk or damaged, such ships could not be used for this purpose.

The Rep Officer then asked if the Japanese Government had taken any steps to inform our various governments or the international Red Cross of the situation, so they could make arrangements to send supplies. In amplification of this the Rep Officer gave the example of the monthly parcel being sent to POWs in Germany.

Continuing the conversation the Rep Officer said that there must be some mistake as the allies did not bomb Red Cross ships. Lt Takahashi replied that the British might not but the Americans did and sighted the following examples of atrocities.

(a) On entering the Vatican City the Americans went to the Japanese Embassy and committed such atrocities there that the Japanese Ambassador had to protest to America through the medium of Spain.

(b) In the Pacific war the Americans were boasting of using Japanese skulls as curios, and bones as paper knives.

The Rep Officer said this must be propaganda.

It was suggested that the Red Cross supplies could be obtained through neutral countries. The Camp Comdt replied that there was no neutral country of sufficient size for this. To which the Rep Officer quoted Russia. Lt Takahashi then said that the Russian situation was finally poised. The Rep Officer's request that he himself might have contact with the International Red Cross was not approved.

2. AIR RAIDS. The Camp Comdt said that air raids might be expected any time now.

Thursday August 17th

It's the start of another long hot day and Joan dear it's our third wedding anniversary and my third as a Prisoner of War, anyhow on this day my thoughts, memories and also hopes are with you dear. I have great hopes of being with you for the fourth one, what a happy day that will be.

A storm breaks while marching back to camp soaking me and my only pair of shorts. We didn't need the rain so much as the water came on again yesterday, but I had to borrow some shorts from my friend "Nobby" for the night.

Saturday August 19ᵗʰ

Another letter from mother who tells me that my youngest sister is a nurse. Inoculations are on again for us and I have just received a dysentery jab and tomorrow it's to be TAB with a doubling of these in a few days time.

31. On this day... August 23, 1944... Paris liberated. Romania surrenders.

Saturday August 26ᵗʰ

Dock workers tell of a battleship and three destroyers in port. I now get my second dysentery jab followed by the second TAB all within a matter of hours, my arm and shoulder is really sore and I myself feel rather feverish, glad tomorrow is Sunday, a rest day. Dock workers report another six cruisers arrived. Is the war closing in?

Sunday August 27ᵗʰ

I spend a rotten night pitching and tossing on my bed and I am glad when morning arrives. All I want at this moment is a cup of tea to relieve my aching head and limbs, to get the fever out of my system, I feel horrible. At breakfast I am one of the first to get my tea, raw tea but to me just now it's nectar. I have no appetite so I swap my rice for another measure of tea and after slowly drinking this second cup I feel somewhat better. I spend most of the day relaxing on my bed space.

It is now 4 o'clock, I pick up my rag of a towel and what's left of my tiny soap ration, then take myself off for a shower. I stay a bit longer than usual, as it is so soothing to my aching body. Back to my quarters and then for tea, which is rice and green stew. I manage to eat it, but enjoy my cup of tea. This over I get ready to go to a band concert, they have managed to get together enough instruments to form a credible band. As I listen to the band I also study the faces of the men as they stand in the half-light thrown from the bandstand, they are grim, sullen looking and in most cases unshaven faces. They show outstanding cheek bones and the hollows of malnutrition, the whites of their eyes enhanced by the tan of the skin, their shirtless bodies, thin with shoulder and rib bones easy to see, to me every man looked twice his age. In this dim light they appear to be a half savage horde, frightened by their own grimness. I vaguely hear the band as it draws to a close; I have been lost in thought. I ask myself how much longer can we hold on, another year must seriously deplete our smitten ranks. Rather more sad than cheerful after the concert I walk slowly back with the others, not much chatter, it's get back and to fall upon the ramshackle contraptions, they deem beds.

Monday August 28th

It's 6.30am Have just collected my breakfast when a "Sumatra" breaks, this is a fierce storm, a back lash they tell us from Sumatra across the straits of the same name. It lashes Singapore, it bends the coconut palms over and moves any movable object in its way. It is accompanied by heavy rains. It holds up the work parties for an hour. The storm passes and we are on our way to routine work on the cemetery, it is very hot and everywhere is steaming and I am steaming sweat with it. This kind of heat just gets one down, getting very fed up with life, the only hope is the odd letter and hard contemplation of the future, this only makes life worth living. More men from Malaya have been seen in Singapore, another close friend of mine has been named.

Saturday September 2nd 1944

On writing up this diary I find it is my mother's birthday, "Many Happy Returns" mother, but afraid I shall not be one of them, but this does to the day make my fifth year of war service. Will the sixth one see me home? I hope so, otherwise I may qualify for the thin man competition.

It is said that 2,000 men from Singapore camps have left for Japan, I expect my two friends seen there have gone with them. In my heart I wish them all the luck in the world as rumour has it that Japanese ships carrying prisoners have been attacked and sunk.

The air raid alert has sounded, is it for real or just a practice? We can only hope, the war, for us must finish soon as I don't think the daily ration of 16 ozs of rice and 2 ozs of vegetable and oil will sustain us for much longer. I find the work gets more difficult to cope with and the grave being dug could just be your own.

Sunday September 3rd

When I awakened this morning it was with a sore throat, but as it is Sunday again I can take it easy. I expect it is due to lack of vitamins and the hard work. The day passes uneventfully, just talking amongst ourselves and watching some men stripping the bits of wood that make up their beds, to rid themselves of bed bugs that live there by day in the crevices, only coming out at night to bite them all over.

*32. **On this day...** September 3, 1944... Allied forces enter Belgium.*

Monday September 4th

My bad throat persists, but it is work all the same. Feeling as I do the day seems very long, with the dreary march back to camp along a ribbon of a road, shining white in the overpowering dazzle of the sun. We have a permanent squint and begin to look like the Chinese. Water shortage in camp again, but we are allowed to wash with the aerodrome workers and get a bucketful of water each. It's enough to get the muck and dried body salt off oneself.

After this I reported sick as my throat is terrible and I feel fit to drop. The MO puts me on green leaf vitamin extract, I feel sure no ones medicine ever tasted so horrible. It is extracted from all types of leaves and grass by the Dutch troops, but it works. Also I have to have hot gargles. I find it difficult tonight to swallow my food, but find the tea a relief. This last month I seem always very ready to get to bed.

33. *On this day...* September 4, 1944... Antwerp and Brussels liberated by Allies. Allied forces enter Holland.

Tuesday September 5ᵗʰ

After spending a choking sort of night I am ready for a cup of tea. The food is no problem as it is a half pint of pap rice, but I have only negotiated about half of the 70 step stairway to my floor when I have to set down and drink it off to get enough strength to reach the top.

I have got to see the medical officer again this morning so I take my place on sick parade. I am later seen by him, severe tonsillitis, my tongue is now swollen and my lips are getting sore. At the other end, my scrotum is sore and peeling. I am told pellagra (a breakdown of tissues) or if you like slowly going rotten seems to be my trouble. I'm getting a bad case and my only hope is my green leaf medicine and rice polishings, if I can get any. It is now raining heavily after a very hot dry period which will freshen the air and that could be a help.

338

Friday September 8th

The "Nips" don't want us to get too cheerful as they have banned us from singing.

*34. **On this day…** September 8, 1944… First V2 rocket lands on England.*

Sunday September 10th

Another visit to the MO who tells me to see him daily for a week. I have to pull all the willpower I have to keep going these days. Another batch of letters have arrived, the sorters say that some of it was posted in May this year, it appears that the "Nips" are pushing it through faster.

Eating and drinking utensils have always been somewhat varied, from half coconut shells to a variety of tins, mainly in use by the men, but now the engineers have the use of cutting and welding equipment and the army type metal lockers are being cut up and formed into mess tins and mugs for those in need.

Tonight sees the start of a new darts competition, the last one being won by my cemetery workers. I have been given the honour of darts captain this time.

News has just come to hand that in the event of the allies invading Malaya vegetable supplies to us would virtually cease. They have placed in Changi jail enough rice and salt to last us until the end of the year, enough oil until end of October . This gives us something to chew over, are things at last moving? Are the "Nips" being pushed back? Anyhow there is some hope in this sort of discussion.

One of my main gravediggers has gone to hospital with stomach trouble and another has a bad mouth and has got seven days light duties in camp. These casualties make things very difficult on the cemetery.

Monday September 11th

On my visit to the medical hut I was weighed at 8st 8lbs, still recommended light garden work on the cemetery. The few "fit" men here jokingly say that I'm a "Bludger", our term for a work-shy type.

Wednesday September 13th

Well at least I've made another year as today I have reached my 33rd birthday. I expect I am the topic of conversation around the tea table at home. The wife will begin to think that she has married an old man, five years wasted on a crazy madman's war. I've got to make up for these lost years so let it be soon. Went to a lecture, the subject, "Paying for the war". What a prospect, it proved interesting, but hardly the thing for us.

Thursday September 14th

Told by the MO not to go to work today, so to help pass the time I walk around the prison's circular road, an area walled on the outside by concrete 24ft high and on the inside by one 18ft high so one sees nothing only a mass of concrete, what can be more dismal. Later I help plant some "Paw paw" seedlings, a dwarf tree which carry fruits like a green melon.

*35. **On this day...** September 17, 1944... Battle of Arnhem begins.*

Monday September 18th

After a quiet weekend I arise to face another sick parade and get a return to work, but to report back in fourteen days time. On the sick parade with me is my third and the last of my permanent grave-diggers. To my dismay he is sent to work on the gardens for a fortnight as he is in need of vitamins. The extra green stews the gardeners get may help him. With no regular grave-diggers (the heavy work is slowly killing the four of us) I do the best I can with what men have enough strength to use a spade for a short time. It's something that the death rate has slowed up but for how long? The men are in a bad state. My tongue is still sore and my body itches terribly at night, there is nothing to be seen, but it keeps me awake for long periods of time.

Thursday September 21ˢᵗ

I have saved my meagre payouts, I now have enough to buy 1lb of peanuts at $5.80c or 12/-. We have been told that they contain 80% vitamin B, the one I need most.

36. ***On this day...*** September 22, 1944... First battle of the Philippines.

Sunday September 24ᵗʰ

A *"Gaol Gazette"* has been printed and some of the facts contained in it are as follows:-

25 gallons of palm oil is used to fry for 4500 men. The central cookhouse was designed to cater for 800. (When we first came to the jail 7500 was what it had to cater for until we were thinned down to our present number). 2800 gallons of tea are drank by the men daily, using 50lbs. of leaf. 500lbs. of rice is used at each meal, that works out around five men to the pound.

An artificial limb factory has come into operation, to construct a varied mixture of limbs for the camps 62 limbless men. I expect that after two and a half years without they will be pleased to try them out. As we have now got permission to tap more rubber trees for the latex, a rubber factory has come into use, it makes a fairly good type of sandal, the shoe soles are made, I understand, from a mixture of latex and latorite. Men of the Malay Volunteer Force and some Dutch are the ones behind this venture. Then there is the grass and leaf extraction unit as I have mentioned producing "Flavourine" (Vitamin B) also a "toddy" and type of gruel for bad cases in hospital. The camp workshops also turn out a type of razor although I still manage well with my super sharp table knife. Other useful things are Dart boards, darts, cotton, some shorts, mess tins, spectacle frames and boot repairs. Mine are being repaired at the moment. There are not many pairs of boots in the camp, most men now wear sandals, as for myself and the three permanent gravediggers, they try to keep us in boots, otherwise we could not dig the heavy clay-type soil.

* * *

I seem to have cultivated an itch in the area of my shorts, put it down to a skin irritation, but by noon it gets a bit unbearable so I go to the hut and whip them off and on close investigation, what do you think? My God I'm lousy, plenty of them about the camp but never thought much about it myself. Well fortunately for us they cannot stand the hot sunlight, so I make myself a makeshift G-string and hang my shorts out all the next two days and am clean again, but will have to keep a close watch from now on.

Saturday September 30ᵗʰ

Work for me is very much routine now, not too many burials so can get on with further scrub clearing. Two men found on the roof have been put in the jail tower and are on a rice and water diet for three days.

A cigarette issue today, this has now happened for the third week in succession, I exchange mine to anyone who can provide something edible and managed to get some towgay, it's supposed to have Vitamin B content.

Went along to an Australian concert this evening, they have managed to construct a new "Playhouse" but darts is the rage game at the moment.

Sunday October 1st 1944

The days tick by, it is now our day of rest. I spend mine making a pair of shorts for work as the old ones are just patches strung together. I have salvaged a pair of ladies tennis briefs which I use for a pattern as there is not much material for use. I have a sewing needle (large) and I manage to get some camp made cotton, then I set to work. The finished article fits rather tight and close, without the stretch of the briefs.

Monday October 2nd

For some reason the "Nips" will not allow officers to visit the jail, so RSM Boroughs (5th Norfolks) takes over command of the 500 men in my group.

No burials in cemetery during September.

Tuesday October 3rd

More mail has arrived, I received two from the wife and two from mother, all early 1943 posted. It doesn't matter to me when they were written as just reading them gives me a real lift and renewed hope.

Wednesday October 4th

It's morning and dark as we get into what is mainly our only clothing, a pair of nondescript shorts, but I do hear "Nobby", one of my team, cursing as he tries to find the right hole to put his foot in his well worn socks.

As we get to the "Nip" guard post we are greeted with "Akabar yasima", meaning cemetery workers can go back to camp and rest for the day. Why? We are told that the aerodrome control does not want us down there. Fortunately burials have dropped off a lot over the last month, just the odd one. I expect the weakest have gone until the next wave.

Thursday October 5th

Still am not allowed to go to the cemetery but am told that we must find a new site as burials are to cease at Changi. I shall be allowed to take my party there on two days a week for maintenance only. There are around 600 graves present, all set out and mounded up as in an English churchyard: *"Just some corner of a foreign field that is forever England."* All the graves have wooden crosses and nameplates, made for us by the Royal Engineers.

**A corner of the cemetery
with the mounded and turfed graves in the English tradition**

Friday October 6th

Morning comes with a request that I join a British Officer, Major Bregiel, along with an officer from the Australian forces to go out and look for a site suitable for burials and not too far from the jail. We found an old scout camp only 300 yards from the Jap

General's house and decided it was the place. I managed a quick look around the General's garden, it was a dreamland with its exotic flowers and a picturesque house. I imagine he squatted in one of the best places. I was asked to draw up a plan.

Sunday October 8th

Spent the day drawing up new cemetery plan and submitted it. Later I was told it was accepted.

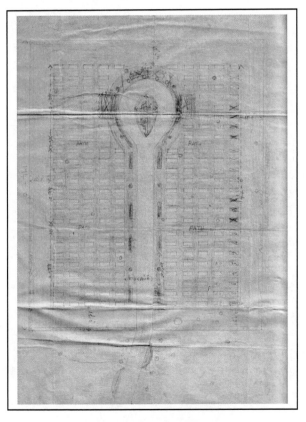

New cemetery plan at old scout camp
accepted 8th October 1944

'The Tobacco Rush'
A cartoon drawn by a cell–mate after an issue of tobacco

Tuesday October 10th

Yesterday was a day off although today we went to work under escort to the Changi cemetery. The "Nip" guard looked as bad off as us, sores around his mouth, skin trouble and a bit of beri-beri. We had heard that the "Nips" on the island have had a bit of a food problem.

Wednesday October 11th

A new order issued by the "Nips" warns us that when work parties are marching outside the jail area there must be no stragglers at any cost.

The day on the cemetery passed off pleasantly, plenty of work as by not being there daily it's become a bit overgrown.

Thursday October 12th

Today I awaken to the unusual sound of a lot of planes flying around, its activity which makes me think that something must be going on not too far away from Singapore. It's another day in for me, nothing has happened about the new burial site yet. I wander around the jail area, down by the boreholes, feel sorry for those poor devils who hardly seem to leave them, they are the dysentery cases who until they get clear of the trouble live there with the myriads of flies. Many men that I have buried have been claimed by the disease. Back to the jail where sick and wasting men sweat the day out, what a dreary existence for humanity. I'm glad the day is over as hanging around this place can get one down to a low ebb. I get to bed early, miserable in mind, sleep is broken by the dive bombing of mosquitoes and the horrible smell of bed bugs as they crawl over me somewhere, but I must be thankful that they never bite me and no-one can understand why this is so, the men are plagued with them biting.

Friday October 13th

Morning brings relief and after the daily rice pap breakfast I am told to report with my three gravediggers. I am to go out to the new site to get it set out for use. Spend an interesting day measuring up, setting out pathways and grave spaces. The "Nip" Commandant, Captain Takahashi, came along and looked it over and agreed that we could carry on. Our working day ends and it's back to the jail, but the march back is not so far as to and from Changi. Not worried about stragglers today as there are only four of us. After tea its just sit around as all camp entertainment ceased as from yesterday because of some breach of The Imperial Japanese Army rules.

*37. **On this day...** October 14, 1944... Allies occupy Athens.*

Sunday October 15th

I go to the hospital to see a friend and am stunned to see malaria and other cases laying on the floor, where are the beds? There were enough when the hospital was at Changi and now we have a lot less patients, there should be a surplus, so who has got them?

Wednesday October 18th

For a few days now we have had air raid practice, the so-called "Brown out", seems to be with us most of the time these days.

Thursday October 19th

Soya beans are back on the menu and how acceptable they are for their vitamin value but as they are always cooked on the hard side one has to chew them well to make sure that they don't pass straight through, thereby losing what goodness they have.

Friday October 20th

Today I have the first two burials on the new cemetery. Black out alarm goes at midnight and lasts for an hour, but earlier in the evening I had to spend sometime doing a patching job to the seat of my shorts which I ripped badly getting over some wire. A new supplement to our food is called "Ragi", a seed grass grown in Ceylon for elephant food and has some vitamin value, but doubt it will give us the strength it gives the elephants.

Sunday October 22nd

An Australian burial today, the poor fellow came in from the "torture-chamber", Outram Road jail notorious for its cruel punishment.

Monday October 23rd

I have come by a book called *"Gone With The Wind"*, it has made hours of enjoyable reading. May have some more letters to read in a day or two, seventy bags have just arrived.

38. On this day... October 25, 1944... Battle of Leyte Gulf – End of Japanese Naval power.

Saturday October 28th

After five weeks we are still getting the 1oz a week tobacco ration, I still sell or swap mine. Camp made soap is also issued but is rather on the soft side. My boots and socks are in a bad state, the socks I now put on in two pieces and by the looks of them it will soon be three, it's getting like a jig-saw puzzle.

Sunday October 29th

It's three years today since I left England and do hope the next year around will see me home, although Singapore could be a nice place to live under the right conditions. "Modern Girl" as the men refer to it (otherwise smelly fish is back on the menu again), at least it gives the rice a flavour.

We pass the Japanese General every day that we go to the new cemetery and today I have a Dutch funeral. Not much to do as this place is flat and fairly clean so we just keep four open graves ahead.

Wednesday November 1st 1944

As for the old cemetery we were escorted to it yesterday at 9.30am, the "Nip" soldier decided at 12.00 noon that he had had enough and brought us back, so two hours maintenance was all we could do. After dinner I go to the canteen, with $2.00 that I have saved. It just buys 1lb of towgay beans, which I shall keep until the soya beans that we are still getting run out. Tapioca root is now plentiful on the gardens; this is a great help to us for it can be made into flour which goes to make bean and vegetable pasties. When we do get a fish issue it's near to being rotten, it's so fried that one can eat the lot, head, fins , bones and tail.

Friday November 3rd

On arising this morning we are told no work as it's a day of celebration for our hosts the "Nips", what it's for I have yet to find out. Not much to do here only sit around discuss food, the possibility of an invasion by our forces and maybe find a book and read awhile. In Changi camp if there was anytime off, at least you were able to stroll around camp under the lovely Flame of the Forest trees, bougainvillea and many other types of flowering shrubs, at the jail it is just boreholes, flies and concrete. Many of us have had tinea very bad and it shows as men stand around

350

scratching their crutch, it is so obvious that it has become known to us as the "Changi salute".

Sunday November 5th

The "Brown out" alert has sounded again. I am about to white-wash my cell with some substance that I have come by, the place is filthy so anything usable will brighten it up. Halfway through the job the alert turns into a black out and in the far distance shell bursts can be seen in the sky. To us this is the most exciting thing that has happened in years. News filtering back from Singapore says 30 or more large planes in the attack, nationality not known. Some unexploded anti-aircraft shells landed well inland close to our dysentery ward but I don't think they made the inmates run anymore than usual. The main talk up to bed time is the planes, who were they and were they bombing the docks?

Monday November 6th

Morning comes, it's very hot, the sweat runs freely at this early hour. I do not feel right so I attend sick parade for pains in my body, mainly stomach pains, but there is no medicine, just take two days off and rest. One of my grave-diggers plays the good Samaritan and brings me tea at unusual times which is highly appreciated by me.

Friday November 10th

I get through the two boring days and start work yesterday, happy to get away from this miserable hole of a prison but no escort turns up today to take us to Changi for maintenance there.

Saturday November 11th

Two minutes silence was held throughout the camp, it was signalled by our bugler sounding the Nipponese Temple Call, not being allowed to use our own calls. I get very hungry these days, which I suppose could be the cause of my stomach pains.

Sunday November 12th

Nothing but routine and petty orders, made almost daily by our own Commander. Today it is no food of any description to be taken out of jail and none to be brought in, I don't know what could be taken out, the food brought in could only be some pilfered vegetables from the gardens. Shaving and hair checks are being made, shaving is difficult enough with the materials available and the barber will not cut your hair without payment from the few cents that we get, so it's a toss up between a hair-cut or something to eat and as you may guess eats come first.

This evening I went to listen to Guy Mitchell and his "Gypsy Serenaders" playing Russian and Spanish music. Quite a lot of music written by him and others is in the camp. The restrictions still stand for entertainment in the main, therefore our nightly recreation is darts which is often interrupted these nights by lighting cuts. As I write up my diary, the siren goes for a "brown-out".

Sunday November 19th

Another day of disappointment for many of the men as the tobacco issue has not taken place. Perhaps we have done something wrong in the eyes of the "Nips".

Monday November 20th

Monday gives me the chance to get out of the jail and to work on the new cemetery. While there another "brown-out" alert, quickly followed by a "black-out". All our eyes turn skyward, straining to see the unidentified plane flying very high up. It looks like a silver bird at the great height.

Wednesday November 22nd

This evening I watch the league champion darts team play the rest and loose among much excitement and noise. The group championship was also played off and won by my floor, a team of 4th/5th Norfolks VRA. An eventful night.

Sunday November 26th

As over the years their are again rumours of Red Cross ships coming, to date we have only had one and that was a long time ago. If one did really materialize now we could say, "All this and heaven too", as I feel very hungry. My mother used to say, "Leave the table when you feel you can eat another crust", well I feel that I could just eat six crusty loaves.

Monday November 27th

Another week starting, but only a few burials so life is a bit easier for us. Another air raid warning, it lasts over an hour but nothing to be seen. We are advised to dig more slit-trenches where we can so as to get some cover in the event of a raid, certainly things seem to be moving, although the "Nips" still tell us that we are here for 99 years and, "See wife no more".

Tuesday November 28th

Escorted to old cemetery with only six men as our camp officer has cut the number of volunteers who can help with maintenance for no reason. We spend four hours toiling in the sun, grass cutting, clipping the graves and general work, before setting off on the long march home, we are tired and leg weary. As we gaze ahead along the glaring road, the prison comes in sight and soon we are walking through its gate to spend yet another night in our concrete shell.

Thursday November 30th

To help out my rice at tea-time, I had some towgay bean shoots that I had germinated on a cut open old sock, which at least should give them a flavour. The real reason is that the shoots are supposed to be good for ones eyesight also for beri-beri. Talking of socks, they are a sore problem, not many around now, what are consist of tops as the feet are worn out. A large batch of mail in, 80,000 letters it is said. I have so far received 11, one 1944, the remainder 1943, six from mother and five from the wife. My mother writes of an operation concerning the wife which naturally worry me as she gives no idea what it is about. The wife's letters say nothing of it.

Friday December 1st 1944

There was spare rice this morning, it was decided to give it to men going out to work, it was just plain, but for once I went to work with a full belly.

Sunday December 3rd

Cramp is among our troubles now, many of us being bothered with it, the doctors say it's salt shortage, evidently they have been unable to evaporate enough sea-water lately.

I get myself weighed and go eight stone, that's more than two stone lighter than three years ago.

More camp statistics tells us that 200 acres of gardens are now under cultivation, a lot of tapioca and sweet potato, all seen after by disabled, permanently sick and the daily not so sick men.

Monday December 11th

My memory is getting terrible, I don't seem to remember things from day to day. It has caused me to overlook my diary for over a week, not that there is much to note as it's mainly routine work.

Tuesday December 12th

I go to the showers and rid myself of the day's sweat and body smells, we think that these days we smell very fishy. After tea I go off to a pantomime. This show has been commanded by officers of the Japanese Imperial Army therefore restrictions have been lifted on entertainment. The show is "Twinkletoes", it was an excellent concert, followed by an hour of British and Japanese music. The whole thing lasted three hours and appeared to be enjoyed by the Camp Commandant, General Siato and his staff. I feel a bit more contented with life, it's good to have a laugh, these days. I fall onto my bag of grass, that's what my bed has come to as my pallets were compact long ago, mosquitoes are buzzing around and are just as dangerous as dive bombers.

Thursday December 14th

It's soon the start of another day as I hear the noise of the men arising. The air-raid siren sounds a short "brown-out". The day is wet, very heavy tropical rainstorms and high winds, a drop in the temperature to 83°F, it makes us feel cold, I put my rag of a blanket around my shoulders for warmth while I am sitting around. Think a lot about home these days and the good life, thoughts stray to Christmas day, the dinner and the good times had, this perhaps because it's now December.

Friday December 15th

I think about my wife, Joan, and wonder how she is, how is she coping with life and what does she look like? It is now getting very difficult to visualize anyone's face that I left behind, the doctors tell us that because of the way we live, our memory will be the first thing to go.

Saturday December 16th

We spend the day at the new cemetery and as burials are few now, we have developed a small vegetable garden on some of the spare ground. It is now producing enough green stuff so that we can cook up a stew on the job for my small number of workers, it gives us extra vitamins. Recently three of the grave diggers have been out, digging up a few bodies buried outside the camp in the early days, considering the length of time, they are in a good state and the last one has now been brought in. On our way back to the jail a Malay funeral passes by, the mourners on foot and strung out behind the party bearing the coffin on their shoulders. The coffin was draped in a magnificent jewel bedecked black velvet and with the brilliant colours of the followers it was a sight for our tired eyes.

39. On this day... December 16, 1944... Germans launch their last great counter offensive in the Ardennes (Battle of the Bulge).

Sunday December 17th

Japanese General Siato has made a visit to the cemetery but so far no comments from him.

Monday December 18th

One of their planes has crashed on the edge of the Changi 'drome killing the pilot, this is followed soon after by an air-raid warning.

Planted out Tomato plants grown from seeds of a tin of processed ones.

Wednesday December 20th

The weather has turned wet and to us decidedly cool as we start another day. The wet makes the volcanic earth stick like clay to our spades and throwing it out from the grave seems to take my stomach with it, the day leaves scarce energy for the drag home.

Back in jail we learn that the "Nips" are to allow broadcasts home by the British and Australian concert parties and for men who have received no letters. The people involved are busy rehearsing, but it is my guess that the microphone that they play to never goes on the air.

Thursday December 21st

Another day and the heavy rain keeps us in jail. We spend some of the time debugging our bits and pieces of beds and once again the pathway along the cell fronts look as though murder has been committed as blood spatters it. As the bugs are shaken from wooden boxes and crevices in pieces of timber, they are violently stamped on, and so the cheerless day drags on.

Friday December 22nd

The day dawns with the still relentless rain, in my time here I've never known the temperature to fall so low 69°F. We are cold and miserable, huddled around with anything we can get to cover our thin and in many cases emaciated bodies. The only ray of sunshine is brought by one of our officers, Lt Colonel Prattley, he has presented us, the cemetery workers with a cake for Xmas which is only three days away. Where and how he came by it was not for us to ask, but only to enjoy. Vegetable issue is now at a record as the gardens are coming into full production, although they have their problems, such as being often raided.

Saturday December 23rd

Today cash was issued early for Xmas, I get $9.00, its pre-war value was 35c so it will not buy much, coconuts are $2.00 and small at that. The "Nips" have also made a tobacco issue, their largest yet 1½ ozs, I exchanged mine for some "gula malacca" (solidified brown sugar).

Sunday December 24th

It's now Xmas Eve, it's our rest day, but the cemetery workers are getting tomorrow off as well, barring funerals. It's bed time so I will get my head down after I have hung up my holey sock. I can at least dream about the past.

Monday December 25th

Next thing I know someone is shouting "Happy Christmas, you have got rice for breakfast". What an early morning joker. Meals for the day are really good due to a great effort on part of the cookhouse staff. They produced 52,000 "douvers" a form of pasty, it worked out throughout the day to ten a man, but the tea was still raw. "Nobby" washed his shorts so that we could have a table cloth. Six of us sat down for dinner, those that had a knife or fork made use of them, we even had a jar of flowers on the "table", an old box, which was part of someone's bed. The "Nips" are really getting good as they presented each man with six cheroots, but I suspect they were part of Red Cross goods never received by us, anyhow they created quite a fog around us. Everyone seems to have captured the spirit of the day, even the officers got permission to enter the jail and were pleased to mix and chat with us.

We make our own fun, such as guess the weight of a coconut, guessing how many peppercorns in a jar, highest score on the dart board and so on. Charge was 2c a go and the prizes were $2.00 to the winners of the competitions.

As a thought for all of you at home I go to church this evening and at midnight communion, the first time for both since Easter. Only one candle on the altar, no other lights as they always go off at 10pm so everything is a bit of a shuffle.

Menu for Christmas 1944

Tuesday December 26th

Well it was late to bed but up at the usual time for work this morning. There is much moaning going on, not hangovers but stomach troubles causing men to queue at the boreholes. Too much grease in yesterday's food for stomachs to cope with. Mine don't feel too great. Talking of stomach upsets I have not been plagued with dysentery, maybe because I have been ultra careful about the washing and covering of my eating utensils. When eating one is always worried by the flies always trying to get at the food, it means, always when eating that one hand is constantly being waved over my food. If by chance a fly managed to get through my guard and settles, I will sacrifice that particular piece of rice by throwing it away.

Something happens today that gives us a talking point. When the Japs took over Changi jail they took down the Royal Coat of Arms, now two years later they are putting it back in position, why? What is going on? The "Nips" are also making a propaganda film of the better points of our captivity. So many little things which have happened lately gives us much more hope.

Wednesday December 27th

A week ago I had a blood sample taken and today I have been told that I am Group O+.

Sunday December 31st

It's a dead time in camp at the moment as everyone is waiting for the Old Year to end, hopefully the new one will see the end of our time here. It is very hot today and my eyes are sore with the constant running of sweat into them. Some of the men are training frogs to race as they plan a race on New Year's Day. I retire early to bed not feeling too well.

CHAPTER 8

SILVER LADY

Monday January 1st 1945

After spending a restless night I greet the morning with a heavy cold and an attack of internal haemorrhoids, well for all my troubles I spare a thought for all you at home by wishing you "A Happy New Year" and maybe I shall be with you next year although I could be somewhat deteriorated.

Excitement is high as a little gambling takes place at the frog racing, there is no form as they go, stop and sometimes hop clean off the track. My partner and I won the floor darts tournament and shared $2.70c then lost 80c each on "Housie Housie".

Have just heard from one of the docks work parties that a friend of mine, John Jacobs, has been in Singapore, but has now left for somewhere in the north of Malaya. For a long time now word has been filtering through about the horrific life Prisoners of War are having building a railway in Burma. Reports all the time reach us of the disease, starvation and torture of soldiers and civilians in the desperate rush to push the railway through. They call it the railway of death. Not much going on in the jail just now except darts in which my cemetery team stand in 5th position in the league's 1st division.

Friday January 5th

I am putting up with a lot of pain from the area of my backside, so this morning I join the sick parade. The medical officer, who after a close inspection of my rear, tells me that I have an anal fissure and says I am to go into hospital for an operation. So it seems I am being admitted to dry dock to have my bottom scraped.

Sunday January 7th

I am thankful for the "day of rest" as at the moment it is much easier for me to sit down, just to get some relief. I must be in a low state as it is one health breakdown after another.

I wandered over for an evening Communion service, not that it did me much good, it failed to lift me out of my despondency.

Tuesday January 9th

Another agonising day has started, it seems that I have constant neuralgia at the wrong end; certainly work and heat do not help.

On the way out an armoured car flying the "fried egg" passes us. A lone plane flies very high up, so high its movement seems slow, against the blue sky it shines silver. Over the past few weeks we have seen it often, we think it must be American and has been named by us as the "Silver Lady".

Wednesday January 10th

The week is routine except for a variety concert tonight. It was quite a good show "Sweet and Hot", backed by a Gypsy band led by Guy Mitchell who was with "Alfredo's" band in peace time. A Spanish "girl" dancer was very entertaining.

Thursday January 11th

Today I am off to hospital, a long hut behind the jail. As I make my way I see a number of "Silver Ladies" flying over, I think that a number of our people must be slowly moving towards us. This thought and the belief in it is what I need to keep going, and there are many like me. Soon after my arrival someone comes to check me over, then it is to bed.

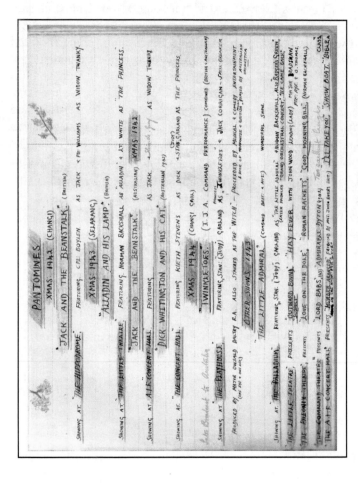

Some of the camp shows that entertained the POWs

Friday January 12th

After breakfast (I get none) I have an enema, not that there is much inside me to clear out. This is followed by an injection, then later my trip to the operation theatre. I am thrown onto a table covered with a red rubber sheet, and I remember being strapped down, with my last recollection being the circle of very bright electric lights glaring down at me. Sometime later I come to in my bed, with a headache out of this world. I have a very large bump on the right rear side of my head, was I coshed? It is said because of a shortage of ether you only get enough to just put you out and then you get the cosh, how tough can they get! The surgical ward seems like the chamber of horrors, all kinds of cutting cases going on.

Monday January 15th

Three days have gone by, much of the time very boring and sometimes painful as I daily sit my behind in a basin of extremely hot water. I am still a bed patient and am surviving on a pap diet.

Tuesday January 16th

Morning comes once again and I am soaking with sweat, the night has been very hot and uncomfortable. Breakfast over and I make my first trip to the "boreholes" since my operation. My God the pain, I thought it was to be my last. Soon after this I am racked with pains darting through my body from head to toe. An orderly comes and takes a blood slide. The night for me is terrible with tortuous stomach pains and they bring me a hot water bottle, which eases the pain.

Wednesday January 17th

After 24 hours the fever subsides and I am feeling better, but very nervous of my next trip to the latrines. The fellow in the next bed has been circumcised and when he wants to pass water yells his head off with pain. Further along an Australian moans, he cut his throat yesterday, has been stitched up and his neck swathed in bandages, perhaps he moans because the cut was not deep enough. Managed to buy a piece of toilet soap for 60c from my amenity grant of $1.20c. The poor fellow with the cut throat died in the night, so he did go deep enough.

40. On this day... January 17, 1945... Russians capture Warsaw.

Tuesday January 23rd

Today is the wife's birthday, my thoughts for a happier one next year go out to her. It's also the anniversary of my coming under fire three years ago and this time I am in hospital.

Thursday January 25th

During the night there was an air raid warning. We are halfway through the morning when we get another alert.

I am to be discharged tomorrow. Two of my men have kept me informed about the cemetery.

Some 200 men came back to us from "River Valley" camp in Singapore area, the remainder, some 3,000 men including John Jacobs, go to Thailand.

Friday January 26th

The doctor says I can go, but to report back in a week's time. Because I am sick my amenity pay has been cut to 75c for two weeks, not enough to buy half a coconut.

I arrive back at the jail to find them at the start of a 48 hour air-raid precaution practice.

Saturday January 27th

I have to join sick parade this morning, after the operation I have been rather constipated. The MO gives me seven days convalescence and with it seven days cascara, he is going to keep me on the run. I have to report every day to get the dose. I have rustled around and got hold of a few good books, which will occupy me for a week, and news has just reached us that swimming parties are to be allowed again as from tomorrow.

Friday February 2nd 1945

Lying around reading does not do much to induce sleep at night, just twisting and turning while waiting for daylight. Later in the morning I go with a party of sick men for sea bathing. I enjoy the warm water, but seem to have forgotten the basics of floating for I doubled up and swallowed a lot of the China Sea, my feet touched bottom and I try out my swimming, manage a few strokes then out to lie on the sand to dry off.

This afternoon I visit the surgical specialist and am told to see him again in seven days time.

Saturday February 3rd

Feeling tired but relaxed, effects of the sea I expect, I slept a lot better. After the usual pappy rice breakfast I again see the MO, he puts me on light duties and stops the cascara, I hope it's the last of it.

It's nice to be with my party to the cemetery, it seems ages since I was there. I notice that quite a number of burials have taken place and I'm glad to be just an on-looker. I manage to do a little work, but am sweating like a pig, mainly from weakness but I enjoy the change.

41. On this day... February 4, 1945... Yalta conference.

Thursday February 8th

Another sticky hot day and I am told that I can join the bathing party for an hour this morning. What a relief to get into the water, to get a bit of swimming practice. We are in areas enclosed by wooden rail fencing called "Pagars" which are to keep the sharks out. Talking of sharks, a few days ago, some Chinese women had been fishing and on passing along our wire fence they furtively looked around, seeing no "Nips" they dropped a young shark over near to where I was working, giving them a nod of thanks I allowed them to get clear then picked it up. Extra to back up tonight's rice, shark steaks. I went to bed feeling well satisfied with the supper we managed to cook on the side, there was enough to help out a few others as well.

Saturday February 10th

Well the day has come round for me to see the specialist again, he tells me that I have not completely healed yet. I am to report sick tomorrow.

A new system of food rationing has been brought in which allows 500 grams of rice for heavy duty workers, 300 grams for light duty and 260 grams for no duties. This has caused a great controversy among the men, but to some extent I think it is a good idea, it could mean the "Bludgers" (don't like work) among us will stop going sick for little or nothing and get to work. Wood to the cookhouses is also being rationed.

Sunday February 11th

On attending sick parade I find myself back on cascara with light duties.

I got a chum who works in the "Nip" workshops to make me a set of dominoes, which I carry with me. They come in very handy for passing the time when it rains, as it has done today.

Tuesday February 13th

I'm always having a re-occurring dream of the wife. She is always in a house and I cannot get in to her and she doesn't try to get to me, I see her pass by the windows, but I don't think she knows I'm in the vicinity. This is a typical dream which I have often. At such times my mind seems to be more disturbed than usual. As I awake this morning I realize that the date is the third anniversary of the capitulation, three hot sticky years have gone leaving us worn out, tired and hungry.

Enough books have been gathered together to set up a small but useful library. Someone has drawn a cookery book and there must be a dozen others all trying to get a look at it. They talk of the good things of the past while others tell them to shut up as they are making their mouths water.

*42. **On this day...** February 14, 1945... Allied bombing of Dresden.*

Monday February 19th

We are to lose some more men, as a party is needed for Blackang Mati Island and some for Singapore. Inoculations are to start in the morning.

*43. **On this day...** February 19, 1945...American Forces land on Iwo Jima.*

Tuesday February 20th

I get my inoculation early, a dysentery jab. I don't think I will be picked to leave Changi. We are allowed out to the old cemetery as we have a cremation to carry out, our small crematorium having been built there by the RE's after an attempt at open burning which was tragic. At the end of the days work, my head grave-digger sweeps up the ashes and puts them into a sandbag which he takes back to the jail, throws them under his bed until the next morning when they are to be taken to the new cemetery for an official burial.

Wednesday February 21ˢᵗ

I also had an unusual burial today, a Dutch civilian from a place called "Palna Darna". Why he was sent to us no reason was given.

A rain storm developed and we played dominoes, I should have left them in camp as it cost me $1.00 from my amenity grant.

Thursday February 22ⁿᵈ

The rain has brought out the snails and we collect some for the officers who pay us $2\frac{1}{2}$ cents a snail as they cook them for the chickens. On delivering them we are offered 5c each for the next lot as they are going to eat them for their protein value. I have tried to cook some, but it took three lots of sea water to clean the filth out of them and after frying you could have soled ones boots with what was left, they were so tough.

Friday February 23ʳᵈ

Rumour says a Red Cross ship is in port, better keep our fingers crossed as the last report came to nothing. Food is pretty tight and grim just now and a ceaseless argument goes on among the men over their rations until bedtime.

Sunday February 25ᵗʰ

Another morning arrives with a sticky heat after yesterday's rain. Most of the day spent in air-raid precaution drill, all this after three years, it appears there must be a push in our direction by the Allied Forces. They cannot get here soon enough for us; I have a cold, sore throat and am still having a very painful time with the fissure despite the operation.

A syndicate have made up a form of football and darts pool, listing the camp teams; so far luck has not come my way.

I'm sorry to say that the dogs that attached themselves to us are slowly disappearing, being killed off for food by the more heartless among us, it is still a punishable offence in the eyes of our own officers.

I have spent along time this evening patching and darning socks with pieces of coarse string, there is hardly any of the original material left.

Tuesday February 27th

Things are looking bad as a further 10% cut in the rice ration is announced, but great news helps counter this. A notice has been posted stating that a ship has docked, and it is carrying 12,000 tons of supplies. It is described as a White Cross ship, the difference between it and a Red Cross one I wouldn't know, unless it may be a neutral one. Naturally the camp is agog and much speculation as to what we will get, mainly in the way of food, goes on until lights out.

Thursday March 1st 1945

The day comes in with much excitement; work parties to off-load the ships cargo are standing by. I go with my party to the cemetery, I think it's been more talk of what they hope to receive than work done, the possibility of food is a big thing in our lives just now. The working day over we trudge back to jail with usual streams of sweat running down our bodies, salt dried on our arms and the flies that followed us out are no doubt the same ones that are pestering us now. Through the prison gate, into that concrete jungle of little boxes that for the moment we call home. The excitement of the morning appears to have gone and despondency has set in. We are soon to know the reason for it, the dock work parties never left for Singapore. Another notice has been posted which rather contradicts yesterday's announcement, worse luck. It reads, "White Cross ship has not yet reached Singapore. All plans have been cancelled". What a sinking feeling this leaves in our stomachs, or should it be empty. Just hope tomorrow will bring better news.

Friday March 2nd

It's still a stalemate situation and to make matters worse we are not allowed out to the cemetery, some trouble over an Australian officer who was with our work party. We spend a horrible day, anywhere outside is better than the jail. On the food front, we are to get three days supply of fresh fish and some damaged rice is coming in. Also reports of air raids on the dock area, this really sounds hopeful. Baths for the hospital are now being made in the camp workshop.

Sunday March 4th

A few days of just routine, pass by, I am on sick parade again, it's just a long line of skin and bone bodies with the bulges of rice bellies. I get light duties, which means a light duty meal of one small rice rissole, which I supplement with some bought food such as palm oil and a tiny chopped onion mixed with water and a pinch of salt This I call palm oil butter. Eight tiny onions weighing 1 oz. cost me $1.00. There is a music concert tonight so after my light tea, I rest for a half an hour then wend my way to the concert area and listen to "Music thro' the Years" represented by what's been composed in the camp, quite a pleasant evening. I walk back with a hospital orderly who tells me that the "Nips" have presented six nanny goats and one billy to them; the idea is to provide milk for T.B. cases. I learn also that the White Cross ship docked this afternoon. Among its cargo is rice for civilians. It's bedtime and I guess I fell asleep with soft music going through my head.

Monday March 5th

I awoke some hours later to the noise of disgruntled men, many of them will be on 6.30am work party for the aerodrome which is devastating on the food they get, loading earth onto rail wagons all day or standing waist deep in sea water clearing mangrove or building revetment walls. Many of these men suffer from bad leg ulcers caused by bites and scratches then worsened by under-nourishment.

Large red crosses are being made around the hospital area by the planting of Red Amaranth in masses; also we eat the leaves as a vegetable. About 200lbs of tapioca root was dug today from the new "Wing Loon" gardens.

Tuesday March 6th

After another wearying day we drag ourselves back to jail and literally drop onto our bed spaces, sweating and exhausted. I shall have to get off the sick list, as these light duty rations are just too small for me. Half an hour goes by and I now feel that I have mustered enough strength to go for a shower. We think life here is very bad, but the reports that are leaking through from Malaya and Burma are horrific, men tortured and starved, others dying in hundreds from cholera. I think now the Sgt Major was right when he told me to stay with the devil I know.

After tea the talk is about the White Cross ship, much conjecture about the crew who are supposed to be a mixture of men from America, Canada, S. Africa and France.

44. On this day... March 6, 1945... Cologne captured by the Allies.

Wednesday March 7th

Recently there have been daily air raids over the docks, but not today, maybe it's because of the ship. It appears more clothing than food is being unloaded according to the 150 men sent to do the work. This is bad from our point of view as our rice ration has now been cut again, twice in a couple of weeks, just hope the bulk can be made up by vegetables from the gardens.

Friday March 9th

The officers of the Japanese Imperial Army have closed down the camp theatre because, they say, of bad thoughts. What they were I wouldn't know except there was a skit on the Japanese Emperor, Hitler and Mussolini running for a bomb shelter, which must have been a bit daring.

Saturday March 10th

The new ration quantities are in force today. Each day's food now produces only 1,400 calories, such scarcity is serious for us, also the camp guards are cut by half, which makes me think that things must be difficult for Japanese shipping.

Sunday March 11th

Our rest day, which is to the good as the midday meal was only half a pint of vegetable stew. It's a cool wet day as well. Parole forms are sent out for us to sign, anyway there is no fear of us trying to escape in the condition of weakness that we are now in. The air raid siren has gone for alert and explosions can be heard in the direction of the docks.

Tuesday March 13th

Morning comes again with that giant red sun rising above the palm trees and within the hour the sweat will begin to run. I am off with my party to the old Changi cemetery for a day of maintenance. The last grave mound is turfed over, now making the total here 581. The men are cutting grass, even being helped by a bored "Nip" guard. I got a sniff of his drinking bottle, whatever was in it contained rum, he was also smoking Virginia cigarettes, what a smell of the outside world. It's a nice quiet day on this cemetery so churchyard English in the way it is laid out. The workday comes to an end and the guard takes us back to the main road, a $2^1/_2$ mile drag to the jail. It seems shortened however, by the interest of passing a small Chinese settlement and seeing their tiny dolly peg children, almost naked, lining up to watch us, the women coolies, still moving a hill to make way for a new road. Before we realized it we are home dumping our bits and pieces and making for the showers, soon to relax cool and clean. I'm terribly hungry and tea is not very much, but a few fried whitebait to add to the rice taste.

Thursday March 15th

Had a bad dream in the night, must be bad because it was of food I could not get. I dreamt that I was in a large restaurant, my wife was the waitress, I was eating porridge, piles of sausages and mash, plates of bacon, eggs and bread and butter, but was very puzzled as I could not tell sugar from salt What a dream, all it did for me was to make me browned off and hungry all day.

Friday March 16th

A mutual help society has been formed in the camp to help Changi prisoners of war after release. I have been asked to join and have done so, but really do not know what future it has got.

Sunday March 18th

The wheels from our trailer have been stolen, they are said to be worth around $6,000 in Singapore, but who could have removed and transported these large lorry wheels from the camp area. We have to take out a huge lorry chassis today as we now have to cart in our vegetables and firewood for the cookhouse. This used to be the officers' work but there are not enough of them available now, it takes a lot of weak men to haul one of these loaded trailers, men on ropes at the front and brake teams at the rear. To make matters worse it pours with rain as we finish the job.

I have come by a few coloured pencils, a swap for "cigs". I have an idea, but I have to search around for a piece of wood large and square enough for a ludo board. Having found a suitable bit of wood I set to work marking it out and colouring it, cutting counters from some cardboard, fashioning a dice, and we are away. It causes a considerable amount of fun for many a night.

Monday March 19th

Heavy rain these last few days have done much damage to the gardens and it will not help our food problems.

Tuesday March 20th

We boil sea water to obtain salt, it takes 16 gallons to produce 4lbs. The cookhouse evaporates about 200 gallons daily for their culinary uses.

Wednesday March 21st

A young man, Ernie Websdale, who used to work as a barman in the "Robin Hood" pub in my hometown died today. It was tragic as he died from liver poisoning, this after being cured of TB. The Royal Engineers had made him a bed of curved metal on which he had laid on for $2^1/_2$ years. He had recovered enough by last Christmas for us to wheel him out to watch a football match and now he had just started to walk again. It seems that his fatal illness was caused by some kind of worms.

Thursday March 22nd

Have been allowed to write home, but often wonder if they are ever received. Camp talk of 3,000 men going to Singapore. The party that went to unload White Cross goods have just returned.

Friday March 23rd

This morning for breakfast we get 50 grams of maize instead of rice, it is mixed with pap. By midday I did not feel quite so hungry, so it appears to have more staying power, the bad point about it they tell us it has no vitamin value and sends you rotten more quickly.

Saturday March 24th

It's rained all night and we have been in all day sitting around and feeling cool as it is still deluging. Tomorrow is Sunday so if there is no backlog of burials I shall be in for another day.

Sunday March 25th

The day comes in fine and steamy hot and in trying to find something to pass the time I make another game, Snakes and Ladders. Its just as well we are not working for it is light duty rations, half a pint of vegetable stew and a little maize to exist on.

Monday March 26th

Today, 100 men leave for Singapore to work, I believe, on the docks. This is dangerous now with the frequent air raids there. General Shito promises Red Cross goods for Easter, also a present, I will wait and see meanwhile holding out no hopes. Dinner was better tonight, a good issue of vegetable hash.

Wednesday March 28th

Around 350 men from the Australian compound leave camp for an unknown destination.

Have tried snails again, cooked a bit different from our first attempt and I feel we shall eat more when we can find them, they are in such demand.

Thursday March 29th

After a 24 hour postponement, 1,000 men are now ready to leave the jail, to go to areas unknown. At least it will give us a bit more breathing space here.

Some White Cross goods are arriving at the jail. So long have we been waiting for it to come. The air raid siren goes in the early hours and gets us straining our ears to try and pin-point where the raid could be, but it's not long before there are more snores than explosions.

At breakfast I enjoy a bit extra for one of my men brings me a fried snail, a bit more protein. Red Cross food is to be issued on Easter Sunday and the IJA wants the empty tins returned on Monday. I wonder why, evidence that they have issued it perhaps. I have enough money to buy some "Blachan", a dried rotten fish but it tastes good mixed with the rice. For dinner I received half pint of rice and half pint of vegetable water with a small rice rissole, what a menu for a top class jail.

Sunday April 1st 1945

Just a few burials this week but it means hard work digging graves, almost too weak to throw the earth out of the hole, but I suppose we have to think ourselves lucky to still be alive to do the work. It brings us to Easter 1945 but no Easter Eggs for us. On second thoughts a form of them has come our way as some of the White Cross goods are on issue of eight raisins, a teaspoon of jam and some salmon in rice rissoles, hardly enough to flavour anything, then tomorrow there is more to come.

When we get around to dinner again, we get a bully beef pasty, sardine rissole, a pat of butter, four sugar cubes and a piece of chocolate, it's small mercies but what a lot of new flavours.

45. On this day... April 1, 1945... American Forces invade Okinawa.

Monday April 2nd

For breakfast this morning we had half a pint of rice pap and two prunes and the stomachs of many of us are now complaining, at any time they are not in very good condition.

A party of Australians have left the jail today. Any other moves have been postponed. The postponement statement didn't last long; for it's just half a day later and 100 more men leave us.

Wednesday April 4th

A little bit of excitement as an "Atap" garage goes up in flames but it did not keep our attention long as a lorry loaded with clothing and boots arrives at the gate. The pickets on duty were hard put to keeping the sightseers within bounds. The main discussion as we take to our beds was the feeling new clothes and boots would have.

46. On this day... April 5, 1945... Russian government denounces Soviet/Japanese neutrality pact. Japan's cabinet resigns.

Friday April 6th

Slapping away at the buzzing but invisible mosquitoes I must have fallen into a deep sleep as too soon it was morning and some burials are coming our way, so besides coping with these it means digging out more graves, as it is I feel almost too weak to lift a spade. After a hard day's graft we drag ourselves back to the jail where there is much excitement as another five loads of the ships cargo has arrived and expectations run high.

Saturday April 7th

A few days ago we managed to send the officers 100 snails for which we are paid $5.00. With my share of the money and some that I have saved I visit the canteen, where I buy 1 oz. curry @ $1.40c, onions (small) @ $1.10c for 1 oz., and 4ozs Blachan @ $2.00, it's all so expensive.

Another party of 400 men leave us. The amount leaving us recently has left us a bit more breathing space.

Sunday April 8th

A chance to rest the worn out shell of a body. Breakfast this morning is rice pap with a dollop of marmalade that tastes good. The day's meals contain small portions of White Cross food as last week. Just lounge around all day, no concert parties as the "Nips" have not allowed us to start up again.

Monday April 9th

I arise tired for another week of what has now become a form of drudgery. When we arrive at the cemetery I inspect the open graves and to my astonishment find that an animal has fallen into one. Poor little devil, for the first thought of the men was food. It was a bit of a tussle to kill it as it was six feet down, eventually he was got out. An Australian officer working with us called it a "Looper", one of my men formerly a gamekeeper said it was a tree rat and he was not going to eat any. The "Aussie" skinned it, the carcass was about the size of a rabbit, it was put in a vegetable stew and eight of us had it for dinner, it tasted very much like rabbit. The normal daily ration is now down to one-third pound of rice supplemented with vegetables from the gardens, mainly green stuff. Anyhow it may get better as another four lorry loads have just arrived from the docks. It is said that it contains some two year old tins of food, warranty expired, only 25% is fit for consumption, anyhow that is better than nothing.

A notice on the board is asking for six fully tattooed men, needed to sing for the Japanese Imperial Army, another propaganda stunt I expect.

Tuesday April 10th

After a bout of facial tinea I have stated to shave again using my well-honed table knife. I feel a bit sore but a lot cleaner. I follow this up with a really good cup of tea, some butter and jam with the rice; it's from the good ship and a delight to taste. We just cannot express words enough to show what these little changes of food mean to us. I even managed to get a cup of coffee; it was out of this world.

47. **On this day...** April 12, 1945... Death of President Roosevelt.

Friday April 13th

Reports are saying that there is trouble in the cookhouse over the dishing out of this new food. The daily topic is food and more food, well what else would starving men talk about?

Saturday April 14th

The "Nips" have now stopped sending in the goods from the ship which doesn't help the situation. No reason given as yet. Rumour also has it that the White Cross ship was sunk after she left harbour.

Our Camp Commandant has allowed the following announcement to filter through to the men. It says news for "World Headlines" is abroad, what could it be? Nothing else has been said, maybe he knows something or it's a timely morale booster.

Sunday April 15th

No rest day for us as we have had four burials during the last two days and have to do some grave digging so as to keep ahead. It has to be one of those hot steamy days and it's a constant job wiping sweat from smarting eyes. We toil on until 4 o'clock and then return dead beat to the jail to fall on our beds, our sweat dries off leaving our bodies salt-covered before we can manage to get to the showers.

The evening passes quietly until 10.30pm when we are hurriedly called out for a roll call. The "Nips" count us over three times, no inclination as to why we have to be messed around at this late hour.

Monday April 16th

More Red Cross food on the menu, a good meat rissole, a sweet cup of tea, with coffee later at night, lips are smacking on the flavours.

Tuesday April 17th

After a heavy shower of rain we all search the cemetery boundaries for snails and what a harvest, over 250 were collected. These were handed to an officer who took them to the cookhouse and promised to bring us $11.00 the next day.

Wednesday April 18th

Red palm oil is on sale at the canteen at $2.00 a small measure and having collected our snail bonus we buy some. Some "Cross" items, not enough to go round, have come our way, we decide to put them in a draw. My ticket wins me a tin of tooth powder, other items are tooth brushes, shaving soap, razor blades, combs, pencils, and toilet rolls, nothing very startling.

Thursday April 19th

At lights out another roll call is called for. We are kept on it until 12.45 am before returning to bed. The reason, an Australian is missing.

Friday April 20th

Morning arrives and after breakfast we are told that we are confined to the jail until further notice. Later in the morning news comes that the "Aussie" has been found, head first down a latrine bore-hole, accident or suicide, no one will ever know. We are going out to bury him this afternoon.

Saturday April 21st

Talk at the moment is of the one thousand gardeners to dig a trench around the jail, I feel this must be someone's idea of a joke. I went to a lecture on bee keeping, it passed away the evening.

Sunday April 22nd

It's now the third week that we have had the little extras from the ship. It's a workday for us again because of more burials, the last three Sundays have not provided much rest.

Back at the jail we hear that a further 640 Red Cross parcels have been delivered. As there is not enough of these to go around, they are opened and the food content goes to the cookhouse and the oddments go into a draw, this time the draw consists of mainly chewing gum. We also learn that the rice ration has been increased by 30 grams, if any part of us agrees that this is good it is our stomachs. The ships part cargo of clothing arrives and naturally we all fall to discussing what we might get, until sleep eventually takes over.

Monday April 23rd

I'm awakened in the early hours by the man next to me, he was cursing and banging his bits and pieces of bed around, complaining he was being sucked dry by hundreds of bed bugs. Others awake and curse him, but with some help he soon settles down again. Apart from a few snores and a few groans from the sleeping all is well.

Morning arrives and the men arise and fumble around in a fed up quiet sort of way, even if they do work a seven-day week Monday still seems to have that feeling. With a rattle of mess tins of all descriptions, only about half the real thing, mugs in some cases are half coconut shells.

After breakfast it is the cemetery for me and the chance to get clear of my concrete home for a few hours is worth something.

Tuesday April 24th

It's a Red Cross food day so we look forward to dinner and discuss it's possible content as we go back. We get to the showers quickly, freshened we set around impatiently waiting for dinner call. Up goes the cry, "Come and get it", we hurry to the dishing up tables and receive a ration of rice hash plus one bacon and tomato pastie and a fruit pie. My God! How that bacon tastes, I swap half a pint of rice for a second one as a fellow didn't like tomato, my good luck. They say that there will be extras for tomorrow's breakfast, so what do starving men do, but go to bed dreaming of what's to come.

Wednesday April 25th

Morning comes and with it the main topic of conversation food, and when we get it, not bacon and eggs as some had hoped for but a knob of butter, which I mixed with my rice.

After breakfast I had to report to the Regimental Sergeant Major where I received a pair of American army type boots, kid leather with rubber soles. Heavy-duty workers received them as there was not enough to go around. I think they are the most comfortable boots I have ever worn, but then two years without them is a long while.

48. On this day... April 25, 1945... Berlin surrounded by Russian troops.

Thursday April 26th

My Colonel took me on a hospital visit, some of the patients we saw were in a terrible condition, some half rotten with pellagra, the swarms of flies kept at bay only by the mosquito nets, the stench was almost too much. We saw a fellow, "Rabbits" White, who lived just a few miles from me back home, normally a thin man but just now his skin stretched to a waxen white, blown up like a balloon. He is down with the last stages of beri-beri and does not know us as he is delirious, seeing only his children running on the grass outside his window. The attendants do not think he will make it. In his case the food ship has arrived just too late. More parcels have arrived so there will be some more tasty morsels. Dinner comes and with it salmon and sardine pasties, to us it's like living at the Ritz.

49. On this day... April 27, 1945... Russian and American troops link up in Germany.

50. On this day... April 28, 1945... Mussolini and his mistress shot by Italian partisans.

51. On this day... April 30, 1945... Adolph Hitler commits suicide rather than face capture

Tuesday May 1st 1945

Spent a few uncomfortable hours before daylight with chronic chest and stomach pains. Before breakfast I was sick, I don't want the sight of food, only the impossible, a cup of sweet milky tea. At midday I eat some rice and the pains come back. I go and see the medical orderly and he gives me a mist alkali, the new food has been too much for my stomach to digest. I soon learn that I am not alone.

The snails that we have gathered and sell have brought us $38, this has been useful in buying flavouring foods to mix with our rice.

Wednesday May 2nd

Red Cross clothes have arrived, also two lorry loads of rice damaged by water, a lot of it can be made use of. Feeling a bit below par I manage to get through some work on a very hot day and only eating a little rice, I get through the day of reckoning.

52. On this day... May 2, 1945... Germany armies in Italy surrender.

Tuesday May 3rd

I arise to another day, which takes us on a $2^1/_2$ mile march to the old Changi cemetery for maintenance and a cremation. Cases of dysentery have to be dealt with this way. A day mainly of grass-cutting, after which the ashes of the cremated are collected and its the march back to the jail. To us, tired and weak with hunger, this seems a long way off. As we finally pass through the gate we are soon told by the others that 10,000 letters are in, the thought of a letter, even two years old, helps to lift our spirits. The aerodrome men follow us in, they say the 'drome is nearing completion and they hope work will ease off. As for my men we feel that work is too much and feel lazy if that's the right word to use. Really there is very little life left in us, we ask when will it all end? But there is no answer to that.

Sunday May 6th

We moan as we heave ourselves off our beds, as there is no rest because we have to work and it is so very hot. Butter and jam on the breakfast menu again, supplemented with sweet tea. It's a case of look out stomach here it comes again but hoping we are getting used to these rich food items. Very pleased to receive two letters from the wife and one from my mother, but many disappointed faces as the Post-corporal passes down our lines. The letters quickly read, we are on our way to the cemetery, mainly to dig graves but the letters will be read over and over again by nightfall and in many cases passed around to one another.

Monday May 7th

It's difficult to keep track of the days as there is no ending to the week for us lately, we have come to know Sunday as it's the day we normally get the choice titbits, so it must be Monday around again and this morning I have to go with the bearer parties to Changi cemetery for two cremations. For over two miles we followed behind the corpses, rather smelly and with the usual stream of flies in attendance. After the burning it's back to the jail, we shall have to collect the ashes on our next maintenance day. We arrive back at the jail to find the Generals from the Japanese Imperial Army are carrying out an inspection of the place, which is unusual.

After showers we settle down for tea, later some of us walk around the inner wall of the jail, our way lit by a large tropical moon. Then it is sitting around until bedtime talking, but it all ends on the same long standing subject, always food and what mother makes, if by a miracle a bakers cart came out of the blue there would be one almighty stampede. I have just received news that from tomorrow I have to give what time I can spare in an effort to get the Changi cemetery looking spick and span again, no reason given.

Tuesday May 8th

Morning comes in once more, the weather is exceedingly hot, and having no imminent burials I decide to go to Changi for a day's clean up as requested.

During the day British Red Cross parcels come in, they are tattered and torn and a lot of the contents are bad, also blown tins. Where has it been all these years? Why has it just arrived here? We are asking ourselves is the war over or nearing its end.

53. *On this day...* May 8, 1945... At one minute past midnight Germany surrenders and war in Europe officially comes to an end.

Wednesday May 9th

A wet day so no work therefore it is light duty rations. I also remember this day as the one I met the girl who later became my wife, it was back in 1937. It seems a long time since we were last together, although always in my mind, I know that we shall meet again. Heaven's knows what I will look like for at the moment I am just skin and bones, at the last weigh in I went just over 7st. Fellows with hatchet faces, sunken eyes, elbows, knee caps and ribs all showing clearly through the skin, I don't think another year like the past will find many of us alive.

Thursday May 10th

The snail fund has enabled my men to buy $10 worth of palm oil, they say it is good for the eyes, I hope this is so as mine are playing tricks and for three days I appear to be rather light headed. Food is about the same, breakfast, ½ pint rice pap; Tiffin, ½ pint rice and vegetable hash plus anything I can pick up; Tea ¾ pint of rice, $^{1}/_{6}$ pint salt fish, mug of raw tea, what a menu.

Sunday May 13th

It's Red Cross time around again, and while out at work we cook a good stew from our cemetery garden sideline. A thick mixture of tapioca, spinach, coconut and pineapple, the last two gifts from some passing Chinese. Dinner at night, a bully beef pasty, a better day for the old stomach.

The 'Changi Boys' Fellow POWs 1945

Monday May 14ᵗʰ

Another week begins, much like the last but I have to say again that the main topic is food, the men talk of what they would like to eat, what they ate in the past and what they hope to eat in the future. So you can understand our state of mind, the minds of very hungry men on the point of starvation.

Friday May 18ᵗʰ

A day passes at the old Changi cemetery, it's very hot and on the march in I ask myself once again, when will the end come? The end has come for some, 150 cookhouse staff have been withdrawn from their jobs by the medical officer who says it's time they did some outside work. They take the place of some of the weaker aerodrome workers, when the "Nips" in charge see them they ask where do the new prisoners come from? Others are surprised and just stare at the giants of the jail.

Tuesday May 22ⁿᵈ

Owing to the prolonged drought, water is now in short supply and with the exceedingly hot weather which can continue for the next four months it's going to be mighty uncomfortable with only a trickle at the showers. It is also said that some days there will be no washing at all. I hope I shall be lucky for a few days, as this excessive heat has brought out a heat rash, I am covered with prickly heat. I thought after three years I would have been immune, it's damned irritating.

Wednesday May 23ʳᵈ

One of the Majors is in trouble with the powers that be, concerning some black market cigar business, hard luck on him being caught. Some Red Cross food for us tonight. With the rice we get a chocolate covered fig and jam cup, excellent, would like a dozen, but then my stomach would suffer, still it gave us something to talk about until lights out.

Friday May 25th

Another scorching hot morning dawns and with it news that 500 men are moving to what is called No 2 camp. I feel like packing up cemetery work and trying to go with them, it is said the food will be better there. I wonder, although I am fed up to the teeth, perhaps it is still better to stay with the devil you know. Anyhow one harsh devil has finished with us, after 20 months the poor fellows who have done the aerodrome work are no longer needed to labour. At least if they survive they can tell others that they are founder members of the great Changi aerodrome. We arrive back to the jail after a scorching days work to learn that 350 prisoners of war have landed here from Sumatra with a 1,000 more to come.

Sunday May 27th

Another Red Cross food day, but only a few titbits issued.

Monday May 28th

The day comes with the news that I have an American to bury, the first in my cemetery but then there is not many of them here. Just over a hundred men buried in the second cemetery. It's stinking hot and everything that's not green just glares in the strong sunlight. Some 100 more men leaving the jail no doubt to make room for a new intake, the news comes via the office clerk checking on a burial. The day over I make my way back with some nagging pain in my rear, I cannot work with it so I shall have to go sick in the morning.

54. ***On this day...*** May 28, 1945... Naval air attacks on Japanese mainland.

Tuesday May 29th

Saw the doctor, he examined me and said I had a breakdown of the anal fissure for which I was operated on some time back. He told me to rest for a few days as he did not want to send me to hospital, he would see how things went. British and Dutch prisoners numbering 11,000 men arrive in camp, 250 of us stand by to leave. The air raid siren blares out but no sign of planes at this end of the island, although almost daily now we see the very high flying "Silver Lady" but no notice seems to be taken of it.

Thursday May 31st

This brings us to the end of the month that seems to have been the longest in my life, everyone is damned browned off. When will it all end? When I think of English menus I could cry.

Friday June 1st 1945

The start of a new month always raises the spirits for awhile. Saw the medical officer this morning, happy with my condition but does not want me to work, but I want to so I can start tomorrow.

Saturday June 2nd

I go with my party to work today but soon find that I have to do the lightest of work. I manage to get through a very hot, tiring day. Back at the jail I soon hear that another 750 men are to stand by for a move.

Monday June 4th

Morning arrives and after breakfast men named for the move gather their bits and pieces and stand about in abject silence, not knowing where they are destined for. Barely had they moved when another call for 1800 men to be put on standby.

Tuesday June 5th

As the days go by work is routine and standby men are still with us, it's a wearying time. The relentless sun almost scorching our skin off, in the time I've been here I have never been so hot. Managed to get on a late afternoon bathing party, it's nice to get into the sea, a very large Red Cross hospital ship is seen passing out at sea, going where or carrying who we could not hazard a guess.

Thursday June 7th

Sweltering days go by with just routine work and doing battle with the myriads of flies, drop a grain of rice on the ground and it is immediately lost sight of, covered by hundreds of them, one swipe and you have a battlefield of the dead. No more standby parties moved yet, I never seem to get on one as the Command don't think I should leave the job I have, perhaps for my sake they are right, not knowing where a move could take you, anyhow I am once again off the sick list, but bored stiff.

Tuesday June 12th

During the last 14 days I have carried out seven burials, nothing like the numbers in the early years but are on the way up once more.

Some Red Cross food is coming up for dinner, but vegetables are in short supply because of drought hitting the gardens. I have got some tomato plants going from cuttings. Other garden news is no tapioca root for at least three months, which is bad news for food rations.

A silver cigarette case salvaged from a bombed house, a war trophy, has been stolen from my pack, it's big money on the black market operated by the "Nip" guards.

Wednesday June 13th

Two burials today. "Rabbits" White, suffering from beri-beri, appears to be holding his own.

Saturday June 16th

A party given the code X8 has now left us and men now seem to be leaving daily. There is a scarcity of water also due to the sizzling drought. Some 1,500 men arrive in the camp so we seem to maintain a balance.

Tuesday June 19th

I arise this morning feeling decidedly cooler, the long drought has broken, it's pouring down with rain, with thunder that sounds like guns of battle. We had two burials yesterday but so far not notified for any today so we can stay in the dry. The time is spent de-bugging and playing cards and dice games.

One of my cell mates has found some lice in his bits of clothing. The puzzle now remains how to keep from catching lice when it's already in ones cell. What a bloodsucking combination, bugs, lice, and mosquitoes, the flea would make the quartet, but as I have never seen one I would imagine that they cannot stand the heat.

Friday June 22nd

On the way to work this morning I picked up a yam (like a sugar beet) it was evidently dropped by some villages. I had some palm oil so I sliced it up and fried it for Tiffin, it made a little extra for three of us. It's hot and heavy and we are glad the day is over, digging graves drags your stomach out.

Dead beat, we slouch rather than march back to jail, my tongue is stuck to my mouth with dryness. Water is still in short supply so the shower is only a dribble. Tea is poor, just rice and a few greens with the usual half-pint of raw tea. Not a lot of life among the fellows tonight, we are very quiet, they ask one another when will it all end, life has become so wearying.

Sunday June 24ᵗʰ

After a nights sleep, disturbed a lot by snoring men, some shouting in their sleep, others cursing or groaning. Nowhere could one possibly come across so many agonised souls. I awake with a thick head to just one more rest day and no Red Cross titbits as the stocks have run out. Our little garden patch on the cemetery produces some bits to help out.

Some more mail in, none come my way as yet.

Saturday June 30ᵗʰ

A week goes by with only routine work but a little excitement tonight as the word goes around that an "Aussie" has escaped, where does he think he is going in his condition? The poor fellow must be deranged.

Sunday July 1ˢᵗ 1945

Tomorrow 1,000 men move to the so-called No 2 camp, 70 of these are from my Regiment, The Royal Norfolks, it will leave us thin on the ground. The moving around has caused the hospital to auction off their source of eggs, 17 ducks, they fetched $13.00 each. Myself, I managed to get an old spring bed also some loose coir which I stuff into my bits of mattress giving them a little more body.

An officer, Major Bregiel, who has worked with me over the years had an operation today for acute appendicitis, also a cell mate, Jack Parker, has been taken in with malaria.

Monday July 2nd

My bed space has been raided again, the thief has taken 5ozs of "Blachan" (fish paste). Received a letter from the wife, it's over a year old but makes good reading and it will get read many times over.

Wednesday July 4th

A further 240 men leave the jail. Myself, I get moved to another cell. I move my furniture, one sawn off cupboard from an old sideboard, my newly acquired bed and then fix up a mosquito net that I came by some time in the past. I spend an uncomfortable night on my bed, at the same time flapping at a "mozzie" I have trapped inside the net.

Thursday July 5th

After one more night I decide this soft bed is not for me, after three years of a concrete base I just could not sleep on it, so I give it away. Another of my men has gone down with malaria and a complication.

Friday July 6th

Lt Col. Dillon takes charge of the cemetery from Lt Col. Newy, who becomes Camp Representative Officer.

Saturday July 14th

Today has been wet so we have been confined to the jail and that has meant light duty rations. With $5.00 I have saved I go to the canteen and buy 2lbs of tapioca root and hope to find someone with some palm oil and share a fry up later this evening. Passed an interesting night talking with an officer from the Shanghai

Volunteers, discussing also our freedom, different little changes going on seem to point to it in the near future, let it soon come.

Sunday July 15ᵗʰ

Major Bregiel, the officer in for appendicitis, is now recovering. We have been very close over the past three years. He tells me he regards me as a son. A very early burial that I carried out was his son who died from battle wounds, the effect was to age him prematurely. On writing up my diary I find that I am missing out some days, my memory has lapses, not to worry as it is very routine work just now, also I have got down to odd scraps of paper as it is very hard to come by.

Air raids in the vicinity are now probable as men are digging more slit trenches close by, this must be a good sign. Some 150 light duty men leave us to go to Singapore.

Monday July 16ᵗʰ

It's the only day that my men are allowed to go to Changi cemetery for maintenance. Today it is for repairs and cross renewal as they get eaten off at ground level by termites. The trouble with Changi is the long march back, in our weak condition it's utterly exhausting and on arriving back at the jail we just sink onto our beds. On this occasion we get caught in a storm, drenched with rain, I really feel frozen stiff in about 80^0F. I ask myself what will I do when I get home if I should arrive in the winter. Well at least there is no need for a shower so I get dried off, wrapping myself in my rags of a blanket I huddle up and wait for that life saving cup of raw tea.

Sunday July 22ⁿᵈ

Later I visit the hospital, see the major and a few other lads, all are improving, even the beri-beri case not expected to live last week has pulled through. Seeing some of the fellows there practically rotting away gives me some hope for at least I can still walk around, although the food barely keeps the skin on our bones. What bits and pieces the canteen holds is in many cases beyond our pockets as our amenity grant of a few dollars will not buy much with whitebait at $34 per lb and gula malacca, a type of solidified brown sugar at $18 per lb The only way is to pool our money, which enables us to get a spoonful each.

Tuesday July 24th

Some orders made in the jail makes one sick, the latest is, if you work outside each man will hand in one shirt, one pair of shorts before he leaves and collect same on return. This clothing being recent Red Cross issue could be lost or sold. The mixing of one's clothing could also make us all lousy.

Wednesday July 25th

Had two more burials, these are now frequent enough to keep us grave digging on Sunday again. The weather is very hot and on this work I just stream sweat for hours on end, running into one's eyes and dripping off my nose and chin. I'm glad to finish and get back for a shower and rest, while doing this I get a smell of stinking cockroaches. I reach for my haversack in which I have some dried tapioca chips, a coconut and some gula malacca which I had put by so that I could have a bit of a celebration on my wedding anniversary, about a fortnight hence. On turning this out I disturbed 18 large cockroaches enjoying themselves. I clean up the food and apart from the nut eat it with my tea rice, just cannot afford to waste it.

Thursday July 26th

The day dawned hot as hell, but it brings a bit of excitement as a number of planes fly very fast over us, some of the men claim to have seen the markings as ours, others say that they were Lightnings, perhaps it is wishful thinking.

Friday July 27th

More burials, all from beri-beri, a vitamin deficiency. Is it catching up with the remainder of us, we test ourselves by pressing a thumb into the skin, if it leaves a hole for some time it's the onset of the complaint.

Our guard of long standing who takes us to the cemetery reported to the guard house, put his rifle under his chin and shot himself. His name was "O-No" and it is said he got too friendly with our officers and was found out.

Saturday July 28th

Another visit to the old cemetery, in the short time we get to work there it is a difficult job to keep on top and under the pressure it becomes very trying and it doesn't help when we learn that some tapioca root sent for our cemetery workers stew pot has gone astray, who got their hands on it while en route is anybody's guess.

Sunday July 29th

Major Bregiel is out of hospital now and has just had a blackout causing some consternation, however, after resting for the afternoon and with some help he gets back to camp.

Some 15 months ago enough books were collected to start a small library, now at last I have managed to get a ticket to become a member, but not much peace to read as the topic under discussion on the floor is that the "Nips" have called for a party of men to work at cement mixing in Singapore. Not many want to go, a few will risk the hard work just to set eyes on women again.

Tuesday July 31st

Morning once more and as I yawn my way to breakfast, I am thinking it's still nice to be alive although I think lumbago has afflicted me. Towards midday a buzz of excitement as anti-aircraft guns open fire on some very high planes, this really gets us thinking that the war must at least be close to us. The thought of this is pushed from my mind as I feel bad, my bones now aching badly. Having dealt with a burial, the corpse coming from the infamous Outram Road jail, I rest in the shade until it's time for the homeward trek, arriving at the jail I for go a shower and take to my bed.

Wednesday August 1st 1945

I spend another troubled night, awakening to a new month, to me it's another month of living hell. When will it end? I am feeling very queer, miss my breakfast and join the sick parade, malaria is suspected, a blood slide is taken but later proved negative. I spend a horrible day and at 7pm another blood slide is taken which again proves negative.

Thursday August 2nd

A sleepless night but I am glad that I can still appreciate the daylight as it comes in sharply around 6.30am I am also glad of my cup of tea, although eating little of my rice. During the day I get two further blood tests which also turn out as negative. When I got the last one I collapsed on the table, I am very weak having suffered three blackouts during the day. The medical officer thinks I have dengue fever coupled with a chill, but has nothing to give me.

Friday August 3rd

I get through the night with bone breaking pains, the symptoms of dengue. After two days suffering they find some medicine which I am given twice a day, another 24 hours and I come out of my semi-delirious state and begin to take some notice of what's going on around. One of my men has just been brought back from the cemetery on a handcart after collapsing; he is a recent malaria case.

Saturday August 4th

I have a more restful night and awake feeling much better. I eat breakfast, walk around for a bit to keep my legs working then lay on my bed until Tiffin. My man, brought in yesterday, is back in the hospital suffering from malnutrition and complications. Another party of men left for cement mixing and bricklayers' labourers in Singapore. Reports of men coming back from Malaya. I report to the medical hut and get two more days to take it easy.

Monday August 6th

I report to company gardens where I work for half an hour, by doing this I get full daily rations.

55. On this day... August 6, 1945... The Japanese city of Hiroshima destroyed by the atomic bomb.

Tuesday August 7th

Only by keeping this secret diary do I know the date. I am told to take the day off. My men are coping with a flow of burials, men are dying of various complications, very little body resistance left.

Wednesday August 8th

I join the sick parade MO says I can start light work tomorrow. It's now raining hard, the temperature drops enough to make me feel cold, I cover myself with what bits and pieces I can find as I'm worried about getting another chill. After a few hours the sun breaks through and for once it's a treat to feel its heat.

At bedtime I am plagued with an attack of the irritating prickly heat. For some hours I lay listening to a variety of sounds made by men suffering from minds in turmoil.

Thursday August 9th

Thankful for the arrival of daylight I get myself out to find some water for a wash, then breakfast, still rice pap, but the mug of tea is more than welcome. It's time then for work once again. While on the cemetery a party of villagers dump a large sack by the fence and with a furtive wave they went on their way. Discreetly two of my men go and bring it in, to our pleasant surprise it contains about 1 cwt of red apples. They were shared around and many of us tasted apples for the first time for four years. The natives have always been friendly in a quiet way but this latest gift must mean something exciting is in the wind. We are still hoping that the day of our freedom is not far off, this year we hope.

After tea I feel rather ill with stomach pains, I go to bed early and am alone in the cell moaning in agony, someone hears me and fetches a medical orderly. At 11pm he brings the doctor, it's dark as lights are out. I hear a voice exclaim, "Where the hell is he?" As he reaches my cell he says, "It's a bloody dog kennel". He sends me some tablets and a hot water bottle to place on my stomach.

Have a fair night and this morning I see the MO, he checks me over, makes no diagnosis, says something to do with the food.

There is an undercurrent of talk going through the jail. It is that the war is over and as we leave for work we are addressed by

402

our Camp Commandant, who quietly tells us that there may be headline news in a few days and we may hear things that might excite us. He asks us to carry on and also look normal so as not to upset the "Nips". This we do, although inside we feel very excited, but to our guards we are as poker faced as ever. In the evening we ask each other has the war ended, all day I have asked myself this. I cannot grasp the realisation of it, am I dreaming, anyhow it's to bed with something to lay and think about.

56. *On this day...* August 9, 1945... Second atomic bomb destroys Japanese city of Nagasaki.

CHAPTER 9

HAPPIEST EXPECTATIONS

Monday August 13th 1945

We work as usual, however, by the look of the Japanese Army activities and the fact that the air raid siren is sounding it does not seem that the war is over, or just another rumour monger at work. It's really better not to take too much notice of what one hears for we are all on edge, upset by false news but it persists throughout the day, no one talks of anything else. Somehow we struggle with burials and grave-digging only glad to get back to the jail, exhausted by the work and war news.

Tuesday August 14th

It is much the same as yesterday, rumours again rife, talk of official statements to be announced cause trembles of expectations and moods of sheer exasperation owing to conflicting reports, try as I may I cannot ignore them as the day passes.

57. *On this day*... August 14, 1945... Japan surrenders unconditionally to the Allies.

Wednesday August 15th

Another day follows with the same undercurrent of excitement. It creeps into you, I take my mud stained wedding photograph off the wall, kiss the wife a couple of times then find a few flowers to put in jar beside it. I try not to show my feelings too much, the men, also are trying hard to hide them but I think everyone is boiling inside. What a catastrophe if all these rumours are untrue, even so I feel a warm thrill of expectancy in my blood.

Friday August 17th

Two more days pass and this one, a day of nervous tension, getting as we thought mixed up in a riot, as rifle and machine gun fire cracks just beyond the trees close to the cemetery. Somehow we get through our work, we get back to the jail in a sweaty state of nervous exhaustion, the rumours of so many ways and dates that the war finished, coming from all over the area. The saying "patience is a virtue" is one I must abide by at this time.

Saturday August 18th

No 2 camp gets a holiday, which make things look better as they have been engaged in digging defences. I now get a nasty setback as a lone plane gets fired on as it drops some bombs. It's only a moment's setback as more POW's arrive here from Singapore with their rumours of good news. The rice ration has gone up, more Red Cross food is promised. We have not been definitely told that war is over. Are they just letting it sink in gradually for fear of trouble? The "Nip" guards are still on duty, it seems with a smile. More men arriving here all seem very happy. We get a half day off work, lots of work parties appear to have finished. Although not yet told officially that the war is over, a message says, we can send a five-word message home as soon as the relieving troops arrive, they must be close by in Malaya.

Monday August 20th

The jail is one big bustle and uproar, overcrowded with men it reeks with sweat. It's 10.30am and 2,000 more men from Singapore are unloading from lorries, it will soon be standing room only. Eleven loads of Red Cross food arrive with them. Rations are soaring as more and more trucks arrive. It's like Christmas Eve here as men and food continue to arrive throughout the day. Plenty of happy badinage and broadly smiling faces from this motley crowd of skin and bone men with rice bellies. Happy because they have come through the horrible years.

Well it is plenty to eat, also sweet coffee. Had three helpings of sago pudding with lashings of sugar given to me by my cellmates, it was issued to them when they broke camp in Singapore.

Still no official news from the "Nips" or our own people but all the signs say that the war is over. For the five-word message home I put, "Freedom, Happiest Expectations", but was told to cut out freedom. Why, no explanation is given, so I wrote "Felicitations". Red Cross food for breakfast and tea, so go to bed contented with the marvellous thought that I shall see you all at Christmas and at last we hear that tomorrow they hope to pronounce us free.

Tuesday August 21ˢᵗ

All up bright and early this morning waiting for the promised news, however, it does not come. The whole place is rife with rumours, such as a fund started for us in London has reached the million pound mark. We are to be allowed to draw extra food on ration cards and so they go on. Rice and chocolate for tea and I get two pints of sago.

My day was spent on the old Changi cemetery tidying up the graves. Saw the Japanese burning up some dummy planes on the 'drome, they seem as happy as us and I wonder if they also are waiting for official news of the war's end. The march back after a days work doesn't exhaust us so much with the extra food in our stomachs giving us a bit more strength.

Food and clothing has been arriving all day and this evening I get an issue of a pair of Japanese army shorts, a coloured shirt and a vest, we all certainly look cleaner although somewhat overdressed. The medical officer gives out a warning against beriberi increase owing to an unbalanced diet. Many men are being taken into hospital with severe stomach pains.

Wednesday August 22nd

The tension and excitement is great as we still await the final word and so the days go by and I've just had to bury two unfortunate fellows at this stage.

Have just been issued with a Japanese G-string, why at this time? Could have done with them when our shorts were falling to bits, it will make a souvenir of the past.

Ten American cigarettes handed out, the place seems a smoke haze, the food is fit for a king, it's made up of rice with milk and raisins, salmon and cheese hash, chocolate and butter cup, whitebait pasty, sweet tea, it's too rich for us. Beriberi is still on the increase. The puzzle is what's going on, is the war over? Are the "Nips" trying to put some weight on us before our troops get here. It has been said over the last weeks that the "Nips" intended to drive all Prisoners of War between them and any invading Allied Forces, but it appears that this will not happen now.

Friday August 24th

Nippon General sends for Camp Representative, is this it? We wait for news but when it comes the notices say that the "Nips" have lifted the ban on concerts, music and clapping.

Impromptu concerts have sprung up and the "King" has been sung in many places. It is rumoured that our planes are to drop medical supplies tomorrow. It is a curious atmosphere not knowing exactly what the situation is. I begin to think that it is all suddenly ended and we have not been told because of the possibility of trouble between our "Nip" guards and us. For the third day running we have had Yak meat, the first for around two years.

Saturday August 25th

We awake this morning to find large POW signs, also ground signs marked POW. These have been put in position since midnight and this tells us it must be the end. The expected planes do not arrive. Why? Perhaps because the Singapore Radio has said that the POW's have received medical supplies and much extra food. Many concerts going on in the camp and the various hues of the hundreds of coloured shirts that we have been given makes the place look like Brighton beach.

A day off has been given but three men and myself had to go out for a burial. The whole jail and areas around are crowded with men who have come back from Malaya and Burma, hundreds are ill with stomach troubles, many in hospital with diarrhoea. They just cannot digest the Red Cross food, it's far too rich for us. When I take my party past Japanese guards I no longer have to give saluting commands in their language but have been told to revert to English. Our Colonel has spoken to us, he shook hands all round and just said there was a lot of interesting news coming in.

Sunday August 26ᵗʰ

An open air service was held today, 16 Padres were in attendance for this thanks giving demonstration of freedom, thousands of men took part. We are now getting a bit impatient while waiting for something to happen, so many rumours as to how and when we shall be going home, they are going to fly us home, take us by warship, liners and so the talk goes on.

At dinner we each received a quarter pound of butter and some salt, according to the boxes the butter was packed in 1926! After a long evening in which we discussed the many things that might happen to us I got wearily to my bed and with a comfortable stomach I must soon fall asleep.

Monday August 27ᵗʰ

Morning seems to have arrived very quickly. During the day Red Cross planes flew twice over us dropping leaflets printed in English and Japanese advising us to be careful what we eat and how to carry on for the time being. Well I have never been told officially that the war has ended but events of the last few days have proved it. Tonight we each received 6ozs Kraft cheese, delicious!

Tuesday August 28th

A day later and I am just once more suffering from a bad stomach. Our living quarters were inspected by the Camp Commanding Officer. Why after so long?

A wireless report has come through saying medical men and supplies are being dropped by parachute on Changi aerodrome tomorrow. They are more than welcome as the drugs could save lives that hang in the balance.

Wednesday August 29th

It's 1.30am and I awake to the droning of a plane overhead. In the morning we are told that it parachuted in two medical officers and two orderlies along with two infantry officers. Like myself their introduction to Singapore was a very wet one as it has been raining heavily.

A burial this afternoon so shall have to venture out in it. What a terrible thing to have to bury men now that they are free. With it over and feeling a bit downcast, the weather not helping, we get back to the jail, where we find a radio has turned up. From whence it came no one bothers to ask as they crowd around to listen to a broadcast from Ceylon, the first radio news for nearly four years. More supplies expected to be dropped tomorrow.

Thursday August 30th

I am at work on the Changi cemetery when I hear the drone of some large planes. We excitingly watch the sky in the direction of the sound, soon three Liberators are circling the near-by 'drome, getting lower each time around, then a straight fly up the runway and large packages are parachuted down from each plane. One small parcel without a 'chute went astray and fell close by, this one I retrieved. We have a crowd around as we tell of the planes dropping packages; every happening is something to be talked about. We go to bed rather excited at night, it's a wonder we get any sleep.

Friday August 31ˢᵗ

As I awake to another day I wonder what it will bring, anyhow to start with it's another day at Changi. I rather think it is to keep us out of any mischief by keeping us occupied. As we march out, with no escort now, I notice that the "Nip" guards are acting rather self-conscious, the reason for this, their rifles have been replaced with dummy ones with a rubber blob on the end, one sentry has a puppy on a string. We salute and pass as though nothing has happened but having a good laugh further down the road.

A Chinese society has presented the camp with ten pigs, in many small ways the Chinese have been helpful over the years, this gift will make for a few tasty stews. We spend a hard day cleaning up, grass cutting and attending to the flower beds. Getting lost in work is the best thing to calm our over excitable minds, the day passes more quickly and we are soon on our way back to the jail, the march no longer the hard drag as our stomachs are better filled.

After a shower we settle down to listen to the radio, which is such a wonderful thing to us, we listen to programmes from Ceylon and even England, from where we hear Frances Day singing in London. The paratroop officers recently dropped here have been able to get a transmitter from the Japs. They are checking off our names for transmitting home.

Saturday September 1st 1945

I awake this morning not feeling very well, all this delightful but different food is upsetting the system. I am now suffering from beriberi and protein fever.

Sunday September 2nd

I realise that it is my mother's birthday. Many Happy Returns mum, will soon be seeing you, but don't things just happen to me on your birthday. My call-up the day before outbreak of the War, the Selerang (Black Hole) incident and today we have been told that the war is officially over, great news. Also today a number of large four-engine planes have been dropping supplies on the aerodrome for over an hour while Mosquito bombers flash across the sky at, to us, amazing speeds.

A draw was made this afternoon for the odds and ends from broken up Red Cross parcels. I managed to draw a packet of razor blades, useful when I get a razor, at present I still get through a scrape with my table knife. Listen to some more news from Ceylon and Delhi.

Eight strange Chinese soldiers appear in our area, they have red tabs on their collars, we are told that they are guerrillas and are taking over some duties.

58. On this day... September 2, 1945... VJ day celebrated. WWII officially comes to an end.

Monday September 3rd

The weekend has gone by with nothing outstanding evolving. The start of a new week takes me and my small party, now down to four, to the No 1 cemetery for more maintenance work. With all the noisy excitement around these days it is a pleasure to get to somewhere with peace and quiet and spend a nice morning

411

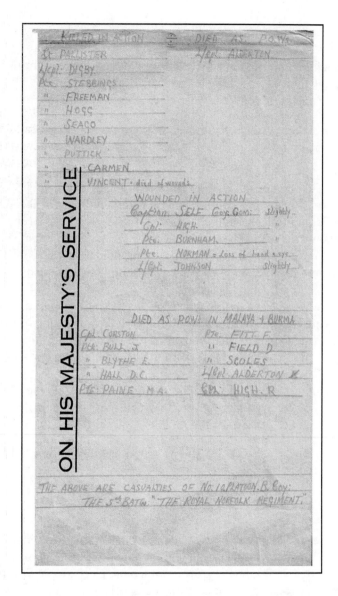

ON HIS MAJESTY'S SERVICE

KILLED IN ACTION | DIED AS P.O.Ws.
Lt. PALLISTER | 2/Lt. ALDERTON
L/Cpl: DIGBY
Pte. STEBBINGS
" FREEMAN
" HOSS
" SEAGO
" WARDLEY
" PUTTICK
" CARMEN
" VINCENT - died of wounds

WOUNDED IN ACTION
Captian SELF Coy. Com: slightly
Cpl: HIGH. "
Pte. BURNHAM. "
Pte. NORMAN = Loss of hand & eye.
L/Cpl: JOHNSON slightly

DIED AS P.O.Ws. IN MALAYA + BURMA
Cpl. CORSTON | Pte. FITT. F.
Pte. BULL. J | " FIELD. D
" BLYTHE E. | " SCOLES
" HALL D.C. | L/Cpl. ALDERTON K
Pte. PAINE M.A. | Cpl. HIGH. R

THE ABOVE ARE CASUALTIES OF No. 10 PLATOON. B. Coy.
THE 5th BATN. "THE ROYAL NORFOLK REGIMENT."

Some of those that didn't make it home.
Casualties of No. 10 platoon, B Company, 5th Royal Norfolks

clipping the grass on the graves of our unfortunate comrades. Still sweating profusely but not now getting so exhausted. It's Tiffin time and just as we get sat down the heavens are shattered by the roar of large planes coming in to drop more supplies on the runways close by. With Tiffin over, washed down with a pint of now sweet tea, but still no milk, we get back to work with sweat streaming down our bodies, no doubt made worse because of the extra hot tea ration. Our workday over we march the few miles back home, now in a much happier state of mind, however imagine our surprise on approaching the jail to see the Union Jack flying from its flagstaff, on its right the Dutch tricolour and to its left the Stars and Stripes of America. The site of the old flag made our hearts leap, it brought tears to my eyes and to many others, we all agreed that it was the best sight in the world. All the natives in the area were very excited at the sight of it, they greet us with huge grins on their faces, saluting us as we pass.

Tonight more planes arrive and drop supplies, including four more parachutists made up of three press men and a Colonel. News goes around that Lady Mountbatten is paying us a visit tomorrow. A press ship carrying 100 pressmen is due in. A Lt Colonel from the 2nd Norfolks has also just arrived along with a high up from the 5th Infantry Division. I am told that the 2nd Norfolks have fought their way across Burma.

Tuesday September 4th

Many civilians have come to the jail including ex-internees; they have come to see friends, a lot of whom are Singapore and Malay volunteers. It makes one a bit homesick but my time will soon come. In the meantime I write up my diary and I am a bit downcast when I see that over the last month I have buried 19 men who have died in freedom, how unlucky can some be.

Wednesday September 5th

The Chinese here are really going to town, greatly enjoying their freedom, flags everywhere, many national ones waving in the breeze. There is great and intense excitement among them as the 5th Indian Division lands and looks prepared for any eventualities.

Tea is so much more appetising now; tonight we get an issue of butter, jam, cheese, and biscuits also vitamin tablets, what a party meal it is to us after the long years of rice and more rice. I don't think I shall ever stand the sight of a rice pudding again. At least we sit around after tea until bedtime talking about the new foods that fill our stomachs, some getting pains of indigestion while others make tracks to the latrines. I expect it will take some time to get used to the change of diet, anyhow to enjoy the new flavours we are prepared for a bit of discomfort.

Thursday September 6th

Three more parachutists have dropped in but who they are nobody seems to know. The men are now allowed to walk out in a three-mile area in organised parties. Saw some of the Indian Forces in our area today also a few British soldiers, including two officers who stopped and talked to us.

Later I wrote my first airmail letter home, it's around four years since the last one. The clocks are changing tonight, back 1½ hours, I don't seem to remember it before, well under the "Nips" maybe it hasn't. I am told that I am to go for a medical inspection, a check up now I expect by doctors that have recently come in.

Friday September 7th

Today I saw the first plane land on the aerodrome, looks like a small transport. It made a number of taxi runs up and down the runways as if it were testing them out, then it took off again. I watched it as it disappeared into the distant sky; the fact that a

British plane could come and go so safely to me seems like a miracle.

On the day of his release a prisoner has been given permission to marry, I don't know who it is but suspect he must be someone who was on the island previous to its fall to the "Nips".

Saturday September 8ᵗʰ

I am still doing cemetery work and today I am struck down with a fever. An ambulance had to be called to fetch me in. What a headache I have, it's like a violent storm without the noise. The medical officer comes to see me, says I have a high temperature. I am given some aspirins and a sleeping draught.

Sunday September 9ᵗʰ

Feeling a little better this morning but have to stay in bed for two days, so it sounds like another attack of dengue fever.

Monday September 10ᵗʰ

On the second day I am able to take more notice of what's going on. I am told that two officers of the 2ⁿᵈ Battalion, The Royal Norfolks, have arrived on staff work here. My room-mates tell me that many men are roaming all over the place, some jumping lorries going into Singapore, others visiting the surrounding Malay kampongs, no doubt to try and chat up some of the pretty girls that live in them. I am also told that men of long service here are now being flown home to England and that hospital ships are taking the wounded and long-term sick on board, all sounds very encouraging.

The Major connected with me on the cemetery has been ill for sometime, he has been taken on board. The floor all around me has been washed with "Lysol" disinfectant, its smell is rather strange to me. I am given a newspaper, rather old, it's the

"Norwich Mercury", its reading proves rather interesting. I read of a local woman's accident (a person who I knew very well and who was very good to us Territorials), the burglary of a shop owned by an aunt of mine, also read of two girls who were caught cutting down trees in the water company's area, must be short of fuel. An article on the setting up of a nursery for homeless babies, it is so bad that many children are left unwanted.

Tuesday September 11ᵗʰ

I write another letter home, I can now tell them that the food is getting much better, only get rice pap for breakfast now, the other meals consist of meat and vegetable stews. I am still trying to shake off the effects of the fever.

Lady Mountbatten visits the area with Admirals and Generals in the party. Men are now moving steadily away in small draughts, some for planes, others for ships, some for the long way home via Australia and America.

Wednesday September 12ᵗʰ

Another hot humid day dawns. At last I am allowed out so with two friends I hitch-hike to Singapore, about 11 miles, we are going to watch the victory parade. I saw Lord Mountbatten, the people of Singapore cheered and rushed around excitedly. The march route was lined by British and French sailors. As I talked to one of the sailors from *HMS Nelson* I realised what a small world it is, when in conversation he told me of a girl he knew in my home town, she happens to be the daughter of a friend of mine. After the parade we visited the docks and was invited aboard the *HMS Sussex*, saw the *"Nelson"* and the French warship *"Richelieu"*. The day was out of this world for us, so much freedom and excitement, to cap it all we were driven back to camp in a jeep. Slept well, being tired out.

Thursday September 13th

It is my 34th birthday, the fourth one out here. I am now waiting patiently for a ship to take me out of all this. Yesterday was a bit too much, I feel rather rough, still suffering the effects of the fever.

Daily issues of tinned food are now made to us and cigarettes are plentiful. I swap mine around for other bits and pieces. It's very routine for us that are waiting. I long for the day when I can leave all this behind. Shall I look back one day and wish for some part of the life I have led for nearly four years, no I don't think so, perhaps only the sunshine will be missed when I arrive home in an English winter. I expect I shall feel very cold after this hot climate.

Saturday September 15th

The days move slowly by as parties of men leave the Changi camp for Singapore on their first stage home, elated and singing as they go make me and a few others left here in the jail feel rather dejected as we look around at the rubbish left behind, such as makeshift beds, bits of broken furniture, boxes and miscellaneous rubbish that was once home for the departing men.

Relieving troops are now moving into this area to take over administration duties. I meet some of them for an occasional chat and learn something of what has been going on in the world outside ours. Was glad to receive a letter from Mother today getting all the family news, it appears I have a lot of new nephews and nieces, also the fact that my brothers and sisters have survived the war was great news.

Sunday September 16th

A grand day with the early mists rising above the trees and a huge red sun edging through, soon it will be quite hot. I can enjoy the days now that the rigours of war are over. Although free I still have some work on the cemetery, I am taking a party there as soon as we have collected some rations. The work is mainly to set up some new crosses; the termites soon eat them off at ground level. The two and a half mile march to the cemetery comes much easier now accompanied by cheerful banter. The place looks lovely now that I see it through the eyes of freedom, the grass of the mounds clipped and green. The straight lines of the crosses and neat grass pathways, the main gravel road through with a large raised bed in the roundabout - a colourful mass of Bougainvillea, the dark green tulip trees (planted three years ago as 12 inch cuttings have now attained the height of 12 feet) are resplendent with their huge orange-red blooms. The Lych Gate stands out with its trim fence of small mauve flowers on either side of its entrance path. As I stand under a huge tree that grows on a bank a few yards from where the cemetery commenced I contemplate all the hard work and heartbreak, the weakness, starvation, the weariness, I wonder how we managed to bury around 800 men in graves dug with worn out tools, dug from sticky volcanic clay. I heave a sigh, look up at the spreading branches of the tree above me, it is a cachou tree, it has provided us with yellow peppery fruit in abundance over the years gone by if you could beat the large brown ants to the ripe ones as they had a passion for the taste as well. I step out of its shade, look up once more, thinking goodbye old friend you saw me come and you watch me go, I feel sorry that it may not be long before you have to go too as the construction of the nearby aerodrome advances upon you. I gather the men together, we leave the cemetery, I with a twinge of sadness look once more at the mounds thinking of those beneath but at the same time thankful that I was not with them. The work for the last three and a half years is left behind.

A lot of men invited by sailors of *HMS Nelson* did not return for two days, army discipline caught up with them, they were locked in their cells for punishment. I have just finished writing two letters home which I hope will leave with the above mentioned ship which is due to sail.

Monday September 17*th*

The war has been over several weeks but a lot of us are still patiently waiting, some I imagine just bored to tears at the delay. Saw a talking film, "The Pirate and Princess" (Bob Hope), it was a quite exciting event after so long.

Tuesday September 18*th*

Slept well for once perhaps it was the calming effects of the film. I awake refreshed wondering what the day has in store, however, it's not long before I know the prospects for the day. A number of crosses sent up by the Royal Engineers have to go to the cemetery, so with two men I set off to the place I thought a few days ago I had seen for the last time. Having replaced the crosses we spent the rest of the day trimming the grass on the graves. We were given a lift back to the jail in a jeep driven by one of the relieving forces.

After tea we parade for our first army pay for around four years, so I and my men are looking forward to the day we will be allowed to go into Singapore.

Wednesday September 19*th*

The day arrives with the usual heat and frustration as we get no leave and rumours of postponements of moves towards the day of embarkation disappoint us, no ship yet available it seems. The place has become a veritable rubbish heap as the litter left by daily moving men heaps up. I am suddenly aroused from my thoughts as a group of men from my floor burst upon me yelling with pleasure that a pint of beer per man is being issued after tea, it is a wonderful occasion for the vast majority of us. I expect the flavour will be new to us after three and a half years, it certainly should help us sleep.

Thursday September 20*th*

It did, and another day of sitting around. Flies are breeding in their thousands, it's a constant job flicking and swatting to keep them from eating you alive. The reason for their sudden increase is our new food supply, so much tinned food individually handed out, means empty tins which are not being collected are black with flies, also waste food and fruit lays about instead of being buried by those who discard it, thrown away because many are suffering from bad stomachs due to the change in diet. It has now reached a time when a lot of men don't want food. The beer issue went down well, some couldn't stop until they saw the bottom of their glass, whilst a few slowly savoured it to the last drop. New clothes are slowly being issued, its been going on over the last two days and has caused some chaos, I am getting mine anytime now. Making my way to the rows of tables heaped with jungle green shirts, shorts and trousers, green mugs and plates, in fact everything is jungle green, the first time for us. Well the clothes are army issue alright, if you are lucky as I am it's reasonable but on many it fits where it touches, making us a misfit looking lot. After some interchanges among each other we see the humorous side of it and the men laugh and joke with one another, anyhow it is evening now and we go off to collect a further half pint of beer which was quickly consumed by all.

Some film apparatus has been set up in our area so it's to the talking pictures we go, we begin to feel civilised again. Many Chinese children from a nearby village come among us, they enjoy "Donald Duck". These children look so tiny but they smoke like old hands. After the film we learn that the advance party of our group leaves at 10am tomorrow, it's getting exciting.

Friday September 21*st*

I watch the advance party leave but with a sinking feeling in my stomach, it has not been very comfortable for the last five days, got the "squitters". Hope it's not dysentery after keeping clear all the past years, perhaps just the new food.

Saw another open air film complete with the Chinese kids chattering away and ear to ear grins creasing their little faces, they are enjoying freedom too.

Due to the condition of my stomach I feel very low, but cannot pass up a chance to go with some of the fellows to visit Singapore docks. We walked alongside the *HMS Nelson*, I was surprised to see her still here as she was supposed to have left for home a week ago. She stands high out of the water because of the high tide, she towers above us with sailors in their "whites" hanging over the deck rail shouting to us below. One was calling me and my two mates to the gangplank beckoning us up. Arriving on deck he said he had recognised me, apart from being thin he said my face had not changed. He told me he came from Cley (a village 8 miles along the coast from my home town) and that his father had been one of my Territorial squad. He says he is allowed to invite one POW aboard for the night, he also got two of his mates to do the same for my two friends. They lashed us up with a good tea, real bread, it was a Godsend, and afterwards we were given a camp bed each to sleep on deck. This was all right until a storm around midnight drove us below.

Saturday September 22ⁿᵈ

Around 3am I awoke racked with terrible pain, the young sailor heard me groaning and he fetched his officer who spoke with me for a while. He thought that I had eaten too much bread and fetched me a bottle of Milk of Magnesia from the Officers' Mess. After a good dose I slept better and when I was awakened by the clatter of sailors going about the ship's duties I went up to the deck but to my astonishment could not see the dockside, only a blur of buildings some distance away. During the night for some reason we had moved, why we never learned, perhaps they wanted the space for other ships as there are quite a lot around. We are given breakfast but after my experience during the night I am very careful what I eat. After it is over, at 8.30am a ship's launch took all who had stayed onboard the four miles to shore where my friends and I got a lift for a few miles. Later we were picked up by a truck driver and taken the rest of the way to Changi jail. After cleaning myself up I just laze around for the rest of the day. It still seems strange not getting my men together at 7.30am to march off to the cemetery for a day's toil and sweat. I turn into my bed early.

CHAPTER 10

HOME FROM HELL

Sunday September 23ʳᵈ 1945

I arise to a lovely fresh morning with freedom, I now admire much more the nature of this island. The war has been over five weeks, many have departed but there are still a lot of us here. We are told there is a shortage of ships but it could be any day now.

We were paid some money this morning and three of us got permission to go into Singapore to experience its nightlife, for which it is renowned. We find an amusement place called the "Great Wall". The Chinese girls look so dazzlingly pretty, almost irresistible; maybe it is because we have not seen well-dressed females for such a long time. Whisky is drunk tonight as though it was water, however it could well be diluted. Later we found a restaurant but food is still scarce except for eggs of which I eat 18, but then they are not much larger than a bantams. The night has gone and feeling very happy we find a taxi to take us back to Changi jail.

Monday September 24ᵗʰ

I slept very well and am ready to visit Singapore for the day, it could be the last, if the talk we hear is right. I could be on my way to England any day now. Get a lift in an army truck into a very busy town, mooch around for a time watching all that's going on, street vendors trading in almost everything. I haggle with one for a pair of ladies real silk pyjamas, a present for the wife, something from the Far East. We find a cafe for a bite to eat and drink during which I have an interesting talk with an English speaking Chinese girl, Ni Ling, working in the Baltimore cafe. I must try and remember to send her a card when I get home. The meal was good, steak and eggs. After washing it down with tea we make for the "Great World" amusements. We listen to a dance band with wonderful girl singers; well they are to me as it is years since I've heard such. One of the songs by a tiny Chinese girl, "My Heart Belongs To Daddy", went down very well. Tired of the fun and excitement we find another restaurant for food and drink before we set off back to camp. We sample some Chinese wine, it must be rather potent for the three of us are getting pretty lively. In the corner stands a spiky tree, to us it seems like an Xmas tree so we collect some small currency notes from others of our like around and trim the tree up with it. We partake of some more wine and enjoy the evening. Later I let two little Chinese boys and their sister take the money from the tree, for this I get my first kiss in four years as the happy little girl comes and gives me a hug and a kiss, it's made my day. It's been two glorious nights, something forever to remember. I think "Goodbye Singapore" as I start to look around for transport back.

Tuesday September 25ᵗʰ

I awake remembering nothing of the journey back, I talk to my companions but they are as vague as I am, anyway must have been some good Samaritans around who brought us back to camp. No one is to leave the jail as embarkation is on the agenda for anytime now, an advance party has left. It's just wandering around all day, it seems years instead of hours, night comes and we are still here. We get a bottle of beer and a tot of brandy, so manage to keep our spirits up, roll into bed with the promise that we move tomorrow.

Wednesday September 26ᵗʰ

I am awakened at 5am by shouts of, "Get out of bed if you don't want to miss the boat". Have a hurried breakfast and a last look around at the jail and areas beyond which have been my abode for the best part of four years. Spare a thought for the cemetery, which because of the interest it gave me kept me from being buried in it. I am now dragged from my thoughts by shouts of, "Embus", the trucks to take us to the docks have arrived.

It's 8 o'clock and we are rumbling through the jail entrance for the last time, all has gone somewhat quiet, no doubt nostalgia has momentarily gripped the men. We travel through the villages exchanging friendly waves with the Chinese, Malays and others.

By 10.20 we were embarking on the *HMT Sobieskia*, a Polish ship (which also came out with us) was the only one available to take us home, but a ship with a marvellous record so we are told. She has landed troops in almost every theatre of the war. We spend all day in the dock spending much of our time watching the bustle of activity that goes on around the ships. The night comes on, bed is the only place really to go, I am sharing a cabin with two other Sergeants who feel much the same as me, tired and virtually drained after the last two days.

Thursday September 27ᵗʰ

Morning comes and to my surprise we are still in dock. A morning of general activity of Naval and Army officers up and down the gangplank, watching them helps time pass by. It's now midday and the ships engines are throbbing beneath us. 1 o'clock arrives and a huge shout goes up from the deck, the dockers are casting us off, slowly we drift from the dockside. We are leaving Singapore, for some the sooner the better, for others a tug at the heart strings, after all there is something mystic about the Far East. The dockside is receding and only one dusky maiden wiping a tear from her eyes as she waves goodbye is seen. So finally we have left, somewhere we will remember for the rest of our lives.

During the last 24 hours we have covered 287 miles, slowly through the Malacca Straits because of the danger of mine fields. We get a few boat station drills. The food on the ship is good but plain, although butter is plentiful, as quarter pounds have been issued to each man. This was a bit upsetting for a few airmen with us as some men thinking that they lacked "Brylcream" rubbed butter into their hair. It was all light-hearted stuff and went off in

HMT Sobieski – A Polish ship that took us home

good spirits. Spent most of the day watching the coastlines of Malaya and Sumatra disappear into the mists.

* * *

Another 24 hours has passed, again we are told the mileage logged this time, it has increased, 357 miles. We are now rolling badly, in a heavy ground swell. Many are now sea-sick, not a happy event. A battleship with her destroyer escort passes by, they flash us a signal. Apparently we are in the Indian Ocean, the ship has become very hot. I am perspiring from every pore, just streaming with sweat. A flying-boat passes overhead. Now the outlook is nothing but sea, thousands of miles of rolling ocean with us bobbing around like sausages on the boil. After some hours we pass other ships, the swell gets heavier and with a strong wind blowing hot air, sleep does not come easy.

* * *

We are on deck early this morning, 07.00 hours to watch the ship enter Colombo docks, Ceylon, it's a great moment, the first stage from Singapore. As we passed the lighthouse we were given a welcome by the Harbour Master's daughter waving from its platform. We spend two hours hanging over the ships rails waving to the hundreds on the dockside.

At 10 o'clock we are given shore leave until 3pm As we leave the ship it is fantastic the difference the service girls stationed here make, one put an arm around my neck, a hug and a kiss makes life worth living again. Having got clear of the crowd, two friends and myself make for the town. We must somehow look so much different from other people; by the way we are stared at we must be misfits. Perhaps it is our haggard looks, thin bodies with rice bellies and ill-fitting clothes, really we must look terrible.

I'm standing outside a jewellers, I think I will buy the wife a present from Ceylon. I go in and a young native girl comes to serve me, she speaks good English, and after a good look around

427

she suggests a Moonstone necklace with its superstition of good fortune. She wishes me "Bon Voyage" as I leave the shop to join my friends, we think it's time we had something to eat so we set out to find the NAAFI. Having found it we had an excellent lunch, it was good to see the smiling faces of the English girls.

At the dock a lot of girls of FANY (a nursing unit) were talking with the men. I say hello to one and soon we are deep in conversation as she comes from Norwich, only a few miles from my home town. As we talk for some 30 minutes she fills me in with a lot that has happened over the past four years. Leaving her I chat to a WREN who tells me she has been here for two years and how sorry she feels for us. We are feeling very happy now I tell her as I shake hands and depart for the ships gangway.

* * *

Some 24 hours later at seven in the morning we are moving out, a mixture of people are watching, among them some pretty Singhalese girls, all are waving and cheering as the ship pulls away, soon to be clear of the port and the vast number of ships that are around, some still hooting us "God Speed". I seem to have got a rotten cold; I suppose it is the changing conditions.

While we were in Colombo the first medal ribbon was issued.

* * *

Another day has dawned and it presents just another great expanse of sea. I'm afraid we are now getting just a little bit impatient. It's mid-morning and a message is coming over the ships loudspeaker system for us to go to our mess decks for an issue of comforts. These turn out to be 300 cigarettes and six chocolate bars, the latter being very welcome, as for the cigs, with this cold they don't appeal. The day passes we just sit around talking, playing cards or sleeping. The previous excitement is now telling it's suddenly become very tiring.

Friday October 5th 1945

We arise once again from cooler nights to very hot days of the Indian Ocean, which is always changing colour to various shades of blue. While I watch these colorations two ships appear on the horizon. Word is going around and men are coming up from below to line the rails, it's something to break the monotony. We watch as we steadily close towards each other, they are two warships, which are soon to be recognised as the *HMS Glasgow* and *HMS Jamaica*. The sailors line the rails of their ships and wave to us. A signal is flashed over, we are told it reads, *"Best Wishes and Happy Landing"* and *"God Speed Sobieskie"*. While we have been watching a cruiser has joined them, but I cannot read its name. After watching with interest the other ships it has brought us quickly to lunchtime and with this over it's the usual ship's pastimes until lights out.

I am ready for my bed which means lying just in ones pants, sweating the night out and arising in the morning feeling like a dish rag until revived with a cool shower.

Sunday October 7th

Well we have now been at sea for 11 days and it's coming up to breakfast time, a shout goes up from the main deck, "Land Ahoy". We are told that it is the Island of Socotra (Arabian Sea). By 10 o'clock it appears as a huge rock mass, I learn that it is hot and dry with little vegetation other than dates and such like, no Europeans live there. A lonely shore outpost lamp signals us, *"Good Luck Soldiers"*. The sea is a marvellous blue with lots of spouting whales, sharks and porpoises to be seen.

At 8 o'clock in the evening we are told to look out for the shore lights of British Somaliland as we are now in the Straits of Aden. Soon it's time again for bed, God it's hot, can't sleep, everything touching me is wet with perspiration.

I get up early and have a wash down then go on deck until breakfast, hanging over the rail, watching the wash of a ship trailing in the distance. I think to myself that I am feeling stronger these days, due to the good food and countless vitamin pills, but I am losing too much sweat to increase my weight, which still has not reached eight stone. It must be close to breakfast now and on my way to the mess deck I stop to read the days orders which tells me that I am in charge of tonight's fire picket, at least it will help pass the night. The day passes with little to note and it's now 8 o'clock and I take over my picket duties setting out my men at vantage points which through the night I shall patrol.

* * *

It's midnight and the naval duty officer informs me that we are in the Red Sea and as we talk 15 destroyers slip silently by in the misty moonlight. I doze in a deckchair between patrols. Daylight comes and with breakfast the end of my duties. During the morning I watch the crew firing 4" guns at practice smoke targets. It is exceedingly hot, a dry heat, everybody lying around like dead things as the ship ploughs on through the calm waters.

I am told that to keep up with time our watches should be retarded by a half hour each night. It's mid-afternoon and I am hanging over the deck rail trying to catch what little air there is. I feel better having now shaken off the cold I picked up earlier. I see two black specks appear in the distance, land I think. I watch with interest, as we get closer, a third comes into vision. I am told they are two coral islands and the larger one is Shadwell Island.

After tea I am back on deck, it's much cooler now with a high wind that has our ship rolling. Getting near Suez an officer tells me, I pass the word around, it causes a stir of excitement and much speculation.

Friday October 12th

The ship is alive bright and early, all eyes on a distant coastline. Later we arrive at a place called Ataka, near Port Suez. As we dock the welcome is amazing with hooting sirens of ships, everywhere bedecked with hundreds of flags, bands playing on the dockside, girls everywhere offering food and drink. We were soon allowed on the dockside to partake of this new found hospitality. After a marvellous time we were taken off in parties to collect kit suitable for winter in England.

Later a young lady, a Miss Pegg from the Church Army found me, she had seen my name on the ship's passenger list and had spent the last hour tracing me. What a nice surprise for both of us, she came from Sheringham, my hometown and is now stationed at Suez. We found up two more local lads (Ted Copeman was one) and had our photos taken. Later she took us around to do some shopping. Altogether it has been a wonderful day. Picked up two radio telegrams and 11 letters that have been held here for me.

Saturday October 13ᵗʰ

Slept well and after an early breakfast I am on deck to see what's going on. Must have moved in the night. It's 7.30am and we are about to leave Albedaya, which I understand is sort of a war time dock, may be so, who cares, we are moving again towards home. We have to wait at Suez for a few hours to get passage through the canal. Standing on the bank waving us off is our Church Army sister and many others. As the ship passes through the 90 miles of the canal all there is to see is desert on both sides strewn with rocks and in places Army camps.

Sunday October 14ᵗʰ

We drop off our pilot and mail at Port Said at 1pm and are now off for a cruise through the Mediterranean en route for home.

* * *

During the night the weather has become much cooler with rather rougher seas. This morning I sort out the clothing issued the other

Jack. Miss Pegg and Ted Copeman in Suez, 12th October 1945

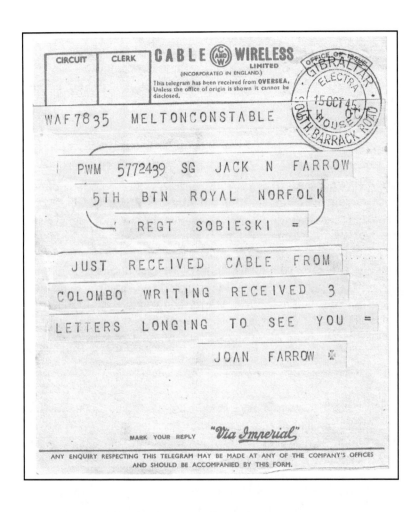

Copy of telegram sent to the Sobieski October 15th 1945

day for colder climes, I try on my battle dress, it's not a bad fit and in a few days time I think I shall need it. We have just been told to throw any ammunition that we may have over the ships side. For the rest of the day most of us loll around making the most of the sun's warmth which in a few days time will be gone from us. We missed the sight of Malta's shoreline having passed it while we slept and see only the distant coast of North Africa as we cruise towards the Spanish end of the Med.

* * *

Two days have passed with routine things occupying our minds but excitement is running high as we are told that we shall soon be seeing the "Rock of Gibraltar" against the skyline, later we see the black smudge emerging from the haze. Soon we are with it close enough to see signal lights flashing to our ship, people waving and ships hooting as we pass into the Straits of Gibraltar on our last leg of a memorable voyage. This passed, we push up the coast of Spain and into a wintry and rough Bay of Biscay. I am glad to get into battle dress to keep warm. The ship moves away from the coast of Spain, heading into more open water.

Monday October 29th

A few days have passed at sea but now we see land ahead, it's the Irish coastline and as the ship steams towards it I am able to see grass on the cliffs, grass so green in fact greener than I ever could have imagined after years of looking at the dull shades of the tropics. I think the "Emerald Isle", how else could it be described. A few hours pass then another distant shore is spotted. Cheer after cheer rings out from the men lining the deck rails, it's England. After a while the noise subsides, the men, like me no doubt thinking, four years to the day and we few are back, leaving behind a great number of comrades who never sustained the rigours of POW life under the "Nips".

The ship moves on into the mouth of the River Mersey, it's getting late into the afternoon, the ship stops, the anchor is run out and we learn that we shall not enter Liverpool dock until morning. All we can do is to watch the various coloured shore lights, listen to the hoots of other ships as they pass us in the dark. I am cold and tired so I go to my cabin and early to bed to try and think of morning and what it may bring.

Tuesday October 30th

It seemed a very long night, not sleeping too well but at last dawn arrives and, for us, it's the last time the ship comes to life. Breakfast over, the men are lining the rails of the ship from stem to stern, excitement is running high and suddenly it explodes as at 10.30am the anchor is weighed, cheer after cheer rings out as we start to move once more and in the direction of the shoreline buildings. Within a half an hour we are being nosed by a tug into the dockside. The dock is crowded with people, bands are playing and flags flying, shouting goes on from the men to the people below.

We are told to get our kit together also to take our ship's blanket with us. To me after the years spent in a prison camp and the excitement of coming home everything suddenly seems to take on a vague and trance-like atmosphere. I see the people, the buildings all distant and in a dream. I leave the gangplank, turning for one last look at the ship that has brought us home, it's goodbye to a good friend. I find myself getting on to an Army truck and soon we are moving away from the noisy dockside through what I think is the Mersey Tunnel and through the streets of Liverpool. My thoughts go back to just over four years ago when I spent several nights here fire-fighting during the 13 night blitz. I was in the Bootle area and the devastation was terrible. I am brought back to present day as the long line of trucks enter a camp where we are to spend our last day and night, tomorrow we will be getting off to our various homes.

Wednesday October 31st

The day goes by with the tidying up of loose ends and the issue of passes to cover the next six weeks, at the end of which I have to report to a rehabilitation centre near Peterborough for my demob clothes and papers to end my six years of war service. The evening is spent talking with friends about the past and future, saying, "Cheerio" and "Perhaps I will see you again soon".

Thursday November 1st 1945

The morning comes cold and with drizzle. Breakfast over I am among the first to be transported to the railway station as I have a day's travelling before me. Trance-like I am put aboard a train and soon we are moving, the journey is travelled in a dream with stops at some stations for a cup of tea. Everywhere seems crowded and the kindness of the people gets one near to breaking point. Eventually I get to within 40 miles of home, there is one other soldier in my compartment going to my home town, he tells me he had married a local girl before going abroad. We are putting on a strong front but beneath it all is a mixture of anxiety and general weakness, as if one might break down. The train is now slowing, I can see the station lights, I get my kit together, the door is flung open, we tumble onto the platform, I find myself surrounded by people, family, but in the half light I fail to recognise them, my senses desert me, I am floundering, and all that's going through my head is that I am home, HOME FROM HELL.

THE END

Jack kitted out on return to UK in 1945

**Jack with brother Billy,
outside the family home in Brook Road
in 1940 before going to Singapore**

Jack reunited with his family, November 1945. Back row: David, Geoffrey, May, Billy, Peggy, Arthur. Front row: Elsie, Father, Jack, Mother, Winnie

BUCKINGHAM PALACE

The Queen and I bid you a very warm welcome home.

Through all the great trials and sufferings which you have undergone at the hands of the Japanese, you and your comrades have been constantly in our thoughts. We know from the accounts we have already received how heavy those sufferings have been. We know also that these have been endured by you with the highest courage.

We mourn with you the deaths of so many of your gallant comrades.

With all our hearts, we hope that your return from captivity will bring you and your families a full measure of happiness, which you may long enjoy together.

George R.I.

September 1945.

**Copy of a letter from George VI
sent to the returned FEPOWs**

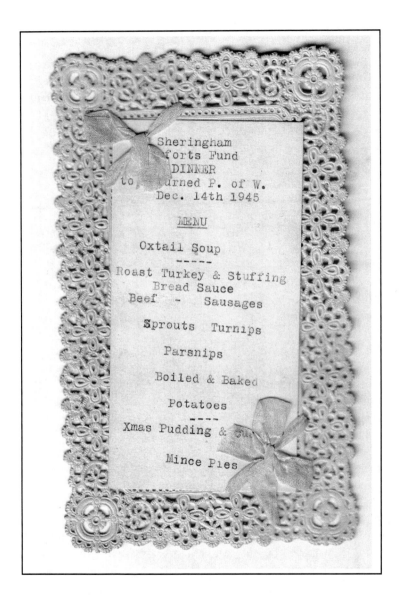

**Copy of the menu for Sheringham Comforts Fund Dinner
for returned POWs, December 14th 1945**

EPILOGUE

Jack and I were married on August 17th, 1941 and after just four days together he was ordered back to his regiment. Later, in October, Jack was given another four days leave; it was then I said goodbye to my husband of less than 2 months and I wasn't to hear of him until the fateful communication from the War office in 1942 – "missing in action". Details were sketchy and later the local paper ran the following:

> *"The man who made the first move to form a Territorial Unit at Sheringham and was one of the first to join, Sgt. J N Farrow, of the Royal Norfolk Regiment, reported missing at the fall of Singapore, is a prisoner of war in Malaya.*
>
> *His parents are Mr And Mrs F. Farrow, of Y-wurry, Brook Rd, Sheringham, and his wife's address is Manor Farm, Thurning."*

We had heard very little of the "Forgotten Army" during the war and in 1945 we received news that the men were returning to Britain. I remember that dark November evening, quite late, standing on Sheringham Railway platform, with my mother-in-law and the rest of my husband's family. It was drizzling with rain and cold.

Soon we saw the train approaching. I don't know what my husband Jack was feeling, but I was very apprehensive. He stepped from the train and walked past me and up to his mother, but he didn't know it was her. He thought it was his aunt. He never asked about me at all, his poor mind must have been in turmoil. He seemed to be in a trance, his eyes were vacant and staring. He was wearing the suit he had been issued with when he arrived in this country. It was two sizes too big, making him look even thinner.

As we all walked back to his mother's house in Brook Road, the common was ablaze, set on fire by his younger brothers, to welcome him back. None of this appeared to register with him, his thoughts were not yet of home. We never knew what his thoughts were as he walked up that familiar road. Was his neighbour and friend, Jim Tuck, whom he buried in Singapore, with him in spirit at this time?

We had to get to know each other again, for apart from having a few days together around the time when we got married we hadn't seen or had any contact with each other for nearly four years.

From the outset of Jack's return one of the hardest things for him was to be indoors, especially a small room. He wanted to be outside as much as he could. We would go on long walks together, away from people. He never did get used to crowds and we soon had to give up going into Norwich for as soon as we reached the shopping centre he would panic, sometimes faint. In these early days getting to know the prices of everyday things was also a challenge. There had been so many changes. No one was given or even thought of counselling in those days.

For the first five or six years Jack would have recurring bouts of Dengue Fever. This was known also as break-bone fever because of the chronic pain felt in all the limbs. Awful dreams also, so bad that he would shout out and wake me. I could never get him to talk about them and he did say that I should get out of bed before I attempted to wake him as he was afraid he might do me harm, thinking I was a guard. These dreams never went away and lasted on and off for the rest of his life and on occasions were accompanied by bouts of depression. I had hoped he would have written about his experiences early in an effort to help cleanse his mind, but despite my urging he put it off and threw himself into work.

Soon after returning home from the war he decided to go to Northampton to train as a carpenter and joiner, however, within a few months his father died suddenly and he returned to take over his work as a landscape gardener (also he thought his mother would need him). After taking over his father's work he expanded the business including opening one of the first Garden Centres that we both ran for 20 years. Looking back, this outside occupation, growing things and working with the seasons was probably the best thing to restore the mind. Gardening was his life he wouldn't have enjoyed a joinery shop. He designed and ran a small leisure park consisting of a putting green, tennis courts and bowling green at the Grand Court, Sheringham (formerly the Grand Hotel).

Even with this heavy work involvement he could not relax and ran local units of the Army and Air Cadet forces. He was also a Local Councillor for 12 years, throwing himself into many projects, not least the abortive attempt of creating a sports complex at the old Beeston Priory. It was partly a way to forget, to block the horrors of his imprisonment, for if he had nothing to occupy his mind the nightmare would return.

Despite these difficulties we had a family, a daughter, Annette (b.1947) and a son, Francis (b. 1948). I suffered from post-natal depression after my second child and Jack had the added burden of coping with two small children. This he did in his quiet way, which probably concentrated his mind on other things. We also had animals about the house, he loved living creatures, especially cats and dogs. He was hardly ever without his dog. It was at work with him, also at weekends when we drove out with the children. Kelling Heath was one of our favourite places, also Morston. In those early days, after the war, we were lucky to have those places almost to ourselves.

Another of his many interests was being involved with the Sheringham Branch of the Royal British Legion, including a period as Chairman. Jack was also a founder member of the Tyneside Club. He remained an active member for most of his life, organizing many events. The club was adjacent to our house so quite convenient. When he became too ill to continue actively in the club's affairs, he was made President in recognition of the many years of service he had given.

In retirement, without the demands of business, Jack was able to devote more time to another interest, conservation. He spent many weekends on Beeston Common helping the local Management Group restore the Newt Pond, which had been neglected since the war and was no longer a permanent feature.

He cleared overgrown and silted streams that fed the pond and with the Management Group and myself installed outlet pipes under the main tracks to prevent flooding. After clearing out the rubbish and replanting, the pond soon returned to its former beauty, with sticklebacks, dragonflies and moorhens. Much work followed with path and scrub clearance, enabling people to enjoy the pleasant walks. Sadly this heavy work had to be given up.

Our daughter was married and lived in Blackpool, however, each summer she would return to Sheringham with her four children. Jack enjoyed being a granddad and loved to take them to the common and point out the different wild flowers and watch them playing around the pond. Our son is also married with two children and has a house backing onto the common. He loves the place as much as his father did.

After all Jack had been through we had had a very happy life together, celebrating our Golden Wedding day on August 17th 1991, with a splendid garden party for family members, just a year before he died.

Joan Farrow
January 2007

Jack and Joan in 1946

**Jack and Joan celebrate their Golden Wedding Anniversary
17th August 1991**

Jack Farrow 1911-1992

POSTSCRIPT

Changi cemetery as laid out and tended by Jack Farrow and his comrades did not survive the post war development of Singapore, particularly the expansion of the airport. The focal point of his captivity could not remain undisturbed and in 1946, the Army Graves Service, decided to move all the graves to Kranji on the north of the island.

To-day the Commonwealth War Graves Commission has responsibility for the Kranji War Cemetery and memorial, with its 4,458 Commonwealth casualties of the Second World War, which are either buried or commemorated within its grounds.

POETRY

It may be you

Surely this was heaven
The thought flashed through his mind
As down from the wharf he jumped
And to his wife he said
At last we are together
And never shall we need,
But hurry up my loved one
I'm dying for a feed.
So off they set together
a loving man and his wife
Wedded to each other
To live a happy life
And in the beauty of their home
He waited for the meal
Dreaming of most beautiful food
Of Steak, Ham and Veal.
He mused his awful waiting,
But his wife sure could bake,
And wasn't this a wicked world,
A place of give and take.
At last she flitted in the room
And cooed I've something
You'll never guess my hero,
'Tis a bowl of steaming rice.
They took away her body
They placed him in a cell,
Convicted him of murder,
And condemned his soul to hell.
Take heed you thoughtless woman,
Or pay the awful price,
for serving up a `Changi' man
A bowl of steaming rice.

To Her

She's sitting by the fireside
The kiddies are at play.
She's thinking of their Daddy
so many miles away.
When will she get a letter?
When will she see his face?
When will he be among them?
In his accustomed place.
His chair is in the corner,
His pipe is in the rack,
She looks towards his picture
And says "Dear God, send him back"
The kiddies may grow noisy,
But she won't wear a frown,
Her man said 'Just keep smiling',
She'll never let him down.
And so for the love of Daddy
Who's miles across the foam,
She joins in with the kiddies
To make it 'Home Sweet Home'.
One day he'll be there with her.
Then life will be serene.
She's just "a soldier's missus"
But she is every inch a Queen.

Singapore Fortress

Almighty Island fortress
The guardian of the East
Impregnable as Gibraltar
A thousand planes at least.
It simply couldn't be taken
And will stand a siege for years
We'll hold the place forever
T'will bring our foe to tears
Our men are here in thousands
Defences are unique
The nips did not believe it
So they took it in two weeks.

Tribute to Hospital Orderlies

When the days were torment
and the nights were clouded terror;
When the power of darkness
had dominion on our soul;
When we fled consuming
through the seven hills of fever;
These put out their hands to us
and healed and made us whole.

Never-mind

Never-mind if the skies are dull and grey
Or the clouds look dark or black,
Just remember there's always a lining
And a sun that will soon come back.

Never-mind if you feel tied and weary
Or fed-up with the world upside down,
Just remember to keep smiling brightly
It's worth much more than a frown.

Never-mind if you're feeling lonely
Or your loved one has gone away,
Just remember to do your duty
With helping by smiling each day

Never-mind if the whole world's against you
Or your burden feels as heavy as lead,
Just remember to make yourself cheerful
And try to help others instead.